Boom for Whom?

Boom for Whom?

Education, Desegregation, and Development in Charlotte

Stephen Samuel Smith

State University of New York Press

Cover concept by Chris Ayers
Photographs by Jennifer Miles

Published by
State University of New York Press, Albany

For information, address State University of New York Press,
90 State Street, Suite 700, Albany, NY 12207

Production by Michael Haggett
Marketing by Michael Campochiaro

Library of Congress Cataloging-in-Publication Data

Smith, Stephen Samuel, 1942–
    Boom for whom? : education, desegregation, and development in Charlotte /
Stephen Samuel Smith
        p. cm.
    Includes bibliographical references and index.
    ISBN 0-7914-5985-3 (alk. paper)—ISBN 0-7914-5986-1 (pbk. : alk. paper)
        1. Busing for school integration—North Carolina—Charlotte—History. 2.
Education, Urban—Political aspects—North Carolina—Charlotte. 3. School
improvement programs—North Carolina—Charlotte (N.C.)—Politics and
government. 5. Charlotte (N.C.)—Economic conditions. I. Title.

LC214.523.C48S63 2004
379.2'63'0975676—dc22   2004041673

10 9 8 7 6 5 4 3 2 1

Contents

List of Maps, Tables, and Figures

Preface and Acknowledgments

As I complete this book in June 2003, preparations are well under way to commemorate the fiftieth anniversary of the Supreme Court's landmark decision in *Brown* v. *Board of Education*. A month ago, the attorney general and secretary of education announced the creation of a high-profile commission to, as their press release said, "encourage and coordinate activities that will commemorate the 1954 ruling, one of the most important decisions ever issued by the U.S. Supreme Court." Here in Charlotte, plans are being made for a series of events including a retrospective, a symposium, a play, a museum exhibit, and an ongoing community dialogue about the city's desegregation experience. That experience has national relevance because Charlotte is the city whose segregated school system gave rise to the Supreme Court's *Swann* decision. While not as epochal as *Brown, Swann* was a turning point in school desegregation history because it allowed mandatory busing for racial balance. In the aftermath of the decision, Charlotte eventually implemented what is generally considered one of the nation's most successful mandatory busing plans.

This book is about *Swann's* consequences for Charlotte. Here, however, I want to talk about some of *Swann's* consequences for my family in the hope of conveying the disappointment, anger, and sense of the irony of history that helped prompt the writing of this book.

In the 1980s, when my family moved to Charlotte, both of my children—who are white, as am I and my wife—were bused in grades 4-6 from our predominantly white, suburban neighborhood to First Ward, an inner-city elementary school where they received a fine education. Located just a few blocks from downtown, First Ward bordered Earle Village, a run-down public housing project virtually all of whose residents were African American. Prior to desegregation, almost all of First Ward's students were black, and the school was a dilapidated and neglected one. However, with mandatory busing came middle-class white families with the kind of political clout and resources to help transform the school, so much so that it was generally considered one of Charlotte's school desegregation showcases and in 1988 received a National School of Excellence Award.

In 1988—when my daughter had just graduated from First Ward and my son had just entered—approximately 32 percent of the school's students were black. At that time blacks constituted 40 percent of the school system's total enrollment, and First Ward's enrollment was well within desegregation guidelines. In the subsequent fifteen years, local developments led to a decline in mandatory busing for desegregation in Charlotte, and the reopening of the *Swann* case led to its end. The Charlotte schools have seen considerable resegregation and, in that respect, generally exemplify the national and regional trends documented by many scholars, most notably Gary Orfield and the Harvard Civil Rights Project. In First Ward, this resegregation is especially stark: blacks now comprise 90 percent of the school's students, more than double the system-wide figure of 43 percent.

My son, recently a counseling intern at First Ward, has run into some of the extraordinarily effective and dedicated people who played a large role in his education fifteen years ago. Their continued presence at the school augurs well for the current cohort of students, as, I am sure, does the presence of a new generation of caring and effective educators. Nonetheless, it is difficult to reflect on the almost total resegregation of this one-time desegregation showcase as well as the national trends without asking, Would not the upcoming fifty-year commemoration of *Brown* v. *Board of Education* more appropriately be called the last rites for much of that ruling's landmark promise of school desegregation and racial equality in public education?

The question is a polemical one that exaggerates the situation. The Charlotte schools are not likely to return anytime soon to the extreme racial segregation of the Jim Crow era, nor are many other school systems. Moreover, some school districts—such as the one in Rock Hill, the South Carolina city that is home to Winthrop, the university where I teach—are trying to swim against the national tide by pursuing greater socioeconomic and/or racial balance in pupil assignment. But the intentionally polemical nature of the question serves to raise a less polemical one, "To the extent school desegregation has been dying, why has it been doing so?" This book provides an extended answer to that question, at least in the case of Charlotte.

In providing that answer, the book deals with many other aspects of Charlotte's recent history. A word about them is appropriate here. In the eighteen years that I have lived in this city, it has become more affluent, cosmopolitan, and diverse, with many more exciting things to do and places to go than it had in 1985. It has also become an uglier, more congested, and more polluted city. In Charlotte, as elsewhere, there is an ongoing debate about whether these costs of development are worth its benefits. Here, I am not especially concerned with that debate.

However, as both scholar and citizen, I have a considerable stake in emphasizing that Charlotte would not have developed the way it has absent school desegregation. Whatever their educational consequences, both *Swann* and the busing plan had huge economic and political consequences for Charlotte that are profoundly laced with the irony of history.

This irony can be summarized by a reference to Atlanta, the prototypical New South city with which Charlotte, in the eyes of its civic boosters, has been playing catch-up for most of the twentieth century: from an economic and a political standpoint, busing in Charlotte did more to help Charlotte catch up with Atlanta and to help Charlotte's business elite catch up with the business elite of Atlanta than it did to help Charlotte's blacks catch up with Charlotte's whites. Perhaps the same thing can be said of the entire Southern civil rights movement, that is, that by many criteria, it turns out to have done more to help the South catch up with the rest of the nation than to help black Southerners catch up with white Southerners. But it would take a book at least as long as this one to investigate the validity of that conjecture.

This is not to dismiss the palpable improvement that the civil rights movement made in the lives of black (and white) Southerners or to say that from an educational perspective, mandatory busing for desegregation was a failure. Just the reverse. As my disappointment and anger at First Ward's resegregation suggest, from an educational standpoint, there is much to be said—as well as not to be said—for Charlotte's mandatory busing plan, and it is precisely because there is much to be said for Charlotte's pursuit of school desegregation that the situation in 2003 is so terribly and distressingly ironic: the most lasting effect of *Swann* and Charlotte's nationally praised busing plan is not a desegregated school system. Rather, a much more lasting effect is a booming Charlotte in whose prosperity and benefits the people who fought the hardest for school desegregation, African Americans, continue to share much less than whites.

In substantiating these claims about *Swann's* many consequences and disparate benefits, this book will use concepts (e.g., regime theory and civic capacity) employed by many contemporary political scientists, myself included, who study urban politics. These concepts, I am convinced, illuminate Charlotte's desegregation history, and this history, in turn, will help deepen how political scientists understand urban regime theory and civic capacity. Because these political science concepts are not exactly everyday terms, even among people who read and write about desegregation and education policy, I have devoted a large part of the Introduction, chapter 1, to explaining them.

As the Introduction indicates, my understanding of regime theory draws heavily on the work of Clarence Stone, but my debts to him go much further. Like scores of people who study urban politics, I have repeatedly benefited from the depth of his knowledge, the loftiness of his vision, and the largeness of his heart. While Clarence's name is a household one among urban politics scholars, that of the late Glen Broach is not. But Glen, too, provided indispensable support. During my first ten years at Winthrop, he chaired the political science department in a way that helped maximize the university's many charms and went a long way toward minimizing its drawbacks, especially those stemming from a shortage of resources. His leadership produced a wonderful department culture whose strength is illustrated by how it continues to flourish three years after his sudden death.

I have numerous other professional and personal debts. The most important are to the literally hundreds of Charlotteans upon whose experience and knowledge I have drawn. Scores kindly agreed to formal interviews as part of the research that went into this book. When quoted, their names appear in the text and/or notes, but for each interviewee quoted, there are five or six whom I did not have occasion to quote, but whose comments nonetheless deepened my understanding and without whose time and insight this book could not have been written. There are also many other people from whom I learned in the course of our joint efforts to improve public education through service on various committees or membership in a range of organizations. I hope they share my belief that this book helps place our efforts in a broader historical context.

Tom Hanchett, Steve Johnston, Tim Mead, and Don Rosenthal read the manuscript with a concern for its main themes and an attention to detail that improved the earlier drafts significantly. I also benefited from the helpful comments of Luke Largess, Wilhelmenia Rembert, Stephanie Southworth-Brown, Louise Woods, the late Annelle Houk, and SUNY Press's anonymous reviewers.

Thanks also to Debbie Agata for help analyzing data on student and faculty racial balance; Ted Arrington for numerous conversations that helped bring me up to speed on local politics; Tom Bradbury for sharing his intimate knowledge of local educational issues; Bill Culp, Michael Dickerson, and the staff of the Mecklenburg County Board of Elections for the many ways that they helped me obtain data; Sara Klemmer of *The Charlotte Observer* for graciously facilitating my access to the paper's library of clippings; Mike Weinstein for helping me think about the census data; Patrick Jones of the University of North Carolina at Charlotte's Cartography Lab for providing the map showing the location of Mecklenburg's black population; Joanne Miller, Art Director of *The Charlotte Observer,* for supplying the computerized file used to create the map showing the location of schools in Meckenburg County; Chris Ayers for adapting that file to produce the map; State University of New York Press's Priscilla Ross for believing in the book and Michael Haggett for shepherding it through production; Lori Schmidt and April Lovegrove for wise, skilled, and gracious clerical support; and Aset Abdualiyev, Stephanie Southworth-Brown, and Sally Sevcik for proofreading assistance. I also repeatedly benefited from the generous and expert assistance of librarians at Winthrop's Dacus Library, as well as at the Charlotte-Mecklenburg Public Library's Robinson-Spangler Carolina Room and the University of North Carolina at Charlotte Atkins Library's Special Collections.

As indicated by the frequency with which her name appears in the text and notes, I owe an immense debt to my colleague and wife Roslyn Arlin Mickelson. To this book, to things of much greater consequence, and to our life together, she makes the kinds of contributions that could only be made by so wifely a scholar and so scholarly a wife. The experience of our children, Ginny and David, in the Charlotte school system added, of course, to my understanding of it. Much more importantly, they have enriched my life immeasurably and given me a much deeper appreciation of what really matters in it.

Early reports of many of the topics discussed in chapters 5 and 6 appeared in "Education and Regime Change in Charlotte," a chapter in the book *Changing Urban Education* (University Press of Kansas, 1998) edited by Clarence Stone, and in "Hugh Governs? Regime and Education Policy in Charlotte, North Carolina," an article in the *Journal of Urban Affairs* (vol. 19, no. 3, 1997). I am grateful to the University Press of Kansas and the Urban Affairs Association for permission to use material from those two publications. Figures 5.1 and 5.2 originally appeared in an article that I wrote with Roslyn Arlin Mickelson, "All that Glitters is Not Gold: School Reform in Charlotte Mecklenburg," that appeared in *Educational Evaluation and Policy Analysis* (vol. 22, no. 2, summer 2000). I am grateful to the American Educational Research Association for permission to use those figures and other material that appeared in that article. Thirteen of the chapters' epigraphs are quotations from *The Charlotte Observer.* They are reprinted with permission from *The Charlotte Observer;* copyright owned by *The Charlotte Observer.*

A sabbatical from Winthrop and generous funding from the Parker Foundation, the Spencer Foundation, and the Winthrop University Research Council provided the time and resources that made the book possible.

It should go without saying that I alone am responsible for any errors of fact or interpretation that might mar the book.

Maps

———————————————

Mecklenburg County

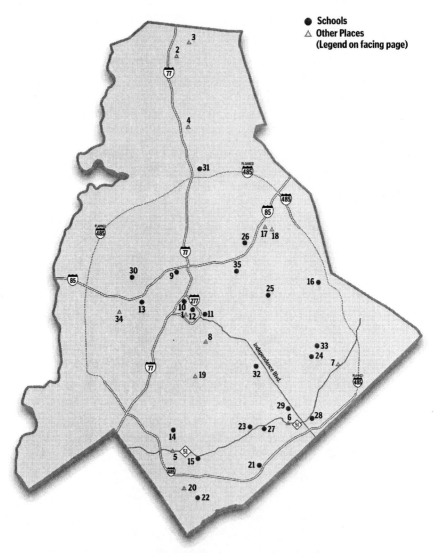

Map of Mecklenburg County Showing Location of Schools and Other Important Places Discussed in Text

Legend For Map of Mecklenburg County

BY NUMBER

1	Downtown
2	Cornelius
3	Davidson
4	Huntersville
5	Pineville
6	Matthews
7	Mint Hill
8	Eastover
9	West Charlotte High School
10	Irwin Avenue Elementary School
11	Piedmont Middle School
12	First Ward Elementary School
13	Harding High School
14	South Mecklenburg High School
15	McAlpine Elementary School
16	Reedy Creek Elementary School
17	University Place
18	University of North Carolina at Charlotte
19	SouthPark Mall
20	Ballantyne
21	McKee Road Elementary School
22	Hawk Ridge Elementary School
23	Providence High School
24	Lebanon Road Elementary School
25	Devonshire Elementary School
26	Education Village
27	Elizabeth Lane Elementary School
28	Butler High School
29	Crestdale Middle School
30	Allenbrook Elementary School
31	North Mecklenburg High School
32	East Mecklenburg High School
33	Independence High School
34	Charlotte-Douglas International Airport
35	Hidden Valley Elementary School

ALPHABETICALLY

Allenbrook Elementary School	30
Ballantyne	20
Butler High School	28
Charlotte-Douglas International Airport	34
Cornelius	2
Crestdale Middle School	29
Davidson	3
Devonshire Elementary School	25
Downtown	1
East Mecklenburg High School	32
Eastover	8
Education Village	26
Elizabeth Lane Elementary School	27
First Ward Elementary School	12
Harding High School	13
Hawk Ridge Elementary School	22
Hidden Valley Elementary School	35
Huntersville	4
Independence High School	33
Irwin Avenue Elementary School	10
Lebanon Road Elementary School	24
Matthews	6
McAlpine Elementary School	15
McKee Road Elementary School	21
Mint Hill	7
North Mecklenburg High School	31
Piedmont Middle School	11
Pineville	5
Providence High School	23
Reedy Creek Elementary School	16
South Mecklenburg High School	14
SouthPark Mall	19
University of North Carolina at Charlotte	18
University Place	17
West Charlotte High School	9

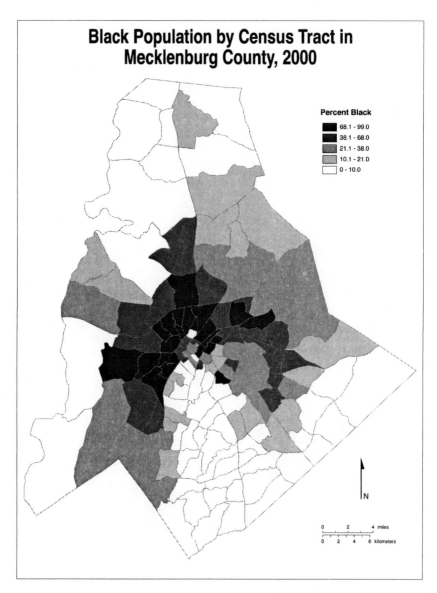

Black Population by Census Tract in Mecklenburg County, 2000

Percent Black

- 68.1 - 99.0
- 38.1 - 68.0
- 21.1 - 38.0
- 10.1 - 21.0
- 0 - 10.0

N

| 0 | 2 | 4 miles |
| 0 | 2 | 4 | 6 kilometers |

Map of Mecklenburg County Showing Distribution of African American Population

Chapter 1

Introduction

Charlotte-Mecklenburg's proudest achievement of the past 20 years is not the city's impressive new skyline or its strong, growing economy. Its proudest achievement is its fully integrated school system . . . [that] has blossomed into one of the nation's finest, recognized through the United States for quality, innovation, and, most of all, for overcoming the most difficult challenge American public education has ever faced.

> —1984 editorial in the *Charlotte Observer* entitled "You Were Wrong, Mr. President," commenting on President Reagan's claim during a visit to Charlotte that busing was a failed social experiment.[1]

I believe public school desegregation was the single most important step we've taken in this century to help our children. Almost immediately after we integrated our schools, the Southern economy took off like a wildfire in the wind. I believe integration made the difference. Integration—and the diversity it began to nourish—became a source of economic, cultural and community strength.

> —2000 statement by Hugh L. McColl Jr., CEO and chairman of the Charlotte-based Bank of America, the country's largest consumer bank.[2]

It seemed a telling moment in Charlotte history, and in many ways it was. There was President Reagan on a 1984 campaign stop denouncing busing because "it takes innocent children out of the neighborhood school and makes them pawns in a social experiment that nobody wants. And we've found that it failed."[3] But whatever reaction the president may have expected to this comment about busing, the white, otherwise cheering and

1

enthusiastic Charlotte audience responded with a silence that was "uncomfortable, embarrassed, almost stony."[4] What more dramatic indication than this silence among Reagan partisans in Charlotte that its residents, like observers nationwide, saw its busing plan as a success and something special, worthy of great civic pride?

However, almost twenty years later, the *Observer's* rebuke of the president—excerpted in the chapter's first epigraph—commands as much attention as the crowd's silence because even a cursory familiarity with Charlotte indicates how things have changed in the subsequent eighteen years. To be sure, the city's skyline has become more impressive, featuring the tallest building between Washington, D.C., and Atlanta, the headquarters of Bank of America, the country's largest consumer bank. Several other corporate towers have also been added, including one that houses the headquarters of Wachovia, the country's fifth largest bank.[5] As the presence of these two banking powerhouses suggests, the local economy has continued to boom, with Charlotte becoming the country's second largest banking center, trailing only New York.

Accompanying this economic growth has been Charlotte's expanding reputation as a quintessentially prosperous and congenial Sunbelt city, a reputation exemplified by the U.S. Conference of Mayors naming Charlotte as the nation's "most livable" city of its size in 1995.[6] Moreover, Charlotte is typically viewed as a good place for blacks, was named in 1998 by *Essence* magazine as the best city for African Americans, and ranks very high on many similar lists.[7]

Yet time has been much less kind to the Charlotte-Mecklenburg schools (CMS), especially the system's efforts to pursue desegregation. Within a year or two of Reagan's Charlotte visit, CMS began witnessing an increase in resegregation that would continue through the turn of the century. Moreover, CMS' desegregation policies became increasingly enmeshed in political and legal controversy. By the start of the twenty-first century, the same federal judiciary whose decisions had given rise to Charlotte's vaunted busing plan was now issuing rulings prohibiting CMS from pursuing the desegregation policies that a majority of school board members favored.

The contrasting trends between Charlotte's skyline and the racial balance of its schools—the first climbing upward since Reagan's campaign stop, the second dropping downward—might initially seem to belie any claim, such as that of Bank of America's CEO Hugh McColl in the second epigraph, linking economic growth to school desegregation. That claim, however, does have considerable merit, and one of this book's main goals is to specify the links between desegregation and economic growth, emphasizing that they involved the cold realities of urban politics at least as much as the warm glow of racial diversity. Those linkages can be summarized in a series of observations laced much too fully with the irony of history: school desegregation was the product of a long struggle initiated and waged primarily by African Americans seeking their just share of the American Dream. Yet given CMS' increasing resegregation, the most lasting consequence of this struggle is not a desegregated public school system. Rather, a much more lasting consequence of school desegregation was its crucial contributions to Charlotte's development and economic boom whose many benefits black Charlotteans are still a long way from fully sharing. Moreover, the economic development facilitated by Charlotte's school desegregation accomplishments made it increasingly difficult to sustain them. Similarly, the increase in civic capacity—a term from regime theory, a perspective frequently used to study urban politics—that resulted from school desegregation did more to help Charlotte grow than to help Charlotte's school system deal with the consequences of this development. While civic capacity flowed easily *from* education to development, the difficulty in transferring it *to* education was so great that it can be likened to getting water to flow uphill. That task is not impossible, but it requires the political equivalent of a pump, in this case the kind of broad political mobilization that has largely been absent in Charlotte since the civil rights era.

The history provoking these observations is a complicated one, but its main characteristics can be summarized here: CMS gave rise to the 1971 *Swann* decision in which a unanimous Supreme Court affirmed the 1969 decision of a federal judge in Charlotte allowing busing for desegregation. Generally considered a turning point in desegregation history, the Supreme Court's decision in *Swann* quickly led to the desegregation of numerous school districts throughout the South. However, it took almost three years for CMS to adopt its busing plan. Although the perseverance and courage of black Charlotteans was the sine qua non of the plan's adoption, Charlotte's business elite also played an important role. While the business elite generally sat on the sidelines prior to the decision by the Supreme Court, its ruling made clear to the business elite that the best and perhaps only way to end the crisis rocking public education in Charlotte was for CMS to adopt a busing plan. Leading corporate executives thus threw their considerable weight behind, among other things, the election of school board candidates who would implement busing. Business elite support for busing was intimately related to a broader political alliance between it and many key black political leaders. During much of the 1960s, 1970s, and 1980s, this alliance played a pivotal and frequently decisive role in local politics, helping secure the election of pro-growth mayors and the passage of the bond referenda necessary to build the roads and other infrastructure necessary to sustain economic development.

Adopted in the mid-1970s, Charlotte's busing plan continued until the early 1990s, with its heyday coming during the 1977–1986 administration of Superintendent Jay Robinson. During these years, CMS maintained very high levels of racial balance, received widespread national praise, and also claimed substantial progress in improving black academic achievement and reducing racial disparities on standardized tests. In retrospect, those claims were exaggerated, but the available evidence, though frustratingly fragmentary, continues to suggest that CMS did a relatively better job of educating black students during the heyday of the busing plan than it would do as the school district began resegregating. These accomplishments notwithstanding, many racial disparities continued during the Robinson administration. Black students were bused much more than white students. Moreover, while busing may have allowed CMS to achieve high levels of racial balance between schools, within them there was considerable racially correlated tracking, with blacks being heavily concentrated in the lower tracks. Moreover, some schools had considerably more resources than others, with the political clout of a Parent-Teacher Association (PTA) heavily influencing its school's ability to get resources.

From an educational perspective, school desegregation may not have fulfilled its many promises, but politically and economically it was a huge success. Within Charlotte, it laid a basis for black-white cooperation that, among other things, helped achieve district elections on the city council and the passage of bonds for the airport expansion without which Charlotte could not have grown the way it has. On a national level, the busing plan fueled Charlotte's reputation as a city characterized by racial harmony and progressive race relations. In the intense competition for mobile capital, Charlotte benefited greatly from its image as "The City That Made It Work" rather than being just another city that, like Atlanta, was too busy to hate.

However, even as the busing plan flourished in the 1970s and 1980s, the seeds of its demise were sprouting. Although they milked Charlotte's reputation as "The City That Made It Work" for all it was worth, many business leaders pursued development policies that drastically undermined CMS' ability to pursue desegregation. Despite the national praise lavished upon the busing plan, local funding for public education was worse than that in comparable places. CMS' decisions about the locations of new schools also undermined its ability to pursue desegregation on a racially equitable basis. Although CMS' black enrollment was growing more rapidly than white enrollment, almost all new schools were built in predominantly white neighborhoods.

Moreover, the very growth facilitated by the busing plan helped undermine it. Moving to Charlotte as a result of its growth were people from all over the United States who had not lived through the desegregation battles that preceded the adoption of the busing plan and thus lacked the attachment to it that many more-established Charlotteans had. Also, many of these transplants were accustomed to suburban, predominantly white school districts and thus had especially little use for busing. Whereas in the early 1970s proponents of desegregation were the political wheels squeaking most loudly, by the late 1980s, the most noise was coming from opponents of busing and critics of CMS. It was this clamor that now attracted the business elite's ample supply of political grease, with leading corporate executives, among many other things, lending their considerable political support to candidates who would seek alternatives to mandatory busing.

That alternative was adopted in 1992, the first year of the administration of CMS Superintendent John Murphy. The new pupil assignment plan was a magnet plan that tried to have the cake and eat it too: to maintain desegregation but placate those, especially whites, opposed to mandatory busing. The plan also sought to hitch CMS' wagon to the rising star of school choice and help increase public confidence in CMS. As important as the change in desegregation strategies was the adoption of a sweeping program of school reform including a new curriculum and standards, a numbers-driven accountability system for measuring progress in achieving specified educational outcomes, financial bonuses for personnel and schools that achieved their goals, tougher discipline standards, and site-based management. The program thus embodied much of the early 1990s conventional wisdom about the way to improve public education. Consequently, in the early 1990s, CMS attracted the same kind of national publicity for school reform that it had for desegregation a decade earlier.

Despite lavish praise in prestigious national forums, CMS' reform program faced growing problems at home. Some arose from the superintendent's abrasive management style, flirtations with other jobs, and frequent demands for pay hikes, but others were rooted in the program itself. The increased resegregation and the disparities between magnet and non-magnet schools alienated many white liberals and African Americans, thus eroding the black community's historically high support for school bonds. Moreover, the reform program was unable to overcome the many centrifugal tendencies in local politics stemming from Charlotte's growth and the increased influence of conservative Republicans in local affairs. All these political difficulties came to a head in 1995 when CMS suffered the first defeat of a major bond referendum in a generation. Moreover, school board elections resulted in a board with whose chair Superintendent Murphy had an especially strained relationship, and he resigned the day before the newly elected board took office.

Although it was not apparent at the time of Murphy's resignation, it subsequently became clear—from both the much-publicized results of North Carolina's accountability program and scholarly analysis of additional data—that the much-touted reform program could claim very little progress in boosting outcomes. Moreover, on some key measures, CMS' progress lagged that of comparable places, even though the latter lacked a high-profile reform program.

Further compounding the unfortunate history of the reform program was how the magnet plan brought about the litigation that forced CMS to abandon its pursuit of racial desegregation. Although the plan had been developed to placate largely white opposition to mandatory busing, the use of racial guidelines in magnet school admissions triggered a lawsuit from a white family. That lawsuit led to the reopening of the entire *Swann* case and a 1999 trial in which the key question was, Had CMS done enough to desegregate public education in Charlotte to be released from the court supervision required by the original litigation? In contrast to many school districts all too eager to claim that they have done all they can to achieve desegregation and should thus be released from court supervision, CMS maintained it could still do more and was thus not yet ready to be released from judicial oversight. However, after a trial lasting more than two months, a federal district court judge, who had been active in anti-busing movements while a private citizen thirty years earlier, issued a sweeping order requiring CMS to abandon its pursuit of desegregation. That ruling precipitated more than two years of turmoil and uncertainty. Legally, CMS sought to reverse the district court's order by appealing to higher courts. While initially successful, CMS ultimately failed to reverse the most important part of the district court's decision. During the two and one-half years that the case worked its way through the appeals process, CMS struggled to develop a new pupil assignment plan. Although a majority of the school board sought to preserve CMS' long-standing commitment to desegregation, it faced intense pressure from, among others, the business elite and school superintendent to minimize, if not abandon, desegregation in exchange for programs that provided extra and compensatory resources to schools with large numbers of children of color, especially those from low-income families.

Eventually the board adopted a race-neutral choice assignment plan that gave priority to students choosing to attend a school near their home. The plan went into effect in the 2002–03 school year, with the result that the previous twenty-year drift towards resegregation accelerated markedly. At this point, June 2003, it is much too early to ascertain the extent or effectiveness of the additional resources that CMS hopes to provide the increased number of schools with high concentrations of low-income children of color, but one would be extremely hard pressed to argue that CMS is the school desegregation showcase it once was.

Subsequent chapters will elaborate upon this brief summary. But for now it is worth noting that any one of the main characteristics in Charlotte history—CMS' desegregation accomplishments, a high-profile school reform program, the area's prosperity, the reported congenial atmosphere for African Americans, and a school board with a stated commitment to educational equity—would make the city and its school system an interesting place to study. Taken together, these characteristics make Charlotte an especially intriguing case study because in toto they seem to create the potential for addressing two of the most pressing items on the country's domestic policy agenda: improving educational opportunities for African American students and alleviating the black/white disparities that constitute so prominent an aspect of the political, economic, and social landscape of the nation's cities.[8] Before beginning to address these issues, it is necessary, however, to explicate regime theory, the perspective that I will use to discuss and analyze the relationships among education policy, desegregation, politics, and development in Charlotte. My aim is similar to that which guides much scholarship of social and political phenomena: to use a theory, in this case, regime theory, to better understand the Charlotte experience, as well as to use this empirical material to develop and critique the theory itself.

URBAN REGIME THEORY

Probably the most influential theoretical approach to urban politics at the start of the twenty-first century, regime theory receives its most important exposition and application in the work of Clarence Stone whom one book reviewer has called "the most influential urban politics scholar of this generation."[9] Stone's oeuvre is noteworthy because the careful empirical work in his seminal study of Atlanta is informed by a theoretical synthesis that brings together elements of earlier theories about power and urban politics that were often viewed as incompatible.[10] Equally important for this book's concerns, Stone has spearheaded efforts to apply regime theory to urban education through the multi-city, multi-investigator National Science Foundation-funded Civic Capacity and Urban Education Project, the largest effort ever by U.S. political scientists to apply the insights gained from the study of urban politics to urban education. For these reasons, I draw heavily on Stone's formulation of regime theory in this book.

This formulation, on my reading, has four defining characteristics: the social production model of power, an emphasis on the political advantages that stem from control of investment capital, attention to the operation and maintenance of political coalitions, and the recognition that governance is not an issue-by-issue process.

The first of these characteristics arises from regime theory's most basic concern: to understand how the different resources that various local actors (business leaders, educators, community organizations, and so forth) bring to the task of governance can be organized to create an enduring set of arrangements (a regime) whose operation will facilitate local goals. Governance, from regime theory's viewpoint, is problematic because society—especially, perhaps,

U.S. urban society—is characterized by a loose, incohesive network of institutions in which there is "no overarching command structure or a unifying system of thought."[11] This lack of cohesion has several sources. The most fundamental is the defining characteristic of capitalist parliamentary democracies: a division of labor between state and market in which there is private control of business enterprise but (in principle, at least) more public control, largely through elections, of governmental institutions. Other sources include federalism—which disperses power among the national, state, and local levels—and the weakness of other political institutions such as parties. In such a fragmented world, "the issue is how to bring about enough cooperation among disparate community elements to get things done."[12]

That perspective leads to the first defining characteristic of regime theory, what Stone calls the "social production model of power." From this perspective, the key aspect of urban political power is not how it is used by one actor to control another but how it is produced to accomplish goals. Stone does not deny the existence of what he calls "the social control model of power" (power *over*), but he argues that the social production model (power *to*) is more useful for understanding urban politics in much the same way that, say, the wave conception of light is much more useful for understanding certain physical phenomena than the particle conception.[13] Since the study of power has long occupied philosophers, political scientists, and sociologists, it would not be surprising for the social production model of power, as Stone enunciates it, to have antecedents, and indeed it does, most notably in the work of Talcott Parsons. Arguably the United States' most influential sociologist in the 1950s and 1960s, Parsons also emphasized what he called the differences between positive-sum and zero-sum conceptions of power, with the former involving "the capacity to mobilize the resources of the society for the attainment of goals for which a general 'public' commitment has been made." In contrast, according to Parsons, the zero-sum conception of power viewed it as being exercised by one group in society to further its own interests at the expense of another.[14]

Parsons elaborated these two conceptions of power in a critique of C. Wright Mills, another prominent sociologist of the 1950s, whose work, according to Parsons, exemplified the zero-sum conception of power.[15] Paralleling the differences in the two men's conceptions of power were broader sociological and political differences that largely defined the poles of social science discourse in the 1950s. With its emphasis on the positive-sum conception of power, Parsons's sociology paid relatively little attention to the conflictual and exploitative aspects of U.S. society and thus provided considerable ideological justification for the prevailing social order. Mills, however, was one of the academy's most trenchant critics of U.S. society, with his work calling repeated attention to the many disparities in wealth, power, and privilege that existed in the country. In that respect, Mills's work is generally viewed as representative of stratification or elite theory, a body of scholarship which, noting the large stratification in income, wealth, prestige, and education, argued that those (i.e., elites) who possessed such resources dominated both local and national politics.

Although Stone's conception of power resembles Parsons's, the importance he attaches to the stratification of resources is much more reminiscent of Mills.[16] Of particular importance to Stone are disparities in investment capital, the access to which, in his view, plays a unique role in local politics. However, for Stone, the key point is not that access to investment capital allows corporate executives to dominate politics by winning all political battles. Rather, he follows Charles Lindblom in emphasizing the "privileged position of business."[17] While that term may conjure up images of luxurious country clubs, it has much more to do with the operation of a political system, such as the United States,' that is embedded in a capitalist economic system. In such cases, business control of investment capital distinguishes it from all other political actors and participants because the resources engendered by such control make corporate participation the sine qua non of effective, especially activist, governance. Little of an activist agenda can be accomplished without the business elite's cooperation because even though it "has no power of command over the community at large and can be defeated on any given issue, it is nevertheless too valuable an ally—especially for those who are oriented to change and accomplishment—to be left out of the picture."[18] That is why, despite recurrent outbreaks of anti-business sentiment in the politics of Atlanta, the city that Stone has studied the most closely, "the striking feature of the Atlanta experience is the inclination of those in positions of community responsibility to pull back from conflict with the business elite and seek accommodation."[19]

Regime theory's recognition of "the enormous political importance of privately controlled investment"[20] in facilitating governance is its second defining characteristic. However, despite considerable emphasis on how control of investment capital affects local politics, regime theory is sharply critical of the economic determinism characteristic of some variants of both Marxist and rational choice approaches to urban politics. Such approaches largely deny the ability of urban political leaders to improve significantly the situation of low-income residents because the generic political advantages of investment capital are typically magnified in the local context by the structure of U.S. federalism that requires local governments to compete with each other for mobile wealth, especially investment capital. The need to pursue policies—often labeled developmental ones—that will attract such wealth makes it extremely difficult, so the argument goes, for localities to adopt policies that serve economically disadvantaged groups and classes at the expense of their more affluent counterparts.[21] The latter policies (typically called redistributive ones) are viewed as impeding a locality's ability to attract mobile capital by sucking up resources that could otherwise be used to attract investment.

In contrast to such theoretical claims, regime theory asserts that the consequences of developmental policies and redistributive policies are not written in stone but are affected by the characteristics of a locality's regime. "Politics matters" is a rallying cry of regime theorists who deny that the policies that localities should and do pursue are overwhelmingly determined by the structure of the U.S. federalist system and/or the logic of capitalist accumulation. Rather, urban political outcomes, are, according to regime theory, very much affected by politics, in particular the characteristics and operation of coalitions and understandings, both formal and informal.

The attention that regime theory pays to the formation, operation, and maintenance of coalitions is its third defining characteristic. This concern with coalitions suggests important similarities between it and the classical urban pluralism, exemplified by Robert Dahl's *Who Governs?*, which developed in large part as a critique of stratification theory for neglecting the process by which political bargains were struck, coalitions assembled, and decisions made. That similarity notwithstanding, regime theory's first two defining characteristics—the social production model of power and the importance of private investment—distinguish it sharply from classical urban pluralism.[22]

Moreover, regime theory differs from classical urban pluralism in yet another way. Pluralism, according to Stone, erroneously assumes that political preferences are developed independently of the likelihood of their being realized and, consequently, that governance is an issue-by-issue process. Rather, Stone argues, preferences "evolve through experience and therefore are informed by available opportunities."[23] These opportunities are, in turn, shaped by the prevailing pattern of political coalitions and understandings. There are several reasons such coalitions and understandings frequently embrace a range of issues:

> Once formed, a relationship of cooperation becomes something of value to be protected by all of the participants. Furthermore, because a governing coalition produces benefits it can share or withhold, being part of an established coalition confers preemptive advantages . . . Hence, there is an additional reason to preserve rather than casually discard coalition membership. . . .
>
> [T]he unequal distribution of economic, organizational, and cultural resources has a substantial bearing on the character of actual governing coalitions, working against the kind of fluid coalition and power dispersion predicted by pluralist theory.[24]

The recognition that governance is not an issue-by-issue process, the fourth defining characteristic of regime theory, has important ramifications. Because governance is not an issue-by-issue process, it is possible to characterize governance arrangements—i.e., the regime—which typify a locality. One set of characterizations involves the main players in the regime. In Atlanta, for example, Stone's work calls attention to the leading role played by the coalition between the city's business elite and leaders of the African American community. Another set of characterizations involves the issues and goals around which a governing coalition is organized. Stone distinguishes among several different kinds of issues, the most relevant here being the difference between regimes whose goal is development and those whose goal is the expansion of opportunity for low-income urban residents.[25]

By its very nature, economic development is in the interests of a wide range of businesses (such as utilities, the daily paper, and developers) that stand to profit from this growth. Because these actors who play such a large role in local politics stand to profit from economic development, it can proceed largely by coordinating the activities and interests of institutional elites, often through the use of selective material incentives. In addition, economic development issues impose "no motivational demands on the mass public and are advanced easiest when the public is passive." For this reason, "development activities are often insulated from popular control."[26]

In contrast to development regimes, those devoted to the expansion of opportunity for low-income citizens are organized around a very different set of issues, for example, "enriched education and job training, improved transportation access, and enlarged opportunities for business and home ownership."[27] Just as the issues are different, so too are the political arrangements, with those characterizing lower-class opportunity expansion regimes being much more demanding than those characterizing development regimes. While both development and opportunity expansion require coordination among institutional elites, in the latter case such coordination cannot be achieved on a strictly voluntary basis but requires regulation and coercion.[28] Such regulation and coercion are "most sustainable when backed by a popular constituency."[29] In addition to providing the political clout necessary to sustain the regulation and coercion of institutional elites, mass mobilization is also necessary to ensure the effective functioning of the educational, health, housing, and employment programs designed to serve the poor. But such mobilization is not easily effected; lower-class constituencies lack the resources of their middle-class counterparts, and the long history of many programs that failed to meet the needs of the urban poor has contributed to cynicism and withdrawal.[30]

As this summary of regime theory suggests, its normative concerns were initially much more implicit than explicit, with much of its early attention, exemplified by Stone's work on Atlanta, focused on land use issues, often considered the very stuff of urban politics. The explicit focus of this work was empirical; few regime theorists were motivated by a desire to help local authorities devise more effective coalitions to develop downtown. If anything, they sought to understand why challenges to development were so often stymied or diverted. However, drawing on the understanding developed from this study of land use issues, Stone has sought to develop regime theory's insights through the Civic Capacity and Urban Education Project to the more explicitly normative concern of improving urban education. A discussion of the concept of civic capacity indicates how regime theory can be applied to education policy.

CIVIC CAPACITY AND URBAN EDUCATION

Civic capacity "refers to the mobilization of varied stakeholders in support of a communitywide cause" and involves two elements.[31] The first is involvement: the greater the participation of key stakeholders, the greater the civic capacity. The second is an understanding that an issue is a community problem requiring a collective response, what Stone calls "social-purpose politics."[32] While actors may continue to differ on some points, "ideally they are able to come together in a coalition with a shared responsibility to act on their common concern. Civic capacity, then, is presumed to be manifest in cross-sector mobilization (a coalition that encompasses multiple categories of actors) around a community issue."[33] That mobilization is necessary to "establish a new set of political arrangements commensurate with the policy being advocated."[34] These new arrangements largely come about "not by coalition *pressure* on the school system, but by coalition contributions to critical policy tasks."[35] In the area of education, such arrangements, Stone emphasizes, must include educators. He draws on a 1989 RAND study's analogy with the DNA double helix to emphasize that a school reform strategy must have two complementary strands: the outside one involving support by noneducators and an inside one of educators oriented toward academic performance. Leadership plays a key role in connecting the two strands; without such connection, civic capacity is minimal.[36] In general, the focus of these arrangements would be furthering "the goal of academic achievement for all students."[37] In toto these arrangements would constitute what Stone calls a performance regime, which would be organized around improving education just as a development regime is organized around improving land use values.

The merits of thinking about urban issues in terms of civic capacity become apparent by contrasting it with what is usually called social capital, a trendy staple of discussions of cures for whatever ails urban education, cities, indeed, the entire country.[38] Although there is considerable debate over the full and precise meaning of social capital, its gist is generally viewed as involving "connections among individuals—social networks and the norms of reciprocity and trustworthiness that arise from them."[39] Stone notes that "civic capacity can be thought of as a category of social capital,"[40] but he emphasizes the difference between the two concepts. Social capital calls attention to the manner in which small-scale instances of cooperation can foster reciprocity and trust, but these kinds of *interpersonal* habits do not necessarily translate into the kind of *intergroup* cooperation that is the essence of civic capacity. One consequence of the slippage between interpersonal trust and intergroup cooperation is that small-scale collaborative successes in, say, developing effective programs at several schools can rarely be reproduced throughout a city. Another consequence is that civic capacity in one area (e.g., downtown development) need not necessarily carry over into another (e.g., education).[41] In other words, even if bygone years witnessed much greater participation in activities such as the bowling leagues to which Robert Putnam has so famously called attention,[42] there was not a concomitant community ability to address social and political problems. As Stone tellingly points out, "No matter how rich our associational life was in the past, it never yielded much in the way of a community-wide capacity for problem-solving. The American city has always been 'the private city' in which little energy has been directed into serving the whole community and responding to its problems."[43] As what Stone calls an "intergroup form of social capital,"[44] civic capacity thus calls attention to the importance of developing and sustaining local political arrangements that are commensurate with the changes in education policy that are being advocated.

In calling attention to the creation and sustenance of these political arrangements, Stone's view can be distinguished from two other perspectives on the politics of education. The first is that school reform has an inevitable political aspect, and that even the most carefully researched and best financed reform initiatives will likely falter unless proponents consider certain political issues, e.g., who benefits from the status quo. Underlying this first perspective is a view of politics as an activity that is necessary but not especially lofty, as something that helps clear the underbrush so that the more worthy work of paving the school reform highway with the most educationally sound approaches can proceed. The second perspective accords a much more positive role to politics. It sees politics not just as necessary for removing obstacles but as playing a crucial role in securing the community involvement without which, a voluminous body of literature now recognizes, meaningful change in education policy and practice cannot take place. According to this second perspective, the ability, say, of a superintendent to negotiate with key players is as important as an understanding of curriculum issues. The concept of civic capacity, as Stone explicates it, draws on the second approach but goes considerably farther by emphasizing that community involvement must be institutionalized for major changes in policy and practice to be effected and sustained. From the perspective of this third approach, it is not just that politics matters and its exercise is a lofty calling, but that its goal should be the development of pervasive and durable political arrangements, both formal and informal, conducive to education goals. Given the monotony with which commentators on the contemporary United States cite the proverb that it takes an entire village to raise a child, it is worth noting that many African villages were characterized by institutionalized and durable political arrangements. It is to the role of such arrangements in facilitating academic performance that the notion of civic capacity directs attention.[45] In so doing, civic capacity renders important service in efforts to change urban education. Although very useful in this regard, both the term itself and regime theory in general entail certain difficulties that must be discussed before attempting to apply regime theory to the Charlotte experience.

CRITICISMS OF REGIME THEORY

Many of the difficulties with regime theory and the concept of civic capacity are suggested by the unreflective acceptance of the social capital problematic that is indicated by Stone's comment that civic capacity can be thought of as a category of social capital. In asserting that linkage, Stone opens up the concept of civic capacity to the many criticisms that have been leveled at the theoretical clarity, empirical relevance, and ideological implications of the concept of social capital.[46] Especially pertinent here are the problems exemplified by the question, Can social capital mend what financial capital has torn? The question is especially relevant to the older cities and close-in suburbs of the North and Midwest that have been severely affected by profit-driven deindustrialization, capital flight, gentrification, and construction projects that ignore the needs of the urban poor. Given the political and economic difficulty of addressing the causes of such adverse developments, it is much easier to think and talk about dealing with their effects by, say, boosting the stock of social capital in urban areas. However, to focus on social capital is to befog many key issues:

> It is surely one of the great ironies of contemporary social thought that at the very time when the inequities of income and wealth of actually existing global capitalism are skyrocketing, there has been an explosion of both professional and lay literature that views a broad spectrum of social problems in terms of social capital. Such a view

suggests that all parties can gain access to capital, just different forms, and that appropriate "investments" in social capital will compensate for gross inequities in financial capital. But whatever social capital might be embodied in a plethora of bowling leagues, PTAs, church groups, and other neighborhood organizations is rarely sufficient to oppose successfully the sway of financial capital or even approximate the social capital (e.g., institutional affiliations and networks of powerful people) enjoyed by those with access to the most financial capital. Moreover, as the erosion of ghetto neighborhood organizations and networks by the loss of jobs indicates, the operation of financial capital constitutes the neighborhood and community organizations to which discussions of social capital typically refer much more than the operation of these organizations constitutes financial capital.[47]

Given the many problems with the literature on social capital as well as with the term itself, little is gained by viewing civic capacity as a category of social capital. Rather, civic capacity is sturdy enough to stand on its own two feet, especially because with its attention to intergroup cooperation, governmental actors, and the development of durable political arrangements, it (civic capacity) avoids many of the criticisms leveled at the theoretical clarity and empirical relevance of the concept of social capital.[48]

However, even if civic capacity is not viewed as a category of social capital, problems with it remain. One of the most important problems indicates a fundamental difficulty with regime theory and can also be illustrated by a question, Civic capacity for whose benefit? That question gets to a difficulty at the core of regime theory, the social production model of power from which the notion of civic capacity is derived. As noted earlier, the social production model views power in terms of *power to* not *power over*. In making that distinction, Stone recognizes that there is a point "at which the two kinds of power merge,"[49] but he minimizes the importance of such convergence. However, the relationship between the two kinds of power must be taken into account, as Anthony Giddens once noted in critiquing Parsons' positive sum conception of power to which Stone's social production model is closely related. Even if viewed from the Parsonian perspective, Giddens notes, "power is always exercised *over* someone." However much it is true, Giddens continues, "that power can rest upon 'agreement' to cede authority which can be used for collective aims, it is also true that interests of power-holders and those subject to that power often clash."[50] Although tension between such clashes and the pursuit of collective aims is fully evident in Stone's empirical work on Atlanta, it receives insufficient attention in his subsequent theoretical discussions of civic capacity.

Perhaps the best illustration of this insufficiency is Stone's view, noted earlier, that broad mobilization of civic capacity to improve education happens "not by coalition *pressure* on the school system, but by coalition contributions to critical policy tasks."[51] Insofar as the statement indicates that pressure on the school system is *insufficient* to produce change, the statement can hardly be faulted and accords with much contemporary thinking about urban politics. Not only are many scholars nowadays saying that traditional zero-sum models of political protest and pressure are inadequate,[52] but activists are making similar statements. For example, even the Industrial Areas Foundation (IAF)—whose experience with community organizing for school reform is among the most comprehensive in the nation—now talks about the importance of "reweaving the social fabric" and "realigning relationships."[53] That language is very different from that of the IAF's founder, Saul Alinsky, a community organizer to whom confrontations such as picket lines and sit-ins were the essence of effective politics.

However, to acknowledge that pressure is frequently *insufficient* to produce major change is not to say that it is *unnecessary*. As numerous studies indicate, the education arena, like most policy arenas, is characterized by competing and conflicting interests.[54] Life would be easier if all of these conflicts could be resolved by strengthening identification to the larger community and the pursuit of social-purpose politics, but the extent to which such identification suffices to secure policy goals is problematic. The political tasks involved in improving urban education parallel the governance ones associated with lower-class opportunity-expansion regimes which, as noted earlier, require regulation and coercion. "Pressure" is the name usually given to key aspects of such regulation and coercion.

Moreover, the boundary between the exertion of pressure and the realignment of relationships is a porous one because today's pressure can easily become tomorrow's realigned relationship and contribution to critical policy tasks. That point is especially well illustrated by the civil rights movement. Although many of its more farsighted participants may have envisioned a world in which relations among races would be very different in a mutually beneficial manner, an appeal to a shared identity was hardly the movement's main strategy, to say nothing of its tactics. Rather, the sine qua non of its success was pressure by African Americans and their allies, not just on school systems but on many local, state, and national institutions. Where successful, that pressure frequently realigned relations between those institutions and African Americans in a productive way that allowed the latter to make contributions to long-standing key policy tasks, such as improving education. To note such long-term consequences is, however, very different from asserting that to contemporary participants and/or observers the civil rights movement was primarily about realigning relationships, rather than exerting pressure.

In addition to neglecting the theoretical difficulties inherent in the concept of civic capacity, regime theory can be criticized for paying insufficient attention to another basic theoretical issue: the relationship between the dynamics of capitalism and local politics. Such criticisms basically take two forms; the first criticizes regime theory for what it does not do, the second for not effectively doing what it says it is setting out to do.

According to the first line of criticism, regime theorists content themselves with studying what takes place within localities and fail to study the relationship between the operation of the globalized capitalist system and the formation, maintenance, and change of urban regimes. As a result of insufficient attention to such issues, the purview of regime theory is viewed as a limited one that cannot get beyond what Lauria calls "middle-level abstractions."[55] Saying that "I plead guilty to working in the vineyard of middle-range theory," Stone basically grants the first criticism but questions its relevance.[56] Many interesting and useful things, he asserts, can be said about the politics of cities without rooting such comments in comprehensive theories about the way the world capitalist system operates. The reply is an effective one, if only because the widespread interest in, and respect for, Stone's work provides ample empirical support for his assertion. In fact, it is largely because regime theory rests content with middle-range theory that it has so far managed to avoid many theoretical standoffs (such as those between pluralists and stratification theorists) and still motivate many intriguing research agendas.

According to the second line of criticism, regime theory underestimates the extent to which the local corporate pursuit of profit and the accumulation of capital constrain urban politics. The second criticism is much less easily dismissed because it attacks regime theory on the very turf that it has staked out: understanding urban politics and using this understanding to improve the lot of low-income citizens. Developed by David Imbroscio in a 1998 exchange with Stone in the pages of the *Journal of Urban Affairs,* this second line of criticism asserts that such attempts will fail "absent a fundamental change in the corporate-dominated character of most current urban regimes."[57] Such changes are possible, Imbroscio asserts, by giving community organizations, small businesses, and local government itself much greater control over investment activity. Moreover, he continues, if regime theory took its shibboleth that politics matters more seriously, it would devote considerable attention to ways of developing effective political challenges to corporate domination. As part of developing his critique of Stone's focus on improving urban education, Imbroscio draws upon Anyon's poignant analogy that trying to change urban education without making broader changes in urban politics and economics is like trying to clean the air on one side of a screen door.[58]

On theoretical grounds, there are at least two replies to Imbroscio's critique, both of which Stone makes. The first is that Imbroscio's suggestions for increasing the role of community organizations, small businesses, and local government itself in the accumulation process are too marginal and/or impractical to address the deep-rooted structural causes of inequality in contemporary urban society. The second is that while the accumulation imperative of contemporary capitalism profoundly affects urban politics, this imperative is not "determinative" because "modern society has low coherence and that the presence of multiple, loosely coupled structures is a foundation for contingency." As a result, there are "multiple sources of system bias to be overcome, not just the mode of production."[59]

Whatever the merits of Stone's and Imbroscio's positions, it is worth emphasizing that the claims of both men are largely theoretical. The kinds of opportunity-expansion and performance regimes of which Stone speaks are largely hypothetical, as are the community-based, petty bourgeois and local-statist ones that Imbroscio touts. There is considerable need to subject both sets of claims to what has, and is, taking place in urban politics. The extent to which opportunity-expansion and performance regimes can be built absent sweeping changes in corporate power in urban politics is a complicated question, a comprehensive answer to which hinges on empirical investigation. Also requiring empirical investigation are questions related to the realignment of relationships and the exertion of pressure in the development of civic capacity and social-purpose politics. This book addresses both sets of questions by relating them to Charlotte's experience. Admittedly, this experience leaves crucial aspects of the questions unanswered.[60] However, the Charlotte story does illuminate many aspects of the complex relationships among corporate power, improving urban education, and the operation of local regimes. Before beginning this story, however, it is necessary to discuss some methodological and conceptual issues.

METHODOLOGICAL ISSUES

In his history of the Detroit public school system, Jeffrey Mirel offers some prefatory observations about the importance of taking a long perspective that studies the relationship between education and the social, political, and economic developments in a given place and notes:

> Ideally, historians should research educational systems in different cities, each representing different economic and political contexts throughout the country. Unfortunately, efforts to achieve that ideal, even when aided by substantial grants and teams of research assistants, have fallen far short of the mark. The reasons for that failure are simple—the amount of material that is necessary to consider in studying the history of even one large urban system is enormous. . . .

For the time being, individual case studies may be the only feasible approach to longitudinal research on the history of twentieth-century urban education.[61]

Since Mirel made that observation, the results of the Civic Capacity and Urban Education Project have been published and bear witness to the fruitfulness of research that employs an explicitly comparative framework to study the politics of urban education.[62] But this project was an extremely large one that drew on the efforts of over twenty scholars for the eleven cities being studied. My thinking about the politics of urban education draws heavily on the work of this project, and many of my concerns overlap its.[63] However, neither Charlotte nor I were part of the project, and my research questions and interview protocols differed considerably from its. Moreover, working without what Mirel calls "teams of research assistants," I found it necessary to focus on Charlotte.[64] Thus, while I will occasionally make reference to the results that have emerged from the Civic Capacity and Urban Education Project, as well as from other studies of urban education, this book is a case study of education policy and regime politics in one city rather than a comparison of policy and politics in several cities.

However, while this book is about Charlotte, I try, when possible, to illuminate its experience by selected comparisons with other cities. In particular, while I was unable to conduct the labor-intensive interviews and archival research necessary to study politics and policy formation in any city other than Charlotte, I can draw on more readily available quantitative data about other school systems to put the Charlotte experience in perspective.[65] For example, as chapter 5 will indicate, it is possible to draw upon data available from North Carolina's Department of Public Instruction (DPI) to compare academic outcomes in CMS with those of other North Carolina consolidated urban districts during the early 1990s when CMS' ambitious school reform program was drawing national praise.

Quantitative data is also readily available about the funding that each North Carolina county provides its public school system. Contained in the annual reports of the Public School Forum of North Carolina, this data provides detailed information on each county's wealth, the actual funding for public education, and the extent to which the actual funding is commensurate with the county's wealth. I will make extensive use of this data because the fiscal dependence of CMS and other North Carolina school systems upon their county commissions, discussed in chapter 2, makes local funding of public education an extremely good measure of the "mobilization of varied stakeholders in support of a community-wide cause," i.e., of civic capacity. The Appendix discusses the methodological issues involved in using the Public School Forum's reports.

In discussing Charlotte's success in building civic capacity, I will, as regime theory's second defining characteristic dictates, pay special attention to the actions and attitudes of the high-ranking executives of major businesses operating in Charlotte, a group that I will call the *business elite*. I am not all that happy with the term because it reflects and contributes to the unfortunate practice, all too common in contemporary political discourse, of avoiding class as a category for both understanding and changing the world.[66] But whatever the theoretical, empirical, and normative shortcomings of *business elite*, the term appears frequently in the literature on urban regimes and has an intuitively plausible meaning. In Charlotte, as in many other cities, local politics are especially influenced by members of the business elite whose businesses' fortunes are heavily tied to local land-use values and are thus key constituents of what Logan and Molotch call the growth machine.[67] Among such businesses are those that benefit from particular land-use decisions (e.g., developers and builders), as well as those who benefit from growth in general (e.g., utilities and the media). Of Charlotte's media, an especially important role has been played by the *Charlotte Observer*. Currently, Charlotte's only daily newspaper, the *Observer* exemplifies Logan and Molotch's characterization of the metropolitan newspaper as the "local business [that] takes a broad responsibility for general growth machine goals," and I will pay particular attention to its editorial stance.[68] Particular attention will also be paid to the activities of the top executives of Bank of America and First Union, the Charlotte-based bank that was the principal forerunner of the bank that in 2003 bears the Wachovia name.[69] The explosive growth of Bank of America and First Union in the 1980s and 1990s provides excellent examples of "the fortunes of some of the most crucial local actors [being] less tied to their old home base."[70] However, each bank has maintained a lively stake in Charlotte's growth and civic health. Moreover, the CEOs of both banks have taken a personal, frequently intense interest in many aspects of local politics, including education, even as the banks have grown dramatically. Despite their business rivalry, on civic and political matters the two CEOs have generally seen eye to eye. As Ed Crutchfield, First Union's CEO from 1984 to 2000, remarked, "On business, we do compete, but that is only true in business . . . It's exactly the opposite way in civic and political affairs."[71] Despite the general agreement on political matters between McColl and Crutchfield, the business elite has not always acted cohesively on educational issues, and such divisions have at times played an important role in local education politics.

PLAN OF BOOK

This book's organization is straightforward and generally chronological. Chapter 2 provides background by discussing Charlotte's economic growth, the political battles of the 1960s, the alliance between the business elite and black political leaders, the political fluidity in the 1990s, and the economic situation of black Charlotteans. Chapter 3 turns to education by discussing the origins and consequences of the *Swann* case, paying special attention to the 1977–1986 administration of Superintendent Jay Robinson that was the heyday of the mandatory busing plan. In addition to discussing the main characteristics of Robinson's administration, the chapter considers shortfalls in civic capacity and the extent to which the desegregation glass was half full or half empty. Chapter 4 deals with the transition years following Robinson's resignation, during which CMS witnessed increasing challenges to the busing plan, more shortfalls in civic capacity, and a range of other problems.

Chapter 5 deals with CMS' high-profile school reform program of the early 1990s. Again, the emphasis is on historical narration, with a particular focus on the operation of the reform program, the events that facilitated its implementation, and the conflicts that led to the resignation of the superintendent who was its architect. As part of that discussion, the chapter discusses battles over desegregation, the extent to which the business elite influenced education policy, and the conflicts that weakened civic capacity. With outcome data more readily available for these years than the 1980s or 1970s, chapter 5 also investigates the extent to which the reform program accomplished its ambitious goals, as well as the reasons for the lack of accomplishment.

Chapter 6 begins the book's discussion of more recent events by considering the increasing pressure upon CMS to abandon its commitment to desegregation. Among other things, that pressure led to the creation of a citizen task force whose efforts and their relation to civic capacity the chapter examines. More importantly, the opposition to CMS' desegregation efforts led to the reactivation of the *Swann* case, and the chapter discusses both the political context of the renewed litigation and its key legal aspects.

Chapter 7 considers the turbulent aftermath of the federal district court's ruling that CMS could no longer pursue desegregation goals. That aftermath included CMS' decision to appeal the court's ruling, pivotal school board elections, intensified battles over pupil assignment, and conflict over school funding. In discussing these issues, the chapter focuses on the extent to which black Charlotteans, especially those on the school board, were willing to follow the course of Atlanta and many other communities in forsaking desegregation in exchange for extra resources for largely segregated schools.

The conclusion, chapter 8, brings together the themes that emerged in the earlier ones. As part of summing up the history of desegregation in Charlotte, the chapter argues that desegregation benefited black children and also enhanced civic capacity. However, the civic capacity resulting from Charlotte's desegregation accomplishments, the chapter emphatically argues, did more to help Charlotte grow than to benefit African Americans or to strengthen public education. Based on this discussion of the asymmetric transfer of civic capacity, the chapter also considers the extent to which education can be improved for black children absent the regulation and coercion of institutional elites that, as this Introduction has noted, is a hallmark of opportunity expansion regimes. The chapter also discusses ways of developing civic capacity despite intense conflict over CMS' continued commitment to desegregation, and it ends with some brief comments about the Stone-Imbroscio debate.

Chapter 2

Background
Regime Politics and the Purest Strain
of the Southern Booster Gene

Charlotte . . . may edge out Dallas and Atlanta as home to the purest strain
ever discovered of the Southern booster gene.

> —-*New York Times* writer Peter Applebome,
> in his 1996 book, *Dixie Rising.*[1]

They would elect Martin King or Malcolm X mayor if somehow one of
them could give them a guarantee of no labor unions and no minimum wage
for laundry workers.

> —1964 comment about what he called the city's "managerial class"
> by Harry Golden, Charlotte journalist, publisher,
> and author of the 1950s' best-seller, *Only in America.*[2]

That's how the old guard thinks—let me go up to NationsBank and ask
Hugh (McColl, Jr.) for his permission.

> —1994 remark by an African American political activist
> criticizing other blacks' relations with Charlotte's
> white business elite, such as Hugh McColl, CEO of
> NationsBank and subsequently Bank of America.[3]

Education in Charlotte has been shaped by the area's demographics, political structure, and growth; the economic situation of African Americans; and
the overall characteristics of local politics. The relations among education and
these other aspects of the Charlotte situation are complex ones with causal
arrows pointing in many different directions. Before trying to discern these
complex causal relationships and focusing on education, it will be helpful to

highlight the demographic, political, and economic context in which CMS operated in the last third of the twentieth century.

DEMOGRAPHICS

Since 1960, CMS has been a consolidated district covering all 530 square miles of Mecklenburg County, over 75 percent of whose population lives in the city of Charlotte, according to the 2000 Census. North Carolina's annexation laws are among the nation's most permissive, and as economic growth has taken place beyond its boundaries, the city has annexed many of these outlying areas, increasing its area from 30 square miles in 1950 to 241 square miles in 2000.[4] In fact, the ease with which Charlotte has been able to annex outlying areas goes a long way toward explaining why it was the only major U.S. city in the 1990s whose population was growing faster than that of its suburbs.[5] Mecklenburg also contains six smaller municipalities located on the county's periphery: Cornelius, Davidson, and Huntersville in the north; Pineville and Matthews in the south; and Mint Hill in the southeast. A few farms can still be found in outlying regions of the county, but they have been rapidly giving way to development.

The 2000 Census listed Charlotte as having 541,000 people, making it the country's twenty-sixth largest city and one whose population had grown by 37 percent in the previous ten years.[6] Mecklenburg had grown by approximately the same amount, reaching a size of 695,000 people in 2000.[7] This increase in population has had profound effects on the public school system, with enrollment growing from 76,000 K–12 students in 1990–91 to 109,600 students in the 2002–03 school year, making CMS the country's twenty-third largest school district.[8]

According to the 2000 Census, blacks comprised 33 percent and whites 58 percent of the population of the city of Charlotte. The corresponding figures for Mecklenburg were 28 percent and 64 percent. In part because the boundaries of the city of Charlotte have been so elastic, its demographic composition stayed relatively constant between 1970 and 2000, with blacks comprising 30 percent of the city's population in that earlier year and 24 percent of the county's. African Americans are heavily concentrated in the center of the county, especially in the area west of I-77 that, not surprisingly, is typically referred to as the westside. Although too recent a development to be discussed in this book's history of regime and education politics, the area's biggest demographic change was the approximately 600 percent jump in the Hispanic population in the 1990s. As a result, by 2000, there were 45,000 Hispanics in Mecklenburg, approximately 6 percent of the county's population.[9] Similarly, while the 1990s also saw a jump in Mecklenburg's Asian population, that change is also too recent a development to be addressed in this book.

Of special interest to this study of education is, of course, the ethnic and racial composition of the school system. In *Swann,* the Supreme Court noted that blacks comprised 29 percent of the district's student body in the 1968–69 school year.[10] Ten years later, after the busing plan had been implemented, blacks comprised 37 percent of CMS' enrollment. But in the twenty subsequent years, the percentage increased very slowly, equaling 38, 39, 39, 40, 42, and 43 percent for the school years beginning in August 1982, 1986, 1990, 1994, 1998, and 2002, respectively.[11] Until recently, almost all of CMS' nonblack students were non-Hispanic whites. Thus in 1992–93, blacks comprised 40 percent of CMS' enrollment; whites, 56 percent; Asians, 3 percent; and Hispanics, 1 percent.[12] However, while the percentage black enrollment had edged up only slightly to 43 percent by 2002–03, the percentage Hispanic enrollment had skyrocketed to 8 percent by that year, with Asians increasing to 4 percent and American Indians and multiracial students comprising 2 percent. As a result of the increased percentages of students of color, non-Hispanic whites constituted 43 percent of CMS' students in 2002–03. Thus over ten years, CMS' percentage of non-Hispanic white enrollment dropped sharply, even though the district had 3,000 more such students in 2002–03 than it had a decade earlier.

A Fragmented Political Structure

The relationship between politics and education is greatly affected by the structure of local government that fragments educational policymaking. It will facilitate a discussion of regime politics to summarize these structures and the ways that they have changed over the years.

The present method of choosing the mayor of the city of Charlotte largely dates to 1935 when, after experimentation with a system in which a five-person council had selected the mayor from among its members, the direct popular election of the mayor was adopted.[13] Also in that year, the size of the city council was increased to eleven members elected at large. However, like the election for mayor, those for city council remained nonpartisan. Although the council would shrink to seven members in the 1940s and several other changes were made in that decade,[14] it was not until the 1970s that the system of representation underwent major changes. In 1975, elections for both mayor and city council became partisan. Two years later, a hotly contested referendum passed by a margin of eighty votes that replaced at-large representation on the city council with a combination of at-large and district representation. The city council currently contains eleven members—four at large and seven from districts—who are chosen in partisan elections held in odd-numbered years on the same day as the general election. Both the mayor and members of the city council serve for two years. Although Charlotte has a city manager and the mayoralty is generally considered a weak one, many of its occupants have played pivotal roles in local politics, and mayoral elections have been extremely important in both shaping and reflecting regime politics.

Mecklenburg County is governed by a county commission, which, prior to 1986, had been elected at large in partisan elections. However, in that year, the county also adopted a hybrid form of representation that evolved by the mid-1990s to a system in which three county commissioners were elected at large and six were elected from districts. Partisan elections for all nine slots are held in November of even-numbered years. The county commission elects its own chair and hires the county manager.

The method of electing members of the school board has also changed over the years. In the years immediately following consolidation, the board consisted of twelve members, the city board having had seven members and the county, five. However, the consolidation agreement allowed for a drop to nine members, all of whom served four-year terms and were elected in at-large elections in May on the same day that primaries were held. Unlike elections for county commission and city council, those for school board remain nonpartisan. However, as a result of political developments (to be discussed in chapter 5), the method of representation changed in 1995 to a hybrid system, with three members being elected at large and six from districts identical to those from which county commissioners are elected. Like the county commission, the school board elects its own chair, but unlike both the city council and county commission, members of the school board serve for four years, with the terms being staggered so that the three at-large seats are at stake in one year and the six district seats are at stake two years later.[15] Moreover, the changes in 1995 also involved moving the day of school board elections from the spring to the general election in November.

The local politics of education are complicated by the manner in which education is financed. As a result of legislation enacted during the fiscal crisis of the 1930s, North Carolina has generally footed more of the local education bill than have most state governments, with slightly over 60 percent of CMS' budget coming from the state in recent years. Moreover, CMS, like school districts generally in North Carolina, lacks taxing authority and must rely on the county commission to issue bonds and provide a significant portion of its operating revenue (recently over 30 percent). As a result, the county commission—elected in partisan elections in years different from those in which the nonpartisan school board is chosen—plays a key role in education issues in Charlotte, frequently using its control of the purse strings to influence school policy. As a result of this influence, education policymaking in Charlotte is frequently fragmented despite the fact that North Carolina's liberal annexation laws and the consolidation of city and county schools have minimized the political balkanization that elsewhere impedes the cohesive development and implementation of policy.

Economic Development

Charlotte's civic leadership has long been preoccupied with growth and economic development. Noting that Charlotte had given rise to the "world's bluntest Chamber of Commerce slogan, the lyrical mid-1970s' corporate rallying cry, 'Charlotte—A Good Place to Make Money,' "[16] Peter Applebome also characterized Charlotte by saying: "If there has to be something called the Museum of the New South, I'm kind of glad it's in Charlotte, where the town's most famous Chamber of Commerce executive was Booster Kuester, where the *Charlotte Observer* is forever running stories with headlines like 'Charlotte Hits Big Time: We Need 2 Phone Books,' where they threw together a whole fake nightclub district for the one weekend of the 1994 Final Four basketball tournament, lest anyone think Charlotte wasn't sufficiently world class."[17]

Especially important from the standpoint of civic leaders has been the attempt to catch up with Atlanta, the prototypical city of the New South, situated 250 miles down I-85, which has set the standard by which, for much of the twentieth century, Charlotte's civic boosters have judged their city's accomplishments: "Atlanta," noted an editorial in the *Observer*, "is the big brother/big sister—the one that was first with big league teams and international flights and an outerbelt highway."[18]

As was the case with Atlanta, trade and distribution have played a key role in Charlotte's development. Charlotte emerged in the 1870s as a leading railway hub, and a combination of the legacy of its importance in rail transport, North Carolina's Good Roads Movement of the 1920s, and federal highway construction allowed the area to remain an important distribution center. In the late 1960s, civic boosters would claim that "only Chicago served as a home base for more tractor-trailer rigs than Charlotte,"[19] and in the 1990s, the Chamber of Commerce would point to the Census Bureau's count of wholesale sales as an indication that Charlotte was the sixth largest distribution center in the United States.[20]

Manufacturing, especially that related to textiles, also has played an important role in the economic history of Charlotte, with the Cotton Mill Campaign beginning in the 1880s bringing a large number of mills to the Charlotte area with the result that it very rapidly become a textile center.

Although the textile industry had virtually disappeared from Mecklenburg by the end of the twentieth century, the industry's boom 100 years earlier fueled the growth of the banks that, many mergers and acquisitions later, would become Bank of America and the Charlotte-based Wachovia.[21]

It is these banks' rise to international prominence and Charlotte's concomitant emergence as a financial and business service center that exemplify the area's dramatic growth. In 1951, *Business Week* had approvingly called Charlotte "a paper town—because most of its business is done on paper,"[22] and subsequent events would make Charlotte even better known for business done on paper, especially banking. No single event better serves to illustrate the intimate relationship between banking and Charlotte's growth than what happened on October 1, 1998. Even before that date, the explosive growth of Charlotte's two major banks, NationsBank and First Union, had made the city the nation's second largest banking center, trailing only New York City in that regard. But October 1, 1998, marked the completion of the merger between NationsBank and the San Francisco-based BankAmerica to create the largest consumer bank in the United States. Although this new bank's name was Bank of America, its corporate headquarters was not the venerable City by the Bay, traditionally considered one of the most eminent and financially important cities in the country, but an urban upstart that even in the 1990s still suffered from the "Ch factor": frequent confusion among non-Southerners between it and Charleston, South Carolina; Charlottesville, Virginia; and Charleston, West Virginia. Another indication of the primacy accorded NationsBank in this merger was that the CEO of the new Bank of America was not the CEO of the old BankAmerica but NationBank's CEO, Hugh McColl.

From the vantage point of 1998, the emergence of Charlotte as an international banking powerhouse was, like so much else in the history of any locality, a combination of geography, politics, and the ambition and acumen of local businessmen. Although nowadays Charlotte is rarely considered a gold-mining region, the area was, until the discovery of gold in California in the 1840s, the United States' leading producer of gold and continued, with the aid of Northern capital, to produce the precious metal after the Civil War.[23] The presence of gold mines helped Charlotte secure one of three branch mints awarded by the federal government in 1835. That two natives of the Charlotte area occupied high positions in the federal government—President Andrew Jackson and House Ways and Means Committee Chairman James Polk—"no doubt helped the process" of Charlotte's securing the mint, as a local historian notes.[24] Although the mint would eventually close in 1913, its seventy-five plus years of existence, together with Charlotte's importance in regional trade, helped establish the city as a regional banking and financial center. In the late 1920s, when the

Federal Reserve Bank of Richmond sought a branch to serve western North Carolina and adjoining regions of South Carolina, Charlotte provided a suitable location since the city already had "more banks, capital, deposits, and resources than any other city in North Carolina."[25]

Of the many advantages that accrued to Charlotte's bankers from having a branch of the Fed located in the city, among the most important came in 1960, when the Charlotte-based American Commercial Bank merged with the Greensboro-based Security National Bank to create North Carolina National Bank (NCNB), the main forerunner of NationsBank. That Charlotte housed a branch of the Fed helped secure the bank's headquarters for the city.[26] Although NCNB's charter was in fact a national one, the various mergers that led to its creation were facilitated by liberal North Carolina banking laws. In 1814, North Carolina's legislature had allowed the branching of state banks, and unlike many other states, it had not imposed any significant restrictions in the subsequent 150 years.[27] In addition to facilitating mergers within North Carolina's banking industry, such as the one leading to the formation of NCNB, this permissive environment gave the state's bankers the kind of experience with mergers and consolidations that provided a leg up when barriers—both at the state and federal levels—were removed to interstate banking in the 1980s. Leading first NCNB's and then NationsBank's charge into interstate banking was Hugh McColl, whose drive and business savvy were noted in a cover story in a 1995 issue of *Fortune*. Taking into account his fondness for hunting, the cover featured McColl in hunter's garb, shotgun in hand, and was summarized in the issue's table of contents with the comment, "McColl's reputation as a skin-you-alive dealmaker makes other big bankers sweat."[28]

Among the many consequences of the growth of Charlotte's two main banks, two are especially relevant here. The first is the area's growing importance as a center of other financial and business services. In 1991, four years prior to its cover story on McColl, *Fortune* had rated Charlotte as having the best pro-business attitude of any U.S. city, noted McColl's contribution to Charlotte's development as a financial center, and concluded by calling attention to its "terrific back-office reputation" that helped bring Hearst Magazines' accounting operations to Charlotte in that year. By 1998, Hearst had committed to placing its name on a forty-six-story office building whose development Bank of America had initiated in downtown Charlotte, near the bank's corporate headquarters.[29]

Called the Hearst Tower, this office building illustrates the second consequence of the growth of Charlotte's banks: the impetus it has provided to the development of downtown Charlotte. Exemplifying their competition for financial preeminence, Charlotte's major banks have built skyscraping downtown corporate headquarters. First Union's 1971 thirty-two-story building was topped by NCNB's 1974 forty-story tower. In 1988, First Union completed a forty-two story headquarters, and in 1992, NationsBank opened its sixty-story headquarters. These projects, along with Charlotte's growing importance as a financial center, helped fuel a series of other high-profile downtown construction projects in addition to the Hearst Tower.[30]

Along with this growth in downtown Charlotte, there also has been considerable commercial, as well as industrial and residential, development on Charlotte's periphery. Two such developments are especially important and directly affected education policy in the 1990s, as chapter 6 will indicate. The first, and older one, is University Research Park. Located approximately eight miles from downtown in the northeast part of the county near the University of North Carolina at Charlotte (UNCC), the park was initially developed in the 1960s and by the turn of the century covered 3,200 acres that housed forty corporations, employing approximately 23,000 people.[31] The second is Ballantyne, a 2,000-acre upscale commercial, residential, and recreational development located in the southern periphery of the county. Once the hunting preserve of Cameron Morrison, who served as North Carolina's governor in the early 1920s, the land stayed within his family and remained largely undeveloped until the mid-1990s, when Charlotte's growth and the opening of southern sections of the outerbelt, an interstate highway encircling Charlotte, provided a propitious opportunity for development. Noting how the former hunting preserve was becoming "a 2,000-acre edge city," with 4,500 homes, 1,150 hotel rooms, and a 525-acre business park, the *Observer's* business columnist aptly noted that this "intense development illustrates the power of Interstate 485 . . . to spawn residential and commercial development."[32] The outerbelt also had profound consequences for educational policy, as subsequent chapters will indicate. Also affecting education policy was the complex interplay among race, class, and Charlotte's economic growth.

RACE, CLASS, AND DEVELOPMENT

As this short account suggests, local politics have long pivoted around economic growth. The political arrangements associated with this focus on growth can very appropriately be called a development regime. This is not, it should be emphasized, to suggest that these arrangements invariably work smoothly and harmoniously. Just the reverse is the case. For example, conflict, often very sharp, over the location of particular projects is the very stuff of development politics, and is as common in Charlotte as elsewhere. One such instance was the dispute in the early 1980s over whether a new coliseum should be built downtown or near the airport. However, while there was considerable disagreement about where the coliseum should be located, there was much less about the need for a new coliseum to facilitate development.

A shared understanding among developers, banks, utilities, the daily newspaper, department stores, and other major businesses that benefit from economic growth is only one aspect of the arrangements characterizing a development regime. A second aspect involves securing the election of pro-growth government officials and the passage of the bond referenda necessary to facilitate this growth. Critical to the success of such electoral endeavors has been a coalition between the business elite and the political leaders of the black community. Because Charlotte's blacks have comprised only about 30 percent of the area's population, their votes were obviously never sufficient to win elections. But given divisions among the white population, the black vote—when cohesive, as it typically was in key contests—could hold the balance of power.

Further contributing to African American political influence was a situation in Charlotte basically captured by Stone's observation about the state of political organization in Atlanta: "Labor unions are weak, and the working class has little political voice. By contrast, the business sector is well organized, and it has a long history of exercising leadership . . . The only other substantial sector of local public life is that of the African American community."[33]

To be sure, since blacks comprise a much larger percentage of Atlanta's population than Charlotte's (approximately 62 percent, as opposed to approximately 33 percent in 2000), Stone's statement is not fully applicable to Charlotte. In particular, groups based in predominantly white neighborhoods have played important roles in local politics, but these organizations have lacked the long-term staying power of organizations and networks rooted among the (predominantly white) business sector and among African Americans. Moreover, while labor unions played a significant role in Charlotte's political life earlier in the century, during the post-*Swann* years, upon which this book focuses, they had a minimal effect on education policy and politics in general.[34] Thus, compared to many cities, especially in the North, Midwest, and Pacific West, Charlotte's recent political history has seen a relative paucity in the *sustained organized* expression of interest and sentiment, with the business sector and African Americans being the main groups capable of maintaining an ongoing and influential organized political presence. For this reason, even though Charlotte's black population is smaller than Atlanta's, what Stone says about the latter also holds for the former: "In most communities, business leaders invest resources in a network of civic organizations and informal contacts through which they create a private capacity to cooperate and promote community projects . . . Having long recognized the value of black allies in the city's politics, they [Atlanta's business elite] have put substantial resources into *creating a direct business tie with black business interests and other black leaders with important institutional affiliations.*"[35]

These efforts were especially fruitful from approximately 1963 through 1987. During those twenty-plus years, an alliance between the business elite and political leadership of the black community dominated major aspects of local electoral politics. However, the very growth facilitated by this alliance undermined its clout. As will be indicated below, the 1987 mayoral election signified this change, and while still organized around development, Charlotte's politics have been much more fluid since 1987 because of both economic growth and the altered influence of this alliance. Here I will sketch the origins and characteristics of this "biracial coalition around economic growth,"[36] saving for subsequent chapters a more detailed discussion of the relationship between education and regime politics. Of course, this coalition did not include all African Americans or every Charlotte business executive. It generally did include though the main players in the business elite and most of Charlotte's influential black political leaders. Moreover, the generally harmonious relationship between the business elite and black political leadership was occasionally punctuated by sharp conflicts, perhaps most notably the 1977 battle over district representation on Charlotte's city council. However, when the dust cleared, that battle served, I will argue in chapter 8, to strengthen this coalition and facilitate Charlotte's development.

The operation of the coalition was especially evident in city politics. Even though the school system is coterminous with the county and important differences exist between city and county politics, what happens at the city level greatly affects county-wide developments, if only because North Carolina's permissive annexation laws have allowed the city to continue to include within its borders over three-fourths of the county's population and most of its economic activity. Moreover, the division of labor between city and county involves the county assuming primary responsibility for the provision of health and human services, while the city is more typically concerned with providing physical infrastructure, such as water and sewage facilities, and high-profile development projects, such as the airport and sports arena. Given the precedence that development issues generally have over those involving human services, it is hardly surprising that the political arrangements that characterize city politics have done much to shape the county's as well. In a 1988 political atlas, two keen observers of local events—a local political geographer and Mecklenburg's longtime supervisor of elections—noted that "in every sense of the word Charlotte dominates Mecklenburg County politics."[37] However, county politics have never been reducible to those of the city, and the most high-profile electoral battle of the late 1990s followed the county commission's decision, discussed below, to cut funding for the arts. But in this election, too, the alliance between the business elite and black political leadership played a key role.

From Populism to the New Deal

A discussion of recent events can be usefully framed by some prefatory comments about earlier years. In the 1890s, Charlotte, along with all of North Carolina and many other parts of the South, was rocked by a populist insurgency that saw large numbers of African Americans and whites come together, in the words of one black Charlottean, to oppose "the oppression of the poor by the rich" and "the weakness of the government in securing liberty to all its citizens alike."[38] The electoral manifestation of this insurgency was a Fusion ticket between the Populist and Republican parties that in 1896 elected North Carolina's governor and captured 78 percent of the seats in the state legislature. In Mecklenburg, Democrats lost all county-wide contests. Among the precincts the party lost were those near Charlotte's textile factories, leading one historian to conclude, "Working-class Charlotteans as well as farmers and blacks were clearly deserting the Democratic Party and its traditional vision of government."[39]

In Charlotte, as elsewhere, the Populist insurgency was defeated largely by an appeal to the importance of maintaining the color line and white supremacy. With the defeat of the insurgency, large numbers of African Americans were disenfranchised by terror, poll taxes, literacy tests, or other forms of repression, so much so that by the spring of 1903, the *Observer* would gloat that "the negro in Charlotte is the most maimed, ineffectual voting element in a body politic that has ever existed since the grant of the magna charta."[40] Although the *Observer* underestimated the intensity with which blacks in Charlotte would struggle to overcome the effects of disenfranchisement and other forms of repression, relatively little research has been conducted on how these struggles manifested themselves in Charlotte's politics during the first third of the century.[41]

More information is available about the 1930s, especially the election of 1935, the year in which, it will be recalled, the city of Charlotte enlarged its city council and returned to direct mayoral elections. On Election Day, the *Charlotte News*, the afternoon paper, carried a front-page story about the brisk turnout, with its second sentence noting, "At 3 o'clock this afternoon 4,985 votes had been cast, of which 3,684 were cast by white persons and 1,301 by negro voters."[42] Although the article also reported "a slackening in the negro vote at about noontime,"[43] even if no additional blacks voted, those 1,301 votes would have constituted about 12 percent of the almost 11,000 votes that were cast for mayor, not an insignificant percentage.

Motivating this turnout was the candidacy of an African American that merited special commentary in the *News'* post-election editorial. Entitled "More Congratulations," the editorial illustrated the patronizing discourse that passed as an enlightened approach to race relations:

And since the day has started on a congratulatory note, it had as well be sustained as long as possible . . .

The municipal campaign saw the early entrance of a reputable Negro citizen. There have been Negro candidates before, but they amounted to nothing, not even in their own circles. Bishop Dale was known to be a man of good sense and honor.

He was defeated, as was inevitable, perhaps, yet because of the manner of his defeat both the white and colored people of the city have earned congratulations. No unpleasantness was to be perceived. The city took it much as a matter of course, interesting, novel, but not anything to be alarmed about or to cause dissension between two races which, after all, have got to live in the same town and might as well do so amicably.[44]

Among the reasons for the "inevitability" of Dale's defeat was the at-large method of representation. In the nonpartisan primary that winnowed the field for the eleven seats on the council down to twenty-two candidates, Dale finished eleventh. But with all seats on the council being chosen at large, an African American candidate was at a distinct disadvantage, and in the election, he finished nineteenth out of twenty-one candidates, the twenty-second having dropped out between the primary and the election.[45]

Charlotte Politics at Mid-Century

Since blacks constituted a significant proportion of the electorate, their support was sought by contending groups of white politicians throughout the thirties, forties, and fifties. Additional research is needed to ascertain the nature of local issues in these years and the coalitions that formed around them, but it is at least clear that in the post-World War II years, Charlotte's politics resembled that of many other Sunbelt cities. Political leaders hoisted various reform and "good government" banners, but as Carl Abbott notes:

The men in the foreground during the 1950s and 1960s were the same people who could be found in the Chamber of Commerce board room or at the monthly meetings of the Jaycees, for the sunbelt reform movements operated with the assumption that leadership should come from certain groups within the local business community . . . From one ocean to another, it was difficult to distinguish the members of the Good Government League in San Antonio, the Charter Government Committee in Phoenix, or the Myers

Park [at the time, Charlotte's most upscale residential area] clique in
Charlotte from the crowd in the country club lounge.[46]

The political prominence of the "people who could be found in the
Chamber of Commerce board room" went back at least as far as the election
of 1935. As a local historian noted in 1976, from 1935 through 1975, every
mayor of Charlotte "was the president or owner of his own business, the only
exception being an attorney."[47] The two longest-serving mayors—Stan
Brookshire and John Belk, whose eight-year tenures spanned the period 1961–
1977—both served as chairs of the Chamber of Commerce. Nor was
Charlotte's civic leadership modest about the role of local businessmen. A
1960 *Observer* editorial asked "Guess Who's Boss of Our Town?" and answered that "Charlotte is run, primarily and well, by its Chamber of
Commerce . . . The Chamber of Commerce is not, of course, the sole active
force . . . But the Chamber of Commerce is the greatest force, and the sum
of its labors has been impressive. We are pleased to acknowledge its bossism
and to wish it continued health."[48]

Martha Evans

Despite the ongoing influence of the business elite, the period 1959–
1963 was a benchmark period in Charlotte politics. The significance of the
electoral change that took place between 1959 and 1963 can be understood
by considering earlier mayoral elections. The five that took place from 1949,
the year Charlotte began reporting returns by precincts rather than wards,
to 1957 were lopsided affairs, reflecting the hegemony of what Abbott calls
the people found in the chamber boardroom. In 1955, there was only one
candidate, in 1957, the victor got 87 percent of the votes, and in the other
three elections, the victor got between 66 percent and 69 percent. In 1959,
however, Martha Evans, who in 1955 was the first woman ever elected to
the city council, challenged the incumbent, James Smith. She received 47
percent of the vote, carrying most black precincts and many working-class
white ones as well. Her tally was especially impressive, because she "did
little advertising and hired no poll workers,"[49] the latter being a frequent
local euphemism for individuals who received "gas money" or other financial
compensation for mobilizing the white working class and black vote, often
by whatever means necessary.

As the 1961 elections approached, Smith's prospects for reelection looked
dim because his leadership skills were generally questioned by Charlotte's
business elite, as was his decision to relocate much of his company's business
to another city. Worried about a possible Evans victory, Charlotte's business

leaders persuaded an initially reluctant Stan Brookshire to oppose her. Although Brookshire had never held elective public office before, he had been chair of the Chamber of Commerce. Brookshire would subsequently candidly acknowledge in his family history: "To the political observers and the business and civic leadership, it seemed obvious that Mrs. Evans, a capable but fiery redhead, having built a strong political base (particularly among the minority groups) during her two terms on council, would win over the field. The business and civic leadership of Charlotte was not happy with such a prospect."[50] With the editorial endorsement of both of Charlotte's daily papers and support from the business elite and the leadership of the Democratic Party, Brookshire won the election with 55 percent of the vote. Again, Evans carried both black precincts and many working-class white ones, as well.

Why "the business and civic leadership of Charlotte was not happy" with the prospect of Evans's becoming mayor deserves additional comment. On its editorial page, the *Observer* acknowledged Evans's ability but then endorsed the political neophyte Brookshire because of doubts that "she, as mayor, could work closely and harmoniously with the Council."[51] Forty years later, it is difficult to view those doubts as expressing anything other than the difficulty that Charlotte's overwhelmingly male political and business establishment had in dealing with an assertive, intellectually formidable, and politically savvy woman.

But the apprehension went beyond gender issues. Although, like Brookshire, a supporter of urban renewal (a topic discussed below), Evans, while on the city council, had often sided with the Planning Commission against various business interests. Furthermore, in the years that predated the upsurge of both the local and national civil rights movement, she had been the city council's most outspoken (and often lone) advocate of the appointment of blacks (as well as women) to various city bodies such as the Urban Renewal Commission.[52] Finally, she had strong support among working-class whites and the local labor movement. Weak by Northern standards, organized labor in Charlotte at that time was strong enough to cripple city bus service with a twenty-six-day bus strike in 1958,[53] to unionize firefighters, to threaten the unionization of other municipal employees, and to maintain a strong enough organization in some of the city's textile mills to significantly influence how workers voted in state-wide elections.[54] These were no small feats in a city well known, as one historian put it, for being a "long-time citadel of opposition to unions."[55]

The 1963 mayoral race was both similar to, and different from, 1961's. In 1963, Charlotte's white, working-class precincts again voted for Brookshire's unsuccessful opponent (one Albert Pearson, Evans had been elected to the state legislature in 1962). But in 1963, unlike 1961, Brookshire carried the black precincts, something he would again do in his successful 1965 and 1967

TABLE 2.1
Electoral Support for Brookshire, 1961–1965

Precinct Number and Name		% of Vote for Brookshire		
	year:	1961	1963	1965
White Working-Class Precincts				
13 Villa Heights		41	25	33
14 Hawthorne		48	25	24
24 Enderly Park		49	40	36
27 Tryon Hills		44	52	29
30 Highland		31	26	23
40 Thomasboro		28	44	37
41 Hoskins		32	16	19
Black Precincts				
2 Second Ward		15	90	94
3 Zeb Vance		62	64	89
25 Northwest		7	89	99
26 Double Oaks		19	97	96

Source: Charlotte-Mecklenburg Board of Elections.
Note: Table entries are percentage of vote for Brookshire.

campaigns. Table 2.1 illustrates this change in voting patterns.[56] It indicates that white working-class precincts continued in 1963 and 1965 to vote against the candidate (Brookshire) supported by the business elite. But the black precincts that had previously supported Evans against Brookshire provided him with huge pluralities in 1963 and 1965.

Two reasons account for the change in voting in the black precincts between 1961 and 1963. The first was the generally conciliatory approach that Charlotte's political and business leaders took to the upsurge of the civil rights movement during Brookshire's first term. The second was political developments within the black community. Both of these developments are best understood in the context of Brookshire's lasting impact on Charlotte's growth, as well as that of his successor, John Belk, who, like Brookshire, also served four two-year terms.

The Mayoralty of Stan Brookshire

The foundation for almost all subsequent downtown development was laid during Brookshire's eight-year tenure in office. Under his leadership and that of his successor, John Belk, Charlotte made full use of federal funding to undertake a series of urban renewal projects that lasted well into the 1970s and physically transformed over 250 acres of downtown land. This involved bulldozing two predominantly downtown black neighborhoods, Brooklyn and Blue Heaven, that white civic leaders viewed as slums and replacing them with a showcase park, a hotel, government and commercial office buildings, and widened roads.[57] Virtually no effort, especially in the project's early stages, was made to build housing for the more than 1,000 families who were displaced by the destruction of this housing. Their migration to other parts of the city changed the racial composition of several neighborhoods very quickly, with real estate agents and landlords facilitating the change with tried-and-true techniques.[58] Urban renewal also bulldozed another downtown black neighborhood, this one in First Ward. But now under pressure from Washington, the Charlotte Redevelopment Authority replaced part of the bull-dozed units with a public housing project, Earle Village, which opened in 1967. A third aspect, much more surgically focused than the first two, targeted a three-block section at the very heart of downtown, containing a variety of small businesses whose clientele was both black and white. "With federal aid those enterprises gave way to a Charlotte Convention Center, a luxurious Radisson Hotel, and the skyscraper headquarters of NCNB bank."[59]

As part of putting together the political arrangements that would facilitate this development, Brookshire sought support from blacks early in his administration. Shortly after the 1961 victory, he started publicly talking about the need for more job and housing opportunities for blacks.[60] He also reorganized the city's largely inactive Friendly Relations Committee into a twenty-nine-member Mayor's Community Relations Committee, which, within several months, negotiated the desegregation of several downtown cafeterias in response to demonstrations led by dentist Reginald Hawkins. In turn, the demonstrators agreed to approach the committee before launching future demonstrations.[61]

That agreement typifies the generally conciliatory approach that Brookshire took toward the upsurge of the civil rights movement. The most chronicled example of this approach came in 1963, when Brookshire, the Chamber of Commerce president, the *Observer's* editor, and other business leaders decided to desegregate the city's leading restaurants by taking several black leaders to dine at these establishments. Rarely has a decision to "let's do lunch" assumed such mythic proportions in the accounts of any city's history.[62]

While this generally conciliatory approach may have had strong moral and philosophical components, it also was motivated by fears that the city's image and economic development would be jeopardized by headline-grabbing demonstrations, especially those threatened by Hawkins at the 1963 North Carolina World Trade Fair that was scheduled for Charlotte. Reflecting on the decision to invite black leaders to lunch, Brookshire would note twenty-five years later, "There is no question but that the mass marches occurring at the time in Greensboro, Durham, and Winston-Salem had a coercive effect on us and the timing of the decision."[63] In an article in the *New York Herald Tribune,* Brookshire noted that demonstrations jeopardized "a community's pocketbook," and that discrimination based on skin color was "legally and morally wrong and economically unsound."[64] And an *Observer* editor who played a key role in the decision to "let's do lunch" noted that while morality played a role in the desegregation effort, the economic realities were more important.[65]

In addition to moral and economic considerations, there were electoral ones. Although Brookshire would say that his 1961 defeats in black precincts precluded pejorative interpretations that he was repaying political debts by taking a conciliatory approach to the black demands,[66] his conciliatory way of dealing with the civil rights upsurge helps explain why he subsequently did very well in black precincts.

The Emergence of Fred Alexander

Facilitating the growth of Brookshire's support in black neighborhoods were political developments within them. Such events cannot be reduced to the political activities of individual leaders, but these activities often provide a useful summary. Such is the case with the political differences between Reginald Hawkins and Fred Alexander, a rental agent and realtor for C. D. Spangler Sr., a Charlotte builder and developer whose son, C. D. Spangler Jr., would take over the family business and subsequently play a large role in both Charlotte and North Carolina politics.

Although contemporaries frequently contrasted Hawkins's and Alexander's styles and personalities, here it seems more useful to discuss three programmatic differences. The first involves the importance of mass demonstrations, protests, and picket lines. While Hawkins had long organized voters and would eventually run for North Carolina governor in 1968, he also, as noted above, helped organize and lead a wide range of high-profile demonstrations and other mass, collective political activities. Alexander rarely, if ever, was involved in such activity and argued that they were basically besides the point. "Some feel the scare technique will work," he told a reporter in 1964, and then added, "It's stupid to think you can scare people who build 50-story buildings. You can be a nuisance. But you can no more scare them than you can come in my house and scare me. It's a matter of whether I want to listen to you and see if there is sense in what you say . . . If it had been fear alone, Charlotte would be in the throes of a demonstration still. The willingness of the power structure and the mayor to sit down and talk was the key thing— the ability to find Negroes and whites willing to see if the conference approach would work."[67] Of course, Hawkins's activity on the outside made

Alexander's job on the inside easier because as Harvey Gantt subsequently noted, "Fred could always use the more militant posture of a Hawkins . . . to move the movers and shakers to chart a course for some change."[68]

The second difference involved the candidates the two men supported and the tactics they advocated in the electoral arena itself. One notable example is the 1961 mayoral election in which Hawkins supported Evans, but Alexander supported Brookshire.[69] Perhaps even more important than differences between the individual candidates whom the two men supported were differences between Hawkins's and Alexander's electoral strategies. These differences were especially evident in races for Charlotte's city council, all of whose members, it will be recalled, were elected at large in the 1960s. Hawkins often urged blacks to vote a full slate, while Alexander called upon them to "single shot," that is, to vote only for their favorite candidate, lest that candidate's chances be weakened by votes that other candidates might accumulate. That difference was especially sharp in 1965, the year Alexander became the first black elected to the city council since the 1890s. Hawkins supported Alexander but urged blacks to vote a full slate. Alexander, however, urged them to vote for only one candidate, Fred Alexander. This tactic was widely used and generally credited with Alexander's getting enough votes to finish seventh in the election, thus winning the final seat on the council.[70]

A third difference is the extent to which the two men thought that blacks could get support from working-class whites and their organizations, including organized labor, most of whose membership at that time in Charlotte was overwhelmingly white. While fully aware that white supremacist ideologies and practices interfered with obtaining such support, Hawkins was considerably more willing than Alexander to try to get it, as well as to emphasize the class aspects of the struggle of African Americans. Alexander, on the other hand, claimed, "You can't get anywhere dealing with the poor white man. He's just like the Negro—struggling."[71] He also "said scornfully that labor unions offer little or nothing in the struggle for Negro rights in the South, not even membership."[72] Those sentiments were matched by Alexander's actions. According to the only extended study of Alexander's political career presently available, he was "staunchly anti-union."[73] During a 1968 strike of city sanitation workers, for example, he attempted to get black union members back to work. According to the strike's organizer, a white union staff member, only the high-profile intervention of a prominent black clergyman kept Alexander's effort from being successful.[74]

As a result of these programmatic differences as well, probably, of those in personality, Alexander received considerably more support from Charlotte's business and political elite. Such support came very early in Brookshire's administration with the mayor's decision to name Alexander to the reorganized twenty-nine-member Community Relations Committee but to consciously exclude Hawkins.[75] That support combined with a range of other events to weaken Hawkins's influence and to increase Alexander's. Shortly after Alexander's 1965 election to the city council, an *Observer* reporter summarized his interviews with both Negroes and "white politicians who by necessity have become careful observers of the Negro political scene" by noting:

> One widespread but not unanimous impression is that Dr. Reginald Hawkins, the 41-year-old Negro dentist who drew most of the headlines as Charlotte's militant civil rights leader, has lost some of his influence in the Negro community . . .
>
> Despite occasional suggestions to the contrary, Hawkins remains a substantial power to be reckoned with, both in political campaigns and in civil rights matters. But his influence may have declined since the height of the demonstrations in 1962 and 1963.
>
> At the same time, two other Negro spokesmen are crowding into the public spotlight that Hawkins virtually monopolized for the first half of this decade.
>
> One of them is Fred D. Alexander, a 55-year-old real estate manager, who on May 4 became the first Negro elected to the Charlotte City Council since the 1890s.[76]

One suspects that the white politicians of whom the *Observer* reporter spoke were not just "careful observers of the Negro political scene" but people with a substantial stake in influencing it. Moreover, it is clear that at the very time Alexander was developing a sound working relationship with Charlotte's most powerful business and political leaders, Hawkins was finding himself in increasing conflict with them. In 1964, Hawkins was indicted on felony charges for registering voters in violation of literacy requirements. Although the charges were dismissed in 1968 for lack of evidence of criminal conduct, the extensive legal proceedings helped drain Hawkins's resources and exacerbated his political difficulties.[77] By the end of the sixties, the metaphorical public spotlight of which the *Observer's* reporter spoke shone much less brightly on Hawkins than on Alexander, who was to play a key role in the election of Brookshire's successor.

Regime Politics at the Polls and in the Community

The electoral success of Brookshire's successor, John Belk, another former chair of the Chamber of Commerce and four-term mayor, also was rooted in this alliance between downtown and most of the black community's political leadership. An especially key election was that of 1969, which was the first after Brookshire's retirement as well as the first in which Belk sought office. Prior to running, Belk had discussed entering the mayor's race with Fred Alexander, who had already served four years on the city council. Many years later, Belk recalled how Alexander claimed that "with the experience he had on the council and with me having the contact with the business community, we could really fix up Charlotte and help it grow."[78]

In the 1969 primary, Belk finished second behind Gibson Smith, whose supporters included opponents of both a new civic center and busing for school desegregation.[79] The passage of bonds for projects such as a new civic center is some of the guts of local development politics. Voters had defeated such a referendum, but the issue remained an important one and would again be put before the voters later in 1969. While the mayor of the city of Charlotte has no formal responsibility for education, the district court's desegregation order in *Swann* was first issued several weeks before the 1969 mayoral primary, and Smith denounced it as "wrong, uncalled for, and disruptive."[80] Finishing third, and thus eliminated, in the primary was George Leake, a black minister. Although Belk's silence on school desegregation would be deafening during the ongoing political tumult over the district court's order,[81] he enjoyed Alexander's enthusiastic support, won 75 percent of the precincts that Leake had carried, and thus beat Smith. In subsequent elections, Belk continued to do very well in black precincts.[82]

Given the importance of African American electoral support to the business elite, it is hardly surprising that as Stone noted in Atlanta, Charlotte's business leaders put considerable resources into developing business relationships with African Americans. Fred Alexander's employment by C. D. Spangler Sr. exemplified those relationships, as did a range of loans to black businesses and investments in politically and economically strategic projects. A major source of such loans and projects was NCNB, which in the early 1970s "had more money at stake in Charlotte's central city than any other institution did."[83] Economic support of black Charlotteans benefited the bank in matters that went beyond local politics. As divestiture of South African investment became an increasingly important part of the worldwide anti-apartheid movement in the 1980s, a local group, Charlotteans for a Free Southern Africa, circulated a petition calling for NCNB to close its Johannesburg office and organized a demonstration around that demand at an annual stockholders meeting.[84] However, the petition and demand received less support than other anti-apartheid activities from black Charlotteans, with several citing the bank's economic support of African American businesses as their reason for not signing the petition. When told, almost a decade later, about black Charlotteans' unwillingness to publicly criticize NCNB's presence in South Africa, Joe Martin, the bank's principal corporate affairs officer and close confidant of CEO Hugh McColl, remarked, "There has been a deliberate attempt to cultivate business among black people by this bank even before the bank became really integrated itself. That is for the bank's interest, but that has also worked in the interest of black people to have access to a bank when there were other banks they didn't have good (or easy) access to. So I think that . . . probably made people less suspicious of our motives in South Africa in the first place . . . and also made them less willing to complain about it because on the scale of things that interested them, any difference of opinion about that was not as important as the commonality of interest on some other things."[85]

Harvey Gantt

The electoral alliance between the business elite and black political leaders continued to play a decisive role in Charlotte's mayoral races up through the 1983 and 1985 victories of Harvey Gantt, who in many ways exemplified the success of this alliance and Charlotte's reputation for racial liberalism. The first African American to break Jim Crow's hold on South Carolina's Clemson University, Gantt later received a master's degree in urban planning from MIT, settled in Charlotte in 1971, and quickly built a successful architectural practice. Three years after his arrival in town, he secured a seat on the city council thanks to Fred Alexander, of whom Gantt has said, "I'm sort of a protege."[86]

After Alexander was elected to the state senate and resigned from the city council, the remaining six members of the council, all of whom were white, agreed that Alexander's replacement should be black. As several longtime black political activists jockeyed vigorously for the appointment, Alexander approached newcomer Gantt, asking if he would be interested in the position.[87] The three Republicans on the council opposed Gantt's nomination, but Mayor Belk—a Democrat and, as noted above, longtime ally of Alexander's—cast the tie-breaking vote for Gantt.

After an unsuccessful attempt in 1979, Gantt was elected mayor in 1983 and again in 1985. Although some developers opposed Gantt, he had the support of the business elite's heaviest hitters and got enough white votes, especially in more prosperous precincts, to defeat his Republican opponents. By making Charlotte the first large Southern city with a majority white population to elect an African American to the mayor's office, Gantt's victory contributed to Charlotte's reputation as a progressive, racially liberal Southern city. In addition to a formidable intellect and personality, Gantt brought to the job an urban planner's sensibilities and concern with balanced growth designed to benefit all sectors of the population and areas of the city.

A sympathetic journalistic biography notes that when Gantt first became active in Charlotte politics in the 1970s, "his lexicon was that of an urban planner, not a civil rights activist,"[88] and that characterization is equally applicable to his mayoralty. Although Gantt addressed some traditional civic rights concerns, such as black participation in city contracts, much of his focus was Charlotte's development, with three of the four points in his 1985 campaign literature stressing "economic development, balanced growth, and paying for growth fairly."[89] Despite that moderate perspective, enthusiastic support from business executives such as Hugh McColl, and his growing national prominence, Gantt was upset in the 1987 mayoral race by Republican Sue Myrick.

Gantt entered that 1987 campaign a heavy favorite. In addition to having the traditional advantages of incumbency, he benefited from the fact that many of the city's established political leaders (whatever their party affiliation) considered Myrick unpredictable, somewhat of a loose cannon, and having too many ties to the right wing of the Republican Party. As a result, the Gantt campaign was overconfident and poorly organized, one consequence of which was that it failed to mobilize black voters the way it had done in previous elections. As mayor, Gantt took the heat for the downside of Charlotte's growth, especially the increased traffic congestion to which Myrick effectively pointed during the campaign. Also hurting Gantt were the changes in the city of Charlotte's electorate and political geography wrought by the prosperity that attracted migration from all over the country. While the party affiliation and race of these newcomers varied, those who were white and Republican were more likely than others to settle in outlying areas of the county. As noted earlier, the city of Charlotte has benefited from North Carolina's liberal annexation laws, and Gantt's planning background led him to support and facilitate annexation. However, Myrick's plurality in these outlying, heavily Republican areas was such that it is possible to argue that annexations cost Gantt the elections.[90] As Joe Martin remarked, the business elite and Gantt "all ignored the suburbs. They ignored them for partisan reasons because they were Republicans. They ignored them for traditional reasons because they were newcomers and outsiders . . . and they ignored them out of ignorance, just out of narrow focus on what had been the traditional concerns of Charlotte. And Sue Myrick took them apart."[91]

Charlotte Politics in Flux

Gantt's defeat marked a turning point in local politics. From 1963 until 1985, the Democrats lost only one mayoral election, 1977, and that was a very unusual one.[92] During these years, again only with the exception of 1977, the victorious candidate always won Charlotte's predominantly black precincts. However, from 1987 through the most recent mayoral election of 2001, Democrats have lost every time, frequently by large margins. Moreover, during this period, the victorious mayoral candidate has always lost Charlotte's predominantly black precincts, an important indication that the alliance between Charlotte's business elite and the political leadership of the black community lacks the electoral clout it had from 1963 to 1985. Accompanying that declining clout has been much greater fluidity in local politics in the years since Gantt's defeat. That greater fluidity was publicly, if euphemistically, remarked upon by Hugh McColl himself: "For years, Charlotte enjoyed a consensus built by business, government, and the citizens groups. But consensus eludes us today."[93]

The extent of the flux in local politics even amidst crucial vestiges of pre-1987 political patterns can be seen in the two local elections that preceded the turn of the century. The 1998 election for the county commission saw the coalition between black political leaders and the business elite flex the kind of muscle in local politics that it had flexed prior to 1987. The most bitter commission campaign in years, the 1998 election for county commission was dominated by controversy over a 5–4 commission vote in April 1997 to cut public funding for the arts in the wake of the Charlotte performance of "Angels in America," the Pulitzer Prize-winning play that had a homosexual protagonist and dealt vividly with AIDS. The *Economist, Washington Post,* and *New York Times* ran stories about the county commission's vote, hardly the kind of publicity sought by an aspiring world-class city whose downtown businesses were aggressively recruiting executives from cosmopolitan financial centers such as New York. Moreover, the cut occurred at the time that NationsBank was aggressively pursuing its merger with BankAmerica, whose San Francisco location would presumably make it especially sensitive to the anti-gay sentiment displayed by county commissioners who publicly talked of "artsy-fartsy people," "queers,"[94] and shoving homosexuals "off the face of the earth."[95]

As a result of such statements and the 5–4 vote to cut arts funding, the business elite, together with many other groups, launched an all-out and eventually successful campaign to defeat what the *Observer* incessantly called the Gang of Five. With prominent developer Johnny Harris playing a key role, the business elite spearheaded the formation of two organizations, the Alliance for a Better Charlotte and A Better Charlotte Political Committee. In addition to having the same acronym, ABC, both groups were headed by Stan Campbell, an experienced local politician who had previously served on the city council and on the staff of Congresswoman Sue Myrick. Although the Alliance was conceived as a nonpartisan civic think tank, the political committee's explicit goal was to help recruit and financially support candidates for local political offices.[96] The latter's ability to fulfill these goals largely hinged on the ample support of the business elite. Initial contributions (in 1997) came from three sources: NationsBank's PAC, First Union's PAC, and Johnny Harris. The year 1998 again saw NationsBank's PAC and First Union's

PAC contributing heavily to the ABC Political Committee, as did numerous individual members of the business elite.[97]

From an electoral standpoint, an important aspect of the campaign against the Gang of Five was the emergence from retirement of Jim Richardson to seek one of the three at-large seats on the board. A popular and an influential former state legislator, Richardson, a black, joined the two white Democratic at-large incumbents in running as a slate. Several tactical considerations governed the decision to run as a slate: all three candidates would benefit from the business elite's fundraising activities; black Democrats and black political organizations would urge their constituents to vote for all three Democrats, not single-shot Richardson; and white Democrats would campaign vigorously for Richardson. African American turnout was extremely high, and the two white candidates polled almost as many votes in the black precincts as Richardson, an indication of the effectiveness of African American political leaders in mobilizing black support for white candidates. All three Democrats won, as the alliance between black political leaders and the business elite demonstrated in this county commission race the same kind of clout it had displayed in mayoral elections prior to 1987.[98]

However, the 1999 mayoral election did not follow the pre-1987 patterns. Rather, it resembled post-1987 mayoral elections, with the business elite backing a moderate Republican, who also benefited from the advantages of incumbency. His challenger was Ella Scarborough, an African American woman who several years earlier had been elected to the city council with support from the business elite. However, the 1999 mayor's race saw her receive only 39 percent of the vote.

The same Election Day that saw Scarborough soundly defeated also saw two black school board incumbents beat back strong challenges from white candidates. In addition to indicating the complexity of local politics, that school board election had a major effect on education politics and will be discussed in chapter 7. Before turning to education, the focus of the next five chapters, it will be useful to discuss the economic situation of black Charlotteans.

THE ECONOMIC SITUATION OF BLACK CHARLOTTEANS

Having discussed the political and demographic context within which Charlotte's desegregation story unfolded, it is useful to talk also about the economic context, in particular the economic situation of African Americans. The issue has many aspects, even if no attempt is made to discern causal relationships, but rather only, as I will do here, to explore briefly the question, To what extent did black Charlotteans make economic progress during the years that Charlotte was booming and becoming one of the nation's main banking centers?

The answer is a complicated one. Over the past thirty years, the economic situation of black Charlotteans has markedly improved relative to that of African Americans in comparable places. However, Charlotte's progress in reducing black/white economic disparities has in many ways lagged that of comparable places, especially during the years of Charlotte's dramatic growth and increasing national prominence.

Before discussing the data that lead to this answer, it is necessary to consider at least three methodological issues:

1. *Over what time period is economic progress measured?* The answer to this question is determined by the nature of the data, the most relevant of which became available only with the 1970 Census and have appeared in each of the three subsequent decennial censuses. Taken together, those four censuses provide both a baseline (1970) prior to the implementation of the busing plan and, perhaps more important, information on the twenty-year period (1980–2000) during which Charlotte boomed and emerged as a nationally important financial center. Since these censuses did not all occur at the same point in the business cycle and the economic situation of African Americans (as well as its relation to that of whites) is affected by the business cycle, it is risky to hinge too much of the analysis on data from any one census. However, that risk is largely unavoidable because these four censuses are the only source of the relevant data.

2. *By what indicators is economic progress assessed?* Of the many possible indicators, three seem especially useful. The first is per capita income, a widely used measure of living standards.[99] A second indicator is home ownership, a good measure of wealth since during the years under consideration, it was generally "the largest component in most Americans' wealth portfolios."[100] The third indicator is the rate of poverty, which provides a measure of the prevalence of economic hardship, the alleviation of which is an important criterion for assessing the consequences of economic growth.[101]

3. *By what standard is the economic progress of Charlotte's blacks assessed?* Useful as it may be to investigate economic trends in Charlotte alone, the investigation acquires additional significance by drawing comparisons with other areas because such comparisons facilitate distinguishing between trends unique to Charlotte and more generic ones affecting other localities, either in the South or within North Carolina. Thus, it is useful to compare Charlotte to the state's other large urban areas: Greensboro, Winston-Salem, Raleigh, and Durham, all of which have sizeable black populations.[102]

However, the choice of the unit of analysis within these urban areas requires some discussion. Because of annexations, city boundaries have changed since 1970, making longitudinal comparisons among cities problematic. Similarly, the boundaries of what the Census Bureau considers the metropolitan statistical areas associated with these cities also have changed over the years. Also militating against the use of the metropolitan areas as the unit of analysis is the fact that Charlotte's metropolitan statistical area has recently included York County, South Carolina, and the relationship between the economic situation of African Americans in that county and both politics and education policy in Charlotte, major foci of this book, is hardly an obvious one. For these reasons and the fact that the Charlotte-Mecklenburg school system has been coterminous with Mecklenburg County since 1960, the county would appear to be the best unit of analysis, with the economic situation of blacks in Mecklenburg being thus compared to that in Guilford, Forsyth, Wake, and Durham counties.[103] To help put the comparisons among these five North Carolina counties in broader perspective, comparisons with the entire state and with the United States also are included.

The comparisons for each of the three indicators appear in a series of tables. Table 2.2 compares the per capita income of both blacks and whites in each of the five counties and the state of North Carolina with their national counterparts. Tables 2.3 and 2.4 do the same for home-ownership and poverty rates. These three tables thus indicate the economic progress of black and white Charlotteans relative to that of blacks and whites elsewhere, most explicitly in the United States. However, from those three tables it is difficult to discern the magnitude of the black/white gap in any particular place or the rate at which the gap has changed over time. This information is provided in Table 2.5, the left side of which provides data on the magnitude of black/white disparities in all four censuses, on all three indicators, and for all seven places. The right side of the table shows the rates of change on these indicators from census to census as well as that between two other pairs of censuses: 1970–2000 and 1980–2000. Generally speaking, these last two rates of change are most relevant here because they indicate each place's progress in alleviating black/white disparities over the two time periods of greatest interest: the thirty-year period for which data are available and the twenty-year period that saw Charlotte boom and become a national financial powerhouse.

The conclusions that emerge from the comparisons among the five North Carolina counties depend, in part, on the indicator being used:

Per capita income: As Table 2.2 indicates, since 1970 the situation of blacks in Mecklenburg County has improved relative to that of blacks nationwide.[104] So, generally, has the situation of blacks in the other four counties and in the state as a whole. Similarly, the situation of whites in Mecklenburg, the four other counties, and in the state has improved relative to whites nationwide. Thus, for example, according to the 2000 Census, the per capita income for blacks in Mecklenburg was 114 percent of the national average, and for whites it was 138 percent of the national average. The corresponding

TABLE 2.2
County and State Per Capita Income as Percent of National, By Race, 1970–2000

	Whites			Blacks		
Place	Per Capita Income in $	Per Capita Income as % of U.S.	Place	Per Capita Income in $	Per Capita Income as % of U.S.
1970						
Mecklenburg	3848	116	Guilford	1819	100
Guilford	3577	108	US	1818	100
Forsyth	3496	105	Forsyth	1762	97
Durham	3477	105	Durham	1716	94
Wake	3466	105	Mecklenburg	1654	91
US	3314	100	Wake	1414	78
NC	2839	86	NC	1342	74
1980						
Mecklenburg	9113	117	US	4545	100
Wake	8680	111	Guilford	4519	99
Forsyth	8457	108	Mecklenburg	4514	99
Guilford	8438	108	Durham	4484	99
Durham	8216	105	Forsyth	4408	97
US	7808	100	Wake	4395	97
NC	6873	88	NC	3778	83
1990						
Mecklenburg	19850	127	Durham	10228	115
Wake	19331	123	Wake	9827	111
Forsyth	18406	117	Forsyth	9534	108
Durham	18116	115	Mecklenburg	9424	106
Guilford	17752	113	Guilford	9197	104
US	15687	100	US	8859	100
NC	14450	92	NC	7926	89
2000						
Mecklenburg	34291	138	Wake	16925	117
Wake	31208	126	Mecklenburg	16461	114
Durham	30706	124	Durham	16108	112
Guilford	28320	114	Guilford	15236	106
Forsyth	27472	111	Forsyth	14740	102
US	24819	100	US	14437	100
NC	23237	94	NC	13548	94

Source: U.S. Census

numbers from the 1970 Census were 91 percent and 116 percent. A comparison of these figures with those from the other six places indicates that Mecklenburg experienced more progress in boosting black per capita income than any place other than Wake and North Carolina, and more progress in boosting white per capita income than any place other than Wake.

However, while Mecklenburg experienced steady progress in raising black per capita income, it did not experience a steady reduction in the black/white income gap. As Table 2.5 indicates, within Mecklenburg, the gap decreased considerably (15 percent) from 1970 to 1980. But from 1980 to 1990, the gap *increased* by 4 percent, and from 1990 to 2000, it decreased by 1.1 percent. Thus, if Mecklenburg's progress is compared to the other places, a complicated picture emerges. Over the thirty-year period, 1970–2000, Mecklenburg's progress (12 percent) in lowering the black/white gap in per capita income trailed only that of Wake's (33 percent) and North Carolina's (23 percent). But most of Mecklenburg's progress occurred from 1970 to 1980. From 1980 to 2000, the twenty-year period in which Charlotte boomed and became a national economic player, the black/white gap in per capita income *increased* by 3.0 percent. During this twenty-year period, only one other place, Durham, did worse in narrowing this gap.

The comparison to Wake—the other North Carolina county that boomed in the late twentieth century—is especially unfavorable to Mecklenburg. According to the 1970 Census, the black/white income gap was slightly greater in Wake than in Mecklenburg, but by 2000, it was noticeably smaller. Thus Wake's economic growth is clearly associated with a steady narrowing of the black/white income gap, but Mecklenburg's boom is not. Moreover, the data from Wake make it difficult to argue that Mecklenburg's lagging progress in reducing the black/white gap—as well as the magnitude of the gap, the largest of any of the seven places for all but the first census—results from Mecklenburg's white income being the highest of the five counties. If a higher white per capita income automatically translated into slower progress in reducing the gap or a larger magnitude for it, then Wake would do worse on both of these measures than Durham, Forsyth, and Guilford (since per capita white income is lower in these three counties than it is in Wake). But Wake does better than all three of these counties, and better than Mecklenburg.

Home ownership: As Table 2.3 indicates, the situation of Mecklenburg's blacks relative to their counterparts nationwide has improved steadily since 1970. The same can be said of Forsyth, but its improvement has not been as great. The other places present a more complex picture, but none shows the same steady gains or overall increase in black home ownership that Mecklenburg does. Within Mecklenburg, the black/white gap in home ownership presents a picture that is even more complicated than that for per capita income. Unlike per capita income, the black/white gap in home ownership in Mecklenburg narrowed more from 1970 to 2000 than it did in any of the other places, as Table 2.5 indicates. However, like per capita income, the most favorable decade for Mecklenburg was the 1970s. Between 1980 and 2000, Mecklenburg's progress in narrowing the gap dropped considerably, with the result that three of the other places made more progress in these twenty years.

TABLE 2.3
County and State Home Ownership Rates as Percent of National, By Race, 1970–2000

	Whites			Blacks	
Place	Home Ownership in %	Home Ownership as % of U.S. Rate	Place	Home Ownership in %	Home Ownership as % of U.S. Rate
1970					
Forsyth	72.5	111	North Carolina	45.5	109
NC	70.1	107	US	41.6	100
Guilford	68.7	105	Wake	40.8	98
Mecklenburg	67.0	102	Guilford	39.8	96
US	65.4	100	Durham	36.5	88
Wake	63.0	96	Forsyth	36.0	87
Durham	60.0	92	Mecklenburg	34.6	83
1980					
NC	72.8	107	NC	51.0	115
Forsyth	72.3	107	US	44.4	100
Guilford	69.2	102	Wake	44.1	99
US	67.8	100	Mecklenburg	40.0	90
Mecklenburg	66.8	98	Forsyth	40.0	90
Wake	65.6	97	Guilford	40.0	90
Durham	62.1	92	Durham	37.4	84
1990					
NC	72.9	107	NC	49.6	114
Forsyth	70.6	104	US	43.4	100
Guilford	68.4	100	Wake	40.3	93
US	68.2	100	Forsyth	40.0	92
Mecklenburg	66.2	97	Mecklenburg	39.6	91
Wake	66.1	97	Guilford	39.4	91
Durham	62.8	92	Durham	36.3	84
2000					
NC	75.7	105	NC	52.6	114
Forsyth	75.5	104	Wake	47.5	103
Wake	72.9	101	US	46.3	100
Guilford	72.5	100	Forsyth	45.0	97
US	72.4	100	Mecklenburg	45.0	97
Mecklenburg	72.0	99	Guilford	43.9	95
Durham	67.1	93	Durham	43.0	93

Source: U.S. Census

Poverty rates: As Table 2.4 indicates, there was a steady decrease in the rate of black poverty in Mecklenburg in comparison to the situation nationally. Durham, Forsyth, and Guilford do not show this kind of steady decrease relative to the national black poverty rate, but Wake does. Further examination of the data on Mecklenburg and Wake—the two counties that do the best on this measure—indicates that in the thirty years from 1970 to 2000, Wake shows greater progress than Mecklenburg in reducing black poverty. However, during this same period, as Table 2.5 shows, Mecklenburg shows greater progress in reducing the disparity between black and white poverty rates than Wake (or any other county) does. Moreover, unlike the situation with the other two indicators, Mecklenburg experienced more progress in reducing the black/white disparity in poverty rates after 1980 than before it, with the greatest progress coming between 1990 and 2000.

Taken together, these three indicators present a complicated picture of black economic progress in Mecklenburg. In comparison to their counterparts in these other places, Mecklenburg's African Americans were markedly and obviously better off in 2000 than they were in 1970 on all three indicators. Mecklenburg also saw more progress over the past thirty years in reducing the black/white disparity in poverty rates than any of the other places included in this analysis. Over this same thirty-year period, Mecklenburg also saw more progress than the other places in reducing the racial disparity in home ownership, but most of this progress occurred prior to 1980. In the subsequent twenty years, Mecklenburg's progress in reducing the racial disparity in home ownership puts it exactly in the middle of the pack. The data on per capita income are the most unfavorable to Mecklenburg. Over the thirty-year period Mecklenburg does relatively well (third out of the seven places) in reducing the black/white gap on this indicator, but almost all of the progress was prior to 1980. From 1980 to 2000, Mecklenburg shows the second worst progress. Given the per capita income data, *uneven* may be the best one-word summary of Mecklenburg's relative (compared to the other places) progress in reducing racial economic disparities during the years that Charlotte became a national financial center.

To these comments about Mecklenburg's relative rate of progress in reducing black/white disparities should be added observations about both its rank relative to the other six places and the magnitude of its black/white economic disparities. In 1970, Mecklenburg had the second largest disparity in black/white per capita income; in 2000, it had the largest. In 1970, Mecklenburg had the second largest disparity in black/white home ownership rates; in 2000, it had the third largest. In 1970, Mecklenburg had the largest disparity in black/white poverty rates; in 2000, it had the second largest. In other words, on none of these measures of black/white economic disparities was Mecklenburg anywhere near the top of the pack in 1970 or 2000. Indeed, it was generally much closer to the bottom. Thus in 2000—very close to the culmination of the longest economic expansion in U.S. history—black per capita income in Mecklenburg was 48 percent that of whites, home ownership was 63 percent that of whites, and the poverty rate for blacks was 340 percent that of whites.

TABLE 2.4
County and State Poverty Rates as Percent of National, By Race, 1970–2000

	Whites			*Blacks*	
Place	*Poverty Rate in %*	*Poverty Rate as % of U.S. Rate*	*Place*	*Poverty Rate in %*	*Poverty Rate as % of U.S. Rate*
		1970			
Mecklenburg	6.1	56	Guilford	27.7	79
Guilford	7.8	71	Mecklenburg	32.9	94
Wake	8.0	73	Forsyth	34.7	99
Forsyth	8.4	77	US	35.0	100
Durham	9.1	83	Durham	36.3	104
US	10.9	100	Wake	40.6	116
NC	13.1	120	NC	44.5	127
		1980			
Mecklenburg	5.5	58	Wake	23.4	78
Wake	6.2	66	Guilford	23.8	80
Guilford	6.8	72	Durham	24.9	83
Forsyth	6.9	73	Forsyth	25.6	86
Durham	7.6	81	Mecklenburg	25.7	86
US	9.4	100	US	29.9	100
NC	10.0	106	NC	30.4	102
		1990			
Mecklenburg	4.9	50	Wake	19.0	64
Wake	5.3	54	Guilford	20.2	68
Durham	5.9	60	Durham	21.4	72
Forsyth	5.9	60	Mecklenburg	21.9	74
Guilford	6.4	65	Forsyth	23.9	81
NC	8.6	88	NC	27.1	81
US	9.8	100	US	29.5	100
		2000			
Wake	4.6	57	Wake	15.1	61
Mecklenburg	4.7	58	Mecklenburg	16.2	65
Forsyth	5.6	69	Guilford	18.6	75
Guilford	6.0	74	Durham	19.4	78
Durham	6.4	79	Forsyth	21.2	85
NC	8.1	100	NC	22.9	92
US	8.1	100	US	24.9	100

Source: U.S. Census

TABLE 2.5

Changes in Black/White Economic Disparities, By Place, 1970–2000

	Year of Census				Percentage Change Between				
	1970	1980	1990	2000	1970–1980	1980–1990	1990–2000	1970–2000	1980–2000
Black Per Capita Income/White Per Capita Income									
Mecklenburg	0.430	0.495	0.475	0.480	15%	-4.0%	1.1%	12%	-3.0%
Durham	0.494	0.546	0.565	0.525	11%	3.5%	-7.1%	6.3%	-3.8%
Forsyth	0.504	0.521	0.518	0.537	3.4%	-0.6%	3.7%	6.5%	3.1%
Guilford	0.509	0.536	0.518	0.538	5.3%	-3.4%	3.9%	5.7%	0.37%
Wake	0.408	0.506	0.508	0.542	24%	0.40%	6.7%	33%	7.1%
NC	0.473	0.550	0.549	0.583	16%	-0.18%	6.2%	23%	6.0%
US	0.549	0.582	0.565	0.582	6.0%	-2.9%	3.0%	6.0%	0.00%
Black Home Ownership Rate/White Home Ownership Rate									
Mecklenburg	0.516	0.599	0.598	0.625	16%	-0.2%	4.5%	21%	4.3%
Durham	0.608	0.602	0.578	0.641	-1.0%	-4.0%	11%	5.4%	6.5%
Forsyth	0.497	0.553	0.567	0.596	11%	2.5%	5.1%	20%	7.8%
Guilford	0.579	0.578	0.576	0.606	-0.17%	-0.35%	5.2%	4.7%	4.8%
Wake	0.648	0.672	0.610	0.652	3.7%	-9.2%	6.9%	0.62%	-3.0%
NC	0.649	0.701	0.680	0.695	8.0%	-3.0%	2.2%	7.1%	-0.9%
US	0.636	0.655	0.636	0.640	3.0%	-2.9%	0.63%	0.63%	-2.3%
Black Poverty Rate/White Poverty Rate									
Mecklenburg	5.4	4.7	4.5	3.4	-13%	-4.3%	-24%	-37%	-28%
Durham	4.0	3.3	3.6	3.0	-18%	9.1%	-17%	-25%	-9.1%
Forsyth	4.1	3.7	4.1	3.8	-9.8%	11%	-7.3%	-7.3%	2.7%
Guilford	3.6	3.5	3.2	3.1	-2.8%	-8.6%	-3.1%	-14%	-11%
Wake	5.1	3.8	3.6	3.3	-25%	-5.3%	-8.3%	-35%	-13%
NC	3.4	3.0	3.2	2.8	-12%	6.7%	-13%	-18%	-6.7%
US	3.2	3.2	3.0	3.1	0.0%	-6.3%	3.3%	-3.1%	-3.1%

Source: Computed from Tables 2.2, 2.3 and 2.4

In some respects, the fact that Mecklenburg experienced less progress relative to the other places in reducing black/white economic disparities is less significant than the fact that the county has experienced more progress in improving the economic condition of African Americans. In other respects, however, the disparities are extremely important because they are a stark measure of ongoing black/white economic inequality in a place touted for its progressive race relations. The significance of such continuing inequality for this book's concern with school desegregation, civic capacity, and economic development is best discussed after the next five chapters' detailed consideration of these topics.

Chapter 3

Swann's Way and the Heyday of Charlotte's Busing Plan

The neighborhood school concept never *prevented* statutory racial segregation; it may not now be validly used to *perpetuate* segregation.

> —Federal District Judge James B. McMillan in his 1969 *Swann* decision that would give rise to Charlotte's busing plan.[1]

Although "separate but equal" is again a shibboleth apparently tempting to many high-placed people, it has not tempted the present School Board.

> —Judge McMillan, ten years later, dismissing a challenge to the busing plan.[2]

The pupil assignment plan . . . has rested for a decade on a fragile consensus . . . But there is a potential impatience perpetually bubbling beneath the surface of community consensus.

> —The *Charlotte Observer*, in a 1986 editorial, "Playing with Fire: The Dangers of Resegregation," cautioning two new school board members who had raised questions about the busing plan's fairness and operation.[3]

Most aspects of CMS' recent history begin with two events in the 1950s, one national in scope, the other primarily of local interest. The first was the Supreme Court's 1954 decision in *Brown;* the second was local voters' approval of a 1959 referendum that led to a merger of the city of Charlotte's school system with that of Mecklenburg County to create CMS. Although both decisions would eventually transform local education, their immediate consequences seemed less portentous, as the initial section of this chapter indicates.

After considering these immediate consequences, I discuss the *Swann* case, noting the events that led to the busing plan, its main characteristics, the relationship between political and legal battles, the role of the business elite, and African American political cohesion. I then turn to the superintendency of Jay Robinson that represented the heyday of Charlotte's mandatory busing plan, discussing its main characteristics and the extent to which the desegregation glass was half full or half empty. Finally, I discuss the political constraints and shortfalls in civic capacity that affected the Robinson era.

The Struggle for Desegregation

Brown and Consolidation

Concerned with preserving its image of racial moderation, North Carolina engaged in "well-publicized, but decidedly token integration," thus maintaining "an almost completely segregated school system for the first decade after *Brown*."[4] This was certainly true in Charlotte. Starting with the 1957–58 school year, the Charlotte school board, trying to avoid more comprehensive court-mandated desegregation, agreed to the voluntary transfer of a few black students to white schools. Three of these students managed to attend such schools without major incidents, but a fourth, Dorothy Counts, was met with taunting mobs who spit and threw sticks and debris. The continuing hostility forced her out of the school, but photographs of the courageous, dignified young black woman surrounded by scores of jeering white yahoos made newspapers around the world, including one in India, where, tellers of the Charlotte story delight in mentioning, it deeply affected the Counts's family friends, missionaries Darius and Vera Swann. In India, Darius would later write that their son "had never known the meaning of racial segregation," and that they had been "happy to watch him grow and develop with an unaffected openness to people of all races and backgrounds."[5] But when the Swanns returned to Charlotte in 1964, their son was assigned to an all-black school. Unable to persuade either the superintendent or school board to change the assignment, the Swanns contacted civil rights attorney Julius Chambers and joined other black families in the litigation that would bear their name.

As Charlotte's school desegregation history unfolded, it was greatly affected by the fact that the district was a consolidated one, if only because its large size made it difficult for whites so inclined to avoid desegregation by moving to another school district.[6] At the time of consolidation, some Charlotteans, such as city schools Superintendent Elmer Garinger, realized the implications that consolidation could have upon desegregation.[7] However, there was little public discussion of these implications, perhaps because that goal may have seemed even more remote than earlier; in the 1959–60 school year, the number of black students (one) attending white Charlotte schools was less than in 1957–58.[8]

The main push for consolidation came from civic leaders concerned about improving rural schools, increasing administrative and fiscal efficiency, avoiding the redundant construction of new schools, and minimizing conflict between the city and county. Both daily newspapers also supported the proposal, and the referendum leading to consolidation passed by a 3–1 margin in June 1959, creating CMS the following year.

Pressure to Desegregate

Initially focused on the administrative issues stemming from consolidation, CMS soon faced increased pressure to deal with desegregation. The pressure came from two sources. The first was changes in the legal environment, making it less likely that the courts would accept token measures such as Charlotte's. The second was political, arising especially from demonstrations organized by dentist and civil rights activist Reginald Hawkins at the start of the 1961–62 school year. The site of the demonstrations was a previously white school located near downtown that had been converted to a black school concomitant with the reassignment of the school's white students to a newly constructed facility in an outlying area. Black students arriving at the previously all-white school at the start of the year were met by picketers urging them to return to their previous school. At the head of the picket line was Hawkins, with a sign reading "Desegregate on a Geographical Basis."[9]

At the start of the 1962–63 school year, CMS did just that, at least on a very limited basis. Although only two schools were involved, the effort made CMS one of the first school systems in the South to assign children on some basis other than race. Although the impact of the geographic assignment was vitiated by North Carolina law allowing any student assigned to a desegregated school to transfer elsewhere, that school year saw more African American students (forty-two) attend a white school than in all previous years combined. By 1964–65, the school year in which the *Swann* litigation was filed, fifty CMS schools had geographic assignments. Although the vast majority of CMS' black students continued to attend segregated schools, the district could rightly claim that it was making more progress than most other Southern school systems.

It would continue to do better than most other Southern districts, even before the April 1969 decision in *Swann* by Federal District Judge James B.

McMillan. However, even then, almost 60 percent of the district's black students still attended schools that were all black, or very nearly all black, as the opinion's second paragraph pointed out. It also noted:

> As a group Negro students score quite low on school achievement tests (the most objective method now in use for measuring educational progress) . . . The system of assigning pupils by "neighborhoods," with "freedom of choice" for both pupils and faculty, superimposed on an urban population pattern where Negro residents have become concentrated almost entirely in one quadrant of a city of 270,000, is racially discriminatory. This discrimination discourages initiative and makes quality education impossible. The quality of public education should not depend on the economic or racial accident of the neighborhoods in which a child's parents have chosen to live—or find they must live—nor on the color of his skin. The neighborhood school concept never *prevented* statutory racial segregation; it may not now be validly used to *perpetuate* segregation.[10]

The phrase "or find they must live" was crucial to the reasoning underlying the judge's opinion. McMillan had allowed Chambers to introduce evidence about the causes of the residential segregation that contributed to segregated schooling, and the judge's ruling accorded considerable weight to the role of governmental activity in programs such as urban renewal in producing this residential segregation. Moreover, the ruling also noted, CMS itself had contributed to a situation in which assignment based on neighborhood would lead to segregated education by consciously choosing to build new schools in areas that were predominantly white or black.

In discussing CMS' obligations to go beyond a combination of neighborhood assignment and freedom of choice, McMillan drew heavily on the Supreme Court's 1968 ruling in *Green v. County School Board* to indicate that it was not enough for the school board merely to remove legal barriers to black and white children attending the same school, but rather that "school boards are now clearly charged with the affirmative duty to desegregate schools 'now' by positive measures."[11] How this duty should be fulfilled was up to the school board which, McMillan's opinion noted, "has assets and experience beyond the reach of a judge."[12] However, he made clear that the board "is free to consider all known ways of desegregation, including bussing...pairing of grades or of schools; enlargement and re-alignment of existing zones...and any other methods calculated to establish education as a public program . . . unhampered and uncontrolled by the race of the faculty or pupils or the temporary housing patterns of the community."[13]

McMillan's decision ushered in five years of community upheaval that would include student riots and fighting at newly desegregated schools, frequent bomb threats at these schools, and the nighttime torching of Chambers's law office and his father's business. Anti-busing sentiment also manifested itself in a wide spectrum of legal activities that included demonstrations, petitions signed by thousands of parents, mass meetings, and the formation of an anti-busing organization, the Concerned Parents Association (CPA), whose many activities included fielding a slate for the three seats at stake in the 1970 school board elections.

A comparison between that year's election and the previous one indicates how much McMillan's decision had changed the local politics of education. In 1968, education was so tiny a blip on the local political radar screen that only four candidates sought the three seats that were at stake on the board of education. Of the four candidates, three were incumbents, and all were reelected. In contrast, 1970 saw thirteen candidates, including the three incumbents, seek the three seats at stake. The CPA's president and attorney beat two of the incumbents without a runoff. For the third CPA-backed candidate, Jane Scott, a runoff was necessary against Reverend Coleman Kerry, an advocate of desegregation, whose earlier appointment to fill a vacancy had made him the first black to serve on the board. As Douglas points out, the runoff between Kerry and Scott indicated the geographical, racial, and class complexion of public opinion about desegregation.[14] In addition to sweeping all of the city's black precincts, Kerry carried a majority of the vote in affluent, white southeast Charlotte. Although that pattern of electoral support was normally decisive in most elections, in this hotly contested election it was insufficient to overcome the high turnout in lower- and middle-income white neighborhoods elsewhere in the county as well as Scott's huge margins in them. Her victory brought three new faces to the board, all of them opposed to McMillan's order.

In addition to these political challenges, McMillan's ruling faced the explicitly legal one of appeals to higher courts. Spearheaded by the school board chair William Poe, himself an attorney, the main aspects of the legal challenge to McMillan's decision basically lasted until April 1971, when—almost two years to the day after McMillan's ruling—the Supreme Court issued a unanimous affirmation of his decision in an opinion written by Chief Justice Warren Burger, a Nixon appointee. The affirmation was precedent setting and changed the face of desegregation law and policy. As Douglas notes, the Supreme Court's decision in *Swann* "had an immediate impact across the South. Many lower-court judges ordered school boards to adopt McMillan's desegregation techniques, which the Supreme Court had legitimated. Within a few months of the decision, more than forty judges had entered new desegregation decrees . . . Moreover, within four months of the decision, HEW [the Department of Health, Education, and Welfare] negotiated thirty-seven new desegregation plans . . . Over one hundred school districts across America opened their schools in September 1971 with new pupil assignment plans."[15]

Ironically, some of these other districts may have achieved stability in pupil assignment more quickly than CMS did; it was not until July 1974 that the school board, black plaintiffs, and McMillan reached an agreement on a busing plan for the district. The successful operation of that plan in the 1974–75 school year led to a July 1975 order in which Judge McMillan closed the file and removed the case from the active docket. While that 1975 order reflected the court's satisfaction with CMS' assignment plan and thus marked a watershed in *Swann's* legal history, all did not become completely quiet on the legal front. In 1978, a white parent, George Martin, challenged the constitutionality of CMS' use of race in pupil assignment. Noting "this is the third suit filed by the same lawyers seeking to nullify *Swann,*" McMillan rebuffed the challenge, noting that the findings of fact underlying his denial "amount to a determination that discrimination has not ended."[16] Although the racial composition of CMS' schools was in compliance with the court orders, McMillan pointed to the continuation of ongoing racially discriminatory policies involving the construction, location, and closing of schools; the placement of kindergarten and elementary schools; racially unequal transportation burdens; and the inadequate monitoring of student transfers. Concluding that CMS had the constitutional right to continue to consider race in pupil assignment, the judge further noted, as the chapter's second epigraph indicates, that the school board did not find the separate but equal shibboleth a tempting one.

The Busing Plan

The board may not have been tempted by separate but equal, but a year after McMillan's ruling in *Martin*, CMS sought and received additional latitude in complying with court orders. However, unlike most of the board's requests a decade earlier for greater flexibility in such matters, the one in 1980 was acceptable to the *Swann* plaintiffs. Their acceptance testified to the considerable amity between them and CMS over much of the desegregation plan that had emerged from the struggle between 1965 and 1974. The 1980 order turned out to be McMillan's last in *Swann* and together with the earlier ones provided the legal framework for CMS' desegregation efforts for the next twenty years.

Probably the most important feature of these efforts was the frequent pairing of an elementary school in a predominantly white neighborhood with one in a predominantly black one. Typically, in such pairings, children in the early elementary grades (e.g., K–3) from predominantly black neighborhoods were bused to schools in predominantly white neighborhoods. In the higher elementary grades (e.g., 4–6), children from white neighborhoods were bused to schools in black neighborhoods. However, many elementary schools were not paired and generally contained all elementary grades. When the racial composition of the neighborhood in which such schools were located would not allow them to achieve racial balance, the plan made use of "satellites," noncontiguous areas from which children were bused to the school, sometimes for their entire elementary careers.

From the outset, more black than white children were "satellited," and this disparity was just one of the reasons blacks bore more of the responsibility for busing than whites did.[17] A second reason concerned the structure and operation of the elementary school pairings that perforce meant that African American elementary schoolchildren were typically bused at a younger age and for more years (i.e., four years, grades K–3) than white children (i.e., three years, grades 4–6). The asymmetry of the pairings was viewed by most whites and many blacks as the price African Americans had to pay for desegregation: "Past experience has shown," an *Observer* editorial noted ten years into the operation of the busing plan, "that large numbers of suburban white parents simply will not send their youngest children to school in the inner city. That may not be rational, but it is a reality, and reversing the pairings between inner city and suburban schools is an open invitation to resegregation."[18]

The attendance zones of junior and senior highs could be sufficiently large and the number of years spent in them sufficiently small that pairing was neither necessary nor feasible at the secondary level. Rather, a secondary school's attendance zone was typically an area contiguous to the school supplemented, if necessary, by one or more satellites, there again being, over the years, more satellites in black neighborhoods than in white ones.

However, there were white satellites, and one of them, Eastover, an especially affluent neighborhood in southeast Charlotte, occupies an important place in Charlotte's desegregation history. It was the school board's agreement in 1974 to bus students from this neighborhood to West Charlotte, a historically black high school in which many African Americans took immense pride, that played a key role in forging an agreement on a desegregation plan. That agreement addressed two sets of issues. First, it assuaged African American fears that West Charlotte would become yet another historically black school closed by desegregation. Second, it addressed the widespread perception among whites in other neighborhoods that Charlotte's most affluent white areas (including the one in which the school board chair, Poe, lived) were being spared any responsibility for busing. With Eastover now included in the busing plan, Poe could explain the plan by noting: "This year we have frankly sought stability by consciously giving to every neighborhood some reason to be unhappy about its school assignment at some point between kindergarten and graduation. It's an odd way to gain stability, but it does show some promise."[19]

While every neighborhood may have had some reason to be unhappy, whatever dismay families in Eastover and other southeast Charlotte neighborhoods may have had with their reassignment was eased by two decisions the school board made the same night. It voted to locate at West Charlotte a highly touted optional Open Education program, previously slated for another high school. Placing the open program at West Charlotte, Poe candidly acknowledged in an interview twenty-five years later, was a "sop to whites," aimed at making assignment to West Charlotte more acceptable to Eastover families.[20] Second, the board replaced the school's black principal with a white one, a move that the school board chair, Poe, had earlier suggested as part of an effort "to do everything to make formerly black schools acceptable to white people."[21] Also making West Charlotte more acceptable to Eastover families were other changes in the pupil assignment plan that resulted in the school's attendance zone acquiring middle-class black residences and losing a predominantly black public housing project.

West Charlotte High School also would exemplify another aspect of the pupil assignment plan that would contribute to its stability in subsequent years. The school's Open Education program was one of a small number of optional schools to which students could apply through a lottery that involved racial guidelines. The first optional school was Irwin Avenue Elementary. Located in the inner city close to downtown, Irwin illustrates both the history of the optional schools and the broader struggles over which children would get bused where. In the aftermath of Judge McMillan's 1969 order, CMS proposed closing seven black elementary schools and busing their students to previously all-white schools in outlying areas. Faced with black opposition to such one-way busing (discussed below), CMS agreed to convert Irwin (previously a junior high) to an elementary school and to include in its enrollment many of the black students scheduled for reassignment to these outlying predominantly white schools. As part of that agreement, CMS also committed itself to giving Irwin a "unique and innovative" program.[22] Students enrolled in Irwin's Open Education program were provided transportation, the same as any other CMS students, and could go on to a similar program at Piedmont Junior High (also in the inner city), and then to the open program at West Charlotte. By the heyday of the busing plan in the 1980s, CMS would have six optional programs with either an open or a traditional theme. The open programs attracted the children of some of Charlotte's most prominent families, both black and white, and the existence of the optional schools, whether open or traditional, provided a safety valve for educationally and politically savvy families who were not satisfied with their mandatory assignments.

The history of the many political and legal battles that led to an agreement on a plan in 1974 has been the subject of fine scholarly and journalistic accounts by Davison M. Douglas and Frye Gaillard, respectively. Rather than repeat this already-told story, I want to emphasize three of its most important themes: the intimate relation between the political and legal aspects of the Charlotte desegregation story, the activities of the business elite, and the perseverance and cohesion of the African American community.

The Relation of the Political and Legal

Given the immense legal ramifications of Judge McMillan's decision in both Charlotte and the nation as a whole, it is worth noting the political aspects of the decision's origins as well as its successful implementation. In noting these aspects, I hope to go beyond the commonplace observation that the judiciary frequently pays attention to both public opinion and election returns, though the history of desegregation litigation provides ample evidence of this attention.[23] Rather, I want to begin by emphasizing, as other scholars have done, that if not for the mass civil rights movement of the early 1960s, *Brown's* promise would likely have gone largely unfulfilled. Charlotte was hardly the only Southern locality that saw little school desegregation in the first ten years after *Brown*. In fact, as of 1964, only 2 percent of Southern blacks attended desegregated schools.[24] However, the civil rights insurgency, among its many fruits, produced the 1964 Civil Rights Act, which prohibited racial discrimination in any public or private agency that received federal funding. That provision became a very useful stick that could be combined with the carrot of substantial federal aid to local school districts that was given to Washington by the passage of the Elementary and Secondary Education Act in 1965. Moreover, as part of determining whether a school district would be eligible for federal funds, the Office of Education issued increasingly tough desegregation guidelines. In addition to affecting local policy directly, these guidelines influenced the courts first at the appellate level and then at the Supreme Court in the *Green* decision, upon which Judge McMillan heavily relied in his ruling.[25]

Just as broad political developments affected the legal precedents upon which McMillan drew in making his decision, so too did they affect the manner in which it was implemented. To be sure, the Charlotte experience provides ample illustration of Jennifer Hochschild's observation about school desegregation nationwide: "First, and most crucially, there would have been no school desegregation absent authoritative imposition from an agent out-side and 'above' the school districts themselves."[26] In Charlotte, as in many other districts, this outside agent was the federal judiciary. However, while McMillan emphatically reserved for himself the final say on the efficacy and legality of whatever desegregation plans were submitted to him, he generally left the initiative for developing such plans in the hands of the school board. Not only, in his view, could the board generally bring greater expertise than the court to pupil assignment issues, McMillan believed that giving the board responsibility for developing the desegregation plan would increase the likeli-hood of community support. The frequent recalcitrance of the school board combined with widespread community turmoil tested the soundness of this belief. But it turned out to be a wise one. The key details of the plan were eventually developed by a Citizens Advisory Group (CAG) that grew out of a fall 1973 request by the school board for a broad range of community organizations to provide input on the content of the desegregation plan.[27] In placing the responsibility for initiating the desegregation plan in the hands of the board and ultimately the community, McMillan's approach differed con-siderably from the contemporaneous school desegregation efforts in Boston, where the judge's perceived reliance on a small group of non-residents exac-erbated opposition.[28] By the time that widespread violent resistance to deseg-regation in Boston was making national headlines, Charlotte was well on the road to successful implementation of its new pupil assignment plan, and the difference between the two cities was the subject of considerable national media attention, with local civic boosters deriving considerable mileage from touting Charlotte as "The City That Made It Work."[29]

The Role of the Business Elite

Although by the late 1970s Charlotte's business elite would milk the city's reputation for progressive race relations for all it was worth, the local business elite's role in the desegregation struggle was a complex one. This role in Charlotte's school desegregation battles illustrates a key tenet of Stone's explication of regime theory and the social production model of power that he develops. The business elite may lack control and command power over local politics, but absent a major transformation of local (and perhaps na-tional) political and social structure, the business elite's resources are typically necessary for the implementation of major changes in local affairs. Had the business elite been able to control local politics, school desegregation would not have come to occupy so prominent a place on Charlotte's policy agenda. However, once the business elite saw the need for resolving the desegregation crisis through a busing plan, its resources played a key role in the development and implementation of that plan, as a review of several pivotal events in the early 1970s illustrates.

While the business elite had quickly come together to desegregate public accommodations in the early 1960s, on school desegregation it remained on the sidelines and divided until the Supreme Court's decision. Although the *Charlotte Observer* generally supported McMillan and urged compliance with his orders, other local media generally opposed them.[30] The Chamber of Commerce had played a key role in desegregating public accommodations, but it remained silent about school desegregation, and prior to the Supreme Court's decision, no business executive or government official took the initiative the way former Chamber president and Charlotte mayor Brookshire had in the famous "let's-do-lunch" initiative of 1963. "It was," as one business leader remarked, referring to Charlotte's historically black university, "one thing to go to lunch with a Johnson C. Smith professor; it was quite another to send one's child to school in a black neighborhood."[31]

The Supreme Court's decision convinced the business elite that court-ordered busing was virtually inevitable, and that only the effective implementation of a desegregation plan could restore stability to CMS and tranquility to the community. As the struggle to put CMS on a new course unfolded from 1972 to 1976, the business elite became deeply involved in the process. The Chamber of Commerce, in the words of the school board chair, Poe, "played sort of a partnership with local government."[32] The Chamber funded surveys and provided assistance to a citizens committee trying to devise a busing plan, and its chair, Cliff Cameron, lobbied fellow business leaders.[33] W. T. Harris, head of the area's largest supermarket chain and chair of the county commission, also played a prominent role providing very visible support for the CAG in its efforts to develop a busing plan.[34]

A telling and early illustration of the business elite's change in perspective is provided by the 1972 school board election. This was the first to take place after the Supreme Court's decision and followed the 1970 election in which opponents of busing had won all three seats that were at stake. The business elite had made no coherent attempt to influence the 1970 school board election, but the 1972 election proved very different. An *Observer* article, headlined "Slate-Makers Tap Candidates For Funds," describes how a "lower-level executive of a large Charlotte-based bank . . . wrote a $500 check to the 'Committee for Better Government,' " a group consisting largely of influential businessmen that had been in existence for twelve years. However in a "departure from tradition," the group, for the first time, provided support to candidates for the school board, deciding that it was their "responsibility as community leaders to endorse persons who will join the bitterly-divided board's present majority bloc, which is willing to live with court-ordered busing."[35] Of the sixteen candidates seeking the three vacant seats, four received support from the Committee for Better Government, one of whom later dropped out. The remaining three were Bill Poe, Phil Berry, and C. D. Spangler Jr.

The incumbent chair of the school board, Poe, was initially "devastated" by the Supreme Court's ruling, but he had come to accept the necessity and propriety of finding a way to implement a desegregation plan that would satisfy McMillan and Chambers.[36] Berry and Spangler supported desegregation. Both were Mecklenburg natives, but neither had held public office before. An African American, Berry was, at the time of the election, an assistant vice president at NCNB. By the 1990s, Spangler, a white, would be president of the University of North Carolina, reputedly the wealthiest man in the state, and the largest NationsBank stockholder.[37] But in 1974, Spangler was already a man of considerable means, the president of a group of motels as well as of construction and realty companies bearing the family name. These companies had built large numbers of both single-family homes and rental units in black neighborhoods. One of the companies' longtime rental managers and realty agents was Fred Alexander who, as noted in the previous chapter, by the mid-1960s was the single most politically powerful black person in Charlotte and the first African American to serve on the City Council since the 1890s.

In addition to receiving support from the Committee for Better Government, Poe, Spangler, and Berry were endorsed by both the *Charlotte Observer* and the *Charlotte News*.[38] All three men won election to the school board, and it was this newly constituted board that took the decisive steps in developing Charlotte's busing plan. One of the most crucial of these steps was authorizing CMS staff to work with the CAG in the latter's efforts to develop a school desegregation plan. In these efforts, the CAG benefited from financial backing, lobbying, and highly visible demonstrations of support from some of Charlotte's most prominent corporate executives, further indications of the business elite's general determination to settle the desegregation controversy.[39] Although the board did not adopt the CAG's plan until two months after the May 1974 school board election, that contest further indicated how important a turning point the 1972 election had been. While the 1972 election was intensely fought, the one in 1974 was, according to *Observer* reporters, "remarkably bland," one in which "most candidates worried that voters hardly knew their names, much less their philosophies."[40] Whatever the level of voters' familiarity with the candidates, the outcome was very clear: all three winners supported busing, while both an anti-busing incumbent and a challenger lost, another indication of the declining electoral influence and organization strength of anti-busing forces. Although one of the three members of the victorious 1970 CPA slate would be reelected in 1976, no candidate with an explicitly anti-busing platform would again secure election to the school board until 1988.

While the *Observer* reporters might have characterized the 1974 election as "bland," few people would apply that term to events within the school system itself, even after the key aspects of the busing plan were worked out. Particularly noteworthy was the 1976 public firing of the school superintendent, Rolland Jones. Among the business elite and many CMS staff, there were questions about the superintendent's communication skills, managerial ability, administrative strategy, and personal style.[41] At the urging of W. T. Harris, Spangler introduced a successful motion at a televised meeting of the school board that Jones be fired.[42]

Jones's dismissal, it should be emphasized, involved administrative and managerial matters rather than any fundamental disagreements over desegregation. Indeed, while the busing plan continued to have critics in Charlotte, sometimes black as well as white, the city's most prominent leaders, business and otherwise, were rarely among them. Rather, these leaders generally touted and took pride in what they viewed as Charlotte's school desegregation accomplishment and its many consequences. Especially enthusiastic was W. T. Harris, who, in a 1984 commemoration of *Brown* v. *Board of Education,* commented: "I have looked at a lot of school systems across the country. We have got absolutely the best school system in the United States. I will say to you that any school system that isn't doing what ought to be done ought to get about it because they can make progress. We elected a Black mayor, and we are proud of him . . . I would say to you that prior to school integration, we couldn't have done that, regardless of how good he was. We have grown tremendously."[43]

African American Political Cohesion

Effusive as members of the business elite could be about the busing plan, the perseverance, courage, and cohesion of African Americans were the sine qua non of whatever desegregation progress Charlotte could claim. Local backing among blacks for school desegregation was a tribute to Chambers's legal success as well as his political skill in mobilizing support for his desegregation efforts among African Americans long before local civic boosters realized the benefits that Charlotte could reap as "The City That Made It Work." African American support for the busing plan also was a response to events in both the courtroom and larger community, which served to bring black leaders of initially different perspectives together. Illustrative of the way African Americans closed ranks behind a school desegregation agenda was the changing position of African Methodist Episcopal Zion clergyman George Leake, whose 1969 candidacy for mayor was discussed in the previous chapter.

Prior to McMillan's 1969 ruling, Leake remarked, "I don't feel it's necessary to have whites and blacks in the same school. I'm not concerned about that. I *am* concerned about quality education"[44] and that he did not "give a damn whether they ever integrate" a proposed new high school, "as long as they put a decent facility in a Negro community."[45] More important than such statements were Leake's actions after McMillan's April 1969 decision when he spearheaded opposition to the school board's proposed plans to close many black schools and bus African American students to schools located in white neighborhoods. The opposition to such one-way busing manifested itself in several important ways, the most militant of which were a threatened school boycott and a downtown march of 1,200 people, whose leaders "were flanked on either side by ranks of militant youths in Black Panther dress."[46] Leake also entered direct and separate negotiations with school board chair Poe to keep several of the black schools open. When the board agreed to a modified version of his proposal, Leake then helped operate and arrange financing for the buses that transported black students who had previously attended some of the closed schools to one of the schools that was kept open.[47]

The subsequent year's events changed Leake's position considerably, if not his underlying ambivalence. In February 1970, McMillan issued a sweeping order that put two-way busing at the head of the policy agenda. Moreover, the May 1970 school board election saw the electoral triumph of the anti-busing CPA which, in opposition to McMillan's new order, was urging parents to boycott the schools when they opened. Faced with that threat, Leake announced, "As distasteful as busing is to me, as much as I hate to see the loss of the identity of any predominantly black school . . . the hour of decision is upon this community . . . I today pledge my support to the successful implementation of this order and should there be any subsequent change by the Supreme Court reducing or increasing busing, I pledge my support today."[48] Although the national office of the Congress of Racial Equality (CORE) would file an amicus brief with the Supreme Court challenging many of the *Swann* plaintiffs' demands,[49] the change in Leake's position put an end, for at least ten years, to any significant challenges from within Charlotte's black community to the hegemonic position of Chambers's desegregation efforts. To be sure, the inequities of the busing plan, and sometimes even the plan itself, occasioned opposition. Many school board elections throughout the 1970s and early 1980s would see some black as well as white candidates protest the busing plan, but these electoral challenges were as futile as the legal challenge embodied in *Martin*. Charlotte's mandatory busing plan flourished from the mid-1970s to the mid-1980s, with the superintendency of Jay Robinson being its heyday.

THE JAY ROBINSON ERA

In the aftermath of the August 1976 firing of Superintendent Rolland Jones, CMS was led on an interim basis by three of his deputies until the board chose Jay Robinson as the new superintendent. Whereas Jones's leadership of CMS was sandwiched between jobs in Canada and New York, Robinson was a native North Carolinian who had previously been school superintendent in nearby Cabarrus County. When Robinson resigned from his position with CMS in 1986, it was to take—at the request of C. D. Spangler Jr., then president of the University of North Carolina system—a job as one of the system's vice presidents and its main lobbyist. That appointment was a tribute to Robinson's deep roots in North Carolina as well as his considerable political skills, attributes that, along with a passionate commitment to desegregation, were readily apparent during his nine-year leadership of CMS.

Of the various aspects of Robinson's administration, three will be discussed here. The first involves linkages to the broader political situation; Robinson's tenure overlapped the heyday of the alliance between the business elite and the political leadership of the black community. This overlap facilitated a second aspect of his tenure and the one that was probably its most important defining characteristic: the busing plan. Although almost all of the main features of the plan had been adopted under previous superintendents, Robinson's administration epitomized the success of the mandatory desegregation techniques that would gain CMS national recognition. A third characteristic of Robinson's tenure was his administration's attempts to rein in CMS' centrifugal tendencies.

Black Political Influence

Including as it did the years (1983 and 1985) in which Harvey Gantt was elected mayor, Robinson's tenure as CMS' superintendent coincided with a high tide in local politics of the coalition between African American political leaders and the white business elite. The sway of this coalition was particularly evident in school board elections with African Americans generally holding a higher percentage of seats on the school board than on either the city council or county commission. In 1978, AME Zion clergyman George Battle was elected to the board. With the triumph of PTA activist Sarah Stevenson in 1980 and the reelection of Phil Berry, African Americans comprised one-third of the board's elected members until Berry resigned following his election to the state legislature in 1982. Moreover, the Democratic

Party dominated the school board during these years. As Theodore S. Arrington has pointed out, beginning with the school board election of 1978, not a single Republican was victorious until 1986, and then only one Republican was elected.[50]

These electoral successes in school board elections of blacks in particular and Democrats in general had a variety of institutional and behavioral explanations. Although school board elections were nonpartisan, they took place in May on the same day as primary elections during years in which, as Arrington notes, Democrats had "more primaries and more interesting primary campaigns" than did Republicans, thus facilitating Democratic turnout.[51] Moreover, in the absence of party labels, voter-mobilization drives by non-party organizations could be especially effective, and during those years, the strongest such organizations were located in the black community. This efficacy was illustrated by the 1982 school board election in which Reverend Battle led all candidates, including the two white incumbents also seeking reelection. In explaining why he finished behind Reverend Battle, one of these incumbents who had hoped to lead the field commented, "The black community just out-politicked the rest of Mecklenburg by a good margin. They worked while the rest sat on their cans."[52] The second white incumbent who barely avoided a runoff attributed his narrow victory to African Americans, "Since it was such a low turnout, the fact the Black Political Caucus endorsed me got me at least 300 votes. That gave me the margin to keep me out of a runoff."[53]

In addition to reflecting the influence of black political leaders in their alliance with the white business elite, the 1982 school board election also indicated the importance attached by the business elite to the smooth functioning of the busing plan. After endorsing the three incumbents, the *Observer* noted that of the four candidates for the remaining seat, two were "*highly* impressive."[54] One of these was Ella Scarborough, an African American relatively new to politics, who in subsequent years would successfully run for the city council with the *Observer's* support. But in the school board campaign of 1982, news accounts indicated that she thought maintaining racial balance was less important than "keeping every school up to par." "Those yellow school buses," she said, "don't do it. Teachers and the concepts they teach do it."[55] Her opponent, Karen Gaddy, made no such statements. The *Observer's* editorial commented: "We would find our fourth recommendation a toss-up between Ms. Scarborough and Ms. Gaddy if we were convinced of the depth of Ms. Scarborough's commitment to maintaining, through annual fine-tuning, the school system's current pupil assignment plan. But on that issue, we feel more certain of Ms. Gaddy's commitment. We recommend Karen Gaddy."[56] Gaddy won, and she did not disappoint the *Observer's* expectation of a commitment to maintaining the pupil assignment plan through annual fine-tuning.

Desegregation

Such fine-tuning was one of the hallmarks of Robinson's administration. Virtually every school year saw the board juggle student assignments and sometimes the configuration of grades at some schools in an ongoing effort to maintain racially balanced schools. While the legal standard of racial balance was somewhat ambiguous, CMS generally tried to keep the black enrollment at each school within +/−15 percent of the system-wide black enrollment. That +/−15 percent variance also was the standard adopted by Judge Robert Potter in his 1999 ruling in the reactivated *Swann* case, and it is the standard that will be used in this book.[57] I will call schools falling within that +/−15 percent variance racially balanced (RB) and schools falling outside of it racially identifiable black (RIB) or racially identifiable white (RIW), as the case may be.

The policy of trying to put a ceiling on white as well as black percentages reflected CMS' position that whites, as well as blacks, stood to benefit from desegregation. Administratively, the policy served to increase the likelihood that CMS would have a pool of white students upon which to draw to minimize the likelihood that any school would have too high a percentage of black students. From a political standpoint, the policy made it difficult for white families so inclined to try to avoid desegregation by living in an area assigned to a school that was overwhelmingly white.

Although the annual pupil reassignment process was often a controversial one, it generally succeeded in allowing almost all of CMS' black students to attend RB schools. As Figure 3.1 indicates, in the early 1980s, no more than 10 percent, and typically about 5 percent, of CMS' black students attended RIB schools.[58] Moreover, while the percentage of white students in RIW schools was generally higher than the percentage of black students in RIB schools, it too was much lower than it would be in subsequent years. In addition to paying careful attention to the racial composition of student populations, Robinson's administration kept close watch on the racial composition of faculties and staffs. That effort was dictated by both legal considerations and Robinson's belief that faculty and staff racial balance was an essential component of desegregated education. While the effort bore considerable fruit, CMS never achieved fully balanced faculties, and RIB schools typically had a higher percentage of black teachers than other schools. For example, in a year of relatively high faculty racial balance, 1982–83, African Americans constituted 31 percent of CMS' teachers, but 38 percent of the teachers in RIB schools, 31 percent of the teachers in RB schools, and 28 percent of the teachers in RIW schools.[59] However, faculty racial balance was higher during the Robinson years than it would be a decade later, as chapter 5 indicates.

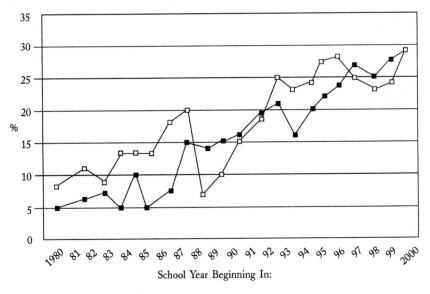

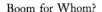

FIGURE 3.1 Enrollment in Racially Identifiable Schools, 1980–2000
Source: Charlotte-Mecklenburg Schools.

Administrative Issues

The ongoing attempts by senior staff to adjust the racial composition of both faculties and student populations reflected an administrative approach that sought to rein in centrifugal tendencies. Whereas Jones had allowed principals considerable latitude in many decisions, CMS under Robinson was much more centralized. Contributing to this centralization was Robinson's reluctance to allow a principal to stay more than five or six years at any one school, a defining characteristic of his administration. For example, just three days before his resignation from CMS became effective, Robinson recommended the assignment of nineteen principals, only eight of which were necessitated by retirements or resignations. As CMS' spokeswoman noted, Robinson was "going out with a recommendation that has been a hallmark of his administration ... [he] doesn't believe in principal ownership of a school."[60] "Jay had the feeling," his longtime deputy superintendent later explained, "that one of the problems with a principal who stays too long in a certain school is that he tends to begin to think wholly of that school as my school, not part of a system, and he begins to judge everything in terms of my school . . . We were trying to generate the feeling that you are part of the Char-Meck schools . . . You are a part of whatever is happening in the whole organization."[61] The frequent shifts also allowed Robinson to assign strong, effective principals to schools especially needing their skills. However, the extent to which a school's "need" was measured by educational criteria rather than the political clout of its PTA was a subject of considerable controversy, as will be discussed later.

In addition to reining in many of CMS' centrifugal organizational tendencies, Robinson generally succeeded in running a tight political ship. Drawing on his political skills and deep roots in North Carolina's political culture, Robinson was usually successful in cultivating members of the business elite. With their help, he encouraged the candidacies for school board of supporters of the busing plan. These same skills facilitated a generally cordial relationship with the school board, the leadership of which was usually supportive of the superintendent.

Half Full or Half Empty?

Because the Robinson years marked the heyday of the mandatory busing plan that earned Charlotte national acclaim, and the merits of such plans, as well as of school desegregation in general, have sparked great controversy, there is considerable reason to note the shortcomings and failures of those years, as well as the accomplishments. Here I will explore the educational aspects, saving a discussion of the broader political consequences for the Conclusion.

Half Full

As already noted, during Robinson's nine-year tenure, CMS achieved extremely high levels of student racial balance among schools, experienced minimal white flight, and maintained a high degree of faculty racial balance as well. These accomplishments explain the national acclaim accorded to CMS.

In describing what these high levels of desegregation meant at the school level, tellers of the CMS story often cite First Ward as the elementary school that exemplifies the school system's desegregation success.[62] Located only a few blocks from the heart of downtown, First Ward bordered Earle Village, a public housing project virtually all of whose residents were African American. Until the mandatory busing plan paired First Ward with two schools located in comfortable middle-class white neighborhoods in southeast Charlotte, it was a dilapidated and neglected school, almost all of whose students were African American. As a result of pairing, First Ward became a grades

4–6 school that had the resources and political clout of middle-class white parents. Motivated by a desire to make desegregation work, a number of these white parents launched various programs to strengthen the school. Among other things, they staffed First Ward's reading program, repainted the principal's office on the weekend, and lobbied both appointed and elected officials on the school's behalf. Robinson facilitated their involvement by giving First Ward a talented principal who helped attract a strong faculty, developed the school's educational programs, and took advantage of First Ward's proximity to downtown by cultivating members of the business elite, thus securing a wide range of intellectual and material resources. Upon this principal's retirement, Robinson appointed an equally talented replacement whose similar efforts facilitated the school's renovation, further enhanced its educational programs, and promoted a bracing esprit de corps among the school's faculty. These efforts were recognized, several years after Robinson left CMS, with First Ward's receipt in 1988 of a National School of Excellence Award.

At the high school level, West Charlotte, the historically black school to which white students from the affluent Eastover neighborhood were bused, is typically cited as another showcase example of CMS' desegregation success. Indeed, at the height of Boston's violent reaction to court-ordered desegregation, a group of West Charlotte students traveled to that city, and some Boston students came to Charlotte in an exchange that symbolized Charlotte's desegregation success. While West Charlotte's accomplishments are most typically touted by journalists and civic boosters, they are not alone. The oral histories compiled by historian Pamela Grundy also bespeak the extent to which West Charlotte afforded black and white students the opportunity to develop interracial friendships and social networks.[63] Such friendships and networks involve more than the racial tolerance and understanding about which it is very easy to wax lyrical. These friendships and networks also are relevant to educators' concerns about the outcomes that can be attributed to desegregation.

Such outcomes can be divided into short-term ones such as improved test scores and long-term ones such as educational attainment, occupational attainment, and social mobility. It is these long-term outcomes that provide the strongest and least ambiguous empirical evidence for the benefits of school desegregation.[64] Such empirical evidence, a wealth of sociological inquiry indicates, makes theoretical sense: a desegregated primary and/or secondary education helps break the intergenerational cycle of racial segregation by preparing African Americans to live and work in settings that in the United States have historically been dominated by whites. To desegregation proponents, such long-term effects are especially important because they substantiate *Brown's* most basic goal which, it should be remembered, was not primarily about boosting test scores. Rather, it was about providing blacks with a gateway to mainstream institutions and to the benefits that such access typically confers.

To my knowledge, no systematic research was ever conducted during the 1980s on the effects of desegregation on students at West Charlotte, or any other CMS school for that matter. However, it is plausible that the interracial friendships and social networks chronicled by Grundy at West Charlotte and remarked on by teachers, students, and observers at many other schools had the same kind of positive effects on long-term educational outcomes documented in research conducted elsewhere.

As for short-term outcomes during the busing plan's heyday, the situation is more complicated. The kind of student- and school-level data that would allow this issue to be addressed with any degree of rigor is presently unavailable for the early 1980s, and it is necessary to rely on system-level data that is, at best, only suggestive. What this data does suggest, however, is that CMS made more progress in improving the academic achievement of black students during Robinson's administration than it did subsequently.

This data involves scores on the California Achievement Test (CAT), which became mandatory for all North Carolina districts during the first year of Robinson's administration. Figure 3.2 displays racially disaggregated scores

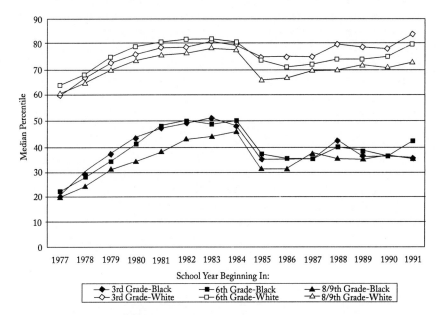

FIGURE 3.2   CMS CAT Scores, 1977–1991
Source: Charlotte-Mecklenburg Schools.

on the total battery for grades 3, 6, and either 8 or 9 for the fifteen years in which CMS was required to administer the test.[65] As is readily apparent, the figure shows that during the early 1980s—years in which Robinson was superintendent, and CMS was more racially balanced than it would subsequently be—white test scores were rising, but black test scores were rising even more rapidly, thus allowing the black/white test score gap to close at a faster rate than in subsequent years. The data summarized in that figure accord with the perceptions that were current in the early 1980s, when both CMS and the local media rejoiced with each year's report of steadily increasing test scores and the narrowing of the black/white gap on them.[66]

However, the picture changed dramatically beginning with the 1985–86 school year, when all scores dropped sharply. Over the next six years, white scores increased only slightly, and black scores generally remained at the same level. This dramatic change has at least two possible explanations. The first involves changes in CMS. The 1985–86 school year was Robinson's last year at the helm of CMS, and subsequent years saw a marked increase in resegregation, as Figure 3.1 indicates. Moreover, as the next chapter indicates, his successor proved unable to provide the leadership that CMS needed.

A second possible explanation for the dramatic change in CAT scores beginning in 1985–86 has less to do with changes in CMS and much more to do with changes in the CAT itself. That year saw the introduction of a new and renormed version of the CAT. There is thus reason to downplay the educational significance of the rising test scores prior to 1985–86 by dismissing this increase as an artifact of things such as greater familiarity with the test, better test preparation, and improved alignment between curriculum and the test. This was the explanation provided by David Armor, the main expert witness on academic achievement for the white plaintiffs in the reopened *Swann* case.[67]

This second explanation undoubtedly has considerable merit, but there are grounds for suggesting that it is not the whole story. Those grounds involve the comparisons between scores in CMS and those statewide that are presented in Figures 3.3 and 3.4, which plot the result obtained by subtracting the median percentile in North Carolina from the median percentile in CMS for grades 3, 6, and 8/9 for each year that CMS administered the CAT. As these figures indicate, both black and white students in CMS did better in comparison to students statewide early in the 1980s than later in the decade. Although the differences are small, the trend is similar in all three grades, and it becomes especially discernible when the differences for all three grades are combined, as these two figures also do.[68] Since it is difficult to attribute the difference between the early and late 1980s to changes in student characteristics or to other reasons,[69] Figures 3.3 and 3.4 suggest that during the early 1980s, as judged by comparisons with the rest of the state,

CMS was doing something better for black students than it was doing in the late 1980s. Without additional data, it is difficult to ascertain whether that "something better" was more effective (but educationally vacuous) test preparation or genuine academic achievement. It is even more difficult to ascertain

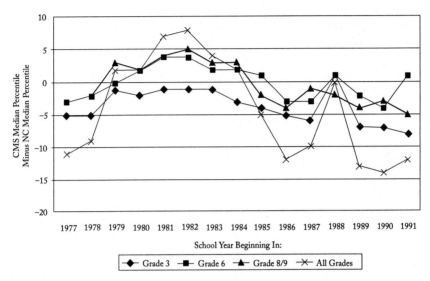

FIGURE 3.3   Black Students' CAT Scores: Difference between CMS and North Carolina, 1977–1991
Source: Charlotte-Mecklenburg Schools.

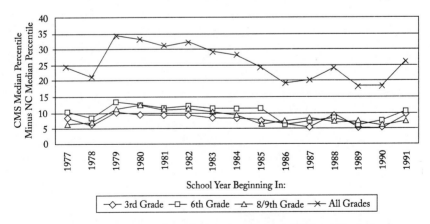

FIGURE 3.4   White Students' CAT Scores: Difference between CMS and North Carolina, 1977–1991
Source: Charlotte-Mecklenburg Schools.

the extent to which that something better—whether it involved test preparation or genuine academic achievement—might have been linked to CMS' greater racial balance at the decade's start and/or to particular policies of the Robinson administration. These many difficulties notwithstanding, the comparisons between CMS and North Carolina combined with the data on the black/white test-score gap within CMS provide some suggestive evidence that, as measured by CAT scores, CMS was making more progress in improving black academic achievement during the heyday of the busing plan than in the other years the CAT was administered.

However, even if CMS was doing better in improving African American outcomes early in the decade than later, black achievement still lagged that of whites by a considerable amount. To address this issue, CMS developed a variety of programs, but it is not at all clear that they had sufficient resources, much less effect. For example, five years after the 1983 implementation of a Minority Achievement Program, its resources consisted of a budget that translated to forty-five dollars per school and a director who had no support staff of any kind. Moreover, the program was operational in less than 40 percent of CMS' schools.[70] Such facts indicate the need to discuss the extent to which even during the busing plan's heyday, many of desegregation's promises remained unfulfilled.

Half Empty

Whatever the accomplishments of the Robinson era, no nine-year administration could possibly be sufficient to overcome the legacy of several hundred years of slavery and state-mandated segregation that was manifest in myriad ways throughout his years leading CMS. Even CMS' most noted accomplishments, the maintenance of very high levels of racial balance and minimal white flight, reflected this legacy because the mandatory busing plan's operation hinged on systematic inequities that required black families and children to shoulder much more of the responsibility for making the busing plan work than their white counterparts did.

Similarly, there is more to the First Ward and West Charlotte stories than the purely upbeat accounts provided earlier would suggest. A significant aspect of the former's success lay in the downtown location that made it an extremely visible school, as well as one with unique access to the financial and human resources of Charlotte's business elite. Moreover, while there was considerable involvement in the school's activities by parents and community leaders in a small satellite black neighborhood on the other side of downtown, there was much less participation in PTA or other school-related activities by the residents of Earle Village or nearby black churches, despite the school's intense efforts to elicit involvement. Both the PTA and almost all parental- and community-support activities were dominated by middle-class parents, the vast majority of whom were the same whites who led the PTAs of the two K–3 schools in white neighborhoods with which First Ward was paired.[71] Moreover, both of the principals whom Robinson appointed to First Ward were white females. Their predecessor had been a black male, and his replacement involved the kind of racial and gender issues whose many ramifications cannot be adequately addressed by interview data obtained twenty years later.

West Charlotte also benefited from unique resources. Its students included children of many of Charlotte's most influential black and white families, and the characteristics of its student body, along with the presence of the Open Program, allowed it to attract exceptionally talented teachers and administrators. These same distinctive aspects placed a premium on CMS' leadership making sure that West Charlotte, like First Ward, had such talent. More importantly, the high level of racial understanding and acceptance among West Charlotte's students notwithstanding, many classes within the school were racially imbalanced, with blacks being overrepresented in the lower tracks and underrepresented in the higher ones. The existence of such second-generation segregation at CMS' desegregation showcase high school requires comment and perforce leads to a discussion of the extent to which—the high level of racial balance among CMS' schools notwithstanding—there was widespread racial imbalance among the classes in any particular school.[72]

Shortly after Robinson assumed office, HEW ruled CMS ineligible for a $922,000 grant because of within-school segregation. That ruling intensified already existing attempts to address the problem, and such efforts continued throughout Robinson's administration. Although year-by-year data on the success of these efforts are lacking, there is little doubt that an especially pernicious aspect of within-school segregation, racially identifiable tracking, remained prevalent throughout CMS. In fact, shortly after assuming CMS' superintendency, Robinson's successor, Peter Relic, noted that "academically gifted classes had too few blacks, and slower classes . . . had too many blacks," and he was praised for his candor.[73]

The best data on the extent of racially identifiable tracking during the Robinson years come from a survey of the racial composition of high school English classes in 1981–82,[74] several years after CMS had intensified its efforts to improve the situation that had cost it the HEW grant. Table 3.1 summarizes this survey by presenting data on the percentages of all black and of all white students enrolled in a given grade who were in each of the four tracks in high school English.[75] The table also provides a rough indication of the magnitude of the racially identifiable tracking by calculating a disparity ratio whose value would be 1 in cases in which a track is not racially identifiable, greater than 1 when blacks are overrepresented in a track, and less than 1 when blacks are underrepresented. For example, as the table indicates, of all

TABLE 3.1
Racially Identifiable Tracking, High School English, 1981–82 School Year

	% of all black students taking English in this grade in the track[a]	% of all white students taking English in this grade in the track[a]	disparity ratio[b]
	12th grade		
	All CMS High Schools		
Track 1[c]	45%	10%	4.5
Track 2	44%	51%	.86
Track 3	5.7%	22%	.26
Track 4	4.8%	16%	.30
	West Charlotte		
Track 1	34%	12%	2.9
Track 2	54%	49%	1.1
Track 3	6.7%	18%	.38
Track 4	5.6%	22%	.26
	11th grade		
	All CMS High Schools		
Track 1	42%	8.9%	4.7
Track 2	49%	53%	.93
Track 3	8.0%	27%	.29
Track 4	1.2%	10%	.12
	West Charlotte		
Track 1	33%	9.5%	3.5
Track 2	52%	56%	.92
Track 3	13%	23%	.56
Track 4	2.2%	11%	.20
	10th grade		
	All CMS High Schools		
Track 1	41%	7.9%	5.2
Track 2	49%	50%	.97
Track 3	10%	29%	.34
Track 4	.071%	13%	.06
	West Charlotte		
Track 1	37%	14%	2.7
Track 2	34%	46%	.75
Track 3	26%	32%	.80
Track 4	2.9%	8.5%	.34

a Entries may not add up to 100% because of rounding.

b The disparity ratio is computed by dividing the entry in the third column into the entry in the second column.

c Track 1 is the lowest track.

Source: Charlotte-Mecklenburg Schools.

the black students enrolled in twelfth-grade English, 45 percent were enrolled in the lowest track. However, of all the white students enrolled in twelfth-grade English, only 10 percent were in the lowest track, yielding a disparity ratio of 4.5. In contrast, less than 5 percent of all black students were enrolled in the top track, but 16 percent of white students were, yielding a disparity ratio of .30. As the table also indicates, the racial disparities in track placement were even greater in the tenth grade, with 13 percent of white tenth-grade English students in the top track, but less than 1 percent of black students in that track. As Table 3.1 also indicates, showcase West Charlotte generally had less racial disparity in track placement than CMS as a whole, but it too was characterized by considerable racially identifiable tracking.

Importantly, the school year in which this survey was conducted, 1981–82, happened to be the one in which, as Figure 3.1 indicates, CMS achieved extremely high levels of racial balance among schools. But if the high levels of racially identifiable tracking in high school English classes are any indication of what was taking place in CMS' other classrooms—and it almost certainly is—it appears that in this district acclaimed for its desegregation successes, relatively few black students experienced a genuinely desegregated education, even in its showcase high school.[76]

This survey also called attention to another aspect of both the West Charlotte and CMS stories: the disparity in course offerings among CMS' schools. Four of the ten high schools did not offer any Advanced Placement (AP) English courses, and of these four, three were on the westside, an area that has typically been on the short end of many policy sticks. Harding was one of these three schools and had the highest percentage black enrollment of any high school. Eighty-five percent of the school's twelfth-grade English classes were in the bottom two tracks, and 15 percent were in the top two tracks (though none were AP). In contrast, the high school with the lowest percentage of black enrollment, East Mecklenburg, in southeast Charlotte, had only 57 percent of its twelfth-grade English offerings in the bottom two tracks, and 43 percent in the top two tracks (including two AP classes).[77]

Harding also illustrates another major shortcoming of the Robinson administration: whatever the other reasons for the frequent reassignment of principals, the policy also served to "reassign" problems from schools with influential parents to schools whose parents lacked clout. Prior to the year in which the survey on high school English classes was conducted, Robinson shuffled principals in a way that transferred South Mecklenburg's principal to Harding. The man's tenure at South Meck had been a controversial one, characterized by "years of tension" between him and some faculty members.[78] News of his transfer to Harding led some teachers at the school to claim it was a "dumping ground" wielding "little power because it has few active, affluent and powerful parents to pressure top administrators."[79] As things turned out, the newly transferred principal was reassigned from Harding to an elementary school after only seven months. However, four years later, a second principal whose leadership of another southeast Charlotte high school, this time Myers Park, was considered ineffective was transferred to Harding, replacing the school's highly regarded principal, who in turn was assigned to Myers Park.[80]

Reflecting on the reassignment of principals to and from Harding several years after he had left CMS, Robinson told a reporter, "We had some leaders whom we transferred there because we hoped that in a smaller situation they might get along better, but those were bad decisions. Then we had some extremely strong principals there, but we probably moved some of them too soon."[81] That these "bad decisions" just happened to benefit high schools in affluent white southeast Charlotte and hurt schools on the poorer and more African American westside was probably not coincidental. As Robinson candidly acknowledged in a different context in the same interview, "At a school where parents are less vocal and not in a position to be strong advocates, there is a tendency not to look after their needs as you might."[82]

Political Constraints and Shortfalls in Civic Capacity

Robinson's comment calls attention to the political constraints under which CMS felt it was operating. Even during the busing plan's heyday, Robinson and busing plan proponents were concerned that a too-vigorous pursuit of additional racial equity in pupil assignment and resource allocation would erode support for desegregation among whites, especially in the increasingly conservative national political climate following Ronald Reagan's election as president. That concern was subsequently summed up by Carrie Winter, who served on the board from 1976 to 1988 and was its chair from 1983 to 1988, "There is a point at which you have to compromise in order to keep what you have gained."[83]

In minimizing opposition to its decisions about where that point was located, CMS benefited from political demobilization around educational issues. Claims of such demobilization would appear to be contradicted by the African American clout in school board elections noted earlier, but the contradiction is only a superficial one. As Adolph Reed has noted in a related context, the kind of political incorporation exemplified by African American electoral success can exert a "demobilizing effect" because such success legitimizes electoral politics "as the primary means of political participation, which naturally seems attractive compared with others that require more extensive and intensive commitment of attention and effort. A result is to narrow the operative conception of political engagement to one form, and the most passive one at that."[84]

Several developments facilitated this demobilization. Many of the activists, both black and white, who had struggled over the past decade to achieve mandatory busing were more than willing to see the desegregation glass as half full rather than half empty. Contributing to that willingness was a complex mixture of political fatigue, a desire to justify earlier efforts, and these activists' ability—more than that of most citizens—to work the system so their children could drink from the part of the glass that was half full. Some key activists—again, both black and white—who had played important roles in the struggle for the busing plan were elected to the school board or assumed other leadership positions in CMS and the community and thus found themselves with the responsibilities and political encumbrances that inevitably distinguish governance from advocacy.

To be sure, some African Americans and liberal whites actively urged CMS to fulfill more of desegregation's promises, but their efforts ran up against the developments facilitating demobilization. Similarly, their efforts garnered little support from the business elite, for whom education was less important an issue in the early 1980s than it had been a decade earlier or would soon become again. A variety of developments contributed to education's low salience to the business elite. The desegregation crisis had been resolved, and Charlotte was receiving favorable national publicity for the busing plan. *A Nation At Risk* was not yet published or was too recent to affect major changes in business policy. Finally, corporate relocation decisions, as Charlotte executives perceived them, were influenced more by factors such as tax rates and access to markets and transportation than by the quality of the school system. Thus, while the business elite used CMS' reputation to help attract new business, it lacked the motivation to get involved in education that it had in 1974 or would have shortly after Robinson left. Finally, one especially important business, the *Observer*, like CMS, worried that too vigorous a pursuit of racial justice in education would jeopardize whatever had already been achieved.

The *Observer's* position was exemplified in an editorial that appeared shortly before Robinson's resignation when two members left the board in midterm, and their replacements called for a freeze on the frequent fine-tuning of the pupil assignment plan until a more stable, long-range one could be developed. The *Observer* responded to this call with an editorial entitled, "Playing with Fire: The Dangers of Resegregation." Acknowledging the "good intentions" of the two newcomers, the editorial noted that the busing plan has rested on a "fragile consensus." Most Charlotteans, it continued, were proud of the fact that Charlotte "has one of the most integrated school systems in the nation—and, all things considered, one of the best. But there is a potential impatience, perpetually bubbling beneath the surface of community consensus" with both the frequent reassignments and the plan itself.[85]

Similarly, the *Observer* was reluctant to subject other aspects of CMS' operations to searching examination during most of Robinson's tenure. Two years after Robinson left CMS, the paper's publisher, Rolfe Neill, noted, "I think the *Observer* inadvertently has done a disservice over the years by failing to look deeply into complaints about our schools. Because editorially we were so intent on preserving the fragile covenant that accepted busing, we may have been too quick to presume that public school dissidents were racists trying to eliminate busing."[86]

As the next chapter will indicate, support for the busing plan unraveled soon after Robinson left, and CMS found itself facing a wide range of criticism. Given how quickly all of this happened, one can easily argue that the *Observer's* concerns about the fragility of the "covenant" over busing were justified, as were its concerns about "playing with fire." Yet I would argue that the manner in which the support unraveled also calls attention to the short-sightedness of CMS, the *Observer,* and other civic leaders in avoiding a more searching examination of CMS' operations in the early 1980s. Neill's remarks about the *Observer's* inadvertent disservice came at a time when, as will be discussed below, the *Observer* and Charlotte's business elite were flipping from being too quick to dismiss criticism of CMS to being too ready to accept it. But both errors were opposite sides of the same coin. The shortage of informed and candid public airing of the accomplishments and shortcomings of desegregation and of other aspects of CMS' operation during the early 1980s would subsequently make it easier for critics to trash the busing plan as well as confuse pupil assignment strategies with those for improving academic achievement.

For CMS to have enjoyed the largely uncritical support of Charlotte's major newspaper during the early 1980s would seem to have been a key aspect of developing civic capacity in support of education, in general, and the busing plan, in particular. But whatever civic capacity might have been built by that support lacked depth because too great a concern about "playing with fire" precluded more searching commentary and evaluation about what CMS was doing wrong as well as right.

Fiscal and Planning Problems

A less subtle and more important shortcoming in civic capacity during the early 1980s involved CMS' relationship with the county commission. A key aspect of building civic capacity on behalf of education is developing support across a locality's many institutions. That kind of support is especially necessary in a situation, like CMS,' where the school system is dependent on another local governmental body for a large percentage of its budget. Yet that support was not forthcoming despite Robinson's formidable political skills and the fact that CMS' chief financial officer was an ostensibly popular former member of the county commission. Although CMS could typically count on the *Observer's* backing in the annual tussles over funding, it was usually unable to marshal support from other influential actors, especially among the business elite, against charges of padded budgets, waste, and a lack of fiscal accountability.

A telling example of the difference between CMS' reputation among educators nationally and its strained financial situation in Mecklenburg came in May 1984. That was the month when the *Observer* delightedly noted the statement from W. T. Harris, quoted earlier, that Charlotte had "absolutely the best school system in these United States," as well as a subsequent report from the National Education Association citing Charlotte's desegregation successes.[87] Just three days later, however, the paper called attention to a very different aspect of CMS' situation in an editorial subheadlined, "County Shortchanges Schools." Asking "what's wrong with Mecklenburg's county commissioners and their county manager, Jerry Fox," the editorial sharply criticized their opposition to a pay raise for teachers at a time when Charlotte was receiving national acclaim, and it concluded: "County finances are in the best shape in years. By continuing to treat the schools as burdensome step-children needing stringent financial discipline, the commissioners and Mr. Fox are unnecessarily handicapping the school board and administration."[88]

Whereas the *Observer* likened CMS' situation to that of a financially irresponsible stepchild, former school board chair Carrie Winter has used an even more graphic analogy, likening annual budget hearings to "one of those cowboy movies where they [the county commissioners] shoot at your feet and you have to keep dancing."[89] Since it is difficult to know what CMS' "real" financial needs were, a useful way of assessing the validity of Winter's and the *Observer's* gripes are comparisons between CMS' fiscal fortunes and those of North Carolina's other large urban consolidated school districts, at that time Winston-Salem/Forsyth and Raleigh/Wake. The best data for such comparisons are the annual reports on local school finances, published by the Public School Forum of North Carolina, beginning in 1987.[90] As the Appendix notes, what the Forum calls Relative Effort (RE) compares a county's fiscal ability to support its public schools with the actual support provided and is thus a good measure of civic capacity. Since the 1987 report's measure for RE was a five-year average of expenditures for K–12 education for the school years 1981–82 through 1985–86, it is a particularly good indication of Mecklenburg County's financial support for CMS during Robinson's administration.

TABLE 3.2
Rankings of Local Financial Support for Public Education, By County, 1987–2001

Year of Report	Ability to Pay County	Rank	Actual Effort County	Rank	Relative Effort County	Rank	Relative Total Effort County	Rank	Relative Current Effort County	Rank	Overall Rank County	Rank
1987	Meck	12	Meck	8	Fors	84					Fors	59
	Fors	23	Fors	11	Wake	94					Wake	67
	Wake	25	Wake	12	Meck	99					Meck	71
1989	Wake	2	Wake	7	Wake	112					Wake	76
	Meck	3	Meck	14	Fors	120					Fors	102
	Fors	5	Fors	16	Meck	123					Meck	111
1990	Meck	2	Wake	1			Wake	54	Fors	60	Wake	31
	Wake	3	Meck	6			Fors	80	Meck	75	Fors	59
	Fors	4	Fors	7			Meck	87	Wake	77	Meck	73
1991	Meck	2	Wake	5			Wake	58	Fors	47	Wake	38
	Wake	3	Fors	6			Fors	68	Wake	68	Fors	48
	Fors	4	Meck	9			Meck	91	Meck	76	Meck	63
1992	Meck	2	Wake	2			Wake	57	Fors	47	Wake	44
	Fors	3	Fors	7			Fors	71	Meck	70	Fors	49
	Wake	4	Meck	8			Meck	82	Wake	71	Meck	56
1993	Meck	2	Wake	4			Wake	60	Fors	46	Wake	40
	Fors	3	Fors	6			Fors	71	Wake	71	Fors	53
	Wake	5	Meck	7			Meck	89	Meck	77	Meck	67
1994	Meck	2	Wake	3			Wake	61	Fors	45	Wake	42
	Fors	4	Fors	5			Fors	70	Wake	75	Fors	46
	Wake	5	Meck	6			Meck	85	Meck	76	Meck	57

(continued)

TABLE 3.2 (continued)

Rankings of Local Financial Support for Public Education, By County, 1987–2001

Year of Report	Ability to Pay County	Rank	Actual Effort County	Rank	Relative Effort County	Rank	Relative Total Effort County	Rank	Relative Current Effort County	Rank	Overall Rank County	Rank
1995	Meck	2	Meck	5			Wake	73	Fors	50	Wake	52
	Wake	3	Wake	7			Fors	74	Wake	72	Fors	54
	Fors	4	Fors	8			Meck	84	Meck	74	Meck	56
1996	Meck	2	Meck	4			Wake	65	Fors	47	Wake	41
	Wake	3	Wake	5			Fors	78	Meck	74	Meck	50
	Fors	5	Fors	8			Meck	82	Wake	75	Fors	53
1997	Meck	2	Meck	5			Wake	67	Fors	47	Wake	57
	Fors	5	Wake	7			Fors	80	Wake	74	Fors	69
	Wake	6	Fors	8			Meck	84	Meck	79	Meck	74
1998	Meck	2	Meck	5			Wake	69	Fors	49	Meck	39
	Wake	3	Wake	8			Fors	77	Meck	73	Wake	46
	Fors	4	Fors	9			Meck	81	Wake	82	Fors	49
1999	Meck	2	Meck	4			Wake	69	Fors	51	Meck	28
	Wake	3	Wake	7			Meck	71	Meck	70	Wake	38
	Fors	5	Fors	10			Fors	73	Wake	82	Fors	45
2000	Meck	2	Meck	2			Wake	61	Fors	53	Meck	40
	Wake	6	Wake	6			Meck	72	Meck	67	Wake	41
	Fors	10	Fors	11			Fors	73	Wake	77	Fors	53
2001	Meck	2	Meck	3			Meck	68	Fors	58	Not available*	
	Wake	4	Wake	5			Wake	73	Meck	71	*	
	Fors	15	Fors	11			Fors	74	Wake	86	*	

*Overall Rank was not computed in the 2001 report.
Source: Public School Forum of North Carolina

As Table 3.2 indicates, according to the 1987 report, Mecklenburg ranked higher than both Forsyth and Wake in Ability to Pay and in its Actual Effort. However, when those two variables were compared to yield RE, Mecklenburg ranked the lowest of the three. As a result of this low ranking for RE, its Overall Rank also was the lowest of the three, further indicating that Mecklenburg's financial support for its school system was less than that of either Wake or Forsyth. Mecklenburg's low level of funding (in comparison to both Wake and Forsyth) strongly suggests that despite CMS' nationally praised busing plan, there was a shortfall in civic capacity in the area of education because the county commission's influence over CMS' budget places a premium on the kind of cross-sectoral cooperation that is at the heart of civic capacity.

Just as CMS' fiscal relationship with the county commission was a strained one, its planning relationship with other governmental agencies also was weak during the Robinson administration. That weakness was unfortunate because, as chapter 4 will indicate, the county's rapid growth was threatening school desegregation. Noting this threat early in the Robinson administration, an editorialist called for cooperation between CMS and other governmental agencies because they needed the school board's "acute understanding" of the growth "patterns that are tearing apart today's pupil assignment plan," and the school board needed "their knowledge of the patterns that will shape tomorrow's schools."[91] But CMS' relationship with the planning commission was not an especially productive one. Critics charged CMS with lacking internal planning expertise, generally ignoring planning issues, and when it did consider them, being myopic and unsystematic. From CMS' perspective, whatever difficulties it faced had other causes, including a lack of funds to hire adequate staff and to purchase land in a manner conducive to long-term planning. While Robinson viewed communication with the planning commission as "good," he doubted "it ever had any effect on where development took place."[92] School board member Don Austin was more critical, claiming, "There's been very little cooperation between the planning commission and the school system, and that's the fault of the planning commission. They don't listen to us."[93]

Whatever the disagreement about why planning was not better coordinated, there was little dispute that coordination was indeed poor. Like the relatively (compared to other counties) poor local funding of CMS, the lack of coordinated planning indicated a shortfall in the cross-sectoral cooperation that is essential to developing civic capacity for public education. That this shortfall occurred during the very years that CMS' desegregation accomplishments were winning national acclaim raises especially troubling questions about the development of civic capacity in Charlotte, which will be discussed in the Conclusion.

Chapter 4

Swan Song for the Busing Plan?

Harris and Brookshire said they didn't really care where the loop is built "so long as it is built."

    —1977 *Observer* report on W. T. Harris's and Stan Brookshire's lobbying for construction of an outerbelt in southern Mecklenburg County.[1]

The board needs new faces, new leadership and new and more energetic ways of communicating with and responding to the public.

    —*Observer* editorial, titled "Schools: Time for Change," containing the paper's endorsements in the 1988 school board election.[2]

BUSING IS A RELIC

    —Late 1980s' Charlotte bumper sticker.

As the 1980s progressed, Charlotte's nationally praised busing plan came under increasing local criticism, as did many other aspects of CMS' operations. Much of this criticism was rooted in developments that began in the Robinson era. This chapter begins by discussing these seeds of change, then turns to the administration of Peter Relic, Robinson's successor, during which challenges to the busing plan intensified. The Relic administration also faced severe planning, administrative, and fiscal difficulties, all of which signified woefully inadequate civic capacity. These local problems resonated with the generic late 1980s nationwide alarm about a putative crisis in public education[3] to make those years extremely troubled ones for CMS and its superintendent, who was forced to resign at the end of his third year in office. Given the brevity of Relic's administration and CMS' drift during this period, the late 1980s are best understood as a transition period between the very different worlds of the early 1980s and the early 1990s.

SEEDS OF CHANGE

Of the many changes that would affect CMS, the most important was opposition to busing. As early as 1978, the *Observer's* education writer pointed out that support for CMS' desegregation policies was hardly unanimous. Although that comment by itself was hardly newsworthy—after all, CMS was still facing *Martin's* legal challenge to its desegregation policies—the source of the writer's observations was more interesting. Rather than being concentrated among Southerners, as stereotypes might lead one to expect, the "most vocal and highly organized opposition comes from suburbs filled with transplanted Northerners transferred to Charlotte by large corporations shifting their operations to the Sunbelt. The parents are disappointed with what they consider an inferior Southern school system, and their irritation is compounded by the forced busing many had expected to leave behind in Northern cities."[4] Said one Northern transplant: "When we moved down here from Albany [New York], we bought a house out here in Providence Plantation [an affluent outlying neighborhood in southeast Charlotte] so we could get our kids out of inner-city schools. But dammit, you got us anyway."[5]

Development and Its Discontents

It would take ten years for those sentiments to affect the school board's composition, but they grew increasingly pervasive throughout the 1980s, as the region's economic development attracted more newcomers. Facilitating the growth of these sentiments was the way the geography of Charlotte's growth affected new school construction. Just as southeast Charlotte's Eastover neighborhood posed important difficulties for desegregation in the early 1970s, now other, more outlying southeast neighborhoods would pose the most daunting obstacles over the next two decades. By the turn of the century, explosive growth in the north of the county also would pose a wide range of problems for CMS planners, but in the years which are the focus of this book, south Mecklenburg's growth posed the most salient threat to desegregation efforts.

Shortly after the 1979–80 school year began, an *Observer* article with the subheadline "Low Pupil Estimate in South Mecklenburg Leaves Classes Bursting at Seams" pointed out how planners' enrollment projections had "missed most dramatically in the 11-school South Mecklenburg area, the hub of surging residential construction."[6] A month later, the ominous implications of unrestrained growth in southern Mecklenburg for school desegregation were noted by Tom Bradbury, subsequently the *Observer* editorial board's education specialist. Entitled "Direct Growth, for Schools' Sake," Bradbury's column called attention to Superintendent Robinson's hope that Charlotte would confront and change growth patterns. "If some of the city's explosive suburban growth could be shifted around to the north and west," Bradbury pointed out, "it would be much easier to deal with school [racial] imbalances."[7]

Based on recognition that the high-growth areas in south Mecklenburg were distant from neighborhoods with large numbers of blacks, Bradbury's point was an obvious one. Its prescience is illustrated by the history of McAlpine elementary school, built toward the end of Robinson's tenure. Located in southeast Charlotte, just below Highway 51 on land that was purchased in 1984, McAlpine was planned as a response to growth, but it also fueled development. "When that site was selected," a developer testified in the reopened *Swann* litigation, "almost overnight there were major subdivisions that came on line. Land values certainly started increasing."[8] McAlpine's southerly location occasioned opposition among some African Americans, including future school board chair Arthur Griffin who, in the controversy surrounding the reopened *Swann* case in 1999, asserted that his opposition to McAlpine fourteen years earlier cost him the 1986 school board election.[9] The Robinson administration also had reservations about the site, but it felt that the judicious drawing of attendance boundaries and the pairing of McAlpine with other schools would allow it to be racially balanced. This hope was realized, sometimes barely, until the 1990s when, as the next chapter will indicate, the mandatory busing plan was scrapped, CMS stopped pairing elementary schools, and McAlpine's African American population plummeted to 4 percent.

McAlpine's desegregation experience was not unique. As CMS would note in the 1999 trial in the reactivated *Swann* case, twenty-seven new schools had been built in the 1980s and 1990s.[10] At the time of the trial, seven of these new schools had so small a black enrollment that they were racially identifiable white (RIW), and six of the seven were in the south of the county. Moreover, of those twenty-seven schools, only one had so large a black enrollment that it was racially identifiable black (RIB) at the start of the trial, and it was in the northern part of the county.

However, even if concerns about the future of school desegregation were ignored in the early 1980s, sound planning dictated a shift in growth to northern areas of the county because of, among other things, greater proximity to both underutilized sewage treatment plants and Charlotte's water supply. "Balanced growth" thus became a major issue in local politics during this time with Mayor Gantt, holder of degrees in both architecture and planning, raising the possibility that the city would impose disincentives to growth in the south as well as provide incentives to growth in the north. The latter were politically popular and spurred commercial and residential development in the northeast part of the county near the University of North Carolina at Charlotte. But political opposition precluded the use of disincentives in the south, which thus continued to experience explosive growth.[11]

The Outerbelt

Spurring growth in the south were plans for an outerbelt, an interstate highway on Charlotte's periphery. Not only would the outerbelt markedly affect CMS, but the battles over its construction and location indicate the role of politics and economic clout in shaping the course of both Charlotte's development and the character of its educational system.

Although North Carolina's Board of Transportation had earlier included a Charlotte outerbelt in its long-term road plan, it was not until 1977–78 that controversy peaked over the location of its first legs, those in the south of the county. The key issue was: where in the south of the county would these first legs be built, the largely undeveloped part of the county below Highway 51 ("the southern route"), or the more developed region above it ("the northern route")?[12] Supporters of the northern route included the planning commission's professional staff, a majority of Charlotte's city council, including Harvey Gantt, editors of both the *Charlotte Observer* and *Charlotte News*, and home owner groups located south of Highway 51. Some of the proponents of the northern route were actually skeptical about the merits of any outerbelt but felt that if one had to be built, the northern route would minimize urban sprawl, was more consistent with previous planning documents, and would fulfill the outerbelt's main goal: easing congestion on Charlotte's streets.[13] In addition, Susan Green, leader of a home owner group supporting the northern route, argued that the southern route would undermine CMS' efforts to maintain a desegregated school system. She noted that the high-density development in the southernmost parts of the county facilitated by the southern route would be predominantly white, thus requiring school children to "ride new routes miles longer than those they currently experience" if racial balance were to be maintained.[14] Prescient as her argument turned out to be, it attracted little attention at the time, and school desegregation concerns played little role in the outerbelt debate.[15]

Whatever the merits of the northern route might be, the southern would almost certainly trigger much greater economic development. It thus attracted the support of the Chamber of Commerce and most of Charlotte's major developers and builders who, along with home owner groups north of Highway 51, also argued that it would involve less disruption of existing development, fewer land acquistion problems, and would be more environmentally sound. [16] Also preferring the southern route were a majority of Mecklenburg's county commissioners, former mayor Brookshire, and former county commission chair W. T. Harris. However, in lobbying Raleigh about the outerbelt, the latter two made clear, as the chapter's first epigraph indicates, that they did not really care where the loop was built, "so long as it is built."

With the county commission and city council taking opposing positions, the state's Board of Transportation, with whom final authority rested, chose the southern route in April 1978. However, the ongoing debate about the route combined with state budgetary constraints, the need for an environmental impact study, and intergovernmental snafus to postpone land acquisition and the start of construction for seven years. By that time, the areas north of Highway 51 had become sufficiently developed to seriously hinder land acquisition. Charlotte's city council was thus less wedded to a northern route. Helping persuade the city council to go along with the southern route was Johnny Harris, one of Charlotte's most prominent developers and the scion of a family that played a pivotal role in local land use decisions for much of the twentieth century. A discussion of Harris's activities further indicates how the erosion of racial balance in CMS and Charlotte's development were the result of political decisions and the exercise of economic clout rather than blind demographic changes and market forces in which human agency played no role.

Harris is the grandson of the former North Carolina governor, Cameron Morrison. [17] At the turn of the twentieth century, Morrison played a leading role in the disfranchisement of blacks in the state, emerged as one of North Carolina's most influential leaders, and touted his advocacy of white supremacy in a successful campaign for governor of the state in 1920. After leaving the statehouse, Morrison returned to Charlotte, where his vast landholdings included a 3,000-acre farm located just outside what was then the city of Charlotte's southern boundary and a large hunting preserve south of Highway 51. Under the auspices of Morrison's son-in-law, James Harris, the post-World War II era witnessed the development of land that had once been the farm into, among other things, SouthPark, a large, upscale mall in southeast Charlotte. A generation later, Johnny Harris and other family members sought to transform the land that was once the hunting preserve into a 2,000-acre residential, commercial, and recreational development called Ballantyne. More than 200 acres larger than the nearby town of Pineville and the largest mixed-use development in Mecklenburg history, Ballantyne was greatly facilitated by construction of the southern route of the outerbelt.

In the early 1980s, with plans for the outerbelt stalled, Harris took advantage of his fund-raising activities in the 1984 gubernatorial campaign to secure an appointment to the state's Board of Transportation. Once on the board, the *Observer* reported, Harris "pushed for completing the southern leg of the outerbelt . . . It will border Ballantyne, increasing the land's value. Harris donated 110 acres in Ballantyne for the outerbelt, U.S. 521, and other roads. In return, the state will relocate and widen U.S. 521 through Ballantyne. That is how the system works . . . Harris's advantage over most developers is the family land."[18] Moreover, Harris drew on the resources that came with being on the Board of Transportation to secure city council approval for the southern route in a complicated deal that netted state funding for a pet city council project, the widening of one of the main roads between downtown Charlotte and outlying areas.[19]

By the time the deals had been consummated that allowed construction of the outerbelt to begin, Robinson had left office. But the boost that the expressway gave to development in the extreme southern parts of Mecklenburg County would affect decisions that his successor, Peter Relic, had to make almost immediately after assuming office.

THE ADMINISTRATION OF PETER RELIC

Following Robinson's resignation at the close of the 1985–86 school year, CMS was led on an interim basis by one of his top aides until Peter Relic assumed the district's helm in July 1987. Relic came to Charlotte from an affluent, predominantly white suburban New England school district with about 10 percent the enrollment of CMS. But his resumé included a stint as deputy assistant secretary of education in the Carter administration that gave him national visibility lacked by the other finalist, the superintendent of the Winston-Salem system. Relic's broad background appealed to many board members, who felt the school system needed to go outside of North Carolina to find a superintendent not enmeshed in the state's network of educational administrators. As things turned out, Relic's lack of familiarity with the educational and political byways and folkways of North Carolina and Charlotte had its downsides. This liability was dwarfed, however, by his preference for being an educator dealing with issues facing teachers and students rather than for being a manager and political leader dealing with the issues facing CMS. During his stay in Charlotte, Relic's talents as a visionary educator would receive frequent praise from teachers and the school board. But influential members of the board grew increasingly dissatisfied with his leadership of CMS. In June 1990, at the end of Relic's third school year in Charlotte, the school board forced his resignation.

Indeed, even a superintendent who relished the administrative and political demands of the position would have found it challenging to lead CMS, faced as it was in the late 1980s with an extraordinary array of problems. Some of these difficulties reflected the growing national critique of public education triggered by the 1983 publication of *A Nation At Risk* and were exacerbated by the United States' economic situation that made public education a convenient scapegoat for the seeming superiority of foreign economies, especially Japan's. Typical of such blame was the oft-repeated statement by no less a person than the secretary of education that the United States had three deficits—a trade deficit, a budget deficit, and an education deficit—and that solving the third was the precondition of solving the other two.[20]

To the problems created by the national distemper over public education can be added four challenges more specifically rooted in local conditions: Charlotte's growth, CMS' budgetary constraints, opposition to the busing plan, and changes in the school board.

The Growing Challenges of Growth

The growth in enrollment posed numerous problems. After hitting a twenty-year low of 71,600 students in the 1983–84 school year, CMS' enrollment began increasing, reflecting both local growth and national demographic trends.[21] The increase affected all aspects of CMS' operations, not least the ability to maintain a desegregated system with equal educational opportunities for black and white children. Among other things, as noted earlier, the growth in enrollment had led to the construction of twenty-seven new schools by the time of the 1999 trial in the reactivated *Swann* case. The vast majority of these schools were built in predominantly white neighborhoods despite the fact that CMS' percentage black enrollment did not shrink but increased slightly from 39 percent to 42 percent during this period.

The location of almost all of these schools in predominantly white neighborhoods inevitably raises questions about the criteria employed by CMS in acquiring land for its schools. As noted earlier, this issue was raised about McAlpine during Robinson's administration, and it became even more salient during Relic's superintendency and that of his successor, John Murphy.

Relic found himself dealing with this issue shortly after taking office, as development in the south of the county intensified, spurred by the impending construction of the outerbelt. In October 1987, his deputy superintendents recommended that CMS acquire three parcels of land for schools that would be located further south than any of CMS' existing ones. Two of the parcels were donations from Johnny Harris's development group in the area that would eventually be part of Ballantyne. Noting that it might be ten years before schools were actually needed in that area, the deputies' memo said that CMS was under no obligation to build the schools, in which case the land would revert to the donors. The memo also addressed desegregation issues by saying that schools "would not be built unless they could be planned with appropriate black/white ratios . . . Such a successful solution would involve paired schools and/or satellites."[22]

By the time, 1996, when CMS had to decide whether to go ahead and build a school on the Ballantyne land donated by the Harris group, the system of paired elementary schools had been abolished, and the likelihood of the school being almost entirely white occasioned considerable debate (discussed in chapter 6) about whether to proceed with construction.

Unlike the first two parcels, the third parcel involved a purchase for a school that CMS staff argued required immediate construction, even though it was extremely close to the county line. The site's considerable distance from any sizeable concentration of African American neighborhoods notwithstanding, the memo claimed that an appropriate black/white ratio could be obtained by busing black students from an inner-city neighborhood. That claim provoked considerable skepticism, and the board's two black members and one white member voted against acquiring the site. Their skepticism proved justified. Although the school, McKee Road, was racially balanced during its first year of operation (the 1989–90 school year), it became racially imbalanced the next year and remained so. With the completion of depairing in 1996–97, McKee's black enrollment plummeted to 1 percent, making it CMS' most racially imbalanced school at the time of the trial in the reactivated *Swann* case.

In addition to illustrating the difficulty of desegregating a school built in such an outlying region of the county, the McKee Road story calls attention to two other aspects of the relationship between growth and desegregation. First, already remarked on in the case of McAlpine Elementary school, is the self-fulfilling character of school siting decisions; they can both contribute to development as well as respond to it. In the case of McKee Road, much of the development near the site may have been planned, if not completed, prior to the school board's decision to acquire that site. But as with McAlpine, at least some of the major development in the area followed CMS' decision to acquire the land for McKee. In particular, the preliminary plans for the 141 residential unit Providence Arbours Development, located one-half mile from the school, were not filed until five months after CMS decided to acquire the land.[23]

Second, the debate about the McKee Road site emphasized the need for new thinking about ways to maintain a desegregated system in the face of the explosive growth in south Mecklenburg. The three members who voted against acquiring the site raised questions about the wisdom of pairing a school in a predominantly black neighborhood with one in a predominantly white neighborhood, given the long distance between the two neighborhoods. Because of residential segregation, they pointed out, there was much to be said for building schools midway between black and white neighborhoods. "We want the staff to look at midpoint schools in a way we haven't before," said AME Zion clergyman George Battle, one of the two black board members to vote against acquiring the site.[24] That exhortation resonated with the *Charlotte Observer,* which viewed the board's vote as perhaps "the best decision under the circumstances, [but] it is not a happy or auspicious one." To avoid similarly unhappy decisions in the future, the paper called for a broad-based community effort to find sites with a "decent access and a price this side of the moon. But the central issue is really one of policy and mandate. What's affordable depends in part on how important the community thinks closer-in sites are."[25] In noting the differential land costs for outlying as opposed to midpoint schools, the *Observer* was calling attention to key financial issues that CMS faced in addressing both growth and desegregation. But in the late 1980s, CMS was not in a good position to pay extra money for land for new schools that could be more easily desegregated. The system faced a variety of fiscal problems, some of them of its own making.

Budgetary Constraints

Several developments combined to make CMS' financial situation in the late 1980s even more difficult than it had been earlier. At the same time that growth in student enrollment was placing additional financial demands on CMS, the school system was facing an increasingly hostile local political environment. A conservative fiscal watchdog group, Citizens for Effective Government (CFEG), many of whose members had played a key role in Sue Myrick's upset of Harvey Gantt in November 1987, was challenging local taxing and spending policies. In criticizing CMS, the group found a ready target in the way that CMS had handled the construction of Providence High School. Located in the south of the county on the north side of Highway 51, Providence was CMS' first new high school in over twenty years. Land for it was acquired during the Robinson administration, with CMS officials believing that, despite its southern location, the typically large attendance areas of high schools combined with the use of satellites would allow it to be racially balanced. Whatever problems CMS would have desegregating the school, it faced much more immediate ones financing it. Providence was originally budgeted at $7 million, but even before Relic appeared on the scene, the projected cost increased to $13 million. Moreover, shortly after arriving, Relic made headlines by charging that this school, expected by Charlotteans to be state of the art, would be only second-rate, unless CMS "went back to the drawing board."[26] Of the $4 million of changes approved by the board in September 1987, at least 60 percent went for improving athletic facilities, making them "exceptionally defined and first-rate."[27] By the time the school opened in August 1989, costs had reached $20 million, almost three times the original budget.[28] The unanticipated overrun caused postponement of other construction projects, contributed to the overall financial problems facing CMS in the late 1980s, and gave credence to charges by the county commission and others that the school system was poorly managed.

The fiscal constraints facing CMS merit additional discussion by drawing again on the data in Table 3.2. As noted earlier, the 1987 report, which was based on data from the Robinson years, indicates that even then CMS received relatively less financial support from county government than did either of North Carolina's other two large consolidated urban systems, Wake and Forsyth. The 1989 Public School Forum report—whose spending data came only from the 1987–88 school year, Relic's first—also shows Mecklenburg ranking lowest in Relative Effort (RE) and in Overall Rank. Beginning with the 1990 report, as the Appendix explains, the Forum began breaking down RE into Relative Current Effort (RCE) and Relative Total Effort (RTE), with the latter dealing with a period several years prior to the date of the report. On this measure, as Table 3.2 indicates, Mecklenburg does poorly for almost the entire period for which data are available; the county ranks lowest in all reports until 1999. Similarly, on Overall Ranking, Mecklenburg generally is lowest in all reports.[29]

Because Mecklenburg did worse than the other counties in most of the years covered by Table 3.2, the Appendix develops four indicators to answer the question, Was there any period during these many poor years that Mecklenburg did especially poorly? These indicators are called Difference in Relative Total Effort (DRTE), Difference in Relative Current Effort (DRCE), Difference in Overall Rank (DOR), and Ability/Effort Discrepancy (AED). Given the way the first three of these indicators are calculated, a negative value means that Mecklenburg is generally doing worse than the comparison counties, and the larger the magnitude of the negative value, the worse is Mecklenburg's performance relative to Wake and Forsyth. The fourth indicator, AED, is a cruder indicator that has only two values, None or Negative, with the latter indicating that Mecklenburg's support of public education is much poorer than that of Wake's and Forsyth's.

As Table 4.1 shows, according to all four indicators, Mecklenburg's support of CMS was generally worse in the late 1980s and early 1990s than in any other years. Indeed, it is on the reports—those issued in 1990 and 1991— that draw heavily on data from the Relic years that CMS does the worst on DRTE and DOR.

These comparisons of educational expenditures among the three districts accord quite well with comparisons among different items in the Mecklenburg County budget. The late 1980s and early 1990s saw county commissioners frequently cut CMS' budget requests. While the absolute amount of dollars

TABLE 4.1
Mecklenburg County Support for Public Education, 1987–2001

Year of Report	Difference in Relative Total Effort (DRTE)	Difference in Relative Current Effort (DRCE)	Difference in Overall Rank (DOR)	Ability/Effort Discrepancy (AED)
1987	−20		−16	None
1989		−14	−44	None
1990	−40	−13	−56	Negative
1991	−56	−37	−40	Negative
1992	−36	−22	−19	Negative
1993	−47	−37	−41	Negative
1994	−39	−32	−26	Negative
1995	−21	−26	−6	None
1996	−21	−26	−6	None
1997	−21	−37	−22	None
1998	−16	−15	17	None
1999	0	−7	27	None
2000	−10	−4	14	None
2001	11	2	Not available	None

Source: Data in Table 3.2.

earmarked for education increased during these years, CMS' slice of the budgetary pie declined so much so that a 1993 newspaper account noted, "Over the past 10 years, no major area of county spending has increased less than schools."[30]

It is impossible to ascertain the extent to which the squeeze on CMS' budget reflected the more pressing needs of other county-funded programs, the generic influence of local fiscal conservatism, specific dissatisfaction with CMS, and/or other developments. But coming as they did at a time when CMS' enrollment was beginning to increase rapidly, the constraints would have long-term as well as immediate effects.

Opposition to the Busing Plan

Growing opposition to the busing plan compounded CMS' difficulties. Moreover, the busing plan frequently provided a convenient scapegoat for other alleged CMS deficiencies. Criticism about the busing plan was, not surprisingly, frequently confounded with criticism about what was at the end of the bus ride. As was the case a decade earlier, much of the criticism was voiced by newcomers. Indeed, it is one of the ironies of Charlotte educational history that much of the opposition to the busing plan came from transplants, both individual and institutional, drawn to the area by the economic development that had been facilitated by Charlotte's racial liberalism and desegregation accomplishments.

Of the many relocations that affected Charlotte's educational history, that of Royal Insurance—which moved its headquarters from New York to Mecklenburg's southern periphery in 1985 and 1986—is among the most important because the large number of jobs made it the prize plum that Charlotte had so far attracted in the battle to attract mobile capital. Many of the Royal employees who moved to Charlotte, school board member Susan Burgess would note several years later, had previously "had their children in public schools in suburban systems [which were] for the most part self-contained, high-budget, all-white school systems and then they came here, and many of them bought [in an outlying area] not realizing that they were in a paired situation with [a primary school located in a heavily black inner-city area]. . . . and that was the first time that a sought-after relocation came in here with executives who said: your schools are bad. And we really don't give a flip about your desegregation, we're not busing our kids down to the ghetto."[31]

The dissatisfaction of Royal employees and company management showed clearly in a 1987–1988 Chamber of Commerce task force on jobs and education convened largely in response to complaints from newcomers to Charlotte. The two most visible businessmen on the task force were a Royal vice president and the local head of another recently arrived company. The newcomers' formal complaint was that CMS was not adequately preparing non-college-bound students for the job market, an issue that became a major item on the task force's agenda. Informally, they also vociferously complained that the quality of education for college-bound students was being sacrificed for integration goals and that, consequently, the busing plan should be overhauled or eliminated. However, the informal complaint never made it onto the task force's formal agenda because the Chamber's officers decided in advance of the first meeting to exclude the topic, lest it open a Pandora's box of issues too divisive for the task force to handle.[32]

Nonetheless, pressure was building to address these complaints. Charlotte's longtime business elite realized "You had to pay attention," in the words of Joe Martin, a close confidante of bank CEO Hugh McColl.[33] Paying attention meant doing several things. McColl became one of the first businessmen to speak out on the schools after the task force's final report, using a speech to the Rotary Club to proclaim that "our schools aren't good enough."[34] Pointing out that longtime Charlotteans had a tendency to dismiss complaints about the schools by Northerners as Yankee racism, Martin, who helped write the speech, subsequently noted that McColl's Southern roots made his criticism especially credible and helped attract attention.[35]

Another indication that McColl and Martin were concerned about education was that the former recruited the latter to run for the school board in

May 1988. School Superintendent Peter Relic had talked with some executives, "asking them to recruit people to run for the school board. . . . And so
the chairman [McColl] came and talked to me about it, and I said, well, I
would be interested myself."[36] Martin thus became the most influential business executive to seek a seat on the board since C. D. Spangler Jr.'s candidacy
at another turning point in CMS history.

The 1988 School Board Election
      The May 1988 school board election showed the pressure on CMS to
change the mandatory busing plan. The election followed hearings about the
busing plan earlier in the year at which opponents had mobilized their forces.
"Angry Parents Call For End of Busing" read the headline of an *Observer*
article about one of those meetings at which, among many other people, a
white parent, Jan Richards, demanded an end to busing, saying it "may have
been appropriate 16 years ago, but times in this community have changed."[37]
To be sure, the hearings also elicited support for the busing plan. But the
opposition was stronger now; it catapulted Richards to a victory in the May
1988 school board elections, making her the first candidate elected to the
board in over a decade on a platform calling for an end to mandatory busing
for desegregation and a return to neighborhood schools.
      Pressure for change also came from the business elite and was reflected
in how the *Observer's* position changed between 1986 and 1988. In the 1986
election, which occurred shortly after Robinson had announced his intention
of resigning, the *Observer* had emphasized the "need for continuity and experience on the board" and endorsed three of the four incumbents seeking
reelection.[38] All of them strongly supported Charlotte's busing plan, and all
three of them won. The only victor the *Observer* did not endorse in 1986 was
self-described conservative Christian Sharon Bynum. More than any other
victorious candidate since 1972, Bynum had called "for doing something
different" about desegregation, and, as a result, she received strong support
from people opposed to busing.[39]
      In 1988, the *Observer* took a different tone. Instead of stressing the
importance of continuity and experience, the endorsements were titled
"Schools: Time for a Change" and called for "new faces, new leadership."[40]
Only one of the three longtime incumbents seeking reelection received an
endorsement, and it was a partial one. Of the three candidates—William
Rikard, Joe Martin, and Jan McIntyre—who received a full endorsement,
only the last was an incumbent, but she was a virtual newcomer, having
been elected to fill a vacancy six months previously. In addition to receiving
a full endorsement from the *Observer*, all three received considerable financial
support from Charlotte's business elite, with Martin and Rikard, an attorney with a downtown law firm, raising approximately three times the amount
of money raised by any other candidate.[41] The two men's fundraising success

reflected their especially strong roots in Charlotte's business elite and indicated its eagerness for change.

All three of the *Observer's* top three endorsements won, as did Arthur Griffin, an African American paralegal, who had received a partial endorsement. The only victor who did not receive any endorsement from the *Observer* was Jan Richards, an indication that while the paper sought change, it was not ready to support an end to the mandatory busing plan and a return to neighborhood schools. No longer on the board were its previous chair and two other incumbents, all of whom had served at least two terms and strongly supported the busing plan.

The board's operation soon reflected the change in its membership. Headlined "School Board Splinters, New Members Change Dynamics," an *Observer* story noted that the board was no longer "the courtly, polite school board to which most viewers are accustomed."[42] Not surprisingly, the splintering involved desegregation and pupil assignment.

While there was considerable sentiment on the board that something had to be done about pupil assignment, the nature of that something remained elusive. Again, the opening of a new school, Lebanon Road, illustrated the problems facing the board as well as the reasons blacks, albeit for reasons different from those of whites, also were criticizing the busing plan. Like the other new schools mentioned earlier, McAlpine and McKee, Lebanon Road was built in a high-growth area in the southern half of the county, but it was much farther east and north than these other two. Consequently, while located in a predominantly white neighborhood that hardly qualified as a midpoint, Lebanon Road was closer than both McAlpine and McKee to neighborhoods with large numbers of black residents. To achieve racial balance at Lebanon, a K–6 school, the board reassigned black students from another K–6 school, Devonshire, much closer to their home. However, this was the third reassignment of black students from the Devonshire neighborhood to more distant schools. In the 5–4 vote on the superintendent's proposal for this reassignment, both black board members voted against it. Commented white board member Joe Martin:

> A slim majority . . . has created another "satellite" in the predominantly black Devonshire neighborhood . . . One result is a serious depopulated Devonshire school. That's the same process that resulted in the closing of schools in numerous inner-city neighborhoods in the 1960s.
>
> The board will now consider options for "revitalizing" Devonshire . . . that means getting white students to go to the school. Curiously missing from the option being considered: creation of a "satellite" in a white neighborhood similar to the one created in Devonshire. Instead, the proposals have to do with "choices" for white students . . . Black "satellited" students were given no "choice" . . .

It should be unsettling, to say the least, that the plan for inte-
grating a school must now be imposed by a white majority over the
objections of the board's black members.

The question is not "How can we maintain—or abandon—the
old busing plan?" but instead "How can we fairly and effectively
integrate our schools for the '90s and beyond?"

We need a new consensus—and a new plan that will be as good
for the '90s as the 1970 plan was for the '70s.[43]

As both a board member and one of Charlotte's preeminent business
executives and civic leaders, Martin would play a pivotal role in the events
leading to that new plan. But these events would not transpire until after the
1990 school board election and the forced resignation of Peter Relic shortly
thereafter, in which Martin also would play a leading role.

The 1990 School Board Election

The change in the board's composition that began with the 1988 election
continued in 1990 when, with four seats at stake, two incumbents, including
the chair, decided against seeking reelection. In its editorial endorsements, the
Observer approvingly took note of the change by likening the school board to
"a team halfway through the rebuilding process."[44] The vacant seats were
filled by two candidates the *Observer* endorsed: community activist Susan
Burgess and First Union banker John Tate, member of a family long active
in Charlotte's business, political, and civic life. Burgess emerged victorious in
the first round, but Tate had to go through a runoff against an outspoken
advocate of neighborhood schools. The runoff for the school board took place
on the same day as the runoff in the Democratic senatorial primary involving
Harvey Gantt, and Tate benefited from a large black turnout that contributed
heavily to his 58–42 percent winning margin.

While the rebuilding process was not as complete as the *Observer* would
have liked—Sharon Bynum was reelected in the first round, despite failing to
receive the *Observer's* endorsement—the composition of the board after the
1990 election was very different from what it had been prior to 1988. Five
of its members had two or fewer years of service, and a sixth, Jane McIntyre,
had been on the board for just over two years. It was this largely rebuilt board
that found itself having to hire a new superintendent when shortly after the
May 1990 election, Superintendent Relic was forced to resign.

Relic's Resignation

At the end of his first year, Relic received a rating of excellent on his
annual evaluation, drawing considerable praise from the board for his candor

in discussing problems ranging from the shortcomings in Providence High School's design to shortfalls in academic achievement. However, by the end of his third year, the board viewed his performance as being so poor that many sought his resignation. The difference between those two evaluations was the difference between pointing out problems and being able to lead CMS in solving them. Viewing everything as "going in the wrong direction," Joe Martin, who was among the board members most critical of Relic, noted that Relic came and opened things up, encouraging "everybody who had a criticism to offer it." But, Martin continued, "If we are going to say, 'Schools are not good enough,' we have to say how we will make them better. We never did that."[45]

In addition to feeling that Relic was not providing leadership in address-ing major issues such as desegregation and academic achievement, the board was sharply critical of Relic's managerial skills. Especially salient were the previous year's events at two elementary schools. The first was the creation of two all-black, sixth-grade classes in response to white parents' complaints about discipline at Eastover, an elementary school in a wealthy white area, and the second was the use of an experimental arts curriculum in Davidson elementary, whose inclusion of a nude photo of a woman upset some parents. In both cases, Relic was criticized for being slow to act and ineffective in his communication with both parents and the media.[46] From the board's perspec-tive, Martin would later say, "We were rocking from crisis to crisis as dissent would get out of hand in one school, or just mismanagement would occur in another . . . and he was not forceful enough in managing those problems before they became crises . . . and he was not giving us much direction in terms of what we were going to do to make the schools better."[47]

Yet Relic hardly bore the sole responsibility for CMS' floundering, for as Martin acknowledged immediately after criticizing Relic, the superintendent was not receiving much direction from the board because it was so divided. During Relic's tenure, Martin would say only half jokingly, "I bet we never had a vote that wasn't 5–4. The votes to adjourn might have been closer . . . but it was never the same five against the same four . . . It was a shifting 5–4 vote on everything, and you can't develop policy on anything with . . . unpredictable 5–4 votes."[48]

The board's lack of cohesion reflected not just whatever leadership and political shortcomings Relic might have had but the rebuilding process through which the board was going, as well as the broader difficulties of maintaining a desegregated system and responding to complaints about academic achieve-ment. It was left to Relic's successor, John Murphy, to develop a plan for dealing with both of those issues. That plan clearly succeeded, initially at least, in getting unanimous support from the board. Whether that plan ac-tually benefited the students of Charlotte-Mecklenburg is, however, less clear.

Chapter 5

Political Fluidity and the
Alchemy of School Reform

The vision is to ensure that the Charlotte-Mecklenburg School System becomes the premier urban, integrated system in the nation.

> —Revised vision statement adopted by the school board in September 1991.[1]

A brilliant superintendent . . . one of the three best in the country, and I can't think of who the other two would be.

> —William Bennett, former U.S. Secretary of Education, talking about CMS' superintendent, John Murphy, December 1991.[2]

I always thought Murphy might get away with all our gold. I just never figured it would be in his teeth.

> —Comment by school board member Susan Burgess about the superintendent's request for reimbursement for $14,000 in dental bills.[3]

With the start of the 1990s, CMS again attracted the attention of educators nationally, just as it had twenty years ago. But this time it was not for mandatory busing but for a high-profile program of school reform, one aspect of which was the dismantling of most of the mandatory busing plan and its replacement primarily by magnet schools. Just as the magnet plan reflected a national movement away from mandatory desegregation strategies in favor of voluntary ones, so too did CMS' school reform program embody much of the prevailing wisdom about ways of improving urban education. The program enjoyed the vigorous support of some of the most influential members of Charlotte's business elite, as well as of some of the nation's most prominent advocates of school reform. But despite initial local and national rave reviews, both the program and its architect, Superintendent John Murphy, became increasingly controversial. Voters rejected two school bond referendums, the first such defeats for CMS in over a generation. Moreover, in November 1995, one of Murphy's bête-noires became chair of the school board, and Murphy subsequently resigned, effective the day before the new board took office. Finally, although it was not apparent at the time of Murphy's resignation, subsequent analyses indicated that although CMS' reform program had received national praise, educational outcomes were—with only one exception—generally the same or worse than those of comparable North Carolina urban districts that did not see such sweeping reform.[4] Events in CMS during the early 1990s thus provide ample material for a discussion of the complicated relations among civic capacity, local politics, the development and implementation of educational policy, and educational outcomes.

This chapter begins by summarizing the reform program's auspicious start and main characteristics. It then proceeds to review the program's political difficulties and the shortfalls in civic capacity that arose from the superintendent's leadership style, conflicts over resegregation, inadequate support for bond referenda, and changes in representation on the school board. After covering such political issues, I turn to educational ones by first indicating how little success the reform program can claim in improving outcomes, and then I consider the program's flawed conceptualization, development, and implementation. The chapter concludes by discussing how the reform program's emphasis on symbol rather than substance also was counterproductive.

A NEW SUPERINTENDENT AND SCHOOL REFORM ON A GRAND SCALE

The Hiring of John Murphy

In choosing John Murphy from among four finalists for superintendent in 1991, the school board hired a man who had already attracted national attention that was exemplified by a front-page *Wall Street Journal* article that appeared shortly before he assumed CMS' helm. Headlined "Forceful Educator Gets Teachers and Children To Be More Productive," the article discussed Murphy's tenure as superintendent of Prince George's County, Maryland, and noted that the county, a suburb of Washington, D.C., had been a laboratory for ideas that President Bush and Education Secretary

Lamar Alexander wanted to apply nationally.[5] It called attention to Murphy's emphasis on magnet schools, *Milliken II* programs,[6] tests, accountability, and a self-described management philosophy of "applied anxiety" that had led to demoting principals, transferring teachers, and freezing salaries "when he didn't see results." Accompanying the programmatic changes, the article indicated, were concerns that magnets were creaming resources and that teachers were teaching to the test. The article also indicated intense conflicts between the head of the National Education Association's (NEA) local chapter and Murphy. It also noted that his desire for additional compensation infuriated some parents who, at one community meeting, "shouted 'here's your raise' and threw quarters at his feet." While the head of the Charlotte-Mecklenburg Association of Educators, the local NEA affiliate, would get along quite well with Murphy, and no Charlotte parent ever threw quarters at the superintendent's feet, much of what was past in Prince George's County turned out to be prologue for CMS.[7]

In embarking on reform at CMS, the Murphy administration benefited from both the national and local mood. Nationally, complaints about public education had become increasingly commonplace by the start of the 1990s. Locally, dissatisfaction with the busing plan, academic achievement, and the legacy of Relic's shortcomings as an administrator and a leader created a situation in which Charlotte-Mecklenburg was looking for sweeping changes and effective leadership. Such sentiments were particularly strong among Charlotte's business elite. Moreover, the reform program's emphasis on a numbers-driven accountability system, financial bonuses, and site-based management resonated with corporate management strategies. Consequently, the Murphy administration received widespread backing from the business elite, particularly in its first years.

Support from Business Executives, Union Leaders, and School Reformers

The most visible aspects of business elite support were *Observer* editorials and signed columns by its publisher, Rolfe Neill.[8] Other support took the form of fundraising for CMS and personal lobbying on Murphy's behalf. Shortly after Murphy took office, the chairman of Duke Power led a drive to create the Charlotte-Mecklenburg Education Foundation, a private foundation that by 1993 was able to disburse over $107,000 in grants to teachers and the school system itself.[9] Heading these efforts was Nancy Crutchfield, the wife of First Union CEO Ed Crutchfield, probably Murphy's most determined supporter among the business elite. In 1993, when the school board met privately to consider a raise for Murphy, who had threatened to leave

Charlotte for a superintendent's position in another district, Crutchfield himself "wanted to speak to the elected officials on Murphy's behalf" and waited in a nearby office while the board deliberated.[10] Two years later, after the unexpected defeat of school bonds, Crutchfield called Murphy "the best guy in the country."[11] In Neill's words, Crutchfield was Murphy's "blocking back, with the school board as well as the business community."[12]

The lack of opposition from employee unions and associations also made Murphy's task an easier one. The relationship between such employee groups and educational improvement is a complex one that varies from district to district. But any program such as Murphy's that involved a high-stakes accountability system with its array of carrots and sticks inevitably raises complex personnel issues and conflicts. Whereas in Prince George's County, Murphy threw the head of the NEA affiliate out of his office, no such action was ever needed in Charlotte, where the generic weakness of Southern unions was compounded by North Carolina law prohibiting local governments from engaging in collective bargaining. Moreover, Murphy got along quite well with the leaders of Charlotte-Mecklenburg's two largest unions, the Classroom Teachers Association (CTA) and Charlotte-Mecklenburg Association of Educators (CMAE). Early in his administration, Murphy appointed the president of the CTA to a full-time position at the Education Center. The president of the CMAE, Vilma Leake, retained her teaching position but was appointed to several advisory positions and given special access to both Murphy and his aides. Early in Murphy's administration, Leake criticized some aspects of his program, but she was generally very supportive of it. When Murphy indicated in 1994 that he might leave CMS, Leake said, "He has the children's interest at heart . . . and I would hope he would not leave. He needs to stay here and finish the job he started."[13]

Ties to nationally prominent educators also aided the Murphy administration. The most visible manifestation of these links was the World Class Schools Panels that met in Charlotte during Murphy's first year. Financed by corporate donations, these meetings involved discussions about CMS' reform agenda by some of the country's most prominent proponents of educational change, including William Bennett, former education secretary; Ernest Boyer, president of the Carnegie Foundation for the Advancement of Teaching; Donald Stewart, president of the College Board; and Denis P. Doyle, education writer and senior fellow at the Hudson Institute. However, some participants were unfamiliar with the agenda, and others lacked knowledge about what was actually taking place in Charlotte. Moreover, the discussion was extremely general. Thus the World Class Schools Panels may very well have been more symbolic than substantive. But from a symbolic standpoint, they were very effective in lending a prestigious national imprimatur to the changes sweeping CMS.[14]

These reforms drew lavish praise from some of the nation's most prominent advocates of school reform. Louis Gerstner, IBM CEO, singled CMS out for praise in his 1994 book about reinventing education. One of the coauthors of Gerstner's book was Denis P. Doyle, who in addition to participating in the World Class Schools Panels served as a paid consultant to the Murphy administration.[15] Together with Susan Pimental, another of the Murphy administration's consultants, Doyle touted CMS' experience in a *Phi Delta Kappan* article, "A Study in Change: Transforming the Charlotte-Mecklenburg Schools," which breathlessly talked about how Murphy had "managed to restore that city's faith in its public schools and "blaze the trail" for district-wide educational transformation.[16] Moreover, Doyle and Pimental subsequently repeatedly cited CMS' reform program as a model worthy of national emulation in a handbook for improving education.[17] Murphy himself was named one of North America's 100 best school administrators in *Executive Educator,* and William Bennett lauded Murphy with the remark in this chapter's second epigraph. Moreover, in an issue commemorating *Brown* v. *Board of Education,* one of the nation's most prestigious scholarly journals, *Teachers College Record,* published an article by Murphy, claiming considerable success for CMS' reform program in solving what he called "the other half of the puzzle" that *Brown* had bequeathed to educators: raising the academic achievement of African American students.[18]

Becoming the Premier School System in the Nation

Several months after Murphy took office, the school board adopted a revised and lofty vision statement whose opening words provide the first epigraph for this chapter. That vision was reflected in the sweep and ambition of CMS' reform program which, for purposes of analysis, can be viewed as having five interrelated major components.

The first was dismantling most of CMS' mandatory busing plan, replacing it with other desegregation strategies, most notably magnet schools. The second addressed academic achievement by calling for a dramatic overhaul of CMS' standards. Closely linked to the changes in standards and curriculum was the third component of the program: a system of quantitative benchmark goals designed to assess the extent to which each school was making progress. The implementation of site-based management strategies and procedures was the fourth component. The fifth involved financial bonuses for the principals and staffs of schools that met their goals, making CMS the first North Carolina district to use a system-wide set of specified financial incentives pegged to a school's performance.

Among these five components, the dismantling of most of the mandatory busing plan occupied a special place because it was seen as the political precondition of the rest of the school reform program.

Adopting a New Pupil Assignment Plan

His experience with magnets in Prince George's County notwithstanding, Murphy denied coming to Charlotte with any preconceived plans for magnet schools. Rather, he told an interviewer in 1993, his decision to try to end the district's long-standing busing plan was prompted by parental complaints about mandatory busing that he heard after he assumed office.[19]

To develop the proposals that would end the busing plan but maintain CMS' vision of being the nation's "premier, urban integrated" system, CMS hired Michael Stolee, a professor of educational leadership, who had considerable experience in desegregation issues. His work became the basis for a new pupil assignment plan, "A New Generation of Excellence," adopted nine months after Murphy took office.[20]

The board adopted the plan by a 9–0 vote, but the unanimous vote was preceded by intense political struggle, much of it focusing on the consequences of the magnet schools. To proponents, the magnets seemed a way to have the cake and eat it as well: to maintain a desegregated school system but placate those—most of whom were white—opposed to mandatory busing; to hitch CMS' wagon to the rising star of school choice; and to increase public confidence in the schools. Many board members understood that, as Murphy explained at one board meeting: "The magnet is not designed to improve the overall quality of instruction. There are other issues we are dealing with to improve the overall quality of instruction. The magnets are simply a way to help us deal with the court ordered busing plan in a peaceful way. If we can do that, we can change attitudes, we can get a positive acceptance of an integrated school system rather than the negativism that is there now, and it simply clears the way to allow us to be more productive."[21] However, the distinction between a school improvement and desegregation strategy was largely lost in public discourse, especially among whites, where to be against the magnets in early 1992 was to defend the busing plan against a widely praised educational innovation, rather than to be against one form of pupil assignment and in favor of another.

Among African Americans, opinion was divided. Early support of the magnet proposal came from some widely respected Charlotte blacks, among them Dorothy Counts-Scoggins, whose unsuccessful 1957 efforts to attend a local high school triggered the events that eventually led to the *Swann* litigation.[22] Moreover, Counts-Scoggins's sister-in-law, an award-winning principal of one of CMS' optional schools and also an African American, was appointed CMS' first magnet school coordinator and worked with Stolee in developing the new pupil assignment plan. However, many African American leaders questioned the magnet plan, with the chair of the Black Political Caucus calling Stolee's initial proposal a "terrible mistake" that would lead to resegregation.[23] While not as critical, a statement by a partner in the law firm that had represented Swann cautioned against the plan's "immediate adoption or implementation because it is fraught with far too many inequities and dangers. That is not to say," he continued, "that the plan has no merit. But what merit there is fades under the cloud of inequities and the pitfalls of danger."[24]

The school board's two black members also differed about the merits of the plan, with AME Zion Bishop George Battle being much more enthusiastic than Arthur Griffin. The March 31, 1992, meeting of the school board exemplified their disagreements. As the agenda formally moved into new business, the first item of which was the pupil assignment plan, Bishop Battle introduced the proposal. He expressed support for Superintendent Murphy, called attention to the need for change, and said that the current pupil assignment plan adopted twenty years earlier had been designed for a community very different from the one Charlotte had become in the 1990s. The first motion following Bishop Battle's remarks was from Arthur Griffin. It called upon the board to approve the new plan but to delay its implementation for a year, a strategy that magnet school opponents were advocating.[25] Griffin's motion died for lack of a second, and later in the meeting he joined his colleagues in voting for the new plan, thus making the vote 9–0. As the proposal passed, whites in the audience applauded enthusiastically, but blacks generally sat silently.[26]

Although the board adopted the new plan unanimously, the objections of many blacks and liberal whites had important consequences. One of these involved the use of other desegregation strategies. As opposed to an earlier draft that relied almost exclusively on magnets, the proposal that Murphy presented to the board on March 31 listed three desegregation strategies. Stand-alone schools in neighborhoods that were racially balanced were listed first; midpoint schools located between predominantly black and white areas were second; and magnet schools were third.[27] Moreover, at the March 31 meeting, the board amended the plan in ways that also reflected the influence of skeptics.

Among the most important aspects of the amendments was a provision that became known as the "10 Percent Rule," designed to address the issue that had plagued CMS for at least a decade: how to maintain desegregation at a time when student enrollment was soaring in outlying, predominantly white areas. The 10 Percent Rule bluntly stated "That the Board not proceed with construction of new schools in any census tracts that have less than a 10% black population."[28] When asked by a board member to comment upon the amendment of which the 10 Percent Rule was part, Superintendent Murphy indicated that its "provisions were constructive and would not adversely affect the plan."[29] The amendment passed unanimously. So too did one calling for the board to establish a committee of twenty-five people to assist "in evaluating the [new pupil assignment] plan, and in making revisions, if any are necessary, to the plan."[30]

Further indication of the support initially enjoyed by the magnet plan came from the May 1992 school board election. Occurring six weeks after the adoption of the new pupil assignment plan, the election was characterized by an *Observer* headline, "School Board Debate Unearths No Discord among Candidates."[31] Of the five incumbents whose seats were at stake, only Joe Martin decided not to seek reelection. Unlike the previous two elections, all incumbents seeking reelection received the endorsement of the *Observer,* its editors presumably now being confident that the board did not need any additional rebuilding. The *Observer's* fifth endorsement went to John Lassiter, an attorney with Belk department stores, who, the *Observer* noted in its endorsement "is a participant in the business community's involvement in education. Nobody will quite replace Joe Martin, but John Lassiter is a good fit for that seat."[32] Unlike the previous two elections, no runoff was necessary in 1992. The four incumbents topped the ten-person field, and Lassiter finished fifth, getting over 40 percent more votes than the sixth-place finisher.

Implementing the New Pupil Assignment Plan

The new pupil assignment plan was at least as complicated as the one it was designed to replace. After listing the three desegregation strategies—stand-alone schools in integrated neighborhoods, midpoint, and magnet schools—it called for the implementation of these strategies and the progressive dismantling of CMS' system of paired elementary schools and most mandatory busing over a five-year period. However, the plan did not envision the end of all mandatory busing for desegregation. In addition to the busing necessary to maintain the midpoint schools, the plan allowed the attendance zones of other schools to include satellite attendance areas.[33] The five-year implementation period was divided into three phases, with thorough evaluations scheduled at the end of the first two.

Over half of the text of the adopted proposal was devoted to the magnets. Included were detailed specifications on the magnet programs that would be created in the first two years of the plan and a section on a "parent information/marketing program" for the magnet schools that called attention to the importance of press releases, posters, billboards, public service announcements, recruiting videos, magnet fairs, and ads on city buses. The plan provided detailed information on the staffing of the magnets: current employees at a school to become a magnet would be the first interviewed for available positions but would not be guaranteed employment at their school once it became a magnet. Moreover, the plan called for a job fair that would allow all CMS employees an opportunity to learn about the magnets and "dialogue" with the magnets' principals. The plan also provided detailed information on the admissions procedures that would be used to achieve racial balance in the magnets but said nothing about how racial balance might be maintained in the schools that students enrolled in the magnets would otherwise attend. In fact, the plan specifically said, "No restriction will be placed upon the number of students who may be admitted to magnet programs from a particular school."[34] Nor was any allowance made for marketing either the stand-alone or midpoint schools.

Although the ensuing five years would see several modifications in the plan, its broad outlines were basically implemented. In the first year of the program, 1992–93, nine schools added magnet programs in areas such as science, foreign languages, and communication. By the time depairing was completed in the 1996–97 school year, thirty-eight of CMS' 120 schools had magnet programs.[35]

Standards, Benchmark Goals, and Accountability
However salient the magnets and other pupil assignment issues were to the public, they were not, as Murphy had emphasized to the board, designed to improve the overall quality of instruction. That was the aim of the reform program's other components, which jibed extremely well with the prevailing policy wisdom of the early 1990s about the way to improve urban education. The fit between the conventional wisdom and CMS' emphasis on quantitative measurement of outcomes, financial incentives, and holding educators' feet to the fire goes a long way toward explaining why CMS received lavish praise from nationally prominent education commentators such as Gerstner, Doyle, and Bennett. This fit also makes clear why the disappointing outcomes of CMS' ambitious program had ramifications that extended well beyond the district's boundaries.

Key to improving academic achievement, in the Murphy administration's view, was a dramatic overhaul in CMS standards. Viewing those mandated by North Carolina as insufficiently rigorous, CMS sought to develop standards that were broader and more complex but that incorporated the state's into CMS' ostensibly more demanding ones. To help teachers gauge students' progress in meeting CMS' standards, the school system developed a set of Criterion Referenced Tests administered during the school year and different from the state-mandated, year-end tests that North Carolina used to gauge both student achievement and a district's progress in improving outcomes. For this purpose, the CAT remained the test mandated by the state during the first year of the Murphy administration. But beginning with the

1992–93 school year, North Carolina switched to its own End-of-Grade (EOG) and End-of-Course (EOC) tests as part of the statewide effort to improve education. Thus required by the state to administer these EOG and EOC tests, CMS used scores on them for charting each school's progress toward meeting its benchmark goals.

These quantitative benchmark goals were the third component of CMS' reform agenda and were designed to measure a school's progress in meeting a range of educational objectives. The system took account of previous performance as well as of a school's racial composition, with the specified increments of gain for black students being different in most cases from those for nonblacks. For example, in 1994–95, a K–6 primary school had six goals: primary grade readiness; reducing extreme absenteeism; scores on social studies tests; scores on the EOG reading and math tests; scores on North Carolina's writing assessment test; and sixth graders' preparation for pre-algebra. These six goals were then typically divided into subgoals. Thus the first goal, primary grade readiness, had twelve subgoals, involving three grades (K–2), two subject areas (mathematics and communication arts), and two categories of students (black and nonblack). Similarly, a grades 10–12 high school had a total of twenty-six subgoals, two of which involved reducing extreme absenteeism, two of which involved reducing dropouts, two of which involved writing, ten of which involved scores on EOC tests, and ten of which involved increasing enrollment in higher-level courses.[36]

Because the school was the level of accountability in CMS' system of benchmark goals, the principal was held responsible for a school's performance. The key role assigned to principals in this accountability system was the fourth component of the reform program. In return for emphasizing the principal's accountability for a school's performance, the program called for giving principals unprecedented flexibility (at least by CMS' standards) in the use of time, the purchase of instructional materials, control over staff development, and the ability to allocate resources.

Financial bonuses, the fifth component of the reform program, awaited principals and teachers in a school that met its goals. Accompanying the carrots were sticks, as might be expected from a superintendent whose management style in Charlotte-Mecklenburg was one of "applied anxiety," just as it had been in Prince George's County. By the end of Murphy's second year, approximately 50 percent of CMS' schools had gotten new principals, and the progress of the system's schools was charted at the district's headquarters on the walls of what CMS staffers typically referred to as the "war room."

After only a year in operation, the reform program seemed to bear considerable fruit as CMS announced in August 1992 that SAT scores of both black and white students had jumped sharply, leading the school board's chair to remark, "I think this shows that the decision to hire John Murphy was the right one."[37] That same week, a group of businessmen approached the school board offering to provide Murphy with a $25,000 bonus. Although the *Observer* argued against the board's accepting the offer, it called his first year an "extraordinary" one, said Murphy was a leader of "rare force and uncommon ability," and urged the board to recognize his "exceptional accomplishment." What they add up to, the editorial continued, is a "revolutionary change in attitude and expectations."[38] The primary disappointment during the first year was that only five of the 109 schools met their goals for increasing student achievement. Murphy subsequently said that these first-year goals were too high and established what were considered more realistic ones for subsequent years.[39] These revised expectations allowed an increasing number of schools to meet their goals each year, with approximately 75 percent of the district's schools being able to make their goals by the 1994–95 school year, the fourth one of the reform program.[40]

FLIES IN THE OINTMENT

Despite the reform program's auspicious start, that first year's events portended many of the difficulties that would eventually cripple much of Murphy's agenda and trigger his resignation. These problems had both political and educational aspects, and while the boundary between the two is frequently a fuzzy one, it is useful to discuss the former first. The manner in which these political issues played out falls into four broad categories: the superintendent's personality, demands for additional compensation, and flirtations with other job offers; controversies over resegregation and resource allocation; conflicts over bond referenda; and school board elections.

Political Conflicts

Personality, Compensation, and Flirtations with Other Jobs
The vision and passion for educational change that Murphy brought to the job were interwoven with other personal characteristics that often made him the worst enemy of his own reform agenda. Among other things, the flip side of Murphy being what the *Observer* had called a leader of "rare force" was a reputation as a "head-knocker" that had made Charlotte headlines even before he was hired. His abrasive management style and frequent arrogance became a source of controversy throughout his tenure. To supporters, this lack of charm—even by Northern standards, as an *Observer* editorialist euphemistically put it—paled in comparison to his administration's many accomplishments.[41] To others, the style was counterproductive. As one critic charged, if

you wanted anything from Murphy, you had to "kiss his ring."[42] Insofar as that critic was a county commissioner whose support CMS needed to pass bond referendums, it typifies how Murphy's personality got in the way of both his and CMS' goals.

His very visible concern with his compensation was equally counterproductive. In Charlotte, as in Prince George's County, Murphy's pay hikes provoked considerable controversy. Especially contentious was a $44,000 increase in compensation at the close of his second year. In addition to making Murphy's salary higher than that of North Carolina's governor and two U.S. senators, the increase included a $25,000 housing allowance to help Murphy pay mortgages on two homes in Maryland that he was trying to sell. That allowance, critics charged, would jeopardize support for an upcoming bond referendum. Prompting the $44,000 increase was Murphy's flirtation with the vacant superintendent's job in New York City. After the compensation package was announced, Murphy indicated that he would not interview for the job.[43]

However, Murphy's repeated public dalliances with other jobs prompted even otherwise enthusiastic public supporters to chide him repeatedly. For example, before Murphy received the $44,000 hike, the *Observer* urged him to stop considering other jobs in an editorial headlined, "Just Stay Home: Supt. Murphy Is Far from Finishing His Job Here."[44] Eight months after Murphy received that large raise, *Observer* publisher Neill found it necessary to echo earlier editorials with a column headlined, "Dr. Murphy, Keep Your Word." Noting that Murphy's acknowledged motto was, "Always keep your bags packed," Neill said the motto suggested "needless bravado; he is eminently employable nationwide and he needn't remind us. But he has a contract . . . Contracts are made for good reason. Foremost is planned continuity. In an institution as large as our public school system, each new superintendent causes seismic shock."[45]

Resegregation and Resource Allocation

The debate about resegregation, resource allocation, and new school construction that preceded adoption of the magnet plan continued throughout the Murphy administration. Although both the League of Women Voters and several black civic organizations and leaders continued to raise these issues, much of the discussion about them was concentrated in the activity of the twenty-five-person citizens' committee (usually called the C25), whose creation had been part of the amendment that helped secure the unanimous passage of the new pupil assignment plan.

Despite considerable racial, ideological, and occupational diversity, a majority of the committee developed a spirit and unity that many of its members found noteworthy. An indication of this unity comes from looking at the membership of the subcommittee whose report on pupil assignment was submitted to the school board in July 1994. Eight of the ten members of the subcommittee were white; its chair was a white small businessman who resided in an overwhelmingly white, outlying area of the county; and another of the whites was a conservative Christian.[46] These are not the kinds of demographics ordinarily associated in Charlotte or elsewhere with a deep concern for desegregation and educational equity, but they were the main foci of the unanimous report. Although it noted various positive effects of the magnet plan, the report's overall tone was critical, claiming that the plan "has enhanced a trend toward a multi-tiered system," "a significant proportion of the system's schools are projected to remain racially isolated," and "the plan does not achieve an integrated system in a more equitable, fairer way than the old plan."[47] Moreover, it also pointed out that CMS was emphasizing magnets at the expense of both midpoint schools and stand-alone schools in integrated neighborhoods, even though the plan adopted in March 1992 ranked these two other kinds of schools above magnets as desegregation strategies.

The C25's other report dealt with resource allocation. It too noted the accomplishments of the magnet plan but also voiced sharp criticisms, saying "Magnets do drain resources that could have been put to other uses." It also said that "magnets draw disproportionately from schools in integrated areas and have contributed significantly to several of these schools approaching or reaching noncompliance [with racial balance standards]. We hear reports that these same schools have lost PTA leaders . . . and high level students."[48]

When the C25's reports were first prepared, the school board's chair refused to accept them until CMS staff had a chance to prepare a rebuttal, which it did. In their rebuttals, CMS staff took issue with many of the C25's criticisms. Among other things, these reports faulted the methodology of the reports, denied that the magnets drained resources, and asserted that most of the resegregation noted by the C25 antedated the implementation of the magnet plan, and/or was the result of "shifting demographics" rather than the school board's pupil assignment policy.[49]

Although the C25 turned out to be correct in pointing to an increase in resegregation,[50] the submission of its reports with their many criticisms of the magnet plan exacerbated an already strained relationship with the Murphy administration and its supporters on the board of education. These board members took action two months after the C25's reports had been submitted. In an un-scheduled vote toward the end of a five and a half hour meeting, the board voted 4–3–1 to dismiss the C25, with board chair Rikard abstaining and Bishop Battle not present. Opposing the dismissal were Burgess, Griffin, and Tate.

A month after its September 1994 dismissal, many of the C25's leading members joined with the Black Political Caucus, leaders of the National Association for the Advancement of Colored People (NAACP), and other groups in convening a meeting to make plans to address resegregation and resource allocation in CMS. However, virtually nothing came of this meeting. The watchdog committee had been put to sleep for barking, and there was insufficient political will and/or resources among its members and supporters—black as well as white—to sustain an organized attempt to address the issues that the C25 had raised. Part of the difficulty lay in the fact that while many African Americans, such as the leadership of the Black Political Caucus, were increasingly critical of the magnet plan, other influential African Americans, such as George Battle, continued to back it. They based this support on the view that, among other things, the reform program was providing schools in black neighborhoods with hitherto unavailable resources, a gain that, in their view, easily compensated for whatever resegregation might be occurring.

Given long-standing scholarly debates about whether, how, and to what extent citizen participation facilitates policymaking and enhances civic capacity,[51] it is instructive to compare the C25 of the early 1990s with the CAG of the mid-1970s. Unlike the CAG, whose role was the proactive one of helping develop a pupil assignment plan, the C25's role was largely the reactive one of monitoring a plan that had already been developed and partially implemented. Moreover, the CAG operated with the powerful support of Judge McMillan, whose judicial big stick backed the carrots of compromise that the CAG offered contending parties. With a strong-willed and prickly superintendent committed to the magnet plan, and many African Americans worrying that the plan would erode much-cherished desegregation gains, the C25—especially because its role was a reactive one—simply lacked the resources to broker the kinds of compromises that could contribute to civic capacity. Created by a 9–0 vote of the board as part of the adoption of the magnet plan, the C25 was unceremoniously dismissed by a 4–3–1 vote. The difference between the two votes and the closeness of the second reflected the sharp differences on the board and in the community over questions of pupil assignment and resource allocation. These divisions, I shall note later, were intimately related to the shortfalls in civic capacity that plagued the reform program.

School Bonds and School Funding

Attempts by CMS to secure funding during the early 1990s also provoked considerable conflict, with the battles over school bonds being especially noteworthy. A large part of the controversy involved issues of resegregation and resource allocation that became especially sharp in connection with the November 1993 school bond referendum. At $192 million, it exceeded any prior county bond package in Mecklenburg history and provided for the construction of seven new schools and the renovation of nine others. Concerned that insufficient money had been allocated for the reno-vation of older and/or inner-city schools, and that the sites for the new schools were too far from black neighborhoods and would thus facilitate resegregation, Arthur Griffin broke ranks with his colleagues on the board and vigorously campaigned against the bonds. However, Bishop Battle cam-paigned equally forcefully on the bonds' behalf, and the two waged an intense campaign in the black community for support of their positions.

Because of Griffin's opposition, the percentage of blacks voting Yes on the school bonds was lower than the percentage of whites voting Yes, the only county bond referendum of the thirty-six from 1985 through 1995 in which that was the case.[52] As a result, the 1993 school bond package barely passed. But pass it did, and in that respect it differed from two other bond referenda during the years Murphy was superintendent. The record of two defeats out of a total of five bond referenda during his administration compares very unfavorably with CMS' track record in prior years. Between the consolidation of the city and county school districts in 1960 and the start of Murphy's tenure, eight school bond packages had been put before voters, and all eight had passed.[53] This unprecedented (at least in Mecklenburg's recent history) lack of support for school bonds merits explanation.

The first defeat was a small November 1992 package that would have financed the conversion of an abandoned downtown department store into a magnet high school for finance and the arts. Insofar as much of the No vote reflected sentiment in outlying areas that the conversion was a downtown boondoggle and even various supporters of the reform program and/or down-town development questioned the viability of the conversion, the failure of this package in and of itself was of relatively little significance. The same, however, could not be said about the package that failed in May 1995.

Unlike the November 1992 school bonds, the May 1995 package was a large one, much larger than the November 1993 package that had barely passed. As a result of the 1992 defeat and the close call in 1993, there were political pressures to include something for many different segments of the community in the 1995 school bond package. The needs of the school system also argued for a large package for a wide range of renovation, repair, and new school construction projects. Auguring in just the opposite direction, how-ever, was the outcome of the 1994 election. Although no school board seats were at stake, all of those on the county commission were. Local results mirrored those nationally, with the result that Republicans opposed to any tax increase gained a 5–4 majority. Especially noteworthy was the victory of a relative newcomer in Charlotte politics, a self-identified conservative Chris-tian, Tom Bush, who became the vice chair of the commission.

As a result of the conflicting priorities of the school board and Repub-lican majority on the county commission, early 1995 witnessed a complicated set of negotiations among the school board, county commission, Chamber of Commerce, and a range of concerned citizens about the size and composition of the bond package. Eventually, a majority of commissioners agreed to a package of $304 million. It went before the public on a special election on May 30, the Tuesday of Memorial Day weekend. That date was part of a low-profile campaign strategy based on the expectation that a small turnout would facilitate passage of the school bonds and smaller packages for the public library and community college. But bond supporters had not reckoned on the determination of the opposition that was spearheaded by Tom Bush. Finding himself on the losing side of the vote on the county commission to authorize the bonds, he took his opposition public, grandiloquently declaring, "I'm up against Hugh McColl, I'm up against the Chamber of Commerce; I am up against all the PTAs."[54] Together with the CFEG—the citizens group that had been vociferously challenging local taxing and spending priorities since the 1980s—Bush led a campaign that questioned the school board's financial accountability as well as the affordability of this bond package and the ones projected for the near future.

While the black members of the county commission had voted to issue the bonds, many African American political leaders questioned whether the proposed new schools could be desegregated, given their likely locations in outlying, heavily white neighborhoods. Black leaders also questioned whether the money projected for renovations would actually be spent on them or, as in the past, diverted to other purposes, such as new school construction. To address the latter concerns, CMS and the bond task force documented the renovations, and in an interview with the *Charlotte Post*, the city's black weekly newspaper, the (white) Duke Power vice president who headed the bond task force emphasized to the black community that "for the first time, there is a comprehensive, documented [list] . . . and that's how you get the assurance of accountability in elected officials."[55] Such statements secured public support for the bonds from the Black Political Caucus, the *Post*, and, most importantly, Arthur Griffin, who said that 1995 was different from 1993, because "this time they didn't take one dime out of renovations. That's the big difference from 1993 to 1995."[56]

Despite these public endorsements, the likelihood that all of the new school construction would be in outlying white neighborhoods provoked undercurrents of opposition, including that of several black members of the C25. In the absence of survey data, there is no way of distinguishing among the distinctive effects of the opposition to the location of the new schools, generic concerns about the magnet plan, the dislike of Murphy, the size of the package, or other factors in explaining the African American vote. Approximately 55 percent of black voters supported the bonds.[57] While higher than the vote on the 1993 bonds, this figure was considerably lower than the 84 percent average Yes vote by blacks on the four school bond packages between 1985 and 1991.[58] Moreover, the Yes vote among blacks was insufficient to compensate for the failure of a majority of white voters to support the bonds. While bond proponents were counting on a low turnout, conservative white activists waged a carefully targeted door-to-door and telephone campaign to get bond opponents to the polls. It is difficult to ascertain with certainty whether their self-described "stealth" campaign made the difference in the 51–49 percent defeat of the bonds, but it is clear that bond proponents, who relied on preelection polls showing that CMS' bonds would pass, had little idea what was taking place among the electorate. Additional indication of CMS' political inadequacy came from the success of the library and community college bonds that also were on the ballot; both of these packages passed, though preelection polls showed them in trouble.

In the days after the May 1995 school bond defeat, Murphy lashed out at certain political officials for misleading the public and decried local political leadership as not befitting the world-class status to which Charlotte aspired. These public outbursts did little to dispel his image as a volatile, irascible superintendent. His obvious anger, resentment, and frustration were ample testimony to CMS' inability to secure public support for its financial needs.

In the aftermath of the May 1995 failure, the school board came back to the county commission with a request for a smaller bond package to be placed on the November ballot. However, it was not small enough for Tom Bush. With the school board and county commission unable to agree on the size of the package, the Charlotte Chamber of Commerce convened a meeting attended by, among others, Bush, Rikard, the ranking Democrat on the county commission, the Chamber's chair, two previous chairs, and the chair of the Bond Task Force. From this meeting emerged a $217 million compromise school bond package that the county commission unanimously voted to place on the November ballot.

With Commissioner Bush supporting the November bonds, CFEG now took no position. The Black Political Caucus endorsed the bonds, as did virtually all black political and civic leaders, including Arthur Griffin. There was thus only scattered opposition among both blacks and whites, and the bond package passed by a margin of 72–28 percent. Although the margin was a comfortable one, the $87 million difference between the November and May packages would exacerbate CMS' fiscal discomfort in subsequent years.

In addition to its problems with bond referenda, the Murphy administration also faced difficulties in the annual appropriation process. None of the annual budgetary cycles in the early 1990s saw CMS suffer the dramatic setback it did on the May 1995 bond referendum. But during the Murphy administration, the county never fully funded CMS' budget request, and even before Tom Bush joined the commission, it was voicing the same kind of doubts about CMS' fiscal management that it had a decade earlier.[59] An indication of CMS' financial difficulties comes from Table 4.1, which shows that, as judged by Relative Total Effort, Relative Current Effort, and Overall Rank, CMS received less local financial support than did the two comparison school systems during the years Murphy headed CMS. In fact, the parallel between the early 1980s and early 1990s is noteworthy. In both periods, CMS was receiving national acclaim—for its desegregation accomplishments in the early 1980s and for school reform a decade later. Such praise notwithstanding, in both periods local financial support of the public school system was worse than that in the state's two other large consolidated urban districts.

The 1995 School Board Election

The Switch in Representation

The 1995 election signaled a turning point in CMS' history if only because, shortly thereafter, Murphy resigned. However, the election's outcome reflected even a more fundamental change. The 1995 election was the first in which six of the nine board members were elected from districts, as opposed to the previous system, in which all members were elected at large.

The change resulted from events that had taken place several years earlier. With both the city and county having earlier adopted a hybrid form of representation, CMS faced pressure to make similar changes. Contributing to the pressure was the fact that at the time the proposed switch appeared on the ballot in November 1993, the residences of six of the board's nine members were clustered in a small number of affluent southeast Charlotte neighborhoods relatively close to downtown. Thus, many whites, including an influential Republican state legislator, in outlying areas, such as Matthews, felt that they would benefit from the new system.[60] So too did most black political leaders who thought it would increase African American representation. The business elite generally opposed the switch and would take some unprecedented steps after the referendum to prevent what it feared would be the consequences of district representation. But it made little effort to influence the vote. Nor did any other opponents. A month before the election, the Observer reported that "to date, no organized opposition to districts has surfaced."[61] Part of the reason for the business elite's quietude was probably a sense that it was a losing cause, that opposition was, in the words of school board member William Rikard, "paddling upstream."[62] Part of the reason also was a "fear that vocal opposition . . . could ignite a voter backlash against" the 1993 school bond package that also was on the ballot.[63] The referendum for the change in representation passed 53–47 percent, with the new system scheduled to begin in 1995.

A Worried Business Elite

Although the business elite had made little effort to oppose the new form of representation, the switch provoked considerable concern. Both the elite and Superintendent Murphy worried that with six members of the board being elected from districts—in which only a plurality was necessary for victory—the new school board would be less concerned with school reform and more concerned with "single issues," such as sex education and school prayer. Compounding this concern was the fact that the Christian right seemed to be on a roll. Having spearheaded the successful fight against the May 1995 bond package, conservative Christian County Commissioner Tom Bush almost single-handedly seemed to be jeopardizing school reform, and the Christian right was making inroads in education politics in neighboring counties.

Exacerbating these worries was the fact that the new board would, of necessity, be very different from the old board because five incumbents decided against seeking reelection. Among the five were some of Murphy's strongest supporters on the board. In fact, concern about the outcome of November's election and dismay over the defeat of May's bond package were among the reasons Murphy gave for a surprise announcement in September that he was preparing to leave CMS by the end of the 1995–96 academic year. However, he left open the possibility that he would stay if requested by the new board. That was the hope of much of Charlotte's business elite, including the *Observer's* publisher, Rolfe Neill, whose pre-Election Day column was headlined "Vote 'Yes' on Murphy." Calling the superintendent "a shadow candidate," the column cited CMS' many reforms and national recognition. It concluded, "If America is clamoring for what Charlotte has, shouldn't we be careful to cherish, celebrate, and retain it?"[64]

Worries such as Neill's prompted a major intervention by the business elite in the 1995 election that was at least as marked as its efforts in two previous electoral turning points: in 1988, which initiated the turnover in school board membership that paved the way for the dismantling of the busing plan, and in 1972, which facilitated the implementation of the busing plan. However, the business elite had less success than in 1972 and 1988, a reflection of the many centrifugal tendencies in local politics in the 1990s.

The most distinctive form of the business elite's intervention in the 1995 election was an unprecedented attempt to educate the public about the school board by the *Observer* and the Charlotte-Mecklenburg Educational Foundation (CMEF). The CMEF had initially viewed its mission as raising and providing the equivalent of venture capital for public education. But the switch to district representation led the CMEF to instead begin "focusing its efforts on school governance and its impact on systemic reform."[65] As part of this new emphasis, the CMEF conducted a series of focus groups with registered voters in December 1994 and commissioned a survey of 1,800 registered voters in January 1995 that probed perceptions of school reform and information about the school board. Claiming "the community lacks an in-depth understanding of the roles and responsibilities of our school board,"[66] the CMEF then launched a broad education campaign, "Make Your Mark on the Board," which included broad dissemination of criteria for effective ser-vice on the board.

Although legal considerations (including concern with its tax-exempt sta-tus) kept the CMEF from engaging in campaign activity, people closely asso-ciated with it and the Chamber of Commerce played a leading role in establishing the Charlotte-Mecklenburg Alliance for Public Schools. The Alliance regis-tered as a Political Action Committee (PAC) and announced that its purpose was to "support those candidates who will continue education reform in Char-lotte-Mecklenburg."[67] Although the Alliance's chair was a relatively little-known PTA and Junior League activist, its leaders and contributors included a virtual who's who of corporate Charlotte. Among its public leadership were Bill Lee, the former CEO of Duke Power who had spearheaded the formation of the CMEF, First Union's president, NationsBank's chief financial officer and in-coming chair of the Chamber, and two previous chairs of the Chamber.[68] The twenty-seven people making $1,000 donations to the Alliance's war chest in-cluded many in its public leadership as well as First Union's CEO Crutchfield, NationsBank's CEO McColl, McColl's predecessor, and a wide range of other prominent corporate executives.[69] Altogether the Alliance raised almost $52,000, most of which was dispensed in $3,000 donations to the candidates whom it supported.[70]

Election Results

At-Large Seats: While the switch to district representation had prompted the formation of the Alliance, its endorsements for the at-large seats were the most controversial. Of the three incumbents—Burgess, Griffin, and Lassiter—seeking at-large seats, only Burgess did not receive the Alliance's endorse-ment, despite having run in 1990 with strong support from the business elite. Given Burgess's acknowledged intelligence, energy, and ability, the Alliance's nonendorsement was attributed widely to the fear that she would lead the at-large field, become the new board's chair, and thus assure Murphy's departure. Although Burgess had generally supported CMS' reform program, she had a range of differences with the Murphy administration, many of which were exemplified by her vote against dismissing the C25. Some of their other clashes had been public ones, and the superintendent's abrasive management style was especially evident in his dealings with her.

However, the Alliance's anti-Burgess strategy backfired. As an incum-bent associated with school reform, she apparently received the votes of many who supported CMS' innovations. Shunned by the Alliance, she also was perceived as being independent of power brokers and willing to stand up to a superintendent whose personality and hefty compensation made him many voters' bête-noire. While the Alliance did not endorse her, the *Observer,* Black Political Caucus, and several other community organizations did. Moreover, her campaign organization was the largest and best organized of any candidate. Finally, as the wife of a prominent physician, a member of one of Charlotte's most affluent Presbyterian congregations, and a respected participant in many civic activities, she was in a position to raise more money than any other at-large candidate despite not receiving any donation from the Alliance.

Whatever its causes, Burgess's electoral victory was stunning. She led the at-large field, receiving almost 53,000 votes, 13,000 more than Griffin, who finished second, and 20,000 more than Lassiter, who finished third. On the basis of this large margin, Burgess laid claim to the chair of the new board. The new vice chair was Griffin, another incumbent whose differences with the Murphy administration, especially over issues involving equity and pupil assignment, had been especially sharp and public. As a result, the new board was led by two of the previous board's most visible critics of the Murphy administration. Two weeks before the installation of the new board, Murphy announced his resignation, effective the day before it took office.

The District Seats: In the two predominantly black districts, there was little doubt about the outcome. In one of these districts, there was only one candidate, and in the other district, one of the two candidates received the support of every organization (ranging from the Alliance to neighborhood groups) making endorsements and got 79 percent of the vote.

In the other districts the situation was more complicated, and the Alliance suffered defeats in two of them. In District 1, the sprawling, heavily white district in the north of the county, there were eight candidates, the most in any district. The Alliance, in part through the efforts of one of its leaders, the former CEO of Duke Power, encouraged a local PTA activist and Duke Power employee to run, and it endorsed him. An advocate of neighborhood schools, this person drew upon the same pool of voters as another candidate advocating vouchers and neighborhood schools. With a third candidate, a Christian conservative, further dividing the conservative vote, Pam Mange, a white for whom desegregation was an important goal, managed to win the election with only 24 percent of the vote.

The Alliance also suffered a defeat in District 4, a demographically diverse district on Charlotte's eastside. Here the Alliance's candidate, a lawyer, was defeated by social worker Louise Woods. A member of several citizens groups that had publicly championed integration, Woods, a white, benefited from twenty years of grassroots activity in school and civic affairs, as well as from superb organization in many parts of the district. Of the nine successful candidates, she was the only one to win without the endorsement of either the Alliance or the *Observer*.

In District 5, which covers many of the city's affluent southeastern neighborhoods, the field included incumbent John Tate. However, Tate so delayed his decision to run that the Alliance had earlier recruited and promised support to another candidate. As a result, the Alliance endorsed and provided equivalent financial support to both men, but Tate won handily.

In District 6, the heavily white district in the south of the county, there were two very different candidates, both white. One was Lindalyn Kakadelis, an education activist and a conservative Christian. The other was Annelle Houk, a liberal whose involvement with school desegregation went back to the 1960s. Although the Alliance had been formed in part because of worries about the growing conservative Christian influence in education politics, it ended up endorsing Kakadelis figuring, correctly as it turned out, that she would almost certainly win because of well-organized support in several key churches and the large Republican majority in her district.

Kakadelis's victory notwithstanding, the board that emerged from the 1995 elections bore every indication of having a strong commitment to desegregation and educational equity. The only three members of the previous board who had voted against dismissing the C25 were on the new board, one as chair and the other as vice chair. Moreover, two of the white district representatives, Woods and Mange, had spoken strongly in favor of desegregation during the campaign, as had the two black district representatives. Moreover, as black proponents of districts had hoped, the board now had a total of three black members, the highest since the early 1980s. How this new board would deal with desegregation-related issues will be discussed in the next chapter. Here I view the Murphy administration's political failures through the prism of civic capacity and then turn to the educational shortcomings of the reform program.

Shortfalls In Civic Capacity

Despite the initial enthusiasm for the Murphy administration, both its political defeats at the polls and the ongoing lower (compared to Wake and Forsyth) level of local financial support for public education indicate dramatic shortfalls in the civic capacity necessary to sustain the reform program. Part of the explanation for these deficiencies lies in the counterproductive aspects of the superintendent's personality, as well as his high-profile flirtations with other jobs and requests for additional compensation, mentioned earlier. Here I will focus on a second part of the explanation: a local political situation characterized by growing centrifugal tendencies, complexity, and fluidity.

A benchmark event in the development of this fluidity was, as chapter 2 notes, the 1987 mayoral election, which signaled a decrease in the electoral clout of the alliance between the business elite and African American political leaders, as well as a decline in what Hugh McColl, as noted in chapter 2, called the consensus among business, government, and citizens groups. This declining consensus was evident by divisions among both African Americans and whites, as well as in the various defeats suffered by the business elite during the Murphy administration.

Divisions among African Americans

Many African American political leaders persistently opposed Murphy's program, especially its perceived threat to desegregation and equitable resource allocation, with Arthur Griffin's campaign against the 1993 bond referendum exemplifying this discontent. His opposition resulted in a historically low Yes vote among blacks for school bonds. Moreover, that low vote was part of a general drop in black support for school bonds after 1992, the year in which the magnet plan was implemented. That decrease was greater than the decline in white support for school bonds as well as greater than the decline in black support for non-school bonds.[71] Consequently, the history of school reform in Charlotte-Mecklenburg calls attention to the following policy dilemma: in substituting magnets for many aspects of the mandatory busing plan, Murphy sought, among other things, to decrease white opposition to desegregation and thus to allow CMS to proceed with other aspects of educational change. But while laying a political foundation among whites for such change, the magnet plan and other aspects of Murphy's program may have jeopardized CMS' ability to meet its growing financial needs by alienating that segment of the electorate, blacks, historically most likely to support school bonds.[72]

Thus the black opposition to key policies of the Murphy administration was undoubtedly part of the complicated causal web that contributed to its demise. But African American opposition to the general thrust of Murphy's program was basically unsuccessful. A precondition of any successful opposition would, presumably, have been substantial cohesion and political mobilization among blacks, given the fact that they constituted only 27 percent of Mecklenburg's population. But that cohesion was lacking, as indicated by Bishop Battle's generally strong support for Murphy's program. Given these divisions among black Charlotteans, probably the best single word that characterizes the relationship between the Murphy administration and African Americans is "stalemate." As the history of bond referenda indicates, African American discontent created significant political obstacles to the Murphy administration's program. Despite these obstacles, black Charlotteans (and their white allies) opposing the program could not bring about any major changes in it, as the events following the firing of the C25 indicate. After the watchdog committee had been put to sleep for barking, there was no follow-through to the meeting called to protest its demise.

In dismissing the C25, the school board thus eliminated a group around which much of the opposition to the resegregation and equity consequences of the reform program had coalesced. Although no organization or group arose to fill the political void created by the dismissal, it did little to convince these opponents that their criticism was mistaken. If anything, coming as it did on an unscheduled, close vote at the end of a long board meeting, the dismissal served mainly to persuade these opponents that the board's majority was operating at the behest of the superintendent and in a manner as high-handed and arrogant as his. Given the salience of desegregation and equity to these opponents, the fact that many of them were politically influential African Americans, and the importance of black support for school reform in CMS, the stalemate between the Murphy administration and black Charlotteans provided a telling indication of shortfalls in the civic capacity necessary to sustain the reform program.

Educational Change and Whites

It is more difficult to summarize the relationship between the Murphy administration and whites, in part because no set of issues defined white involvement in education the way that concerns with desegregation and equity have historically characterized black involvement. To be sure, white families, like everyone else, want "good schools," but that term admits of so many differing interpretations that it cannot easily be linked to specific policy positions.

Perhaps the best single summary of the political relationship between Murphy's administration and whites is that the reform program failed to overcome many of the centrifugal tendencies inherent in the political, economic, and social changes that had affected Charlotte-Mecklenburg in the previous ten years and that made the task of developing civic capacity more difficult. Of these changes, three are especially relevant to the politics of education: the increased clout of the county's rapidly growing outlying areas, the increase in the number of Republicans, and the increased influence of fiscal and social conservatives in local affairs.

The increasing importance of the county's outlying areas was manifest in the events that led to a majority of members of the school board being elected from districts. Although both Murphy and the business elite feared that the switch would jeopardize his program, district representation resulted in part from the desire of outlying, predominantly white areas for a greater voice on the school board. The increased influence of conservatives and Republicans also was evident in the May 1995 school bond referendum, the opposition to which was spearheaded by white, conservative Christian, Republican County Commissioner Tom Bush. Aiding Bush was a predominantly white citizens group that had challenged local taxing and spending policies for a decade. Together they succeeded in defining the public debate as one involving CMS' fiscal accountability and the county's ability to pay for the bonds without a large tax increase. These fiscal concerns also mobilized conservative activists to get out the No vote and thus contributed significantly to the demise of the Murphy administration.

The Business Elite and Civic Capacity

In reflecting on the relationship between the business elite and civic capacity during the Murphy administration, it is useful to recall regime theory's general viewpoint on corporate political influence. According to this perspective, the business elite "has no power of command over the community at large and can be defeated on any given issue,"[73] but it plays a unique role in local politics because the absence of its distinctive set of resources makes governance much more difficult than it would otherwise be. That claim has additional force in discussions of education policy in Charlotte because of the fragmentation of local political authority. While such fragmentation is a well-known characteristic of the U.S. political system, it is particularly apparent in Charlotte-Mecklenburg's politics of education. A county commission chosen in partisan elections controls a large portion of the nonpartisan school board's finances. Moreover, elections for the two bodies do not occur in the same years.

A graphic example of the importance that CMS policymakers attach to business elite involvement comes from Susan Burgess. Sixteen months before becoming the board's chair and at a time when differences with Murphy were jeopardizing her support among the business elite, Burgess noted the employment and political links between many of her board colleagues and the business elite and then added, "I do have a certain amount of freedom, I think, that not all board members enjoy in that I'm not dependent financially on any of those business leaders." Burgess also made clear that she bore no animus toward the business elite, and that the school board depended on it. Noting the importance of having differing views represented on the board, she said: "We can't, shouldn't, have nine members of the Chamber or nine people from the corporate community, but we sure *need* some of them. We can't exist without some of them. We shouldn't have nine members of the fundamentalist Christian community . . . but I'm *glad* we have one of them. We shouldn't have nine people who will rubber-stamp anything Mr. Murphy says, but I'm *glad* we have some."[74]

Asked specifically whether the use of *need* and *glad* was conscious, Burgess said: "We absolutely must have their [corporate] support in this community because they pull the strings. If we do not have their support, we will not pass a bond. They pay for our bond campaigns; we don't pay for it with public money. We go ask them, and they raise thousands of dollars and have beautiful professional bond campaigns. They give us loaned executives to run it. We can't thrive without them, we need them, and we need them on our Board of Education."[75]

A second graphic example of the importance of the business elite to Charlotte's politics of education comes from the events leading to the appearance of the $217 million compromise on the November 1995 ballot. While no government official in all of Charlotte-Mecklenburg had sufficient respect and clout to call a meeting, massage egos, and insist that the feuding parties reach a compromise over the amount of the package, Chamber officials did. Moreover, the location of the meeting at which the compromise was arranged—at the Chamber of Commerce rather than the offices of the school board or county commission—symbolizes the ongoing role of the business elite in the local politics of education.

However, the very fact that the Chamber had to broker the $217 million compromise was a reflection of the political weakness of the business elite, which had supported the unsuccessful $304 million package in May. This weakness also is evident in the Alliance's failure in the 1995 elections to keep Susan Burgess from becoming chair, the defeats it suffered in Districts 1 and 4, and its inability to recruit a more congenial candidate (e.g., a moderate Republican) in District 6. The significance of the business elite's setbacks in the 1995 school board election is best understood by comparisons with earlier elections.

The Alliance represented an umbrella-type intervention in school board elections, the closest parallel to which appears to be the activities of the "slate-makers" in the pivotal election of 1972, discussed in chapter 3. But the differences between the two interventions are striking. Unlike the candidates supported by the Alliance, all of those backed by the slate-makers were victorious. Moreover, the 1972 election saw one of Charlotte's most influential businessmen, C. D. Spangler Jr., run successfully for the school board, but in 1995, no business executive even approaching Spangler's clout sought office. Similar differences also exist between the school board election of 1995 and that of 1988, another turning point in local educational history, as chapter 4 indicated. Like 1972—but unlike 1995—the election of 1988 saw one of Charlotte's most influential businessmen, Joe Martin, seek office, as the business elite intervened much more cohesively and successfully than it would seven years later.

The events leading up to the 1995 elections—in particular, the switch to district representation—also indicate the business elite's inability to rein in the centrifugal aspect of local educational politics. The business elite's discreet silence in the months before the referendum on district representation contrasts sharply with the vigorous public fight it launched against the switch to district representation on the city council eighteen years earlier.

Thus, taken together, the 1995 elections and the May 1995 bond referendum provide ample evidence of another tenet of regime theory: a governing coalition may be very different from a victorious electoral one. However important as the business elite remained to educational governance during the Murphy years, its ability to be part of a winning electoral coalition and to play a major role in shaping such a coalition in 1995 was much weaker than it had been in either 1988 or 1972. The business elite's lessened electoral clout both reflected and contributed to the shortfalls in civic capacity that made it difficult to sustain the reform program.

Also contributing to those difficulties were many aspects of the program itself (e.g., the resegregation and resource disparity it occasioned, discussed above). But even if those issues are set aside, the program's conceptualization, development, and implementation were badly flawed. So widespread and pervasive were these problems that it is arguably a good thing, not a bad thing, that there was insufficient civic capacity to sustain the reform program.

SCHOOL REFORM AS EDUCATIONAL ALCHEMY

Given the contrast between the grandiose claims in national education venues about the Murphy administration's success in "transforming the Charlotte-Mecklenburg schools" and the political defeats that this administration suffered in Charlotte, CMS may seem to provide a classic example of an exemplary program of school reform sabotaged by parochial and fractious local politics.[76] Such a view is wrong on two counts. First, as noted earlier, both the superintendent's personality and the resegregative aspects of the reform program undermined support for it. Second, to the extent that the political and educational aspects of the reform program can be separated, the latter also were profoundly flawed. To be sure, the Murphy administration could claim credit for successfully developing a number of important programs, including an International Baccalaureate Program, a series of language immersion schools, and the Education Village—a K–12, multischool, hi-tech campus near UNCC. It also could point to improved leadership at some schools very much in need of change. However, its progress in boosting outcomes was, with only one exception, generally the same, or worse, than those of comparable districts lacking a nationally touted reform program. Despite the sweeping claims of success, the reform program did only slightly better in transforming education in Charlotte-Mecklenburg than medieval alchemists did in transmuting lead into gold. Although polemical, the analogy with alchemy is an apt one because in addition to extending promises of sweeping

change that were virtually as grandiose as alchemy's, the reform program—
in its conceptualization, development, and implementation—was as inher-
ently incapable of transforming education as the philosopher's stone was of
transmuting lead.

The shortcomings of the reform program are best demonstrated by first
discussing the scant progress in improving outcomes. I then discuss the
program's conceptualization, development, and implementation, after which I
consider how the Murphy administration's emphasis on symbolic politics rather
than on educational substance contributed to its political difficulties.

Academic Outcomes

Many scholars and educators argue that it requires many years for even
the most ambitious reform agenda to produce major changes in educational
outcomes. From that perspective, there is reason to question the relevance of
any discussion of the outcomes associated with Murphy's reform program,
since his tenure at CMS lasted only four and one-half years.[77] However, that
was not the perspective of Murphy himself, nor the reform program's enthu-
siasts, many of whom, as noted earlier, had lavishly praised the program's
apparent success in improving outcomes. Given these many claims, it is appropriate to comment on them at some length.

That the picture was not as rosy as painted became apparent in the summer of 1997, when North Carolina released the results of its newly instituted
ABC accountability program for the 1996–97 school year, the first full one after
the resignation of Murphy and his two top aides. Although a number of CMS
schools fared well under the ABC plan, CMS as a whole woefully
underperformed the state's other urban districts as well as much of the state in
general. For example, only approximately 35 percent of CMS' schools met their
ABC goals. That compared very unfavorably with the corresponding one for
the entire state (57 percent), as well as for Winston-Salem/Forsyth (44 percent), Greensboro/Guilford (45 percent), and Raleigh/Wake (73 percent).[78]
Also raising questions about CMS' performance was the fact that nine of the
twenty-two schools in the lowest category according to the ABC standards
had, in the previous school year, received financial bonuses under CMS' home-
grown accountability program which, as noted earlier, was one of the reform
program's major policy innovations. In fact, among these nine schools that had
qualified for a bonus according to local criteria were the only two CMS schools
where, in keeping with North Carolina's ABC guidelines, the principal was
suspended because his or her school had performed so poorly.[79]

Of course, it is possible that the reform program produced considerable
gains that were lost upon Murphy's departure, thus explaining CMS' poor

performance in the 1996–97 school year. To see if the reform program could be credited with boosting academic outcomes during the Murphy administration, Roslyn Mickelson and I compared a wide range of outcomes in CMS with those in North Carolina's two other consolidated urban districts—Winston-Salem/Forsyth and Raleigh/Wake—and with those of the state as a whole.[80] We used these comparisons as a way of distinguishing between any distinctive effects of CMS' reform program and any progress that might be attributed to other causes, such as the many statewide reforms that are generally credited with improving outcomes throughout North Carolina.[81] Our analysis showed that—with the exception of some outcomes for Advanced Placement and other higher-level courses—CMS' progress was either the same as, or worse than, that of these three other jurisdictions. For example, CMS was not the only district that saw a sharp jump in SAT scores in the early 1990s, as Figures 5.1 and 5.2 show. Immediately apparent from these figures is the similarity in the trends for all four school systems: scores generally rise, with the sharpest increases in the early 1990s, followed by, in most cases, a general leveling off. In CMS as well as Wake, the jump is especially sharp during the first year of CMS' reform program, 1991–92.

The similar trends suggest that something similar was happening in other districts, and indeed it was. Stung by North Carolina's having the lowest SAT scores of any state in 1989, Bobby Etheridge—at that time, North Carolina's state school superintendent, an elected position—staked much of his political future on getting the state off of the bottom rung of the national SAT ladder by, among other things, persuading the legislature to allocate money to pay the fees for students who took the PSAT.[82] As an *Observer* reporter noted: "In 1990, Charlotte-Mecklenburg and other N.C. School districts began requiring 10th grade students to take the PSAT after the state agreed to pay for the privately administered test . . . Two years later, that same batch of students—mostly juniors and seniors—contributed to the school system's largest-ever increase in SAT scores."[83]

The broad similarities in the trends shown in Figures 5.1 and 5.2 and the fact that most of CMS' gains took place during the first year of the reform program—before many of its main features were fully implemented—strongly suggest that these gains were much more due to statewide policy changes than to any distinctive aspects of CMS' reform program. Moreover, if the program was having a marked effect on CMS' SAT scores, then one would expect the scores to increase with time as the cumulative effect of the reforms became manifest, but there is little evidence of such a cumulative effect.[84]

Just as trends on SAT scores in CMS and the other jurisdictions largely paralleled each other, so too did trends in what North Carolina calls its core high school subjects and dropout rates. From CMS' perspective, the parallel trends in dropout rates were especially unfortunate, because the district had

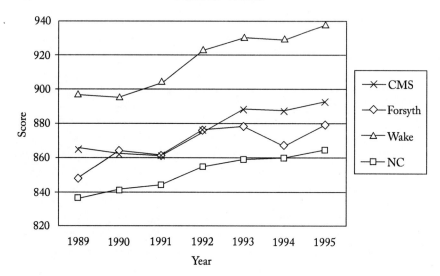

FIGURE 5.1   Average Total SAT Scores for All Students, 1989–1995
Note: Scores not recentered.
Source: Smith and Mickelson, "All That Glitters."

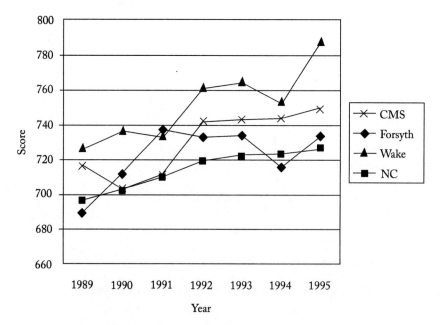

FIGURE 5.2   Average Total SAT Scores for Black Students, 1989–1995
Note: Scores not recentered.
Source: Smith and Mickelson, "All That Glitters."

one of the worst rates in the state. Moreover, CMS' progress in boosting reading and math proficiency in grades 3–8 was generally worse than that in the other jurisdictions. Despite Murphy's claims about CMS' success in solving "the other half of the puzzle" that *Brown* bequeathed to educators, the lags were especially evident for black students. At the start of the comparison period, proficiency levels of CMS' black students were lower than those of black students in Wake, Forsyth, and North Carolina. The gaps were even larger at the end of the comparison periods; in none of the six comparisons (two subjects, three districts) did the gaps get smaller during the four-year period studied.[85] Given the importance of reading and math proficiency in grades 3–8 in and of themselves, as well as for future academic success, CMS' lags in this regard are especially unfortunate. Combined with SAT scores, dropout rates, and proficiency in core high school subjects, the data on reading and math proficiency belie any attempt to credit the reform program with distinctive progress in boosting academic outcomes.

Shortcomings in Conceptualization, Development, and Implementation

In these areas—as in the political aspects of the reform program—Superintendent Murphy was frequently his own worst enemy. Whatever his considerable passion for educational change and ability to inspire some of CMS' employees, the same disputes over compensation and flirtations with other jobs that created such political difficulties for Murphy also undermined the program's educational goals. By its very nature, Murphy's "applied anxiety" approach to management assumed the existence of recalcitrant teachers, principals, and other staff throughout CMS. However, Murphy's continual flirtations with other jobs and the well-known claim that his bags were always packed could only encourage such reluctance and resistance in the hope that he would soon be gone.

However, just as the political difficulties facing the reform program could not be reduced to the superintendent's personality or actions, neither could its educational shortcomings. The educational shortcomings were rooted in the structure of the program and can be grouped into four categories: the "applied anxiety" approach to management, problems in the standards and curriculum, shoddy and uneven implementation, and the downside of site-based management.

Enormous Pressure to Achieve

While the reform program's emphasis on holding educators' feet to the fire may have motivated some CMS personnel, the approach had a huge downside. In the words of an award-winning principal who served before, during, and after the Murphy administration:

> Before Murphy came, if a principal wasn't successful you could hide him or her away somewhere in [a school serving poor children of color]. So I think his biggest contribution was…if you weren't making the mark, you couldn't continue being a principal. If you weren't leading the school and we all knew that there were people out there that just didn't have leadership and they were not leading schools … He made a lot of moves early on. The pressure to achieve after that was tremendous on principals, to a point of intimidation and fear . . . And he seemed to thrive on people being under that kind of tension. And so people produced as a result, but it was a kind of thing that was wearing people out pretty quickly.
>
> When he left, there was this collective sigh across the system. And it wasn't that people didn't want to do well . . . There was this collective sigh that the intimidation factor was not there, and they could still continue doing the job but not feel so threatened and intimidated doing it.[86]

"The pressure to achieve" largely meant achieving the goals established by CMS' accountability system, and it led, among other things, to a variety of strategies aimed at gaming the system. For example, one high school teacher who prided himself on understanding the complex methodology used to assess progress in meeting the goals drafted lengthy memos to his principal, a newcomer to CMS who did not understand the methodology. The memos included a thinly disguised suggestion that the school find ways to transfer low-achieving students to other schools. They also cautioned against the dangers of too much progress in the current year, lest the benchmark goals be set too high the following one:

> English Department . . .
> Currently the White percentage of students in higher level English is 78.3% of the entire white population at [name of school]. We are now exceeding our goal of 64.1% by the system. *If this continues to be this high then next year our goal may be set higher.* This is something we should keep under close watch . . .

> Mathematics Department . . .
> Currently the White percentage of students in higher level Math is 61.7% of the entire white population at [name of school]. We are well off the expected goal of 67.8% by the system. If population

remains constant, then to reach this goal we would need to encourage 54 new White students to enter higher level courses or reduce the total population of Whites by 81 students. *Plans should be considered by [name of high school] to encourage white students into higher level courses and find appropriate placement of students in the Charlotte system.* (emphases in original)

The benchmark goals system created incentives for principals to find what this teacher's memo called "appropriate placement" of students elsewhere in the system, such as the alternative schools for students labeled as having behavioral and other problems. It is thus not surprising that enrollment in these schools jumped much more sharply during the Murphy administration than did CMS' total enrollment.[87] The benchmark goals system also established a framework in which satisfying some goals could conflict with other goals. For example, as noted earlier, a grades 10–12 high school had a total of twenty-six subgoals, two of which involved reducing dropouts and ten of which involved increasing enrollment in higher-level courses. Whether increasing such enrollment merits, from an educational standpoint, five times as much weight as reducing one of North Carolina's highest dropout rates is an issue beyond this book's scope. But it did not take a deep understanding of the accountability system to realize that success in cutting the dropout rate could make it more difficult to increase the percentage of students enrolled in higher-level classes.[88] Thus, there was little incentive for principals to try to reduce the dropout rate. That lack of incentive, combined with the fact that it is generally considered easier to increase enrollment in higher-level courses than to reduce dropouts, makes it not at all surprising that the reform program could show greater progress in achieving the former than the latter.

Poor Alignment and Uneven Implementation

Additional problems with the accountability system arose for those goals upon which progress was assessed by state-mandated standardized tests. As noted above, progress toward meeting these goals was measured on state-mandated standardized tests that were based on North Carolina's curriculum and standards. However, the Murphy administration viewed these state standards as insufficiently rigorous, developed its own, and measured student progress in meeting these standards with its own criterion referenced tests that were administered during the school year. As a result of this situation, there was poor alignment between CMS' curriculum and the tests used to measure progress in meeting the benchmark goals. Moreover, there was considerable variation among schools as well as among classrooms in some schools in the extent to which teachers tried to teach to North Carolina's standards, CMS', or some combination of the two. As an award-winning chemistry teacher, who had been invited by CMS senior staff to help prepare the standards, subsequently remarked:

> I don't see that he [Murphy] gave any support for career development to get to his goals. I think he just said, "There are the goals." And I think the biggest thing that I've always said is I admire him because he had a vision—he knew where he wanted to be in five years, and ten years, but his downfall was that he didn't tell us how to get there. Or didn't suggest what we can do, or anything like that. And I think he needed to do that.[89]

Uneven implementation characterized many other aspects of the reform program, such as the much publicized ProjectFirst. Funded by IBM and staffed in Charlotte-Mecklenburg by Americorps volunteers, ProjectFirst had the stated goal of assisting schools in bringing technology into classroom instruction. However, as Roslyn Arlin Mickelson's study of the project indicates, some of the volunteers lacked a background in computer technology, and none of them had any previous training in teaching computer skills to others.[90] Nor, contrary to the volunteers' expectations, did a two-week preparatory session at IBM headquarters in New York provide such experience. As a result, once they were placed in schools, the volunteers were unable to provide the help that teachers requested. A principal whose service at a ProjectFirst middle school began midway through the project's implementation noted that when she arrived at the school, she

> met with the Americorps volunteer to ascertain his responsibilities. He had not been given "directions" from the previous principal who "did not believe in technology." There was little interest in technology by the previous principal and even less support and resources from CMS to provide needed hardware and upgrades . . . The Americorps volunteer identified five computers purchased through the project, of which three computers were used by the administration . . . The volunteer had limited skills and knowledge in technology and even less in instruction. Teachers expressed concern that the volunteer was unable to assist or to train them. Consequently, the school's computer teacher "trained" the volunteer. The volunteer spent a great deal of time "finding" someone who could help him relative to technical knowledge and curricular issues . . . The placement of Americorps volunteers in needy non-magnet schools wasn't equivalent to a Band-Aid; it was a cotton swab.[91]

The lack of coherence in the reform program's development and implementation was not lost on perceptive Murphy supporters in the business elite.

Although, as noted above, *Observer* publisher Rolfe Neill's columns voiced strong support for Murphy, two years after the superintendent's resignation, he would reflect, "Part of Murphy's problem was he was attracted to every new program. Anything that would get money or attention he went for. Once the attention was over, he went on to something else and left it to a few overworked aides to try to implement still another program of the day. And I think that accreted on the hull of the educational ship and began to slow it."[92] As a result of this buckshot approach, whatever reform actually took place during the Murphy administration was anything but systemic because the myriad new programs were not cohesively implemented at the classroom level, nor coordinated across schools.

Consequences of Site-Based Management

In addition to contributing to the uneven implementation of the reform program, site-based management exacerbated disparities in financial and human resources among schools. Among other things, the Murphy administration implemented a program through which the central office matched—up to a total of $10,000—school-based fund-raising efforts, thus rewarding schools whose students came from affluent families. While the amount involved—$10,000—was obviously a very small percentage of any school's annual budget, the program exemplified how little attention was paid to alleviating disparities among schools.

Equally important, site-based management combined with the high-stakes accountability system to facilitate disparities among CMS' faculties. The evidence is especially clear with respect to faculty racial balance. As noted in chapter 3, even during the years of peak faculty racial balance in the 1980s, racially identifiable black schools generally had higher percentages of black faculty than other schools. That relation is shown in Figure 5.3, which tracks the correlation between the racial composition of faculties and student populations.[93] Positive during the Robinson administration, the correlation remained relatively constant throughout the late 1980s and early 1990s, although student racial imbalance increased sharply during these years. However, the correlation jumped in the mid-1990s and continued at a high level throughout the decade. That sudden increase in faculty racial imbalance can be attributed in large part to the decreased monitoring by the central office of teacher hiring that was part and parcel of the move toward site-based management. As CMS' director of personnel testified during the reopened *Swann* trial:

> Prior to the implementation of site-based management, the human resources department had responsibility for recruiting teachers, for making job offers for teachers, for monitoring the racial balance of the staffing in the schools . . .

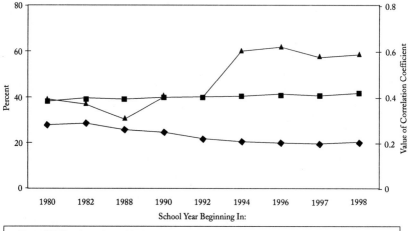

FIGURE 5.3   Correlation between Faculty and Student Racial Composition, 1980–1998
Source: Charlotte-Mecklenburg Schools.

With site-based management, the principals had the ultimate authority for hiring, they could actually go out and recruit their own teachers, and they were no longer held to the diversity staffing issues that had been monitored by the area superintendents . . .

Those schools that were exemplary schools [under the benchmark goals system] tended to be those schools that had large majority [white] teacher populations, and they were schools that received a lot of positive press based on the factors that were included in the benchmark goals. And as a result, teachers started transferring out of schools where they were part of the diversity factor . . .

[N]ew teacher candidates started shopping around. They actually went to those schools and introduced themselves to principals, and principals would hire them as a result of site-based management without any consideration for the diversity needs of staffing in those schools.

We also found that teachers would decline contracts with us if we referred them to a school that had been less successful with the benchmark goals. They would actually say, well, I want to decline that job, I want to look around, or can I go to another school, or are there any other openings, when prior to the benchmark goals, if we assigned a teacher, generally they went to that assignment without question and then later maybe participated in the transfer process.[94]

Symbol at the Expense of Substance

With its buckshot development, coordination, and implementation, the Murphy administration's reform program can be viewed as an example of what Frederick M. Hess has called the policy churn resulting from the way "organizational constraints and professional incentives encourage district policymakers to treat reform as a political exercise."[95] But even if viewed from that perspective, the reform program was a failed political exercise.

Virtually none of the problems in conceptualization, development, or implementation received any significant attention in the Murphy administration's reports to either local or national audiences. Rather, these reports were filled with one-sided, inflated, and premature claims of success. Given the importance of building public support for CMS as well as the nearly universal tendency of administrators to tout their own accomplishments, these exaggerated claims might be overlooked if they did not undermine what are generally considered important aspects of any attempt to improve public education: the development of effective evaluation procedures; the public dissemination of information derived from those evaluations; and increased public understanding of this information so that, among other things, citizens will have a better understanding of what schools and school reform can realistically accomplish.

The reform program took some important and laudable steps to provide the public with data about CMS. The annual report cards, for example, made unprecedented amounts of information available. But the volume of this information—especially that released on a school-by-school basis—frequently emphasized the forest at the expense of the trees. Whether or not the system of benchmark goals was more science than scientism, it is clear that few members of the public understood how it operated. However, the administration's commentary on these goals and the data on school-by-school performance typically did little to help even the attentive public develop a comprehensive understanding of CMS' accomplishments and shortcomings.

Typical examples of these failings were the report cards for the 1993–94 and 1994–95 school years, published as special supplements to the *Observer.* Each included data on the demographic characteristics, academic achievement, absentee rate, and parental satisfaction of each of CMS' schools, along with a list of all of those schools whose progress toward achieving their goals allowed them to receive a bonus. Murphy prefaced each report with a glowing account of CMS' academic progress. The 1994–95 report card—*Building a Legacy of Excellence*—also included a lyrical account of the visit to Charlotte-Mecklenburg by judges from the National Alliance of Business, resulting in CMS receiving an award from that organization.[96] However, nowhere in either report is there any mention that CMS' progress in improving outcomes lagged that of other districts, even though CMS' leadership knew of these lags. For example, in a memo labeled "Confidential," dated January 12, 1995—

ten months before the appearance of the 1994–95 report card—two of
Murphy's aides, including Assistant Superintendent Jeffry Schiller, informed
him that results from the 1994 state report card indicated that CMS' "overall
performance is well below average," "our improvement rate from 1993 to 1994
is generally lower than that of other cluster districts," and "relative performance
in writing is decreasing."[97] Surely that information is relevant to any report
about the state of education in Charlotte-Mecklenburg. Furthermore, in the
absence of that information, even the twenty-four pages of school-by-school
data—to say nothing of the superintendent's glowing reports—serve as much
to obscure the extent of CMS' progress as to elucidate it.

Whatever CMS' leadership was saying to each other about academic outcomes, the Murphy years were characterized by a paucity of informed public
discussion about academic achievement. Such discussion involves difficult issues,
even for professionals, and the extremely complex methodology for calculating
progress under CMS' accountability system did nothing to alleviate this difficulty.
Consequently, it was easier for most Charlotteans to focus on other things, such
as Murphy's personality, management style, and hefty pay hikes. But even individuals and organizations with more explicit programmatic agendas paid little
attention to academic outcomes. Responding to CMS' requests for additional
funding, fiscal conservatives found it easier to focus on charges of financial im-
prudence and the allegedly imminent danger of Mecklenburg's financial house
caving in. Similarly, traditional desegregation advocates found it easier to count
the number of racially imbalanced schools than to dig into the complexities of the
benchmark goals and their elusive relationship to the state tests. Consequently,
neither the conservative fiscal nor liberal social challenge to Murphy's administration included a critique of the system's academic trajectory. The public debate
took the form, "CMS may be making academic progress, but desegregation/tax
rates are at risk," rather than the much more effective, "Desegregation/tax rates
are at risk and many of CMS' claims of boosting academic achievement are
dubious ones." With no other groups developing an effective critique of educational accomplishments, the business elite had scant interest in developing one
either. Murphy's national visibility and close working relationship with prominent
advocates of school reform, such as Denis Doyle and Louis Gerstner Jr., helped
restore confidence in CMS and contributed to the perception that Charlotte-
Mecklenburg had "good schools." That belief, in the eyes of these business leaders, was essential to attracting mobile capital and promoting economic growth.
While some business leaders grew increasingly disenchanted with Murphy's leadership style and flirtations with other jobs, they worried that changing horses in
the midstream of a nationally publicized school reform agenda would jeopardize
CMS' renewed prestige.

If, as claimed earlier, the academic gains attributable to Murphy's program were minimal, then there might seem to have been little political incen-

tive for CMS' leadership to facilitate a candid public discussion of its (the program's) accomplishments and shortcomings. However, I would argue that it had every incentive to promote such discussion, if only because, paradoxically, such candid discussion might have prevented some of Murphy's most notable political setbacks.

A voluminous literature testifies to the existence of the political minefields through which urban superintendents must lightly step. But it is difficult to imagine a more propitious set of circumstances for any reform-minded administration to take office than the one that Murphy encountered in Charlotte-Mecklenburg. Growth and the concomitant economic and demographic changes created a local political situation that was both in flux and amenable to change. Charlotte-Mecklenburg was looking for a change agent, and some of the community's most influential members virtually fell all over themselves trying to build support for Murphy. Moreover, Charlotte-Mecklenburg's relative prosperity, racial composition, and tradition of civic involvement in education also created favorable conditions. Finally, local organizations of school system employees—which in some districts support school reform, but in others may impede it—were historically weak, and even if they had been inclined to mount substantial opposition to the reform program, they were in no position to do so.

These favorable conditions notwithstanding, the Murphy administration collapsed under the weight of its own contradictions. Much of that implosion was precipitated by its defeat at the polls in 1995. Substantive issues such as resegregation and the tax rate clearly motivated many activists and some voters, but much of the controversy swirling around Murphy was of small educational import. Consider, for example, the flap over his pay hikes. Given the high turnover of urban superintendents and the difficulty retaining effective ones, there is merit in the claim of those who argued that CMS should meet Murphy's salary demands. To justify his pay raises, they claimed, in effect, that it is necessary to pay market price for a good superintendent in much the same way that it is necessary to pay market price at an upscale restaurant when you order the catch of the day. However, too much of the debate was over the market price and not enough on whether Murphy—or, more precisely, his program—was the catch of the day. After all, Murphy's compensation was indeed a minuscule fraction of CMS' budget. But these pay raises, especially the thousands that went toward paying his mortgages on unsold homes in Prince George's County, were a potent political symbol that infuriated many Charlotteans. Just as the Murphy administration frequently lived by symbolic politics, so too was it seriously wounded by them. Educational discourse in Charlotte-Mecklenburg, as in many other places, seems governed by a variant of Gresham's law: cheap talk drives out good talk. And cheap talk seems a fitting characterization of the mélange of exaggerated claims of educational progress and grandiose rhetoric about world-class schools to which the Murphy administration repeatedly treated the public.

From this perspective, the Murphy administration could hardly have fared worse had it relied less on symbolic reassurances about CMS' progress and more on a substantive assessment of actual accomplishments. Part of the job of being a public educator nowadays is finding effective ways to educate the public about what can and cannot be expected from any program of school reform. The voluminous data released by the Murphy administration notwithstanding, it fell far short of promoting informed public discourse about developments in the Charlotte-Mecklenburg schools, as well as about what could be expected from any school reform program. Thus, the Murphy administration's shortcomings in educating the public is one reason its attempt to educate the children of Charlotte-Mecklenburg ended as unceremoniously as it did.

To be sure, in CMS, Murphy lived up to his reputation as a "change agent," but his administration left numerous and large pieces for the public, the school board, his replacement, and CMS' students and employees to pick up. During Murphy's watch and in part because of its shortcomings, CMS experienced the first defeat of a comprehensive bond package in thirty years, thus exacerbating both overcrowding and its inability to meet maintenance and renovation needs. During the Murphy watch, CMS also witnessed increasing resegregation and the increasing concentration of black children in dilapidated schools. Moreover, the academic outcomes attributable to Murphy's program were, with only one exception, generally the same or worse than those of comparable districts. CMS' curriculum was both unevenly implemented and poorly aligned with the standards upon which the accountability system was based. Finally, the move toward site-based management exacerbated inequalities in both human and material resources among CMS' schools. Given how frequently the Murphy administration talked about building a legacy of excellence, it is as ironic as it is unfortunate that these many problems constituted so large a part of its actual legacy.

Chapter 6

Desegregation Buried in Potter's Field?
The Reactivation of the *Swann* Case

We feel she was discriminated against because of the color of her skin.

> —William Capacchione, lead white plaintiff, in the reactivated *Swann* case, discussing why he went to court on behalf of his daughter.[1]

Somewhere, somehow, this School Board has forgotten that white kids go to these schools, too. It's okay to be white. The race card has been played so many times, you got people hanging their head wondering whether or not they should be able to go to school in Matthews or at McKee Road or Pineville or South Charlotte. There is nothing wrong with these schools; that's where people happen to live. And the Board of Education is not a laboratory in which to concoct social change. It is a function of that Board to rid the system of the dual system.

> —A. Lee Parks, lead attorney for the white plaintiffs, during his closing argument in the reactivated *Swann* case.[2]

CMS has achieved unitary status in all respects; therefore, all prior injunctive orders from *Swann* are vacated and dissolved.

> —Federal District Court Judge Robert Potter, in his opinion in the case.[3]

With John Murphy's resignation, CMS quickly ceased being a nationally touted exemplar of the conventional wisdom about school reform as well as of how many aspects of this wisdom and its buckshot implementation could be counterproductive. However, within a few years, CMS was again attracting national attention as the reactivation of the *Swann* litigation put Charlotte once

147

again in the middle of the national debate about core issues of race and education. As had been the case thirty years ago, one of the key questions in the debate was, Should, could, and, if so, how can a school system take race into account? This chapter discusses how that debate played out during the trial. It also considers the events that led up to the trial by discussing ongoing controversies over desegregation and resource allocation, the character of the administration that succeeded Murphy's, and the extent to which citizen participation contributed to civic capacity during controversy over pupil assignment.

GROWTH AND DESEGREGATION, AGAIN

Murphy's resignation, along with that of his two chief aides, triggered a search aimed at having a new superintendent in place within six months. From the fifty-four applicants, the school board chose Eric Smith, previously superintendent in Newport News, Virginia, citing his success in improving outcomes for at-risk students, tough disciplinary policies, and a willingness to dismiss incompetent teachers and principals.

In the six months between Murphy's resignation and Smith's arrival, the school board had to deal again with desegregation in the south of the county. Two related events fueled the area's continued growth: the completion of portions of the outerbelt and the Harris group's 1991 announcement of plans for the development of Ballantyne, the 2,000-acre, upscale mixed-use project discussed in chapters 2 and 4.

Included in Ballantyne's 2,000 acres were two tracts of land that the Harris Group had proposed donating to CMS as early as 1987. At that time, as chapter 4 indicated, senior staff had recommended that CMS take an option on the land, postponing a final decision until such time as additional development occurred. By the mid-1990s, that time had arrived, and in the spring of 1996, the school board faced the difficult issue of whether to accept the gift. Budgetary considerations argued for acceptance, especially because CMS faced ongoing huge construction and land acquisition expenses to meet the district's soaring enrollment. However, the proposed location violated the 10 Percent Rule, and its remoteness from any neighborhoods with large numbers of black residents made desegregation a difficult task. With little public controversy among its members, the previous board had built another school that violated the 10 Percent Rule in the south of the county. But the November 1995 elections had produced quite a different board. Several of the board's district members had taken strong pro-desegregation stands during close election campaigns, and the board's leadership—Chair Susan Burgess and Vice Chair Arthur Griffin—had been instrumental in the adoption of the 10 Percent Rule. Moreover, both were considered strong advocates of desegregation and equity, having been the previous board's most outspoken supporters of the C25.

Mindful of the change in the board's composition, desegregation advocates lobbied intensely for the board to use school siting decisions as leverage to require developers to build mixed-income housing that would facilitate desegregation. Typical of such efforts were those of Citizens for an Integrated Education (CIE) which, in the words of member Jane Henderson, saw the vote as a way for the board to take a stand that "we are really committed to integration" by telling developers, "If you want a school in your development that will increase your property values, here's what you have to do."[4] That sentiment was echoed by Louise Woods, a former member of the C25 and CIE, who moved that the school board postpone voting on whether to accept the property until meetings could be scheduled with developers in the hope of obtaining commitments to build housing at a wider range of income levels. Woods's motion failed, and the board then voted 5–4 to accept the donation. The majority included all three board members who, on the previous board, had opposed dismissing the C25. All noted that the vote was a difficult one, but each had a reason for voting to accept the donation. Griffin stressed that the money saved on land acquisition could be devoted to much-needed repairs and renovations of inner-city schools; Tate emphasized the fiscal constraints facing CMS; and Burgess claimed that the school could be desegregated if it were made a magnet, saying that the board would work with planners, developers, and others to avoid similar difficult situations in the future.[5]

Despite Burgess's hopes, when the school opened in the fall of 1999, it was not a magnet, and black students comprised only 2 percent of the school's population, further increasing the drift toward resegregation. More immediately, the board's willingness to violate the 10 Percent Rule exacerbated sentiments that special treatment was still accorded southeast Charlotte, especially when the issue concerned a developer and a family well known for their political clout. The acceptance of the donation in Ballantyne also fueled demands that CMS accept other donations. These demands were especially strong in the large Highland Creek development in the northern part of the county, where many believed that CMS had earlier refused a developer's donation of land on the grounds that a school on that site would be difficult to desegregate.[6]

THE ADMINISTRATION OF ERIC SMITH

Comparisons with the Previous Administration

Shortly after arriving from Virginia, Superintendent Smith removed the security doors that his predecessor had installed to the superintendent's office and removed the parking gates to the Education Center. These changes were physical manifestations of a much more open, accessible leadership style that allowed Smith to mend many of CMS' political fences. The most dramatic example of this improvement was the comments of County Commissioner Tom Bush, who had spearheaded the successful effort to defeat the May 1995 bond referendum. In Bush's view, if you wanted anything from Murphy, "You had to kiss his ring ... [but] Eric Smith has that unique capacity of making people feel very important." Bush also noted that he and Smith had come "to the conclusion that the best way for the school board to deal with Tom Bush is to do it privately through Eric Smith."[7] Bush opposed a 1997 bond package just as he had the one in 1995. But unlike 1995, in 1997, as a result of his understanding with Smith, Bush agreed not to campaign publicly against the package, even though it was 33 percent larger. The tax watchdog group that had also successfully fought the May 1995 bond package supported the 1997 one, citing differences between Smith's leadership style and Murphy's "locked-door policy" and "not being open to dialogue" as one reason for the endorsement.[8] Moreover, in addition to securing the passage of this largest-ever bond package in Mecklenburg County history with 73 percent of the vote, Smith also succeeded in each of his first two years in obtaining the entire hefty budget increases that CMS requested. It had been years since the county commission had not cut CMS' proposed budget increase. The school system's success in winning full funding in two consecutive years dramatically illustrated the political skills that led a community newspaper to hail Smith as the "superintendent of sales."[9]

Almost as different as the two men's leadership styles were their approaches to organizational issues. Smith tried to rein in some of the centrifugal forces to which the Murphy administration, with its emphasis on site-based management, had given full play. He appointed six regional assistant superintendents who would serve as links between him and both parents and principals. "To old-timers," the *Observer* noted, these six regional superintendents "will be reminiscent of the area superintendents adopted 20 years ago and dropped in 1992 in Supt. John Murphy's reorganization."[10] Smith also decreased the instructional and curricular autonomy of CMS' principals and sought much closer alignment between CMS' curriculum and North Carolina standards. Part of the impetus for the increased alignment came from the state's newly instituted ABC accountability program, which graded each school's performance on the basis of student achievement on the state-mandated EOG and EOC tests, with, as Smith noted, "a pretty draconian response if you don't measure up."[11] But the narrowing of principals' autonomy also reflected Smith's insistence that CMS had to function as "one school system, not a system of schools."[12]

These differences notwithstanding, the two administrations had important similarities, especially as CMS continued to wrestle with race and education. Just as Murphy saw the magnet plan as a way of blunting opposition to busing, Smith would propose a much greater expansion of school choice to deal with the complex legal, political, and educational aspects of pupil assignment. In the cover letter accompanying the initial proposal for expanded choice, Smith stressed his commitment to diversity, saying that in 1996 he had "told the board of education in my job interview that the one thing I would not do as superintendent was intentionally re-segregate the Charlotte-Mecklenburg Schools."[13] However, as events unfolded, Smith's position bore increasing witness to the pressure on CMS to abandon desegregation in favor of policies that would provide extra resources to schools with large percentages of students of color. In that respect, many of Smith's proposals to the school board increasingly resembled the *Milliken II*-type strategies that John Murphy had used in Prince George's County. The events leading to these proposals began with the pupil assignment battles that took place six months after Smith assumed CMS' helm.

The 1996 Pupil Assignment Hearings

This round of hearings focused on the 1997 opening of two new high schools, Butler in Matthews and Vance in a K–12, hi-tech, multischool campus near UNCC and University Research Park. When plans for this Education Village, as it was initially called, had been developed during the Murphy administration, Arthur Griffin had opposed placing a high school there, lest it deprive the attendance zone of West Charlotte High School of white neighborhoods necessary for racial balance. But amid all of the fanfare about this hi-tech campus, Griffin's concerns received scant public attention.[14] However, the location of Butler occasioned a broader range of protest when it was proposed during Murphy's tenure.

The site violated the 10 Percent Rule, and plans for its construction triggered objections not just from the usual proponents of desegregation, such as the League of Women Voters, but also from several members of the Charlotte-Mecklenburg Planning Commission, who said that the school was too close to the county line and would require long bus rides for black students.[15] Rather, they said, the new high school should be located farther from the county border, as indicated on the draft of the 2002 Master Plan, a long-range school facilities plan prepared jointly by CMS and county planners earlier in the Murphy administration. Although the board never adopted the plan, the Murphy administration viewed it as generally consistent with existing CMS policy.[16] However, when it came time to acquire land for Butler, the Murphy administration argued that the site indicated on the master plan would require excessive pupil reassignment and went ahead with building Butler on a site in Matthews one and one-quarter miles from the county line.

Facing the simultaneous opening of Butler in the southeast of the county and Vance in the northeast, CMS had a variety of options for rearranging the attendance zones of the system's high schools. Planners developed three plans and solicited comments in a series of public hearings that turned out to be among the most rancorous since the 1970s. Given the fact that both schools were located in predominantly white areas, one might have expected that most of the anger would come from the black families whose children would likely face the longest bus rides to achieve racial balance. But just the opposite was the case. The opposition centered among whites, especially families in three outlying areas whose children were not assigned to the high school closest to their homes. One of these areas was Matthews, many of whose residents felt that the school's location in their town entitled all of its children to attend the school. A fourth proposal was developed by CMS to meet many of these objections, but not all, and resentment continued after the board adopted the new plan.

The 1997 School Board Elections

Anger about pupil assignment in Matthews and other outlying areas triggered the formation, with considerable media attention, of Citizens for a Neighborhood School System (CFANSS) and a PAC established by it. The CFANSS benefited from the support of Matthews's mayor, who was on the PAC's board of directors, and several state legislators from the Matthews area. The group promised to fight for neighborhood schools by lobbying in the state capital and by raising $250,000 to defeat any candidate who did not support such schools in the November 1997 school board elections. However, CFANSS's electoral bite proved not as sharp as its rhetorical bark was loud.

At stake in these elections were the six district seats, the three at-large members not being up for reelection until 1999 under the new system of representation initiated in 1995. Only in the county's two outlying districts could CFANSS and other neighborhood school proponents claim any significant degree of success, with the most pronounced occurring in District 1. There, unlike 1995, conservatives, Republicans, and neighborhood school advocates united behind a single candidate, Jim Puckett, who defeated incumbent Pam Mange by a 54–46 percent margin. And in District 6, the CFANSS-supported candidate, incumbent Lindalyn Kakadelis, fended off a challenge by a 52–48 percent margin from a First Union senior vice president who, at the start of the campaign at least, placed less emphasis on neighborhood schools than Kakadelis did.

However, in the other four districts, desegregation proponents held their own. The decision of John Tate not to seek reelection in affluent, predominantly white District 5 initially raised the possibility that neighborhood school advocates might capture the seat he was vacating, but the CFANSS-backed candidate was trounced 77–23 percent by Molly Griffin, an attorney who was encouraged to run by Tate and received support from a steering committee that included Hugh McColl, Ed Crutchfield, and many other prominent corporate executives and attorneys. In District 4, the county's most ethnically and socioeconomically diverse district, CFANSS was unable to recruit a candidate to run against Louise Woods, an outspoken proponent of desegregation, and she ran unopposed. So did George Dunlap in the predominantly African American District 3. In the other predominantly black district (District 2), incumbent Sam Reid was defeated by another African American, Vilma Leake, a teacher, an ex-president of the Charlotte-Mecklenburg Association of Educators, and the widow of Bishop George Leake. Differences over desegregation played relatively little role in that contest.

Thus, despite the tumult over pupil assignment less than a year earlier, the 1997 school board elections saw neighborhood school advocates gain only one seat, and members who placed a high priority on desegregation and diversity retain six of the board's nine seats. However, the board soon witnessed a dramatic change in leadership. A conjuncture of racial politics, personal ambitions, and differences over policy and administrative issues led a majority of the board's membership to favor Vice Chair Arthur Griffin replacing Susan Burgess as chair, with John Lassiter assuming the vice chair position that would be left vacant by Griffin's ascent. Stung by what she considered behind-her-back maneuvers by people previously considered friends and political allies, Burgess abruptly resigned from the board. Allowed by law to appoint a replacement for the remainder of Burgess's term, the board chose Wilhelmenia Rembert, a vice president at Winthrop University who had played a key role in building consensus on the Committee of 33, a CMS task force discussed later. Rembert's views on desegregation and equity issues were similar to Burgess's, but she was an African American. Thus, the board now had four black members, the most in its history.

As soon as Rembert joined the board, it had to deal with another round of pupil assignment hearings occasioned by the scheduled opening of four new schools, three in the north of the county and one in the south. Assignment to all provoked controversy of one kind or another, but the plan eventually adopted by the board allowed two of the northern schools to be racially balanced. The third northern school opened with a black enrollment that was 3 percent higher than the +/− 15 percent variance allowed by CMS guidelines. However, the situation was quite different at the school in the south, Crestdale Middle School in Matthews.

During Burgess's tenure as chair, the board had paid a premium price for the Crestdale land because even though in Matthews, the site's proximity to a major thoroughfare would make it easier to bus black students to the school from a satellite attendance area in a predominantly African American neighborhood. Consequently, CMS planners had anticipated developing a pupil assignment plan in which blacks would comprise 35 percent of Crestdale's student population, well within racial balance guidelines.[17] However, the plan that Smith presented to the board did not make use of a black satellite in populating Crestdale. Rather, the school's attendance zones were in predominantly white neighborhoods in the south of the county, but 100 seats were set aside for a pilot voluntary transfer program in which CMS would provide transportation for students of color residing elsewhere in the county. A motion to assign, as originally contemplated, a black satellite to Crestdale failed by a 3–3–3 vote. The heavily split vote reflected differences in the importance that board members attached to desegregation, backing the superintendent, and treating different parts of the county equally. Of the board's five white members, two voted for it, two voted against it, and one abstained. The black members also were correspondingly split.[18]

The voluntary transfer plan notwithstanding, when Crestdale opened in 1998, blacks comprised only 16 percent of the school's student population, a figure substantially outside of CMS' guidelines for racial balance. Moreover, as school board member Molly Griffin had noted during the debate, allowing the school to open with a much lower than average percentage of black and poor students would send the wrong message to other parts of the county.[19] This same round of hearings saw bitter protests by white parents in northern areas of the county over assignments to schools—some new, some old—with percentages of poor and African American children that they considered excessive. The Crestdale assignment thus intensified the belief in these northern areas that southern Mecklenburg continued to get special treatment.

The Committee of 33 and the Development of Civic Capacity

Just as the fall 1996 pupil assignment hearings gave rise to CFANSS, so too did they produce efforts by CMS to address the challenge represented by CFANSS as well as to prevent future pupil assignment hearings from being so divisive. The most important of these efforts was a citizen task force created by CMS in January 1997 to develop consensus over pupil assignment and facilities planning. An extended discussion of this task force thus illuminates a key issue: to what extent was it possible to enhance civic capacity at a time when CMS' desegregation policies were facing both political and increasingly severe legal challenges?

Formally called the Future School Planning Task Force, this group had thirty-three members and thus was frequently called the Committee of 33 (C33). Each of the school board's nine members appointed three people, and the superintendent appointed six. Members included leaders of CFANSS and the NAACP's and Black Political Caucus's Education Committees, several prominent corporate executives, and a wide range of citizens and education activists.[20]

Although the issues facing the task force were similar to those with which the C25 had dealt, the C33 reflected the more open and participatory style of the new board and new superintendent. Whereas the C25 was appointed to monitor the operation of the magnet plan that had already been adopted by CMS, the C33 had the more proactive role of developing recommendations to guide future CMS decision making. Because the C25 had been a watchdog, it was easy for the relationship between it and CMS to become adversarial. However, because the C33 role was proactive, it was relatively easy for relations between it and CMS to remain cordial, especially because the superintendent and board hoped agreement within the task force would minimize future pupil assignment donnybrooks as well as prevent neighborhood school advocates from taking CMS to court. Moreover, the task force benefited from a paid consultant, hired by CMS, who acted as facilitator, led virtually all meetings, and provided a conduit for effective communication with CMS staff. All of these considerations augured well for the C33's ability to fulfill the goals that led to its creation.

With the help of the facilitator, the task force produced a unanimous report that was released in August 1997. Among other things, the report called upon CMS to provide equitable resources on an as-needed basis; emphasized the need to bring older schools up to acceptable standards by devoting unprecedentedly large amounts of funds to renovations, repairs, and maintenance; called for the creation of zone-based community planning councils to provide input on pupil assignment and school planning issues; recommended that new schools generally be constructed in areas midway between downtown and the county's boundaries; and identified four goals for pupil assignment—stability, proximity, utilization, and diversity—that quickly became known as SPUD.

The trade-off between proximity and diversity provoked considerable dispute on the task force, just as the tension between neighborhood schools and desegregation had been a recurrent theme in local education politics since McMillan's decision. But the task force tried to shed new light on the issue by seeking quantitative data on how long a bus ride for how many children was necessary to obtain a given amount of desegregation. Based on that data, the task force set goals for both proximity and diversity. For proximity, the task force recommended that mandatory bus rides (as opposed to the voluntary bus rides associated with attendance at magnet schools) not exceed thirty minutes for elementary school students and thirty-five minutes for secondary schools. For diversity, the report recommended adherence to CMS' long-standing goal of keeping each school within +/− 15 percent of the system-wide African American enrollment. It also called upon CMS to give "immediate priority" to addressing socioeconomic and racial diversity in schools containing a large number of students eligible for free or reduced lunch (FRL). Importantly, the report made no attempt to rank proximity or diversity, nor did it attempt to assign priority to any one of the four SPUD criteria, saying that all four were "substantially important."[21] Any ranking of the SPUD criteria would have kept people in one or the other of the task force's contending camps from signing the report, and the C33 did not wish to jeopardize the consensus for which CMS senior staff was so manifestly hoping.

CMS moved quickly to extend the task force's consensus to the larger community by creating five zone-based community advisory councils charged with developing specific proposals for implementing the task force's general recommendations. To facilitate their work, the councils scheduled focus groups at all schools to solicit citizen input. In addition to these advisory councils, CMS also created two additional committees, the first charged with developing a process that would relate CMS' planning efforts to those of the community as a whole, and the second formed to oversee the development of a draft of a long-range school facilities master plan.

Taken together, the hundreds of citizens who were involved in this plethora of task forces, committees, advisory councils, and focus groups represented a level of institutionalized, proactive community participation in desegregation, equity, and planning issues that was unprecedented in CMS' history. Such proactive involvement—as opposed to the reactive mission of the C25—can be viewed as an effort to develop the kind of community support for CMS that the Citizens Advisory Group (CAG) helped build in the mid-1970s. But in building this support, the CAG had benefitted from backing by the formidable political and legal powers of a federal district court whose decision had been unanimously affirmed by the Supreme Court. Also buttressing the CAG's efforts had been those of the business elite. Both of these conditions were missing a quarter-century later, and in their absence, the legacy of the C33 and its offspring is much more ambiguous because participation, in and of itself, is not sufficient to promote consensus and civic capacity.[22]

Indeed, in some respects, it is easy to argue that all of this community involvement did nothing to build consensus or civic capacity. Whatever occurred on this plethora of committees and groups was quickly overshadowed by legal developments. Although the chair of CFANSS, like all thirty-three members of the Task Force, had signed its report, within a month of that report's publication in August 1997, a white parent, William Capacchione—

who was a member of CFANSS and treasurer of its political action commit-tee—filed a lawsuit that led to the reactivation of the entire *Swann* case and would have momentous effects. Moreover, in many of these committees and groups, including the C33, its unanimous report notwithstanding, people with similar views developed and/or strengthened existing relationships in ways that contributed to the political and organizational resources that con-tending groups would bring to the political, electoral, and legal battles that engulfed the district over the next three years.

While this skepticism is merited, it only looks at one side of the coin. There are compelling arguments that the C33 and its offspring did boost civic capacity. Part of this argument involves the 1997 bond package. The C33's unanimous report provided substantive documentation of CMS' needs that was especially effective politically because its signers included a broad spectrum of individuals, some of whom had opposed bond packages in the past and/or who were presently associated with neighborhood school advo-cates planning to show their anger at the 1996 pupil assignment decisions by voting against the bonds.[23] Similarly, the support of task force members for the bonds made it difficult for any groups with which they were affiliated, whether on the liberal or conservative side of the political spectrum, to op-pose the bonds.

Another, and stronger, part of the argument that the C33 and its progeny enhanced civic capacity involves agenda setting, the importance of which is a commonplace in the literature on public policy. As one introductory text's discussion of agenda setting notes: "Policy issues do not just 'happen.' Cre-ating an issue, dramatizing it, calling attention to it, and pressuring govern-ment to do something about it are important political tactics."[24] The C33 helped dramatize and call attention to the many differences in resources among CMS' schools—especially the inadequate physical facilities of schools serving low-income families of color. This had been an issue for many years. But the C33 and its follow-up committees and councils helped push this issue much higher on the policy agenda precisely because it was an issue upon which there was agreement between the otherwise contending proponents of diversity and proximity. Moreover, the sharper the difference over diversity and proximity became, the more salient became the shared recognition of the need to address the inequities in resources.

That liberals and desegregation proponents should advocate remedying these disparities is hardly surprising, but they were not alone. Indeed, on the C33, one of the most vocal advocates of addressing these disparities was the president of CFANSS, who candidly acknowledged that the existence of such differences undermined the moral authority and educational justification of the demand for neighborhood schools. As a result of the consensus on the urgency of addressing these disparities, the first five of the C33's twenty-two recommendations all dealt with the importance of addressing disparities in resources. The prominence given this issue by the C33 was frequently echoed in the many community groups to which the C33 gave rise, again in large part because it was probably the single most important issue upon which the otherwise contending proponents of diversity and proximity could easily agree. Moreover, the C33's recognition of these disparities enhanced the legitimacy of a detailed report on the same subject released in June 1997 by a nongovernmental community organization, Helping Empower Local People (HELP), the Charlotte affiliate of the Industrial Areas Foundation, which had recently begun work in the city.

An indication of the extent to which the C33 helped shape local discourse came during the 1997 campaign for the school board. Both contenders for the vacant seat in District 5, for example, frequently cited the C33, with the CFANSS-backed candidate calling attention to the report's statement of "glaring and unacceptable inequities existing in many inner-city schools" and adding his own view that "giving each student the opportunity to attend the closest school could become a reality with equal resources."[25] The support among C33 members and school board candidates for addressing resource disparities among schools was mirrored in the results of a public opinion poll conducted in October 1997. Support for "making sure that equipment and conditions of all schools are roughly equal" was among the highest of respondents' priorities, ranking far ahead of assuring that "children attend the school closest to their homes" and "making sure all schools are integrated."[26] Another indication of how resource disparity and equity issues soared to the top of the policy agenda in the years after 1997 comes from the results of annual surveys administered by the Charlotte-Mecklenburg Educational Foundation (CMEF). From 1995 to 1997, the CMEF did not even ask respondents whether they supported "improving equity of facilities," the absence indicating how little consideration the issue was receiving from civic leaders at that time. When the item first appeared in 1998, it received stronger support than any other choice, including increasing teachers salaries and providing more computers. In 1999, "improving equity of facilities" received the second-strongest support, slightly trailing salary increases for teachers. Similarly, "renovating/updating schools" did not appear in 1995 and 1996, but in 1998 it received stronger support than any item except "improving equity," and in 1999 the two items received identical support.[27]

Thus, in the two years between the release of the C33's report and the decision in the reactivated *Swann* case, equity in facilities and in the allocation of resources became a buzzword in local discourse on education. Consequently, when CMS had to develop a race-neutral pupil assignment plan to comply with this decision, there was widespread agreement among all board members—proponents of neighborhood schools and proponents of desegregation alike—that the educational, political, and moral effectiveness of this new plan heavily depended on remedying these disparities. This agreement was especially significant given that the judge ordering the new assignment plan found that whatever disparities existed in facilities and resources were not based on race. That finding was only one of his many controversial ones that emerged from the reactivation of *Swann*.

Swann Reactivated

Ironically, given that the magnet program had been largely designed to mollify white opposition to desegregation, it was CMS' use of racial guidelines in admission to the magnets that triggered the reopening of *Swann*. In initiating the litigation, William Capacchione claimed that the use of these guidelines had kept his daughter from gaining entrance to the elementary magnet school of her choice in violation of the 1964 Civil Rights Act and the Fourteenth Amendment. The filing of that lawsuit precipitated a range of legal activity, among which was the intervention of the NAACP Legal Defense and Educational Fund (LDF) and the law firm, now Ferguson Stein, which had represented Swann and other black families in the original litigation thirty years earlier. Arguing that the relief sought by Capacchione would, if granted, prevent CMS from complying with the court orders in *Swann*, Ferguson Stein and the LDF moved that *Swann* be restored to the active docket and that the Capacchione lawsuit be treated as part of *Swann*. That motion was granted, and two black parents with children enrolled in CMS joined the class of black plaintiffs represented by Ferguson Stein and the LDF in the litigation. Eventually joining Capacchione were six other white Mecklenburg parents.

The array of litigants reflected an ongoing theme in Charlotte's desegregation saga, the challenge posed by recently arrived whites living in outlying areas. Six of the seven white plaintiffs were relatively new to Charlotte. Capacchione had moved from California in 1994 and would return there in 1998, six months before the actual opening of the trial triggered by his lawsuit. A second white plaintiff, Larry Gauvreau, who became the most prominent member of the group and won a seat on the school board in 2001, had moved to Charlotte in 1994. A third white plaintiff, a woman who would run unsuccessfully for the county commission in 2000, had moved to Charlotte in the mid-1990s, and a fourth had arrived in 1997. None of the white plaintiffs was a graduate of CMS. In contrast, both of the named black plaintiffs, Terry Belk and Dwayne Collins, had attended school in Charlotte-

Mecklenburg. Moreover, Belk was the only named plaintiff—either black or white—to have been born in Mecklenburg, and Collins had been raised in Charlotte, having arrived with his family while in elementary school.

The litigation also reflected another ongoing theme: the intimate relationship among the legal, political, and ideological aspects of desegregation. Both Collins and Belk were active in local politics, Collins as president of the local branch of the NAACP and Belk as its political action chair. Capacchione had been treasurer of CFANSS' political action committee. At the tumultuous school assignment hearings that gave rise to CFANSS, he had carried his daughter to the microphone where she said, "I go to McAlpine. I don't want to change schools."[28] McAlpine, an elementary school near the Capacchione residence, was the kind of school to which many white families in outlying areas eagerly sought assignment. Located in an economically well-off, predominantly white neighborhood, McAlpine had, in the 1996–97 school year, earned an exemplary rating on North Carolina's ABC accountability system and had a student population in which only 4 percent were black and only 3 percent were FRL eligible. McAlpine's attributes and Capacchione's political support for neighborhood schools notwithstanding, he sought Cristina's enrollment at a communications art magnet because of its emphasis on computers and public speaking. "My lawsuit is completely separate from CFANSS," Capacchione told a reporter. "We feel she [Cristina] was discriminated against because of the color of her skin."[29] Hoping "for all race-based admissions policies to be abolished," Capacchione secured legal representation with help from the Houston-based Campaign for a Color-Blind America, an organization whose goal was "to challenge race-based public policies and educate the public about the injustices of racial preferences."[30] The white plaintiffs' legal team would eventually include Atlanta-based A. Lee Parks, who had successfully challenged the racial guidelines used to draw Georgia's majority-minority congressional districts and had represented whites in many other legal battles against race-conscious public policy. Also on the white plaintiffs' legal team was a local attorney who was the mayor of Matthews and a director of the CFANSS PAC. A third member of the white plaintiffs' legal team was with the firm that, McMillan noted in *Martin*, had filed three lawsuits "seeking to nullify *Swann*."[31]

As important as the ongoing themes were, the litigation also gave ample evidence of thirty years of change in both Charlotte and the federal judiciary. Whereas in the battles thirty years earlier, CMS had vigorously opposed the black plaintiffs, in the late 1990s the two parties' positions substantially overlapped. The extent of this overlap became especially evident in March 1998 as the case broadened from one whose main issue was, Is CMS' magnet school admissions policy constitutional? to one whose key issue was, Is CMS unitary? Although, as the district court's decision in the reactivated litigation would note, "The term 'unitary status' has no fixed meaning,"[32] it is a crucial one in desegregation law. Its importance comes from the 1968 *Green* decision in which the Supreme Court said that school boards previously operating state-compelled dual systems had an "affirmative duty to take whatever steps might be necessary to convert to a unitary system in which racial discrimination would be eliminated root and branch."[33] By the time *Swann* was reactivated, desegregation law viewed a finding that a district was unitary as indicating that the vestiges of the state-mandated dual system had been eliminated to the extent practicable, and that the school district was thus entitled to be released from court supervision and the legal obligation to pursue desegregation remedies. Consequently, black plaintiffs have typically argued against such a finding, which is exactly what the black plaintiffs in the reactivated *Swann* litigation did. However, the very reasons that have typically led black plaintiffs to oppose districts being declared unitary have just as typically led school boards to seek such status. Nonetheless, sometimes districts have preferred not to be declared unitary to avoid challenges to desegregation polices of which the board approves and/or to avoid jeopardizing the funding of certain programs (e.g., magnets).

But it is highly unusual for a school board to vigorously oppose a declaration of unitary status in court. However, that is exactly what CMS' board of education indicated that it was prepared to do in April 1998. Although the vote was not unanimous, the 6–3 margin was a reaffirmation of CMS' longstanding commitment to desegregation. The three negative votes were cast by Lassiter, Kakadelis, and Puckett, all whites. But the fact that the board's other two whites, Woods and Molly Griffin, joined the four black members in voting to fight a declaration of unitary status indicated ongoing support among large numbers of whites for CMS' desegregation polices. As a result of CMS' decision to oppose a declaration of unitary status, whatever differences in legal positions, strategy, and tactics that might have existed between CMS and the black plaintiffs were relatively minor in comparison with those between these two parties and the white plaintiffs, who argued that CMS had removed these vestiges to the fullest extent practicable and was thus unitary.

The large overlap between the legal positions of CMS and the black plaintiffs was symbolized by CMS' legal representation. Earlier in her career, CMS' general counsel, Leslie Winner, had both clerked for Judge McMillan and had been a member of the Ferguson Stein firm before serving in the state legislature and eventually returning to Charlotte to work for CMS. Also included in CMS' legal team was the law firm where McMillan had been a partner before his appointment to the bench.[34] In the battles of the late 1960s and early 1970s, that firm had been one of the few to support McMillan in the face of CMS' intense resistance to his decision. That the school system's legal team now included both McMillan's old firm as well as one of his former clerks (who also was a former member of Ferguson Stein) was a dramatic symbol of the extent to which CMS' legal position, educational policy, and organizational culture had been transformed over thirty years.

As important as these changes in CMS were those in the federal judiciary. In the years since *Swann*, desegregation law had evolved considerably, with three Supreme Court decisions earlier in the 1990s—*Dowell, Freeman,* and *Jenkins*—making the pursuit of school desegregation more difficult.[35] Moreover, because Judge McMillan died in 1995, the reactivated litigation was assigned to Robert Potter, a conservative Republican who had been nominated to the federal bench in 1981 by Ronald Reagan at the suggestion of North Carolina Senator Jesse Helms. A Charlotte attorney, Potter had long been active in local politics and headed local campaigns for Helms in 1978 and for Reagan in 1976 and 1980.[36] Equally important, Potter, then an attorney in private practice, had been active in Charlotte's anti-busing movement in the 1960s, having drafted a petition addressed to the school board on this movement's behalf. On the day before the trial opened in April 1999, the *Observer* ran a picture of Potter, then a private citizen, addressing a school board meeting in May 1969. The article about the meeting described him as one of the speakers "unequivocally opposed to busing for racial balance."[37] And just as there was an overlap in the careers of the attorneys for CMS and the black plaintiffs, so too was there an overlap between Judge Potter and the attorneys for the white plaintiffs, one of them having served as his law clerk.

The trial began on April 19, 1999, almost thirty years to the day since McMillan had issued his momentous decision, and in the same courtroom where the original trial had taken place. More than two months of testimony included a total of fifty-four witnesses, twenty for the white plaintiffs, thirteen for the black ones, and twenty-one for CMS. The witnesses embodied long-standing themes and subtexts of CMS' history, and testimony often seemed a reprise of the parts that many of the people on the stand had played in Charlotte's long-running desegregation drama. Among the black plaintiffs' fact witnesses, for example, were former school board members Sarah Stevenson and Pam Mange, strong proponents of desegregation during their terms. Among CMS' many witnesses were UNCC Chancellor James Woodward and First Union CEO Ed Crutchfield, whose testimony about the importance of diversity in education and the workplace exemplified civic leaders' pursuit of tranquil race relations over the years. In contrast, the white plaintiffs' case featured testimony from past board member Sharon Bynum and current board members Lassiter, Kakadelis, and Puckett, for whom desegregation and the pursuit of diversity were less of a priority than they were for witnesses for the other two sides.

Also serving as fact witnesses for the white plaintiffs were John Murphy and the two chief aides who left CMS with him. Incensed by Eric Smith's remarks during his deposition about the "terribly unacceptable" and "deplorable" aspects of CMS when he (Smith) assumed the system's helm, Murphy testified about his administration's success in boosting black academic achievement and its efforts to do "all we could do to meet the mandate of the court" with respect to desegregation.[38] His two chief aides echoed Murphy's testimony in ways that resembled CMS senior staff's 1994 replies to the C25 that demographic change, not the magnet plan, was facilitating resegregation. Since one of the key issues in the trial was the extent to which demographic change rather than CMS policy was the cause of recent racial imbalance, the testimony of Murphy and his two aides provided the white plaintiffs with extremely important ammunition, upon which their post-trial brief and Potter's decision drew very heavily.

Just as long-standing debates in CMS' desegregation saga were recapitulated by the array of fact witnesses, so too was the national struggle over school desegregation embodied by the expert witnesses whose presence in Charlotte gave the reactivated *Swann* litigation the appearance of being another stop—albeit an especially crucial one—on the nationwide and long-running school desegregation litigation tour. Two of the three expert witnesses engaged by the black plaintiffs had testified on behalf of black plaintiffs in other recent cases,[39] and CMS' team of experts included several with extensive courtroom experience. The white plaintiffs' principal expert witness was David Armor, who had served as an expert witness in eleven other school desegregation cases in the 1990s.[40] On the stand, he admitted that whenever he had taken the stand in a contested unitary status hearing, he had always testified that he considered the district unitary.[41]

The Issues

Because the key issue in the case was whether CMS was unitary, much of the testimony in the trial related to the *Green* factors: those six areas of education which, the Supreme Court said in *Green*, should be evaluated to ascertain whether a school system was operating "just schools" rather than separate ones for blacks and whites.[42] The trial also included considerable testimony about what are generally known as the quasi-*Green* factors (e.g., quality of education and academic outcomes) that also have been subject to judicial scrutiny in unitary status hearings. Testimony and argumentation about both sets of factors hinged on two questions: To what extent are there racially identifiable differences? To the extent such differences exist, what are their causes and legal implications? CMS and the black plaintiffs generally emphasized the existence of these differences, attributed them to conditions over which CMS had control, and viewed them as vestiges of the dual system. These persistent differences showed, the two parties contended, that CMS was not yet unitary. The white plaintiffs generally minimized these differences, viewed them as arising from conditions over which the school board had little control, and claimed that they were not vestiges.

Of the issues covered in the case, the most important involved student assignment, physical facilities, faculties, and academic achievement. The last three can be discussed briefly before dealing in greater detail with the first, around which pivot many of the main themes of this book and the key legal issues that the court faced.

Academic Achievement

The testimony on academic achievement was the most technical with expert witnesses for both CMS and the white plaintiffs using multivariate statistical analyses to address this topic. Legal wrangles over the admissibility of data and reports further complicated the already knotty methodological and substantive issues. Importantly, no party disputed the existence of a gap between black and white achievement. Testimony thus focused on questions such as: What were the gap's causes? What was the legal significance of the gap and its causes? How did the gap in CMS compare with that nationally and statewide? In addressing these questions, David Armor, testifying for the white plaintiffs, presented evidence attributing the black/white achievement gap to differences in family background, especially socioeconomic status, rather than race per se or the effects of what was taking place in CMS schools. He also presented data showing no relationship between the test scores of black students and the racial composition of the schools they attended.

In contrast, the analyses of CMS' expert witnesses—especially William Trent and Roslyn Arlin Mickelson—indicated that black/white differences remained even when socioeconomic status and poverty were taken into account and, moreover, that the racial composition of schools affected academic outcomes. Even if family background were taken into account, Mickelson testified, a negative relationship existed between academic outcomes for black high schools seniors and the amount of time that they had spent in racially identifiable black (RIB) elementary schools and secondary tracks. The diametrically opposed conclusions of the two sets of expert witnesses stemmed from technical, but crucial, differences in samples, variable definitions, and statistical techniques, with Armor's methodology being especially flawed in several ways.[43]

Faculties

One of the *Green* factors being the racial composition of faculties, many witnesses addressed this issue, with the main questions being: What is the appropriate criterion for ascertaining whether a faculty is racially imbalanced?

To what extent do CMS' schools have racially imbalanced faculties? To the extent faculties are racially imbalanced, what are the causes, trends, legal significance, and educational significance of this racial imbalance?

In general, CMS and the black plaintiffs called attention to the growing racial imbalance of CMS' faculties as well as the fact that schools with racially imbalanced student populations also had racially imbalanced faculties. Noting the sharp increase in faculty racial imbalance earlier in the decade, these two parties attributed the jump to CMS' move toward site-based management. The white plaintiffs countered by arguing that the other two parties' criteria of faculty racial balance were too narrow, and that whatever racial imbalance existed resulted from a combination of factors over which CMS had little control (e.g., a shortage of teachers, especially black ones; teachers' preferences to work at schools near their homes; and residential segregation).

Testimony also dealt with disparities in teacher credentials and experience. The black plaintiffs and CMS presented evidence that, generally speaking, RIB schools had faculties with greater turnover, less experience, and fewer advanced degrees than other schools. Moreover, these disparities between the RIB schools and others, especially racially identifiable white ones, had increased in recent years. The white plaintiffs countered that whatever disparities existed were too small to be educationally relevant.

Physical Facilities and Resources

CMS and the black plaintiffs claimed that RIB schools were physically inferior to other schools. In some cases this inferiority was structural (e.g., leaky roofs, malfunctioning toilets), and in others it involved inadequate educational resources such as library books and wiring for computer equipment. The white plaintiffs presented a very different picture, minimizing the disparities among schools and claiming that any disparities were more closely associated with the age of schools than with their racial composition. They also argued that CMS' ability to address these physical disparities had been limited by insufficient funding from the county and the failure to pass the May 1995 bond referendum.

Student Assignment

Just as pupil assignment is the most salient aspect of lay discussion about desegregation, so too was it the pivot of the court case. As Judge Potter's opinion—quoting from the Supreme Court in *Freeman*—would say, "The 'critical beginning point' and 'fundamental' inquiry of a unitary status determination is the degree of racial imbalance in student assignment."[44] At issue was a series of legal questions, with many questions having political counterparts discussed throughout this book: What standard is used to define racial balance? What have been the trends in racial balance since the court's original ruling in *Swann?* To what can these trends be attributed? What is the legal significance of these trends?

What standard is used to define racial imbalance? This question had two aspects: (1) In pursuing racial balance, was CMS obliged by McMillan's orders to place a floor as well as a ceiling on black enrollment? (2) What was the numerical value of this ceiling (and floor)? In general, CMS and the black plaintiffs read the earlier orders and opinions as requiring CMS to place a floor as well as a ceiling on black enrollment, while the white plaintiffs did not. The latter also read these orders as allowing a looser definition of racial balance than did the other two parties.

Changes in racial imbalance: Again, this issue also had two aspects. The first involved system-wide trends in racial balance, a point about which there was perhaps less dispute than on any of the trial's major issues: system-wide there had been a decrease in desegregation, no matter what standard was used, and no matter how it was measured.[45] Moreover, the expert reports for all sides generally showed that racial balance system-wide had decreased since the implementation of the magnet plan.[46]

The second aspect of this issue involved trends in the racial balance of individual schools. In his report to the court, David Armor traced the history of individual schools over the previous thirty years and found large changes during this time in their racial composition. He said that of the sixteen schools that McMillan had declared "illegally segregated" in his 1969 order and that were still operating, thirteen were currently racially balanced and had been so for most of the past thirty years.[47] Conversely, Armor claimed, most of the schools whose black enrollment currently exceeded court mandates were, at the time of McMillan's order, historically white schools. Although opposing attorneys chipped away at the manner in which Armor had classified some of these schools, there is little question that their racial composition had indeed changed dramatically over thirty years. However, there was much greater dispute over the causes of these changes in individual schools as well as of system-wide trends in racial balance.

Causes of changes in racial imbalance: If the most important aspect of a unitary status determination is an investigation of racial imbalance in pupil assignment, then the most crucial aspect of such an investigation involves determining the causes of imbalance. The white plaintiffs claimed that changes in schools' racial composition arose from demographic changes (e.g., the racial composition of neighborhoods and development of outlying areas) over which CMS had no control and thus could not be vestiges of the dual system. For example, writing about Allenbrook, Thomasboro, and Westerly Hills, three schools on the westside whose black enrollment exceeded the ceiling set by the 1980 court order, Armor said: "These formerly white schools were balanced for periods ranging from 20 to 25 years. They are located in the Western area of the county which has experienced considerable demographic change in the past 25 years, characterized by a decrease in the white and an increase in the black school-age populations. They have exceeded the variance in recent years because of these demographic changes in the attendance zones."[48]

In contrast, Fred Shelley, the demographer who provided expert testimony for the black plaintiffs, claimed that CMS' decisions about pupil assignment and attendance zones did more to explain the three schools' racial composition than changes in housing patterns. He compared the time period in which these three schools' racial balance changed with the time period in which nearby neighborhoods changed and noted, "Increases in the black percentages of the schools did not occur at the same time as the neighborhoods themselves,"[49] the changes in racial composition of the schools being greatest at a time when housing patterns were changing relatively slowly. Focusing on Allenbrook, he noted that the school's attendance area included a black satellite, absent which the school would be racially balanced. Moreover, he viewed the school's location as "consistent with the District's definition of a 'stand-alone' or 'mid-point' school, which with appropriate attendance boundary adjustment should be able to reflect the racial composition of the district as a whole."[50]

The difference over the causes of Allenbrook's racial composition was just one variation on the recurrent theme of demographic change versus school board policy as the cause of racial imbalance both system-wide and at individual schools. How, the black plaintiffs and CMS asked, could demographic change explain the increase in racial imbalance over the past thirty years when even the evidence presented by white plaintiffs' expert witnesses showed that residential segregation had *declined* during this period? The declining residential segregation, replied the white plaintiffs, was attributable to a suburbanization of blacks similar to the dispersal of the white population, but residential segregation was still high. Moreover, the white plaintiffs continued, with most of Mecklenburg's rapid growth occurring in outlying areas that remained overwhelmingly white, it was impossible to achieve racial balance without longer bus rides for more students in Charlotte's increasingly congested traffic. But a key reason, countered the other two parties, such long bus rides might be necessary was that almost all of the twenty-seven schools that had opened in the previous twenty years were located in predominantly white, frequently outlying areas. In choosing those sites, CMS and the black plaintiffs emphasized, the school system had ignored its own stated polices, the recommendations of planners, McMillan's orders, and the fact that African American students accounted for approximately 55 percent of the increase in CMS' total enrollment during these twenty years. Moreover, the black plaintiffs and CMS pointed to data on residential building permits and the testimony of a developer to argue that the building of new schools was not merely a response to development; such construction contributed to development.[51] For all of these reasons, these two parties argued, CMS policy, not demographic change, was primarily responsible for the growth in racial imbalance.

Legal significance of current racial imbalance: Because current racial imbalance arose from demographic change over which the school system had scant influence, argued the white plaintiffs, this imbalance could hardly be a vestige of the dual system that existed more than thirty years ago. Moreover, they continued, the fact that few, if any, of CMS' schools were racially imbalanced during much of the 1970s and early 1980s meant that, with respect to pupil assignment, the district had, in fact, achieved unitary status during those years.[52]

Not so, said the black plaintiffs and CMS, drawing on the 1979 decision by McMillan in the *Martin* case, mentioned in chapter 3. Although CMS had, by that time, achieved very high levels of racial balance—much higher than they would be in 1999—McMillan indicated in *Martin* that CMS had failed to fully comply with the guidelines for obtaining unitary status that he had earlier laid down. Among CMS' failures that McMillan noted were: "The construction, location, and closing of school buildings continue to promote segregation," "the Board's continued failure to monitor and control the many thousands of yearly pupil transfers tends to promote and permit resegregation," and "black children and their families continue to bear discriminatory burdens of desegregation."[53] These were the same kinds of problems, argued CMS and the black plaintiffs, that existed in 1999, i.e., almost all new schools were in predominantly white, outlying areas; transfers associated with the magnet school program exacerbated racial imbalance in non-magnets; and the vast majority of satellite areas were in black neighborhoods.[54] The fact that McMillan had pointed in 1979 to the same kinds of problems that would exist twenty years later showed, CMS and the black plaintiffs continued, that 1999's problems were vestiges of the dual system. Thus, the overriding issue, in these parties' views, was not CMS' inability to deal with demographic change but its continuing failure to develop and implement policies to satisfy long-standing court orders. This continuing failure notwithstanding, argued CMS, it was now prepared to take practicable steps—including the implementation of a controlled choice pupil assignment plan—that would allow it to obtain unitary status within several years if the court gave it that time.[55]

The Decision

In a decision announced in September 1999, Potter credited the testimony of the white plaintiffs' witnesses on almost all issues. On academic achievement, he found that most of the black/white gap was explained by socioeconomic factors. Dismissing the testimony of CMS' witnesses as, to one degree or another, methodologically flawed, conceptually inadequate, biased, and/or legally irrelevant, Potter also said that whatever portion of the gap "may or may not be explained by socioeconomics, the Court cannot find that this is related to any discriminatory practice by CMS and cannot identify a cause for which the Court can order a realistic and practical injunction." Therefore, "the Court will not delay the finding of unitary status due to racial disparities in student achievement."[56]

On teacher assignment, he called attention to the much greater degree of segregation that existed prior to McMillan's ruling than in 1999. Adopting the standard of faculty racial balance proposed by the white plaintiffs, he concluded that "CMS undoubtedly has achieved the type of balance one would find in a desegregated system," and that the remaining imbalance was too small to be indicative of segregation and also was "generally attributable to factors outside CMS' control, such as the shortage of teachers and the impact of residential demographics."[57] He also downplayed CMS' and the black plaintiffs' claims that RIB schools had less qualified faculty than others, saying, "The disparities in teacher competence are hard to define and difficult to measure, there are mitigating factors with the alleged disparities, there are practical problems in achieving and maintaining better results."[58] On facilities, Potter said that much of the testimony about the disparities in resources and facilities by witnesses for CMS and the black plaintiffs was anecdotal and/or methodologically flawed. Moreover, he said that while inequities certainly existed, they were primarily attributable to the diverse ages of CMS facilities and shortages of funds rather than to racial composition or intentional discrimination.[59]

The longest part of the decision dealt with pupil assignment. Noting that the effect of previous court orders had left the standard for measuring racial imbalance "somewhat hazy" and "not a model of clarity," he adopted the +/- 15 percent variance for the court's definition of racial balance that CMS had often used for policy purposes.[60] Insofar as this standard provided a floor on black enrollment, it constituted one of the few points on which he agreed with CMS and the black plaintiffs. However, he disagreed with those parties on the legal consequences of applying this standard by emphasizing how little of the racial imbalance of the dual system could be observed thirty years after McMillan's original order. During this period, CMS had "maintained a high level of desegregation" and "relatively few schools in the system have long histories of racial imbalance."[61] "There can be no doubt," he concluded, "that demography and geography have played the largest role in causing imbalance."[62] On other issues, Potter took pains to explain—sometimes quite specifically and scathingly—why he rejected the testimony of the expert witnesses produced by CMS and the black plaintiffs. Here, however, on probably the single most important issue in the trial—the relative importance of demographic change as opposed to CMS' policy in explaining student racial imbalance—Potter made no effort to refute the testimony of either the black plaintiffs' or CMS' demographers. The latter was mentioned only once in passing, and the former was the only expert witness to testify at the trial whose testimony was never cited in Potter's decision.

Overall, Potter found that CMS has "eliminated, to the extent practicable, the vestiges of past discrimination."[63] He thus declared that CMS "has achieved unitary status in all respects" and vacated all prior injunctive orders from *Swann*.[64] In addition, he took several other actions. He issued an injunction prohibiting CMS from taking race into account in "assigning children to schools or allocating educational opportunities and benefits."[65] He also noted that, contrary to the advice of its own consultant, CMS had not secured court approval for replacing the mandatory busing plan with a magnet plan, and thus found that the use of racial guidelines in magnet school admissions exceeded the school system's authority under the then-existing *Swann* orders. In light of that finding, he held CMS liable for $1 in nominal damages, an aspect of the ruling that CMS and the black plaintiffs found especially galling because, they claimed, no prevailing African American plaintiff in any school desegregation case had ever been awarded any financial damages, whether nominal or actual. In contrast, the white plaintiffs were jubilant with the entire decision, and Capacchione, interviewed by telephone from his home in California, declared that he would ask every member of the school board to sign the dollar bill that he had been awarded.[66]

In addition to suffering a legal defeat inside the courtroom, CMS suffered political defeats outside it. The fight against a declaration of unitary status required CMS' attorneys to stress the school system's shortcomings in fulfilling McMillan's orders and the goals of desegregation. As one of CMS' attorneys remarked while preparing a member of CMS' senior staff to testify, "Remember, if it's bad, it's good." In court, attorneys for the white plaintiffs frequently commented upon CMS' reluctance to acknowledge any success, and critics called the school system's emphasis on its own failures a "doofus defense," a term that quickly caught on in the court of public opinion.

At least as important as the difficulties CMS' defense posed for its image among the general public were the morale problems it created for the school system's employees. The much-publicized testimony on the lack of resources in predominantly black schools and the shortcomings in black academic achievement demoralized and angered many CMS personnel, who felt that their hard work was being ignored and dismissed. As one teacher said in a letter to the *Observer* about associate superintendent Susan Purser's testimony that black children were not being taught in Charlotte, "Maybe Dr. Purser should get out of her office in the Education Center and come see where the real work takes place and where the total child is being taught by excellent teachers who don't look at the color of a child's face."[67] Similar sentiment reached into the Education Center itself, where a senior staffer remarked that an expert witness's report documenting CMS' shortcomings in educating black students "trashed everything we've been doing here for years."

The outcome of the trial thus appeared to be a political and legal disaster for CMS. However, within a few weeks, Charlotteans would show considerable support for the leadership of the school board under whose auspices the trial had been conducted. That support was just one of the many developments that occurred in the tumultuous year following Potter's decision.

Chapter 7

The Charlotte-Mecklenburg Compromise?

What we have here is a ruling that has resulted from 30 years of hostility and vengeance of a man [Judge Potter] and people who believe that they have lost power and influence over time . . . This is about a trend in this country that blossomed in the Reagan era, that rendered open season on any civil rights gains . . . This case is deeper in its intent and scope than simply where children will attend school in Charlotte.

—School board member Wilhelmenia Rembert, making a motion that CMS appeal Judge Robert Potter's ruling in the reactivated *Swann* case.[1]

I don't think it matters.

—CMS Superintendent Eric Smith, responding to an interviewer's question about whether concentrating disadvantaged students in inner-city schools makes it harder to meet their needs.[2]

The business community supports (Superintendent) Eric Smith. It does not have the same level of confidence in the board.

—Stan Campbell, head of the Alliance for a Better Charlotte and of the A Better Charlotte Political Committee, in the aftermath of the school board's vote to postpone implementation of a choice pupil assignment plan.[3]

Given Potter's conservative background and anti-busing activities thirty years earlier, his decision in the reactivated *Swann* case was not unexpected. Nonetheless, the ruling plunged CMS into political turbulence, just as McMillan's decision had thirty years earlier. However, in the late 1990s, this turbulence played out very differently than it had in the 1970s. Whereas McMillan's decision required CMS to desegregate, Potter's decision required CMS to adopt pupil assignment policies that could easily occasion massive resegregation. In the 1970s, it was only *after* the Supreme Court affirmed Judge McMillan that the school board and community finally came together around a pupil assignment plan consistent with his order. However, in the late 1990s, the Supreme Court's action merely gave the green light to a plan consistent with Potter's order that had already been adopted by an 8–1 vote of the board.

This is not to say that adoption came easily; that 8–1 vote occurred almost two years after Potter's order, during which CMS was buffeted by conflicting court rulings and a deeply divided school board and community. Much of these divisions hinged on the fact that, with Potter's decision likely to occasion considerable resegregation, Charlotteans—especially black school board members and their allies and supporters—had to confront as squarely as the community ever had the question, To what extent is desegregation a more effective approach—educationally, politically, and/or legally—than approaches that provide extra and compensatory resources to schools with large numbers of children of color, especially from low-income families?

The bargain—either implicit or explicit—in which African Americans have been offered additional resources for segregated schools in exchange for decreasing the pursuit of desegregation has been made in many other districts at many other times.[4] Given the frequency with which Charlotte is compared to Atlanta, it is worth noting that a notable and much-studied example of such a bargain is what has often been called the Atlanta Compromise. In that 1973 arrangement, African Americans accepted large-scale segregation in Atlanta's public schools in exchange for political and administrative control of the public school system and the presumed greater attention to the needs of black children that would accompany that control.[5]

During the very years that Atlanta was embarking on this compromise, Charlotte was taking a different approach to school desegregation. This approach was, of course, the mandatory busing plan that would lead to national praise and allow Charlotte to get much more mileage as "The City That Made It Work" than it could ever have gotten from being merely another city that was too busy to hate, Atlanta's famous boast. As a result, education was one rare area where, throughout the 1970s and 1980s, even the most ardent Charlotte chauvinist never felt any desire to catch up with the big brother 250 miles down I-85.

But in 1999, Potter's ruling triggered growing pressure on desegregation proponents to accept what—in keeping with the tradition of drawing comparisons between the two areas—might be called the Charlotte-Mecklenburg Compromise: additional resources for predominantly black schools in exchange for the acceptance of increasing resegregation. Because CMS had been widely viewed as one of the major successes in school desegregation history, the prospect of such a compromise had obvious national implications, even if CMS' countywide reach combined with Mecklenburg's demographics and relatively large geographic area decreased the likelihood that Charlotte's schools would become as intensely segregated as many other urban school systems. Thus, how CMS dealt with the political as well as the legal pressure to abandon its long-standing commitment to desegregation is this chapter's major theme. To develop this theme, I discuss the legal, pupil assignment, electoral, and funding battles that characterized education politics in Charlotte from 1999 to 2002. I also consider some data on resource allocation to provide a preliminary discussion on the prospects of the Charlotte-Mecklenburg Compromise.

TO APPEAL OR NOT?

While counsel for the black plaintiffs immediately announced that they would appeal Potter's decision to the Fourth Circuit Court of Appeals, there was considerably more doubt about the school board's intentions, with the *Observer* initially noting that "indications are that the school board won't [appeal], unless there's a dispute over legal costs."[6] A CMS press release issued the day after Potter's decision indicated no dissatisfaction with the ruling, instead calling it "a thorough consideration of evidence from all three parties in the case." The release concluded with a statement from school board chair Griffin: "Just as it did 30 years ago, it's time for the community to come together for all children. There are those in the community proclaiming victory, but the only winners must be children."[7]

An even earlier indication that CMS would not appeal was a Unity Rally that had taken place in the ten weeks between the trial's close and the judge's decision. The rally was billed as an event that would unite the community in support of public education, whatever the outcome of the court case. It resulted from more than a month of meetings among political and corporate leaders who feared that the trial was hurting both Charlotte and its image by furthering doubts about the quality of education that CMS provided and by intensifying uncertainty about pupil assignment and magnet school admissions. "The business community is anxious to get on with this business of education," said Allen Tate, chair of the Charlotte Chamber, and one of the main organizers of the rally, "We know we've got to move on."[8]

Attending the rally in addition to Tate were various notables, including the chair of the county commission, the mayor of Charlotte, members of the school board, and many other elected officials and prominent business executives. The rally's highlight was a statement by school board chair Griffin that had been prepared in meetings with a representative of the Chamber of Commerce and other rally organizers. Although this statement reaffirmed CMS' commitment to diversity "to the extent permitted by law," it also said, "Busing, as we know it today, and the existence of inadequate school facilities and resources will end."[9] The latter statement—typically shortened to "busing as we know it will end"—attracted widespread attention. Griffin's statement alarmed traditional proponents of such policies and led opponents to expect that CMS would not appeal an unfavorable verdict as long as the disparities in resources and facilities between predominantly black and white schools were eliminated. As Bill James, the county commission's most conservative member and a prominent supporter of neighborhood schools, remarked to a reporter, "You can't have unity if they're appealing . . . Even though it was unstated, clearly I think the intent of all this unity talk is that there will not be any appeal, and we will return to allowing people to return to schools closer to home."[10]

This commissioner's public statements were echoed in the thoughts of many other local leaders. They believed that in several private meetings Griffin had addressed the business elite's desire to move beyond the disruptiveness of the litigation by agreeing that, in the likely event that Potter ruled against CMS, he would not advocate an appeal. In return, Charlotte's civic leaders and business elite would back an ambitious construction and renovation program in inner-city schools as well as provide support in the upcoming election, or at least remain benevolently neutral. In the view of Stan Campbell, the deal that Griffin "cut was that (business leaders) support him for reelection, and he wouldn't appeal. He took the money and then appealed. Then the money dried up."[11] When claims of the alleged deal were made public several months after the meetings occurred, Griffin emphatically denied that there was one and instead urged critics to try to understand the educationally disastrous implications of Potter's decision.[12] As head of both the Alliance for a Better Charlotte and A Better Charlotte Political Committee,[13] Campbell may have been privy to considerable information about the business elite's political sympathies and views, but the campaign finance reports on file with the Board of Elections provide relatively little evidence for his claim that business elite donations to Griffin's campaign "dried up" after the appeal.[14]

Tactical considerations associated with this election also seemed to militate against an appeal. In the November 1999 school board election, all three at-large seats were at stake, two of which were held by African Americans, Rembert and Griffin. Most local pundits and educational activists thought that if Griffin and Rembert voted for an appeal, their support among whites would drop substantially, thus lowering their chances of defeating the challengers advocating neighborhood schools, one of whom, Larry Gauvreau, was a plaintiff in the case.

In part because of concern that an appeal would jeopardize Griffin's and Rembert's reelection chances, there was considerable doubt about the wisdom of an appeal among many desegregation proponents such as the (predominantly white) memberships of the League of Women Voters and the Swann Fellowship, an organization based in Charlotte's faith community and formed in 1997 to bear witness, largely through educational efforts, to the value of diversity in public education. In the dark clouds of Potter's ruling, many members of these organizations found a glimmer of a silver lining in that the decision did not require the school board to obtain court approval for a new pupil assignment plan but instead gave the board complete leeway to develop one, as long as it was consistent with his ruling. Indicative of this attitude was a statement by the Swann Fellowship's executive director, "It could have been far worse. What this ruling does is give the community an opportunity to forge the new direction of the school system."[15]

Among African Americans there was, from the moment the ruling was issued, more sentiment for an appeal by CMS, if only because the black plaintiffs had indicated that they would appeal Potter's decision shortly after it was announced. This initial sentiment among black Charlotteans snowballed over the next four weeks. This snowball carried both white liberals and a majority of the school board along with it, despite strong counterpressure on the latter from the business elite, many of whose members felt that an appeal, especially of the declaration of unitary status, would distract attention and resources away from what they viewed as more important educational issues.

Contributing to this increasing sentiment for an appeal was the immense prestige among African Americans of the Ferguson Stein law firm. As one of the black school board members remarked after discussing the case with members of that firm, as well as with school board attorneys, "We [CMS] have our own attorneys, but the best civil rights lawyer in town is James Ferguson." Also playing a decisive role in the snowballing of sentiment for an appeal was the recently formed Inter-Faith Committee on Fairness in Public Education, led by clergy at some of Charlotte's largest black churches, several of whom had also met with members of Ferguson Stein. This committee's efforts culminated with a Faith Community Rally on Public Education. Originally and inadvertently planned for the day after the school board was scheduled to vote on whether to appeal Potter's ruling, the rally's date was changed with only a few days' notice for the Sunday evening prior to the vote. With many of the city's black clergy announcing the rescheduled rally at services earlier that Sunday, over 1,500 people, approximately 90 percent of whom were black, packed the sanctuary of one of the city's largest black churches with a spirit and an enthusiasm for appealing Potter's order reminiscent of the mass rallies of the civil rights era thirty years earlier.[16] That spirit was more than appropriate, given the theme of the rally, exemplified in the remarks of one of its organizers, Reverend Casey Kimbrough: "We will not go back to a segregated system. There is a storm in Charlotte, and there can be no peace without justice."[17]

The rally's main speaker was James Ferguson, whose discussion of the far-ranging legal implications of Potter's ruling concluded with a message from Darius Swann. Among the other speakers were representatives of the NAACP, the Black Political Caucus, 100 Black Men, the Swann Fellowship, and HELP, an acronym for Helping Empower Local People, the Charlotte affiliate of the Industrial Areas Foundation. Each of these last two speakers was especially important. The presence of the white speaker from the Swann Fellowship indicated that Charlotte's largest predominantly white, racially liberal organization concerned with education had been won to the necessity of the appeal. The presence of the HELP speaker indicated that Charlotte's largest interracial community organizing effort—and one that had national links—also supported the appeal.

Attending the rally were most of Charlotte's African American elected officials, including all four black school board members. Their attendance presaged the results of the vote at a packed, largely with African Americans, school board meeting three days later. Joined by Louise Woods, the four black board members voted to appeal the declaration of unitary status, and the motion to do so carried by 5–4. The same margin carried a motion to seek a stay of Potter's order. The board also voted on whether to appeal three other issues: the injunction against considering race in pupil assignment or the allocation of any educational benefit, the constitutionality of the magnet lottery, and the white plaintiffs' attorney fees. All three of these motions received six Yes votes, the sixth vote coming from Molly Griffin. The three members—Lassiter, Puckett, and Kakadelis—who had earlier opposed CMS' fighting a declaration of unitary status either voted against appealing any aspects of Potter's ruling or, on the question of attorney fees, abstained because of a possible conflict of interest.

From a political perspective, the impassioned discussion about the vote was almost as important as the vote itself. In making the motion to appeal Potter's ruling, Rembert expressed that passion:

> What we have here is a ruling that has resulted from 30 years of hostility and vengeance of a man [Potter] and people who believe they have lost power and influence over time. They want to be back in the days when no matter how ignorant they were and still are, they believe they deserve preferential treatment over those who do not look as they do. This is about a trend in this country that blossomed in the Reagan era, that rendered open season on any civil

rights gains, any affirmative action gains, and any political gains, that put whites and blacks in the country closer to balance than at any other time in history. This case is deeper in its intent and scope than simply where children will attend school in Charlotte.

It is about race. It is about a growing intolerance for poor people and people of color. It is about power. It is about who had it, who thinks they have lost it, and who is trying like "all get out" to get it back! This case never was about the education of *all* children. But it may have been about the education of some suburban white children, whose parents didn't want them educated in the company of black children in general and poor black children in particular . . .

To effectively educate our children for a rapidly changing diverse society, why in God's name do we seek to segregate them by race or socioeconomic status? . . .

If our children master calculus, Latin, physics and world literature, and do not learn how to get along with others like and different from themselves, we will have failed to effectively educate them.[18]

Similar sentiments animated many aspects of the debate in the election campaign.

THE 1999 SCHOOL BOARD ELECTION

The 1999 school board election was historic in at least two ways. First, it was the first election since the change in representation earlier in the decade when the three at-large seats, and only the three-at-large seats, were at stake. Second, with the election coming two months after Potter's ruling, desegregation was an extremely salient issue, more so than in any election since the early 1970s.[19] In 1970, it will be recalled, challengers prominent in the anti-busing movement rode a wave of white opposition to McMillan's orders, capturing the three seats that were at stake and defeating, in the process, the school board's first black member, Coleman Kerry. In 1999, three seats also were at stake, two of which were held by African Americans: Chairman Arthur Griffin and Wilhelmenia Rembert. However, 1999 saw a strikingly different outcome. Both Griffin and Rembert survived strong and well-organized challenges from white advocates of neighborhood schools who had pledged to overturn CMS' vote to appeal Potter's ruling. Indeed, Griffin's and Rembert's victories marked the first time in the twentieth century that African Americans were elected to a majority of the at-large seats on any governing body in Mecklenburg County.

In some ways, the difference between the outcomes of the two elections indicates that Mecklenburg was more racially liberal in 1999 than it was in 1970. In 1970, it was virtually unthinkable that African Americans would be elected to two of three at-large seats in any county or city election. However, the arithmetic of voting registration also is extremely relevant. In 1999, blacks constituted a much larger percentage of the electorate than they did in 1970s. That jump is probably sufficient to explain the difference between the two outcomes, even if white voting behavior remained the same.[20]

If comparisons with 1970 are set aside, the 1999 election supports several interpretations. Most importantly, Griffin's and Rembert's triumph indicates that their challengers' call for CMS to abandon the appeal failed to mobilize as many voters as neighborhood school advocates had hoped. Because both Griffin and Rembert ran with strong support from the Democratic Party and Democratic candidates for city council also did well, the victories of all of these candidates can be attributed to a strong Democratic tide, buoyed in turn by high African American turnout. However, the third winner in the school board race was incumbent Vice Chair John Lassiter. Insofar as Lassiter was a Republican, had voted against appealing Potter's decision, and received more votes than either Griffin or Rembert, the election can be interpreted as support for the status quo. The election also might be interpreted as a testament to the time-honored advantages of incumbency, since in addition to winning, the three incumbents also raised more money than any of their challengers. Finally, because Griffin, Lassiter, and Rembert were all endorsed by the *Observer*, the election also can be viewed as evidence of the electoral clout of a city's daily newspaper in an election in which candidates' party affiliations do not appear on the ballot despite their close associations with party organizations. All of these interpretations likely have considerable merit, as a detailed discussion of the election indicates.

The Campaign Unfolds

Five candidates initially challenged the incumbents: Pam Mange, the white who had represented the district in the northern part of the county from 1995 to 1997; Larry Gauvreau, a white plaintiff in the reactivated *Swann* litigation; Paul Haisley, a white accountant who had served on several CMS task forces and was a strong proponent of neighborhood schools; Ken England, a white retired education administrator; and Charles Reese, a black pastor. A newcomer to local politics and a recent arrival in Charlotte, Reese raised virtually no money, waged a low-key campaign, and was never a major factor in the race. England dropped out early, indicating the involvement of partisan considerations in the nominally non-partisan contests. Noting that he was a Republican, the *Observer* indicated that the chair of the county Republican Party said that because the four Republicans—England, Gauvreau, Haisley, and Lassiter—"shared the same general beliefs, it didn't make sense for them to compete against each other for only three seats."[21]

Among many of Griffin's and Rembert's supporters, there also was concern about competition from candidates with the same general beliefs. The worry was not about each other—in fact, the two campaigns worked closely together—but about Pam Mange. The concern was that if Mange did well among black voters, her likely lead over Griffin and Rembert among white voters would allow her to beat them countywide. Consequently, the Black Political Caucus did not endorse Mange, even though her positions were quite similar to Griffin's and Rembert's, and she had testified for the black plaintiffs at the recently concluded trial. Nor did the Democratic Party endorse her. Rather, both organizations called upon voters to double shot (i.e., to vote only for Griffin and Rembert, and not vote for a third candidate). In the 1960s, 1970s, and 1980s, black organizations had frequently urged similar tactics, but more recently that approach had been dropped in favor of one that endorsed a full slate of candidates, both black and white. Thus, for example, in the 1995 school board election, the Black Political Caucus had endorsed the white Susan Burgess as well as two black candidates for the three at-large seats for the school board. And, more recently, in the 1998 county commission race, the caucus had endorsed two white Democrats along with a black one for the three seats at stake in that election. That neither the Black Political Caucus nor Democratic Party endorsed the ideologically and politically congenial Mange indicated how much importance both organizations attached to the candidacies of Griffin and Rembert. Noting that the court case had "hit a hot button with people," Eric Douglas, chair of the Black Political Caucus, said, "The judge put a lot of power in the hands of the school board, and it is imperative that we have the right people on the board."[22]

Facilitating black and Democratic effort to mobilize voters was the momentum resulting from the 1998 county commission election in which the so-called Gang of Five had been swept from office, as chapter 2 indicated. Indeed, many of the battle lines in the 1999 school board race resembled those a year earlier. The Five's last remaining member on the county commission, Bill James, urged voters to support Haisley, Gauvreau, and Lassiter in a letter to the *Observer.*[23] In that same forum, Eric Douglas invoked pejorative memories of the Five, then added, "these same forces have identified themselves with a slate of school board candidates. Charlotte, do you want these individuals in charge of 101,000 innocent kids?"[24] Moreover, the races for city council provided additional motivation to mobilize black and Democratic voters because divisions within the Republican Party, strong Democratic candidates, and changes in district boundaries raised Democratic hopes—correctly, as it turned out—that their party could regain a majority on the city council.[25]

Griffin and Rembert also received endorsements from the *Observer*, whose editorial noted that "our integrated school system has helped unite this community; resegregation threatens to divide it."[26] The third endorsement went to Lassiter, accompanied by praise for his analytic ability, composure, and commitment to meeting the needs of inner-city children. Noting that Lassiter had voted against appealing Potter's ruling, the *Observer* opined that he also would represent the neighborhood school viewpoint.

Business Elite (In)activity

Charlotte's business elite shared the *Observer's* enthusiasm for Lassiter. He raised almost $35,000, $11,000 more than in 1995, and he listed contributions from numerous members of the business elite as well as its PACs.[27] Insofar as the three Republicans ran with explicit party support and agreed on many key issues—especially that CMS was unitary and should not have appealed Potter's decision—one might expect that Gauvreau and Haisley would have gotten the same kind of funding that Lassiter received. But that was not the case; financial support for Lassiter did not translate into financial support for Gauvreau and Haisley, who succeeded in raising only $26,000 and $16,000, respectively.[28] In contrast, Griffin raised almost $36,000 and Rembert received $50,000, as the two black incumbents benefited from contributions from Democratic Party-related organizations, many African Americans, and, especially in Rembert's case, a large number of professionals, academics, and businesspeople, white as well as black.[29]

More notable, however, than the money that was given was the money that was not given. As noted earlier, the three most pivotal elections in recent CMS history had seen concerted political intervention by the business elite. In 1972, following the Supreme Court's affirmation of McMillan, the so-called slate-makers sought through judicious campaign contributions to elect candidates who could live with court-ordered busing and end the political turmoil engulfing CMS. That same election also saw one of Charlotte's most influential businessmen, C. D. Spangler Jr., successfully run for the school board. In 1988, through campaign contributions and the candidacy of another of Charlotte's most influential executives, Joe Martin, the business elite also sought to redirect education policy. Finally, the switch to a mixed system of representation in 1995 elicited an even more concerted, umbrella-type political intervention with the formation of the Alliance for Public Schools.

The 1999 election promised to be as important as the elections in 1972, 1988, and 1995. The capability for a concerted, umbrella-type intervention by the business elite very much existed in the form of A Better Charlotte (ABC) Political Committee. As chapter 2 noted, the ABC Political Committee was created as part of the business elite's effort to defeat the so-called Gang of Five in the 1998 county commission elections, but it remained quite active after the Five's ouster. In the first eleven months of 1999, the ABC Political Committee raised over $100,000, its first two contributions of the year coming from a Bank of America PAC and a First Union PAC, each of which donated $4,000. Many of Charlotte's leading business executives also made contributions. The ABC Political Committee subsequently endorsed candidates in both the mayoral and city council races and made donations to its endorsees. But the ABC Political Committee neither endorsed nor donated to any school board candidate despite the obvious importance of the election to the future of education in Charlotte.

The ABC Political Committee's abstention in the school board election partially reflected internal divisions within the business elite about the importance of desegregation and diversity in education, economic growth, and the quality of life. Political considerations also were important. Many members of the business elite thought, as indicated above, that Griffin had agreed not to appeal Potter's ruling in exchange for political support and business elite advocacy of compensatory resources for the segregated schools resulting from the ruling. By the time it became clear that Griffin and other black board members would support an appeal, only a month remained until the election, thus making effective political intervention difficult.

Framing these tactical considerations were broader strategic ones. Given the importance of Griffin's and Rembert's candidacies to African Americans, any obvious effort to defeat Griffin and Rembert by the ABC Political Committee—created and backed as it was by the most prominent members of the business elite—could easily jeopardize key aspects of the multifaceted relationship between it and black political leaders. Moreover, given the past year's extensive (by recent standards) black political mobilization, some members of the business elite worried that the defeat of Griffin and Rembert would trigger additional activity that would not necessarily be limited to organizing rallies at churches, packing school board meetings, and getting out the vote. Finally, a victory by Haisley and Gauvreau would likely strengthen the socially conservative wing of the Republican Party, a result that few in the business elite welcomed, given the recent donnybrook over public funding for the arts. Thus, despite Rembert's and Griffin's insistence on appealing Potter's decision, the ABC Political Committee did not endorse their opponents, or anyone for that matter.

As its endorsements indicate, the *Observer* saw the three incumbents as providing the best available package capable of getting CMS through the tumultuous times ahead. However, it was a package that the business elite had to take, so to speak, off the shelf. Both internal divisions and political considerations made it very difficult for the business elite to customize the package. That difficulty provides additional evidence of how, as chapter 5 indicates, the Charlotte experience confirms a central tenet of regime theory: while the business elite continues to play a unique and crucial role in many area of local politics, including education, it frequently lacks command and control capability.

The results of the election also furnish additional indication of the fluidity of Charlotte politics. Democrats captured control of the city council, and both Griffin and Rembert survived challengers who ran with the backing of the Republican Party. However, as the local chair of the Republican Party pointed out in seeking some consolation from its defeats, a Republican was elected mayor, and Republicans were the highest vote getters in both the school board and at-large city council races.[30] That fluidity was especially apparent as battles over desegregation continued to rock CMS.

PUPIL ASSIGNMENT: DÉJÀ VU ALL OVER AGAIN?

The Pretrial Prologue

Potter's order required CMS to have a race-neutral pupil assignment plan in place by the next academic year. Although the new plan would have to be very different from the one currently in effect, CMS did not have to start from scratch in preparing it. Rather, it drew heavily on a comprehensive planning document, *Achieving the CMS Vision: Equity and Student Success,* which had been developed prior to the trial as a way of showing the court that while CMS did not consider itself unitary, it was taking aggressive steps to achieve that status.

The plan's nine components covered many issues, but the sections dealing with instructional resources and student assignment attracted the most attention. The former noted the many, frequently racially correlated disparities among CMS' schools and then outlined a broad range of specific steps to remedy these gaps and bring all schools up to appropriate standards. *Achieving the CMS Vision* thus put an especially strong and official imprimatur on the need to address the inequities whose existence had become an increasingly salient part of local discourse in the past few years. While the cost of these steps—generally called the equity provisions of the plan—raised fiscal concerns, there was much less controversy about the need to take these steps than there was about the proposal for pupil assignment. Called the Family Choice Cluster Plan, the proposal set out a framework for a controlled choice plan with specifics to be developed later. The framework called for CMS to be divided into three to five clusters that would reflect the entire system's demographics. Families would choose from schools within their cluster, as well as from the magnet schools serving the cluster. The plan sought to allow students living "within a defined proximity zone" of a school to attend it.[31] In the first three years of the plan, "racial preference will be used to promote racial diversity, with a target that each school be within +/− 15 percent of the district average" for white and black students, but thereafter, "the district will use a lottery that is not based on race." Instead, to promote diversity, CMS would use a variety of methods, including intensive recruiting, incentives, and majority-to-minority transfers.[32]

The Family Choice Cluster Plan provoked considerable controversy. In an *Observer* op-ed piece, board member Jim Puckett argued that "controlled choice is the wrong choice for us" because the plan was costly, unfair, illogical, of dubious educational value, and involved, even for only several years, the use of race in pupil assignment.[33] Four days later, another op-ed piece—this one by leaders of the Swann Fellowship, an organization whose views on pupil assignment rarely overlapped Puckett's—also argued that the plan "leaves our community with a number of serious questions."[34] Eventually, however, whatever doubts the Swann Fellowship and other desegregation proponents had about controlled choice were generally trumped by the belief that it was the best they could get, given the legal and political situation facing CMS. Moreover, *Achieving the CMS Vision's* equity provisions had widespread support among desegregation advocates. Consequently, the NAACP and several members of the black clergy mobilized their congregations and constituents to attend the March 31 school board meeting, at which the key vote would be taken. After a motion by Lassiter for a separate vote on the pupil assignment component failed, *Achieving the CMS Vision* passed by a 6–3 vote, the three dissenters being Lassiter, Kakedelis, and Puckett.

The vote signaled the first major overhaul of pupil assignment since the magnet plan had been adopted, exactly seven years earlier to the day. Seven years were not all that separated the two votes; the dynamics on the board were very different. Whatever reservations various board members, such as Arthur Griffin, may have had about the magnet plan, it passed unanimously, amid discussion that was generally characterized by the gentility upon which Charlotte prides itself. Not only did the board fail to reach unanimity seven years later on the replacement for the magnet plan, but discussion prior to the vote was very sharp, with several board members directing pointed criticisms at others.

The dynamics in the audience also were very different. As noted in chapter 5, upon adoption of the magnet plan in 1992, whites applauded enthusiastically, but blacks generally sat silently. Moreover, 1992's vote saw roughly an equal number of blacks and whites in the standing-room-only crowd.[35] But in 1999, the overflow crowd contained few whites, and the predominantly African American audience reacted with jubilation to the plan's passage. That black religious and civic leaders could effect so large a turn-out—arguably the largest by black Charlotteans for a school board vote in at least fifteen years—indicated the same kind of black political mobilization seen in the 1998 and 1999 elections, as well as at the rally at Ebenezer Baptist Church in support of an appeal of Potter's decision.

Despite this strong mobilization, the audience's joy at the outcome of the vote occasions comment. To be sure, the school board had voted to commit unprecedented resources for addressing inequities among CMS' schools, but with its provisions for eliminating racial guidelines in three years, the new plan extended considerably fewer promises of maintaining a desegregated system than the magnet plan had done. These lessened promises reflected how much the terms of discussion had shifted during these seven years and with the trial about to open. Eight months later, as the board wrestled with the consequences of Potter's decision, the new pupil assignment plan would extend even fewer promises, and African American organizations took a position quite different from the one they did in March.

Rush to Adoption

Although the board had appealed Potter's decision and requested a stay, CMS remained legally obliged to implement a race-neutral plan by the follow-ing August unless it received a favorable ruling from the appeals court. Given the Fourth Circuit's conservative reputation, that seemed unlikely to CMS' attorneys. Even hopes of receiving a stay seemed small, with the school system's general counsel estimating the probability as being between 20 percent and 30 percent. "Stays are hard to get," she said, "They're not the order of the day."[36]

The pupil assignment proposal that Superintendent Smith presented to the board a week after the school board election reflected what he viewed as CMS' legal situation. Unlike the plan adopted in March, the superintendent's proposal did not provide for a three-year controlled-choice transition period. That major difference aside, the superintendent's proposal drew heavily on the March plan's framework by laying out a choice plan that divided CMS into five zones and relied on a complex system of magnet schools and geo-graphically determined attendance areas. These areas gave every student a "home school," one near his or her residence, at which attendance was guar-anteed if the student so chose. CMS staff listed this guarantee of assignment to a school close to home as the first principle underlying the new plan. Another principle was cohort continuity; the complex feeder plan was de-signed so that all of the students who attended a particular home elementary school could, if they so chose, attend the same home high school and, in most cases, the same home middle school. Students who did not wish to attend their home school could apply to those particular magnet schools that were associated with them, with CMS providing transportation if the student was admitted through the lottery. In keeping with Potter's ruling, neither the lottery for the magnet schools nor any other aspect of the plan involved racial goals or guidelines. In addition, the plan moved many of the magnet programs from inner-city schools to more outlying ones, the rationale being that inner-city schools would need space for black students who, to achieve racial balance, had previously been bused out of their neighborhoods. All told, it was estimated that the changes occasioned by the plan might result in the reassignment of as many as 65 percent of CMS' students.

Such massive assignment would likely occasion large amounts of racial resegregation since the plan gave the highest priority to students wishing to attend their home school. An analysis published by the *Observer* indicated that the number of schools in which blacks comprised 90 percent or more of the student population would jump from one to twelve.[37] However, with the court order prohibiting CMS from taking race into account, the socioeconomic characteristics of student populations became even more of a focus of attention than in previous reassignments. Here too the projections were for large-scale polarization. With the system-wide average of students eligible for free or reduced lunch (FRL) about 40 percent, the number of schools with more than 80 percent of such students was expected to double (from nine to eighteen), as was the number of schools with less than 10 percent (from eight to sixteen).[38] Moreover, there was considerable variation in the distribution of the high poverty schools among the five zones. Consequently, in some zones, students wishing to not attend their home school might have difficulty finding one that was not high poverty.

This disparity in choices, combined with the projected dramatic increase in high poverty schools, triggered opposition to the plan from many of the groups that had come together at the Faith Community Rally on Public Education to urge CMS to appeal. Among these groups were the League of Women Voters, the NAACP, the Swann Fellowship, HELP, the Interfaith Committee for Fairness in Public Education, and the African American coalition, a group of black business executives. While these groups never came together in a formal coalition, Charlotte had not seen that kind of broad interracial network involved in educational issues since the peak of the desegregation struggles in the 1970s. Drawing on the momentum developed from the rally urging an appeal of Potter's decision, these groups' activities throughout the fall of 1999's pupil assignment battle constituted the broadest mobilization in support of desegregation in a generation. In a variety of public forums, these groups made their case, organizing, in the process, what longtime observers considered the largest attendance of African Americans and their white allies at key school board meetings in over twenty years.

Among the proposals advanced by these groups was one that the priority accorded proximity and cohort continuity in the choice plan be modified by other criteria such as setting a ceiling on the percentage of FRL-eligible students in any given school. Such limits, they noted, would be race-neutral and thus in accordance with Potter's ruling. These limits, they also argued, made fiscal sense as well as educational sense because the Smith administration made clear that costly extra resources would be necessary for many schools with high concentrations of low-income students. Much of this additional funding could be avoided, coalition members argued, if students from low-income families were not concentrated in relatively few schools since dispersing such children, research indicated, was a more cost-effective way of meeting their challenging educational needs.

Dissatisfaction with the plan was not confined to its resegregative aspects. As the comments by hundreds of parents at the lengthy public hearings made clear, there was dissatisfaction from many different parts of the county with the drawing of particular home school attendance zones, the feeder patterns, and the shifting of the magnet programs. In response to these protests, the five-week period between the announcement of the plan and the board's scheduled vote saw a spate of revisions to the plan that continued right up until the day of the vote. These changes increased the number of students who would be "grandfathered," that is, allowed to complete the next academic year at their current school, even though that assignment was not in keeping with the new plan. The revised plan also modified various attendance boundaries, increased the number of magnet schools associated with particular home schools, and moved many of the magnet programs back to, or closer to, the inner-city schools in which they were currently located.

Although the last two revisions addressed a few of the concerns of the NAACP, the Swann Fellowship, HELP, and other groups opposed to the large number of high-poverty schools, these organizations viewed the improvement as marginal. Moreover, in both public and private, Superintendent Smith made clear that none of his revisions would involve changing the plan's basic principles by, say, imposing a ceiling on the percentage of FRL-eligible children at any school. To impose such a ceiling, he said, would make it impossible to fulfill the plan's emphases on choice, guaranteeing a school close to home, and providing cohort continuity. Smith's insistence on a plan that would lead to so large a number of high-poverty and racially segregated schools surprised many members of these groups, given both the outcome of the school board election and CMS' defense of racial equity during the trial. But Potter's ruling had changed CMS' legal situation, and the white plaintiffs were threatening to bring CMS back to court if they thought it was using other criteria such as FRL-eligibility as a proxy for race in student assignment.[39] Moreover, the superintendent saw the emphases on choice, stability, and cohort continuity as a way of dealing with what he had long viewed as intensifying competition from private schools and charter schools. Likening public education to the post office, he told an *Observer* editor, "The Post Office was so interested in being the Post Office that they didn't learn how to compete with FedEx and the fax machine."[40] Smith was deeply committed to boosting the academic achievement of children from low-income families and was aware that the nation's high-poverty schools could claim little systematic success in fulfilling that goal. But he felt that CMS possessed the leadership, personnel, organizational capability, and curriculum already in place to deal effectively with the many challenges such schools posed. Community support also was crucial, he explained to an *Observer* editor: "The question is going to be—however we end up, whether we disperse poverty or whether we concentrate poverty—'does this community have the public will to be successful with these kids?' " Asked whether concentrating low-income kids in inner-city schools made the job harder, he replied, "I don't think it matters."[41]

Among the aspects of community and public will to which the superintendent was referring was support for increased funding, and the discussion of the new plan was intimately related to debate about fiscal issues. In discussions about the new plan with both the Swann Fellowship and HELP, the superintendent called upon them to help rally public support for the increased funding that he viewed as being essential to the success of the new assignment plan. In a meeting with Smith, HELP representatives noted that attendance at the many high-poverty schools projected in the new assignment plan would involve sacrifice by low-income families and asked what sacrifices were expected from high-income families. The superintendent responded that they would have to vote for school bonds and pay higher taxes.

The broad range of dissatisfaction put considerable pressure on the school board to postpone its vote and to spend additional time working on the plan. Even the *Observer's* editorial page—which in recent months had rarely taken even the slightest issue with the superintendent—cautioned "Don't Rush the Job," and noted that doing the new plan "promptly is important, but not as important as doing it right."[42] But the pressure from elsewhere in the business elite and inside CMS for the school board to act quickly was even greater. Superintendent Smith insisted that a vote must be taken before the start of the Christmas break to allow time for all of the massive changes involved in implementing so fundamentally different an assignment plan in August 2000, just eight months away.

The board thus went ahead with a scheduled vote on the superintendent's proposal at a December 16 meeting that exemplified how much the board had been buffeted by legal developments, political considerations, the superintendent's insistence, and time constraints in the past four months. In this exhausting five-hour meeting, the board considered a range of controversial and unsettled issues, including whether to locate an International Baccalaureate (IB) Program at West Charlotte High in the heavily black west side of Charlotte or at North Mecklenburg High in a more northern, predominantly white part of the county. It resolved the matter by giving both schools the prestigious program, and it did the same in the debate over whether an IB program should be placed at Independence High or East Mecklenburg High. Placing IB programs at all of these schools was politically expedient, but it begged the question, as many board members knew, of whether CMS had the resources to support, or the student demand to justify, so many IB programs.

The flurry of amendments and modifications secured the support of seven board members. Among the seven were all of the board's black members, who felt that, with Smith insisting on a vote, it was the best that they could do, especially because the plan was subject to additional modification and contingent upon full funding from the county. Ironically, given that the plan was the first in thirty years to give heavy priority to students wishing to attend a school close to their residence, Puckett, a champion of neighborhood schools, voted against it, saying that several amendments made it not final enough "for me to feel comfortable."[43] Kakadelis, another advocate of neighborhood schools, abstained, saying that she did so because the superintendent and school board attorney had not received all of the amendments in advance.[44]

A Gift of Time and More Conflict

Fourteen days after the board adopted the new plan, CMS' legal situation changed dramatically. On December 30, the three-judge panel of the Fourth Circuit hearing the case stayed Potter's order, pending its ruling in the case. With CMS thus under no legal obligation to change its present assignment plan for a least an additional year, the school board voted in early January not to implement the December 16 plan by August 2000. Instead, the board decided to try to develop a plan by taking advantage of what Arthur Griffin called the "gift of time" given by the Fourth Circuit.[45] But much more was at stake than using the additional time to proceed less frantically than in the weeks leading up to the December 16 vote. The Fourth Circuit's unexpected granting of a stay raised hopes of black board members and their white allies that CMS would prevail at the appellate level in other ways as well. Accompanying these increased hopes was the recognition that if the December 16 plan, or one essentially similar to it, was implemented, the school board would face immense practical and political difficulties in subsequently making any major changes, even if the Fourth Circuit were to reverse large parts of Potter's decision. Not surprisingly, the very developments and considerations that fueled one group of board members' desire to revisit the December 16 plan made it look more attractive to another group. Thus, Puckett, who had voted against adopting the December 16 plan, now voted against postponing its implementation. Kakadelis, who had abstained on December 16, also voted against postponing implementation. Together with Lassiter, they provided the three dissenting votes, the 6–3 margin thus reflecting long-standing divisions on the board.

Little in the ensuing four months would bridge those divisions. Rather, if anything, they were exacerbated by a complex commingling of policy, politics, personality, and conflicting hopes and expectations about how the Fourth Circuit would rule. Moreover, as the school board continued to wrestle with pupil assignment, it became increasingly apparent, as will be discussed below, that the county commission would not fully fund CMS' budgetary requests, thus jeopardizing the chances of high-poverty, racially isolated schools receiving the specially targeted resources which, in the view of many board members, were the sine qua non of these schools having a chance to succeed. These diminished chances buttressed claims that separate could never be equal and served to weaken whatever sentiment there might have been among black Charlotteans and their white allies for a Charlotte-Mecklenburg version of the Atlanta Compromise.

In response to the concerns about the large number of high-poverty schools, CMS staff modified the December 16 plan by decreasing the number of choice zones from five to four, lowering the disparity among these zones in the number of high-poverty schools, and giving students whose home school had large numbers of low-achieving students a greater—and in some cases, a guaranteed—opportunity to transfer to another school. These modifications were not sufficient to secure the support of Arthur Griffin, Rembert, and Leake, who maintained that the plan's basic framework still allowed for too many high-poverty schools without any guarantee of equity. But these modifications went a long way toward meeting the concerns of Woods, Dunlap, and Molly Griffin. Since the ongoing high priority accorded to choice, cohort continuity, and assignment to the home school continued to elicit support from Lassiter, Puckett, and Kakadelis, prospects appeared good that the months of debate on the board and the uncertainty in the community would come to an end with the adoption of a plan at a much-anticipated May 9 meeting.

However, the location of the IB programs remained an issue, with West Charlotte playing as high profile of a role in 2000 as it had in the pupil assignment battles a generation earlier. Although some of CMS' most academically accomplished students continued to graduate from West Charlotte, overall levels of achievement were considerably below those of many of the district's other high schools.[46] Moreover, its nonblack student population had declined from 56 percent in the mid-1980s to 37 percent in 1999–2000, and the school had recently suffered from controversies involving both faculty transfers and the replacement of its principal. If West Charlotte were to regain its reputation—in which many African Americans took special pride—as one of CMS' flagship high schools, it would need a wide range of additional resources. Moreover, placing the IB program at West Charlotte was, in Arthur Griffin's view, consistent with the original purpose of magnets, which "was to create voluntary diversity in the inner city" by drawing white students to the school from the predominantly white northern parts of the county.[47] However, Jim Puckett, who represented those northern parts of the county, said that moving the program from North Mecklenburg to West Charlotte "may be done to help diversity, but it just won't. People can't get from Huntersville and Davidson to West Charlotte."[48] Whether they could not get to West Charlotte because of traffic congestion or would not enroll because of the school's inner-city location was a question that elicited predictably different answers from whites and blacks.

The differences over West Charlotte proved fatal. With the plan before the board including IB programs at both West Charlotte and North Mecklenburg, Arthur Griffin moved that the plan be amended to phase out the IB program at North Mecklenburg, as West Charlotte's was implemented. Reflecting West Charlotte's historic importance to black Charlotteans, all four black board members voted for that amendment, as did Louise Woods. In anticipation of the fight over this issue, she had, at 6:30 one morning, driven from her home in east Charlotte to the northern part of the county and then to West Charlotte to see whether the transportation time between these northern areas and the high school was reasonable. Finding it so, she said, "I'm willing to vote for the plan despite my misgivings, but it has to be a plan that strengthens our inner-city schools." She added, "I cannot make a decision tonight (on a plan) that does not have a strong draw for West Charlotte."[49] The amendment passed 5–4. Its passage was sufficient to cost the plan the support of Lassiter, Puckett, and Kakadelis. Their three votes, combined with those of Rembert, Leake, and Arthur Griffin, killed the plan.

The unexpected defeat of the plan provoked a firestorm of controversy, most of it swirling around Arthur Griffin. To many black Charlotteans and racially liberal whites, he deserved praise for continuing the fight for equity and desegregation. If anyone should be blamed for the plan's failure, argued a leader of the Swann Fellowship in an *Observer* op-ed piece, it should be Lassiter, Kakedelis, and Puckett who, for the sake of the approximately 200 students in North Meck's IB program, had voted against a plan that gave high priority to their cherished goals of proximity, cohort stability, and choice in pupil assignment.[50]

Support for Griffin was, however, drowned out by a wave of anger that went far beyond the whites in outlying areas who were never among his fans. The white editor of the *Observer's* editorial page opined that if school board members would watch the videotape of their meeting, "they'd see why many parents who watched wondered, as I did, 'Why should I trust these people with my child?' "[51] Another *Observer* editor, an African American, generally very supportive of Griffin and critical of the way the plan "concentrates too many low-income or low performing kids at some schools and isolates many students by race," argued that since Griffin never intended to vote for the plan, his "motivation for proposing an amendment is questionable. Such machinations are not worthy of him."[52] In rejecting the superintendent's plan, she claimed, "board members have put a lot more at risk than they apparently know or will acknowledge" because "this school system is in danger of losing the political and financial support it needs to give each child access to a quality public school education. This school system is in danger of losing the economic and racial mix of students that keeps large urban school systems healthy. I'm talking about white flight, but also upwardly mobile black, Latino, and other flight as well. This school system is in danger of losing a school superintendent who has demonstrated his commitment to the educational progress of all children—and has gotten results."[53]

Leaders of Mecklenburg's various governments joined the chorus. Making reference to one of local civic boosters' greatest nightmares, Charlotte's Mayor Pat McCrory all too predictably claimed, "This indecision is causing economic flight," and he called upon the mayors of the county's six towns to join with him "to play a leadership role."[54] Mint Hill's mayor successfully proposed a resolution to the town's board of commissioners about entering talks with the five other small towns regarding seceding from the countywide school system.[55] Given the necessity of state approval, the threat of secession was more symbolic than credible, but comments by Commission Chair Parks Helms required serious attention. If the board failed to come up with a pupil assignment plan by May 31, Helms indicated, the November 2000 ballot could not include the large bond package that CMS felt was essential to achieving equity.[56]

In response to this extensive pressure, the deeply divided school board hired two mediators to try to help resolve differences. The plan resulting from these mediators' efforts phased out North Mecklenburg's IB program, instituted one at West Charlotte, and was largely similar to the one defeated on May 9. But this plan passed 6-3 on June 1, with Griffin, Leake, and Rembert now voting for it. "I don't want to hold up the work anymore with regards to this issue," a beleaguered Griffin told the press.[57] For her part, Rembert indicated that the plan remained difficult to support, but that she could now do so because it allowed the board to develop a race-conscious backup plan

in case the appellate courts found that CMS was not yet unitary.[58] The three
negative votes again came from Lassiter, Puckett, and Kakadelis. In addition
to opposing the loss of the IB program at North Mecklenburg, they took
issue with a provision that allowed the school board to set capacity limits for
each school. That provision raised the possibility, in their view, that the school
board could set limits below the current enrollment of already overcrowded
schools in outlying white neighborhoods. Such limits would, the dissenters
feared, allow the board to assign students from these overcrowded schools to
underutilized ones closer to the central city, thus undercutting the priority
that the plan ostensibly gave to enrollment at a student's home school.

The Fourth Circuit Shakes Things Up

In the wake of the board's adoption of the new plan on June 1, 2000,
staff began scrambling to develop procedures that would facilitate the reassignment of tens of thousands of students in the 2001–02 school year. The
success of the reassignment hinged on families understanding the complex
choice plan and learning about the programs at schools that students, not
wanting to attend their home school, could choose. Toward this goal, during
the week that choice applications were mailed to all of the district's students,
CMS scheduled a Showcase of Schools, a large, much-advertised fair at which
the district's schools would tout their programs to the anticipated thousands
of families who would attend.

But on November 30, 2000—two days before the showcase, and the
same day that the *Observer* ran a forty-eight-page guide, "How to Choose a
School"—a three-judge panel of the Fourth Circuit Court of Appeals issued
its decision. By a 2–1 vote, the panel overruled almost every major aspect of
Potter's decision, including, most importantly, his finding that CMS was
unitary with respect to student assignment. In reaching that finding, the
panel's majority said that Potter had not adequately considered the extent to
which growing resegregation might be linked to the "Board's failure to comply with court orders regarding selection of sites for the construction of new
schools."[59] Noting that in the twenty years since McMillan's decision in *Martin*,
"CMS has built twenty-five of twenty-seven new schools in predominantly
white suburban communities," the majority opinion acknowledged that there
was no evidence that CMS' school siting policies represented an intentional
attempt at segregation. However, it said:

> The Board's practice of siting new schools such that they could not
> reasonably be expected to serve a racially balanced student population
> and Judge McMillan's determination that this practice, in the past,

represented the school system's failure to eliminate the vestiges of segregation, together raise a strong inference that those vestiges remain today. When this inference is viewed in combination with the burden borne by the Capacchione plaintiffs to show that current racial imbalances have no causal link to past discrimination, we are compelled to conclude that a remand to the district court is required.[60]

Thus on the pivotal Green factor of student assignment, the panel overturned Potter's finding of unitary status and remanded the case for additional testimony. In addition, the panel remanded the case for additional testimony on two other Green factors—transportation and facilities—and overturned Potter's rulings that the race-conscious magnet plan was unconstitutional and that the white plaintiffs were entitled to nominal damages and attorneys' fee.

Although the white plaintiffs indicated that they would appeal the three-judge panel's ruling, it had dramatically changed CMS' legal situation. However, board members disagreed about the precise nature of the change and its consequences. Was CMS still under the original *Swann* orders and thus required to continue to use race-conscious assignment policies, which, of course, the plan adopted on June 1 did not? Or could that plan be tweaked in a way that would satisfy the court in the event that the black plaintiffs sought a court order requiring CMS to pursue racial balance? Compounding the board's difficulty in dealing with the changed legal situation was Superintendent Smith's failure—contrary to the board's vote in adopting the new plan—to develop an alternative one in the event that the courts found that CMS was not yet unitary.

With the final preparations underway for the Showcase of Schools, the board held a marathon meeting. It voted 5-4 to postpone implementation of the new plan, to continue to use the current plan (which did consider race), and to cancel the next day's showcase. Comprising the board's majority were its four black members and Louise Woods, the same five members who had voted to appeal Potter's finding of unitary status a year earlier.

In addition to citing the changed legal environment, the board's majority noted that by postponing the new plan's implementation, CMS had minimized the possibility that students would have to be reassigned more than once if higher courts continued to reverse lower ones. This point did little to prevent a torrent of criticism, especially from white parents. The board's vote also dismayed both the superintendent and the business elite. An indication of the latter's sentiment was a Christmas Eve *Observer* article headlined "Businesses Feel Stress of Limbo in Schools." Quoting the president of the Chamber of Commerce and the president of the local realtors association, the article noted that the vote to scrap the choice plan and cancel the showcase of schools "boiled over" the frustrations that business leaders had been feeling about the lack of a new pupil assignment plan. Adopt a pupil assignment plan for the fall of 2002, the Charlotte Chamber's president told school leaders because "the school system needs it, the parents need it, and this community—which prides itself on being progressive—cannot tolerate being under a court order."[61] The article also contained a surprisingly public threat from Stan Campbell, the head of the Alliance for a Better Charlotte and A Better Charlotte Political Committee. In addition to noting the business elite's lack of confidence in the school board, Campbell made reference to the November 2001 school board elections, saying, "There are clearly (board members) who are not going to get supported."[62]

A Plan is Adopted

In addition to facing this public criticism, the board had to deal with the county commission, which continued to link support for funding increases to the adoption of a plan. Under pressure from many quarters, the board wrestled with the details of a choice plan during the first six months of 2001. A key resolution passed on April 3. It linked the adoption of a pupil assignment plan to the implementation of equity, saying "the foundation of equal educational opportunity under the Equity Plan framework is sufficiently sound, if completely developed and adequately funded, to result in the resolution of remaining inequalities over a reasonable time to justify the adoption of a plan of pupil assignment for the 2002–03 school year." It then called upon Superintendent Smith to develop a plan for adoption by the board prior to August 1. That plan, the board resolution indicated, would be based on the Family Choice Plan adopted on June 1, 2000. But it would include several modifications, many of which involved provisions that would be progressively phased in to make it easier for poor and/or low-achieving students to attend schools other than their home schools, especially when their home schools had disproportionately large percentages of students with economically needy or low-achieving students.

With that resolution as a basis, Superintendent Smith presented a plan to the board in late June that was similar to his earlier ones. In accordance with long-standing practice, CMS scheduled public hearings on the proposed plan. However, in contrast to recent previous rounds of hearings, these were ho-hum, badly attended affairs. Contributing to the paucity of interest in the hearings were both their time and timing; they occurred during prime summer vacation weeks and were scheduled with little advance notice.[63] More importantly, the low attendance also reflected cynicism, resignation, and fatigue among activists all across the educational policy spectrum. As the *Observer* reported in explaining the "lowest attendance in recent memory":

The rows of empty seats, several parent leaders say, were not just the result of summer vacations or satisfaction with the plan...

Some parents say they are just weary of the whole topic—and they resent the school board for putting them through it again . . . Others who disliked last year's plan say they see no improvements this time. If the district didn't heed their criticisms the first time around, they ask, why bother to register them again?[64]

Such resignation and fatigue worked to the superintendent's advantage, and the board's discussion of the plan took place in the absence of any significant mobilization by parent groups or community organizations. Especially notable for its absence in these decisive days was the network of organizations that had played a prominent a role in opposing the choice plan in the fall of 1999. But the past eighteen months had taken a considerable toll on this network. The victory of Rembert and Griffin in the 1999 school board election facilitated the kind of demobilization discussed in chapter 3. The Swann Fellowship's one paid staff member had been the linchpin of the network but burned out and with the Fellowship lacking funds, she had resigned to seek other employment and left Charlotte. As the pupil assignment battles dragged on both in the courts and on the board, many desegregation activists took up other concerns. Moreover, many also became as weary with the uncertainty over pupil assignment as had other Charlotteans, and they felt the school board had best adopt a plan, lest public support for CMS plummet.

In this quiescent political climate, board members negotiated among themselves, making changes in various feeder patterns, the drawing of some boundary zones, and the location of magnets and other specialized programs. But even with those changes, the revised plan was, as the *Observer* noted, "essentially a replica of the one the board has bandied about for two years."[65] However, while those two years were frequently ones of bitterness and division on the board, its meeting of July 31, 2001, reflected a complex mixture of the fatigue and political pressure that board members were feeling, as well as their increased desire to finally adopt a plan and move on. In a mutually congratulatory atmosphere in which members voiced pride in the way they had come together to benefit the community and serve the needs of all children, the board voted 8-1 to adopt the superintendent's race-neutral choice plan. The sole negative vote came from Arthur Griffin because of his ongoing concerns about resegregation and lack of equity. But while on other occasions he had fought vigorously over such issues, at this meeting Griffin merely voted No. As he subsequently explained, "As a group, people wanted to move forward. I sensed they wanted to do that. I've been combative before. But there was no need to be combative that night."[66]

The Legal Issue Gets Settled

In adopting the race-neutral choice plan on July 31, 2001, the board had made provisions for an alternative plan that would take race into account if the full Fourth Circuit upheld the three-judge panel's ruling that CMS was not unitary. While important in securing support from desegregation proponents for the race-neutral plan, that precaution proved ultimately unnecessary. On September 21, seven weeks after the board had adopted the plan, the full Fourth Circuit upheld Potter's finding that CMS was unitary by a 7–4 vote. Writing for the majority on this issue, Judge William Traxler drew heavily, as had Potter, on Armor's testimony about trends in racial balance in student assignment and on demographic changes in Mecklenburg County to conclude that whatever imbalances currently existed could not be considered vestiges: "Long periods of almost perfect compliance with the court's racial balance guidelines, coupled with some imbalance in the wake of massive demographic shifts, strongly supports the district court's finding that the present levels of imbalance are in no way connected with the de jure segregation once practiced in CMS."[67] Moreover, as opposed to the three-judge panel, Traxler viewed the record as indicating that "CMS has, to the extent practicable, continually endeavored to site schools in order to foster integration, and has adopted a policy of building schools in areas equally accessible to blacks and whites."[68]

However, two of the seven judges who believed that CMS was unitary were unwilling to affirm other important aspects of Potter's ruling. They joined the four judges opposing unitary status to make a 6–5 majority that overturned Potter's finding that the race-conscious magnet plan was unconstitutional and his awarding of nominal damages and attorneys' fees. Moreover, the court unanimously vacated his sweeping injunction barring CMS from using race in allocating educational opportunities.

The Fourth Circuit's decision could thus be regarded as a compromise with the white plaintiffs winning the most important aspect of the case, the declaration of unitary status, but losing virtually all of the secondary aspects. Indeed, that was the view of the *Charlotte Observer*, which, in an editorial, "Let It Be," called upon all three parties to accept the decision.[69] For its part, CMS was willing to do so. At a special meeting the day the decision was announced, the board voted unanimously not to appeal. For the minority of board members who had always considered CMS unitary, the vote not to appeal was hardly surprising. For the five-member majority who had voted to appeal Potter's finding of unitary status, such speedy acceptance of the Fourth Circuit's vote was more unexpected and reflected a variety of considerations. The Fourth Circuit had rejected those aspects of Potter's decision that CMS had found most onerous. Moreover, those members most concerned about resegregation expected—correctly as it turned out—that the black plaintiffs would appeal, thus keeping alive the presumably slim hope that the finding of unitary status would be overturned. That expectation, combined with recognition that a decision to appeal—especially after the board had recently adopted a race-neutral assignment plan—would infuriate many sectors of the community, tipped the scales heavily in favor of acquiescing in the Fourth Circuit's decision. Moreover, a vote to appeal would almost certainly become a major issue in the November 2001 school board elections, discussed later.

As expected, the black plaintiffs did appeal the finding that CMS was unitary, though most observers felt that the appeal would fall on deaf ears. In earlier major school desegregation cases—*Dowell, Freeman,* and *Jenkins*—the Rehnquist court had gone a long way toward removing the judiciary from school desegregation efforts. Indeed, as Gary Orfield has pointed out, these three decisions "largely displace the goal of rooting out the lingering damage of racial segregation and discrimination with the twin goals of minimizing judicial involvement in education and restoring power to local and state governments, whatever the consequences."[70] The Rehnquist court's action in *Swann* further reflected the perspective it had taken in *Dowell, Freeman,* and *Jenkins.* On April 15, 2002, almost exactly thirty-one years after its initial ruling in *Swann,* the high court announced that it would not consider the appeal, thus letting stand the Fourth Circuit's finding that CMS was unitary and putting an end to the *Swann* case.

Although the Supreme Court also had refused to consider an appeal for attorneys' fees from the white plaintiffs, they had prevailed on the major issue. "It's over and we won," said one of them jubilantly.[71] Conversely, the black plaintiffs and their attorneys lamented the court's decision. In a prepared statement, they accused the court of turning its back on black children, but took comfort in the fact that as a result of the reopened case, the school board publicly acknowledged it "has not met its obligations to African American children," and that "more has been done in the last four years to address the issues than at any time since the mid-'70s, but the task is still not finished."[72]

This statement thus called attention to one of the most ironic aspects of the reopened litigation. The long, highly publicized trial had indeed called dramatic attention to CMS' many failings in educating black children, despite the original *Swann* ruling. Yet the outcome of the trial deprived CMS of the race-conscious pupil assignment techniques that it, along with the black plaintiffs, had insisted at the trial remained necessary to try to remedy these failings.

THE 2001 SCHOOL BOARD ELECTION

Whatever disagreements there were about the merits of the Supreme Court's refusal to hear the case, there was widespread commentary that the finding of unitary status and the concomitant release of CMS from judicial supervision provided greater opportunity for Charlotteans themselves to shape education policy. As a subhead of an *Observer* editorial read, "Supreme Court decision puts the job in our hands."[73] The 2001 school board election provided the first indication of how Charlotteans would do this job with the district no longer under court order. As things turned out, they did it in much the same way they had done it in the three previous elections.

All six district seats were at stake in the November 2001 school board election. By the time it took place, the school board had already adopted a new pupil assignment plan by an 8–1 vote and voted unanimously not to appeal the Fourth Circuit's ruling. By resolving, at least for a while, these divisive issues, the two votes lowered the stakes of the election and addressed what many critics felt were the board's biggest failures. But many crucial issues remained, including whether the new board would elect the controversial Arthur Griffin as chair. Moreover, the votes on the appeal and the pupil assignment plan took place after the deadline for filing for office. Since prior to that deadline it was by no means certain that the board would adopt a plan or how it would react to whatever decision the Fourth Circuit handed down, the stakes in the months leading up to that deadline seemed extremely high. It was these apparent stakes that had led Stan Campbell to indicate, as noted earlier, that the business elite would not support some members of the board.

The most visible target of the business elite's attempt to change the balance of power on the board was District 4's Louise Woods, the sole white person in the five-person majority on many of the most crucial desegregation-related votes in the previous two years.[74] Although the court case had been settled, the District 4 seat was widely viewed as a potential swing vote on many future issues, including any attempt by critics of Arthur Griffin to oust him from the chair of the school board. Thus the *Leader*—which had criticized Griffin frequently and harshly during the previous two years—headlined its major story on the District 4 election, "District 4 Race Key to School Board Balance: Alliances are at Stake as Perpetual Swing-Voter Louise Woods Campaigns to Hang on to Her District 4 Seat in an Election Whose Implications Can Reach As High As the Chairman's Seat."[75]

The district's demographic characteristics jibed in many ways with its being a swing vote on the board of education. Changed only somewhat by the redistricting occasioned by the 2000 Census, it remained the county's most socioeconomically and ethnically diverse district, with African Americans constituting 30 percent of the registered voters. It also was one in which the number of registered Democrats equaled the combined sum of Republicans and Independents. That was a crucial consideration because partisan considerations intruded significantly on this nominally nonpartisan school board election, with the Democratic Party striving to mobilize support for Woods, and the Republican Party doing the same for her opponent, Julian Wright, also white.

An attorney with a major downtown law firm, Wright also was a member of Siegle Avenue Presbyterian Church which, located near a large, inner-city public housing project, is generally considered one of Charlotte's most racially diverse, liberal, and socially conscious congregations. Wright had played a key role in many of the church's community outreach efforts and as a member of a citizens committee overseeing CMS' student assignment efforts had earned the respect of many people who placed a high value on desegregation and equity.[76]

Those aspects of Wright's record notwithstanding, his campaign focused upon Woods's votes as part of the board's five-member majority. Thus, he began an op-ed piece in the *Observer* by contrasting the community's need for "new, effective leadership on the school board" with charges that his opponent had "clung stubbornly to past practices" exemplified by how

> on Dec. 1, 2000, Mrs. Woods had an opportunity to show leadership and move our system forward toward a choice plan . . . Instead, she made the motion and cast the fifth and decisive vote to derail the choice plan, scuttle the long-scheduled Showcase of Schools, and frustrate large numbers of parents, students, teachers, and staff . . .
>
> The toll on our public schools during the past few years of uncertainty has been enormous. We have lost families, teachers, and opportunities to educate all children. My opponent has created much of that uncertainty."[77]

All four of the corporate PACs—including those of First Union and Bank of America—that made contributions in the District 4 race gave their money to Wright, as did the Builders PAC and the North Carolina Realtors PAC. His list of campaign donors included many of the most prominent members of Charlotte's business elite, including Hugh McColl, C. D. Spangler Jr., John Crosland, Johnny Harris, and John Belk. Altogether, his contributions totaled just under $44,000 more than three times Woods's.[78]

While the overwhelming preponderance of business elite support went to Wright, Woods received contributions from several of its members, as well as from PACs associated with the Democratic Party and Democratic candidates. Moreover, Woods did especially well in raising money from within District 4.[79] Those contributions reflected the same kind of grassroots support that had allowed her to first get elected in 1995 despite, as chapter 5 noted, strong support for her opponent from the business elite in that race as well. Woods's neighborhood support and strong campaign organization also allowed her to cover the precincts exceptionally well on Election Day. She also benefited from the traditional constituent service aspects of incumbency, e.g., seven years of responding to parents' concerns and strong ties to the district's PTAs.

Also helping Woods were endorsements from the *Charlotte Post* and the Black Political Caucus. The latter was especially important because with African Americans running for both mayor and an at-large seat on the city council, black political leaders made the same kind of effort to mobilize voters and to cover the polls that they had in 1999. These efforts dovetailed with those of Woods's campaign organization to contribute to her decisive victory by a margin of 58–42 percent. The formally nonpartisan character of school board elections notwithstanding, an analysis of precinct-level data shows a strong relationship between support for Woods and the partisan composition of a precinct, and an even stronger relationship between support for Woods and a precinct's racial composition.[80]

One of the first consequences of Woods's victory was a change in the leadership of the school board, but not one that critics of Arthur Griffin wanted. In the closing days of the campaign, the board's vice chair, John Lassiter, had sent a letter to the district's registered Republicans. Identifying himself as both a Republican and as the vice chair of the school board, Lassiter said that Woods "has been the deciding vote to keep our schools in court, delaying Dr. Eric Smith's student assignment plan and wasting nearly $5 million that could have improved the lives of teachers and students alike." By electing Wright, the letter continued, "You can help trigger a new policy direction on the School Board focused on meeting the needs of children and teachers and not political agendas."[81]

To many, Lassiter's letter was an unprecedented partisan attack by a leader of the formally nonpartisan school board on one of its sitting members. It cost him the support of a majority of the board's members, even some who otherwise thought it important that the board's chair and vice chair, between them, should reflect the long-standing divisions in the community and on the board. Upon installation, the new board reelected Arthur Griffin as chair and chose Rembert as vice chair. The 5–4 margins on the vote for both positions reflected the same divisions that had long divided the board. This also marked the first time in Charlotte and Mecklenburg history that both the chair and vice chair of any elected body was African American.

The longer-term consequences and significance of the 2001 school board elections are less clear. In some ways, the election bore a strong resemblance to all that took place since the hybrid system of representation was introduced in 1995. First, given that, generally speaking, Wright was the choice of the organized expression of business elite political sentiment, Woods's victory again demonstrated the business elite's inability to intervene successfully and decisively in a key school board election. Second, as in 1995, 1997, and 1999, the workings of electoral politics in 2001 produced a board majority with an exceptionally strong commitment to both desegregation and equity. Indeed, the five members who constituted this majority had collectively survived the

1999 and 2001 elections, despite all of the hits it had taken over pupil assignment and the "doofus defense" during the trial. The policy implications of their electoral triumphs were, however, more difficult to ascertain.

RESEGREGATION AND RESOURCE ALLOCATION

Despite the electoral victories of desegregation proponents, CMS saw a marked increase in resegregation at the start of the twenty-first century. The extent of this resegregation can be seen by recalling the data displayed in Figure 3.1. It indicates that beginning with the mid-1980s and continuing through the end of the century, CMS witnessed a slow but steady increase in resegregation that showed some signs of reaching a plateau in the late 1990s. However, that plateau gave way to a sharp rise in resegregation as CMS' legal situation changed, and the district adopted a choice plan. Between 2000–01 (the last school year shown in Figure 3.1) and 2001–02, the percentage of black students attending racially identifiable black (RIB) schools jumped from 29 percent to 37 percent. And in the next academic year, 2002–03, the first year of the choice plan, the jump was even greater, with 48 percent of CMS' black students attending RIB schools. Thus in only two years, the resegregation of black students into RIB schools increased approximately as much as it had in the previous ten years. For white students, the resegregation was equally as great.[82]

Given the intense two-year struggle over the new pupil assignment plan, one can plausibly hypothesize that the electoral defeat of desegregation advocates would have produced greater resegregation. But it is difficult to rigorously evaluate this hypothesis, especially because with the new choice plan just going into effect, it is much too early to assess the effectiveness of the provisions designed to increase the assignment options of poor and/or low achieving students.

It also is too early to assess fully whether these schools with a large percentage of poor and/or African American children will be getting the additional resources required by the Charlotte-Mecklenburg Compromise. As indicated by the April 3, 2001, resolution paving the way for the adoption of the new pupil assignment plan, the school board felt that it had taken crucial steps in this direction. Among other things, in the aftermath of Potter's ruling, CMS developed criteria for designating schools needing extra resources, established standards for the resources required by every school, and implemented a system to monitor progress in reaching these standards. Finally, numerous older schools underwent renovation and extensive repairs.

Writing as I am during the 2002–03 school year—which is when the choice plan takes effect—it would be premature to evaluate the results of all of these efforts. But some comments can be made about the equitable distribution of experienced teachers in the years leading up to the choice plan. Although school-level data provide little information on which teachers are teaching what students for how long, such data figured prominently, as chapter 6 indicated, in testimony during the reactivated *Swann* case, with expert witnesses for both CMS and the black plaintiffs claiming that the experience of faculties at RIB schools was significantly different from those of faculties at other schools. Moreover, as CMS prepared to implement the new choice plan, board members recognized the importance of providing a "reasonable balance of new and experienced teachers in every school" and developed policies with that goal in mind.[83] However, in the years immediately preceding the choice plan, the disparities in teacher experience among CMS' schools were generally about the same as they were in the years immediately preceding the trial, as Table 7.1 shows.[84]

The table presents data on the percentage of new and inexperienced teachers (three or fewer years) in RIB, racially balanced (RB), and racially identifiable white schools (RIW) in the three years leading up to the trial and in the two years prior to the implementation of the choice plan. As a way of comparing percentages in the five years, the table also presents disparity

TABLE 7.1
Teacher Experience by Racial Composition of School, 1996–2001

	1996–97	1997–98	1998–99	2000–01	2001–02
Percent of Teachers Who Are New					
Racially Identifiable Black Schools (RIB)	10	12	15	14	17
Racially Balanced Schools (RB)	8.6	11	11	9.9	12
Racially Identifiable White Schools (RIW)	6.5	6.1	6.9	8.0	8.9
Percent of Teachers with Three or					
Fewer Years of Experience					
Racially Identifiable Black Schools	33	37	41	35	38
Racially Balanced Schools	28	31	32	29	32
Racially Identifiable White Schools	23	22	23	24	25
Disparity Ratios: New Teachers					
RIB/RIW	1.5	2.0	2.2	1.8	1.9
RB/RIW	1.3	1.8	1.6	1.2	1.3
RIB/RB	1.2	1.1	1.4	1.4	1.4
Disparity Ratios: Teachers with Three or					
Fewer Years of Experience					
RIB/RIW	1.4	1.7	1.8	1.5	1.5
RB/RIW	1.2	1.4	1.2	1.2	1.3
RIB/RB	1.2	1.2	1.3	1.2	1.2

Source: Charlotte-Mecklenburg Schools.

ratios, which were obtained by dividing the percentages for the RIB and RB schools by those for the RIW schools, and the percentages for the RIB schools by those for the RB schools. These ratios indicate differences among the categories of schools with, for example, the disparity ratios of 1.5 and 1.4 in 1996–97 indicating that RIB schools had, on average, 50 percent more new teachers and 40 percent more teachers with three or fewer years of experience than RIW schools.[85]

As the table indicates, in all five years, RIB schools had higher percentages of inexperienced teachers than RB schools, which, in turn, had higher percentages of inexperienced teachers than RIW schools. The disparity ratios suggest that the difference between the RIB and RIW schools increased in the years prior to the trial, was highest in the school year 1998–99, and decreased somewhat by 2001–02. However, even in 2001–02, RIB schools had, on average, 90 percent more new teachers and 50 percent more teachers with three or fewer years of experience than RIW schools. While the disparities between the RIB and RB schools were not as great as those between the RIB and RW schools, they were still marked and generally consistent.

Given the jump in resegregation of student populations that occurred in 2001–02, larger percentages of CMS students were affected by these disparities in teacher experience than would have been the case if such resegregation had not taken place. Moreover, the jump in student resegregation was accompanied by an increase in faculty racial imbalance. As Figure 5.3 indicates, the correlation between the racial composition of a school's student population and faculty hovered around .6 through the 1990s. However, in 2001–02, it was .72.[86]

Thus, as CMS began implementing the new choice plan, its situation was a difficult one. Although Judge Potter did not credit it, CMS had produced abundant evidence during the 1999 trial of its shortcomings in providing African Americans with the same educational opportunities that whites received. Moreover, the two elections immediately after the trial, like the two immediately before it, had produced a school board majority with a demonstrated eagerness to address these shortcomings. Nonetheless, in the years immediately after the trial, both student and faculty resegregation had increased and, on average, disparities in teacher experience between RIB and RIW schools were approximately the same as they had been in the years before the trial. Perhaps, when fully implemented, the new choice plan will address these shortcomings, but in this regard, the experience of other districts released from court supervision has frequently been less than auspicious, as the majority of CMS board members recognized.[87] Also adding to CMS' problems on the eve of the choice plan was a very uncertain fiscal environment.

FUNDING IN JEOPARDY?

In adopting the new pupil assignment plan, the school board repeatedly made clear that its success hinged on increased funding. As Table 4.1 indicates, relative to comparable North Carolina counties, Mecklenburg County's financial support for its school system did improve significantly in the late 1990s. That data jibes with chapter 6's discussion of CMS' fiscal success in the first years of Eric Smith's administration.[88] Voters passed the 1997 school bond package, the largest in county history. Moreover, the county commission fully funded CMS' hefty budget request for both the 1997–98 and 1998–99 school years, the first time in recent memory that the school system fared so well for two consecutive budgeting cycles. In subsequent budgeting cycles, CMS did nowhere near as well, an indication of how its fiscal fortunes and the funding necessary for the success of the Charlotte-Mecklenburg Compromise were buffeted by both fiscal constraints and county commission politics.

The initial figures for Smith's third budget were formulated in early 1999 as CMS prepared for the upcoming trial and developed the Family Choice Cluster Plan. Recognizing the sweeping changes required by that plan, Smith initially proposed that CMS seek an increase of 24 percent in funding from the county, a much larger jump than the 17 percent and 14 percent increases that CMS had received during his first two years. Ultimately, the county commission gave CMS an increase of about 11 percent, approximately the same percentage by which the county's overall budget increased. CMS fared no better the following year. Wrestling with the consequences of Potter's ruling, it requested a 20 percent increase in county funding. The commission, however, made clear that such a big jump was unrealistic, and CMS got only 10 percent. In its discussion of the budget, the commission rejected the county manager's recommendation to raise taxes, with the commission's two Republicans being joined by four of its Democrats to provide the 6–3 vote for a budget that kept property taxes constant.[89] Generally strong supporters of public education and other county services, the four Democrats were thinking about the November 2000 election in which the three at-large Democratic commissioners faced what was generally considered an especially strong Republican slate.[90] With that slate including Karen Bentley, one of the white plaintiffs in the reopened *Swann* case, and former commissioner Tom Bush, one of the *Observer's* bête-noires, the paper forsook its characteristic advocacy of increased funding for education. It called the county budget decision "reasonable," acknowledged the upcoming elections, and magisterially opined "responsible incumbents try not to heighten the risk that hot-button opportunists could turn an important choice of leadership into a single-issue referendum on property taxes."[91]

With both Bentley and Bush losing, the Democrats retained their majority on the commission, and the next year's budgeting decisions, finalized in June 2001, proved more beneficial to CMS. The commissioners decided to raise property taxes more than the county manager recommended, with much of the additional increase going for education. As a result, CMS received an increase of about 18 percent, raising hopes that the system would be able to improve equity as well as deal with increasing enrollment. But June 2002 was a different story, as the economic downturn and aftermath of September 11 placed the same kinds of financial pressures on Mecklenburg that local governments around the country faced. Aware of these constraints, CMS requested an increase of less than 5 percent, the smallest in years, but it received only one-sixth of the requested increase. That cut dealt with the budget for the first school year (2002–03) of the new pupil assignment plan. In that year, the number of schools needing extra resources—EquityPlusII schools, as they were called—increased from forty-nine to fifty-four, and K–12 enrollment increased from 106,000 to 109,600.[92] The small budget increase thus jeopardized CMS' ability to deal with growth, to say nothing of its ability to fund the extra resources for schools with large percentages of low-income students upon which much of the success—at least for these students—of the Charlotte-Mecklenburg Compromise depends.

Equity and growth also required massive construction expenditures financed by bond referenda, and CMS faced challenges here as well. An anticipated November 1999 bond referendum was the most visible funding casualty of the pupil assignment battles that raged in the late 1990s. In early 1999, as CMS was developing the first draft of the new choice plan prior to the start of the trial, Superintendent Smith sought to place a $355 million package on the November ballot and initially received encouragement from County Commission Chair Parks Helms.[93] However, in the next few months, a large school bond package suffered a much-publicized defeat in Wake County and, more importantly, CMS' touting of its own failures and shortcomings during the trial gave critics ample ammunition for questioning whether the school system merited additional funding, especially given the uncertainty about how Potter would rule in the case. Such considerations led Helms and a majority of county commissioners to question whether any school bond referendum could pass. "The lawsuit has made it abundantly clear that there are inequities in school facilities that must be addressed, regardless of the court ruling," Helms said, as the county was finalizing plans in June 1999 for the next fiscal year. But he also noted "the uncertainty that has come about as a result of this lawsuit has created an environment where we need to be cautious and absolutely certain when we put bonds on the ballot."[94] As a result, no school bonds appeared on the November 1999 ballot.

Nor was it initially clear that bonds would be placed on the November 2000 ballot because much of the discussion about the proposed referendum occurred in early 2000 as a deeply divided school board grappled with pupil assignment. Whatever differences there were on the school board were frequently writ even larger in relations between the school board and county commission. Many aspects of these relations resembled the chicken-and-egg debate, with some board members, especially African American ones, claiming that they could not support a pupil assignment plan without guaranteed full funding for equity, and the county commission saying that it could not authorize a bond referendum absent the adoption of a pupil assignment plan. With the board adopting a plan in June, the county commission eventually authorized the package of $275.5 million for the November ballot, approximately three-quarters of which was slated for the renovation, repair, or replacement of older schools.[95]

However, one of the board members who had opposed the pupil assignment plan, Jim Puckett, campaigned against the bonds, and another of the plan's opponents, Lindalyn Kakadelis, gave the bonds only a lukewarm endorsement.[96] But other board members vigorously supported the bonds, the Charlotte Chamber spearheaded a drive that raised more than $300,000 in support of a Yes vote, and bond proponents waged a high-profile, effective campaign that reflected how much the need to renovate existing schools as well as to build new ones had become a staple of local discourse since the trial, if not since the C33's report.[97]

Although the school bond package received a slightly lower percentage of local votes than any other package on the ballot, it still passed by a very comfortable 71–29 percent margin. Indicative of the widespread support for the bonds were the facts that they secured a majority of votes in all but one of the county's precincts and received almost as high of a percentage of votes (68 percent) in Jim Puckett's district, District 1, as in the entire county. Moreover, on that same Election Day, Puckett was elected to District 1's seat on the county commission, but support for his candidacy did not necessarily translate into opposition for the bonds. In the precinct where Puckett ran strongest, receiving 69 percent of the vote, the school bonds received 59 percent of the vote. In Puckett's two next strongest precincts in which he received 68 percent, the bonds received 67 percent and 62 percent of the vote.[98] The existence of support for both Puckett and the bonds in a part of the county especially aggrieved by recent pupil assignment decisions suggests that the November 2000 referendum provided some important lessons about how civic capacity could be developed despite intense controversy over educational policy. The Conclusion will consider these lessons.

Chapter 8

School Desegregation and the Uphill Flow of Civic Capacity

The success of Charlotte, N.C. and Mecklenburg County, all this economic success . . . has been based on what I would call racial harmony . . . Had we taken a different course in 1972 (when schools were desegregated), then we would not be enjoying the prosperity that we now have.

—Statement several months before the 1999 reopening of the *Swann* litigation by C. D. Spangler Jr., prominent Charlotte businessman, former member of the Charlotte-Mecklenburg School Board, and former president of the University of North Carolina.[1]

We have got absolutely the best school system in the United States. I will say to you that any school system that isn't doing what ought to be done ought to get about it because they can make progress. We elected a Black mayor, and we are proud of him . . . I would say to you that prior to school integration, we couldn't have done that, regardless of how good he was. We have grown tremendously.

—Statement at a 1984 National Education Association commemoration of *Brown* v. *Board of Education* by W. T. Harris, supermarket magnate and former chair of the Mecklenburg Board of County Commissioners.[2]

What's wrong with Mecklenburg's county commissioners and their county manager, Jerry Fox? . . . County finances are in the best shape in years. By continuing to treat the schools as burdensome stepchildren needing stringent financial discipline, the commissioners and Mr. Fox are unnecessarily handicapping the school board and administration, insulting the good teachers of this county and neglecting the children in their classrooms.

—Editorial in the *Charlotte Observer*, three days after reporting W. T. Harris's comments to the NEA.[3]

The themes that emerge from the previous chapters can be grouped under two main headings: school desegregation and civic capacity. Since desegregation catapulted CMS onto the national stage, it is appropriate to begin there. In discussing the consequences of desegregation, I distinguish between educational and political ones. Without gainsaying the educational benefits of desegregation, I will argue that the political spillovers from desegregation did more to build civic capacity in the area of economic development than in the area of education. As a result of this asymmetric transfer of civic capacity, the spillovers from desegregation, I also claim, did more to help the business elite than black Charlotteans. I then consider how these asymmetries can be decreased by drawing on the Introduction's discussion of the necessity of regulation and coercion in the operation of opportunity expansion regimes. After indicating why the regulation and coercion of institutional elites are indeed necessary to improve education for African Americans in Charlotte, I explore the relationship between the Charlotte-Mecklenburg Compromise and civic capacity. The chapter concludes by using the Charlotte experience to comment on the debate, discussed in the Introduction, about whether the situation of the urban poor can improve absent major changes in the corporate domination of most urban regimes.

WHO BENEFITTED FROM SCHOOL DESEGREGATION IN CHARLOTTE?

As the twentieth century wound down, the country witnessed a large-scale retreat from school desegregation.[4] Almost fifty years after *Brown*, there also was widespread agreement that school desegregation had fulfilled only a small portion of the promises that its proponents had anticipated in 1954. Understanding the complex causal relations among the retreat from desegregation, its unfulfilled promises, and many other factors is no easy matter. Causal inferences are made difficult by, among other things, the tendency of desegregation's detractors—President Reagan being perhaps the most prominent national example—to pursue policies that exacerbate the very problems they decry. As a result, these detractors' jaundiced view of desegregation has a distinctly self-fulfilling aspect.[5] To such individuals and organizations, desegregation proponents can legitimately reply, "Don't spit in our face, then say it's raining."

Scholars have frequently attempted to illuminate the political controversy over desegregation with research, but the academic literature is a very contested one. Probably the closest that academics have come to achieving a consensus on the educational aspects of desegregation is *School Desegregation: A Social Science Statement*, an amicus curie brief signed by over fifty social scientists and submitted to the Supreme Court in June 1991 in *Freeman* v. *Pitts*, a major school desegregation case that arose in an Atlanta suburb. The statement affirmed the long-term benefits of desegregation: "Black students who go to desegregated schools tend to have more friends of other races, work in higher-status jobs, live in integrated neighborhoods . . . and evaluate their own skills and education in more realistic ways when choosing an occupation."[6] Summarizing the results of previous research dealing with short-term effects, the statement said, "Desegregation is generally associated with moderate gains in the achievement of black students, and the achievement of white students is typically unaffected."[7] However, the statement was not signed by several prominent desegregation researchers, including the main expert witness for the white plaintiffs in the 1999 trial, David Armor, who has critiqued the statement at length.[8]

The skepticism of Armor and other critics notwithstanding, there may be more scholarly consensus about the educational benefits of desegregation than about what I will call spillover benefits, the extent to which school desegregation affects a locality's politics, economics, race relations, and other aspects of social life. Skepticism about these benefits takes at least three forms. The first involves the claim that school desegregation undermines potential unity over economic issues between blacks and working-class whites, especially where plans impose heavy transportation and reassignment responsibilities on the latter while exempting upper-class and professional whites. Whatever empirical merit that claim may have, it frequently leads to a political stance in which a narrow conception of the interests of white workers trumps the pursuit of racial justice. Whether or not that political stance is deemed racist—and it is, by most definitions of the term—it precludes the kind of interracial unity that has facilitated the most ennobling and often the most successful struggles in U.S. working-class history.[9] However, the Charlotte experience has relatively little to contribute to the voluminous literature on this subject in part because, as noted in chapter 2, organizations with distinctive roots among white workers or the (multiracial) working class played relatively little role in local politics, especially those involving education, in the twentieth century's last three decades. For this reason, I will confine my comments on this issue to a note and turn to the kinds of skepticism about which the Charlotte experience during these years says considerably more.[10]

Daniel Monti has forcefully articulated such skepticism. He draws on the anthropological literature to liken school desegregation battles in St. Louis to "a ritual that created only the illusion of change" because, despite all of the fuss made over school desegregation, it made little difference in the "community's basic economic or political life."[11] Like all ritualistic crises and reforms, school desegregation involved making "some gesture of concern, a symbolic attempt to heal old wounds, without taxing our institutions too severely or exacerbating the problems that lie at the basis of our disagreement. We move to resolve our differences in short, cautious steps, never taking a definitive action to resolve the problem but also neatly avoiding the chaos that such a resolution surely would bring."[12] Monti's skepticism is paralleled by Derrick Bell's doubts about school desegregation's ability to effect major change. According to Bell, "The interests of blacks in achieving racial equality will be accommodated only when it converges with the interests of whites."[13] In support of the interest-convergence thesis, Bell points to the help that *Brown* gave U.S. policymakers in their fight to "win the hearts and minds of emerging third-world peoples" during the Cold War, and the belief among many white Southerners that an end to Jim Crow was the precondition of the region's economic progress.

In considering what the Charlotte experience says about Bell's and Monti's skepticism, as well as about the harm and benefit of desegregation in general, it is easiest to begin by discussing educational outcomes and then turn to the spillovers, my main concern.

School Desegregation and Educational Outcomes

The testimony presented during the 1999 *Swann* trial provides much of the best available data on this issue. Although the district court did not credit it, CMS and the black plaintiffs presented considerable evidence that racially identifiable black schools received fewer human and physical resources than other schools, especially racially identifiable white schools. Moreover, attendance at racially identifiable black schools had an adverse effect on outcomes, as Mickelson's research has shown. Even controlling for a range of individual, family, and school-level background indicators, the more time high school seniors had spent in racially identifiable black elementary schools during their academic careers, the lower were their scores on standardized tests in the sixth and twelfth grades, and the lower was their track placement in high school. While these effects were small, they were consistent and statistically significant. Moreover, both track placement and sixth-grade achievement affected high school grades and SAT scores, thus indicating that elementary school racial imbalance had indirect as well as direct effects.[14]

Most of the testimony dealt with the years immediately prior to the trial by which time CMS had, as noted earlier, undergone considerable resegregation. A different line of evidence about the benefits of desegregation involves academic outcomes during the early 1980s, the heyday of the mandatory busing plan during which few, if any, of CMS' schools had a black enrollment that exceeded *Swann* ceilings. Educational outcomes during these years received relatively little attention during the trial, and the evidence dealing with them is frustratingly fragmentary. However, the available data, as chapter 3 indicated, currently suggest that during the years of maximum compliance with *Swann*, academic outcomes for blacks were relatively better than in the subsequent years when compliance declined.

In sum, the data from Charlotte—both during the early 1980s and especially more recently—indicate that desegregation is associated with improved short-term academic outcomes for African American students. The same statement can be made about long-term outcomes, as indicated by a wide range of anecdotal evidence and oral histories. Yet it is difficult to read through the oral histories and anecdotal evidence without getting the distinct impression that the most lyrical accounts of Charlotte's desegregation experience are generally those of whites, most of whom are middle or upper class. Whether the overrepresentation of such whites in these accounts is a methodological artifact or of substantive significance is difficult to ascertain.

However, the support that Charlotte provides for the educational benefits of desegregation must be tempered with the evidence that CMS was never a fully desegregated or equitable system. Even during the heyday of the mandatory busing plan, when few schools had black enrollments that exceeded *Swann* ceilings, there was considerable racial disparity in track placement, and as this second-generation segregation declined, there was an increasing return of first-generation segregation. Also, during the heyday of the mandatory busing plan, African American families bore a larger share of the transportation responsibilities. Under the system of paired elementary schools, virtually all of the early grades were located in white neighborhoods. As a result, the youngest children bused were almost always African American, and they were bused out of their neighborhoods for more years than white children were. While many of the transportation inequities associated with pairing were ipso facto eliminated with the implementation of the magnet plan, other inequities became even greater, as indicated by the large discrepancy between the number of black and white students satellited.[15] Moreover, as the 1999 trial made clear, the academic achievement of blacks continued to lag that of whites by a considerable amount, and CMS suffered from significant racially correlated gaps in the allocation of pivotal resources such as experienced teachers. To be sure, in ruling that CMS was unitary, Judge Potter found that the school system had done all it could practicably do to remedy these many disparities and/or that they could not be traced to the era of state-mandated segregation. Thus, the legal significance of these disparities may be minimal. But their political and educational significance remains large because they indicate how far a school system lauded for its desegregation accomplishments and a Southern community touted for its progressive race relations ever were from fulfilling *Brown* v. *Board of Education*'s clarion call for racial equality in public education.

Charlotteans Weigh In

These shortcomings, if not failures, are as integral a part of the educational aspects of Charlotte's desegregation history as the accomplishments. Yet any attempt to view these downsides as the primary aspect of Charlotte's desegregation history must address the response of Charlotteans, both black and white, to the September 1999 court decision prohibiting CMS from considering race in pupil assignment. How Charlotteans view CMS' desegregation experience is hardly a decisive appraisal of its achievements and failures, but it is certainly relevant to such an appraisal.

The viewpoint of African Americans seems especially clear. Public opinion polls consistently show that large majorities of black Charlotteans favored busing for racial balance, even during the period in which the school board was under intense pressure to adopt a race-neutral pupil assignment.[16] This pro-busing sentiment has been reflected in the activities of leading organizations and individuals in the black community. Easily the most visible of these activities was the coming together of a very broad coalition to pressure the school board to appeal Potter's ruling and this coalition's ability to pack Ebenezer Baptist Church on short notice for the rally discussed in chapter 7. Although some black Charlotteans thought an appeal was futile and may have even welcomed a return to (highly segregated) neighborhood schools, there was no organized opposition to the appeal among African Americans, and none of the area's principal black institutions, organizations, or leaders spoke out against the appeal. The absence of public disagreement is especially significant because in many other places African Americans have publicly questioned the importance of desegregation, and in at least one important contemporaneous case, they launched a successful legal challenge to a desegregation order.[17]

Also instructive is the response to the court decision of school board chair Griffin under whose leadership all of the board's black members voted to appeal Potter's decision. Few, if any, Charlotteans, either black or white, have as intimate knowledge of, and experience with, the shortcomings and failures of school desegregation in Charlotte as Griffin. In the mandatory busing plan's heyday, before he was on the school board, Griffin attacked disparities in academic achievement and appeared at disciplinary hearings on behalf of black children whose white teachers were inadequately prepared for dealing with multiracial educational settings. Once on the board in the mid-1980s, Griffin found himself calling attention to lagging black achievement, fighting the construction of new schools in outlying areas of the county, and being accused by the *Charlotte Observer* of playing with fire for raising concerns about what he considered the school board's haphazard approach to pupil assignment. Moreover, on many occasions—such as the 1996 school board vote on whether to accept land for a school near Ballantyne—Griffin was willing to place desegregation below other policy goals, such as securing additional resources for predominantly black schools. Despite that willingness to accept resegregation in specific instances and despite intense pressure from the business elite not to appeal Potter's decision, Griffin was unwilling to accept the blanket resegregation that it entailed. Whatever desegregation's many shortcomings and failures, from the perspective of Griffin and the African Americans who mobilized in support of the appeal, the largely separate and segregated school systems promised by Potter's decision could never be equal. Since, like Griffin, many of the people at the rally were well aware of the inadequacies of CMS' desegregation efforts, their position may perhaps best be summarized by Jennifer Hochschild's paraphrase of Churchill's famous observation about democracy: "School desegregation is the worst option, except for the others."[18]

Almost certainly, fewer white than black Charlotteans would agree with that paraphrase. Nonetheless, surveys of registered voters conducted yearly from 1995 to 2001 show that between 15 percent and 20 percent of whites consistently support "busing students to achieve racial balance," and an additional 30 percent of whites are ambivalent about neighborhood schools if it means "that a number of schools will become racially segregated."[19] Electoral results are even more noteworthy. Although blacks constituted only 25 percent of registered voters, desegregation proponents did quite well in the two elections preceding and the two elections following the 1999 trial. The election just two months after the ruling in the trial was especially noteworthy because two outspoken white advocates of neighborhood schools, Larry Gauvreau and Paul Haisley, failed to unseat Arthur Griffin and Wilhelmenia Rembert, despite the two black incumbents' high-profile vote to appeal Potter's ruling and the board's "doofus defense" during the trial. It would be stretching things, as the previous chapter indicated, to view that election as a referendum on desegregation. But at a minimum, Gauvreau's and Haisley's defeat indicates that a blanket return to neighborhood—and, hence, heavily segregated—schools was not especially salient and/or important to significant numbers of white voters.

Results in 1999 largely mirrored those in the other elections closest to the trial. In 1995, there was considerable speculation that with the switch to the hybrid system of representation, social conservatives would gain the kind of toehold in Charlotte that they had secured in neighboring counties. However, racial liberals emerged from the 1995 election with seven of the board's nine seats. Two years later, neighborhood school advocates scored a net gain of only one seat despite the recent uproar over student assignment and the highly publicized formation of Citizens for a Neighborhood School System, aimed at electing a board whose majority would support a return to neighborhood schools.

And, in 2001, the white board member, Louise Woods—who had voted with the board's four black members on many crucial desegregation-related issues—beat an extremely well financed challenger by a large margin.

Viewed in connection with the courts' ruling that CMS is unitary, these electoral victories suggest that CMS was putting another new twist on the U.S. school desegregation saga in the elections before and after the 1999 trial. Much of that saga, as Jennifer Hochschild has noted, involves a tension between liberalism's focus on rights and democracy's emphasis on citizen sovereignty because of the historical opposition of whites to meaningful school desegregation.[20] Indicative of this tension is the fact that, as noted in chapter 3, desegregation has almost universally resulted "from an agent outside and 'above' the school districts themselves," very frequently the federal judiciary which, it needs hardly be said, is not subject to popular election.[21] Indeed, that was how Charlotte got its busing plan.

But a different dynamic prevailed in the two elections preceding and the two following the trial. Opponents of desegregation had to initiate legal proceedings, and proponents more than held their own in the elections. The election results had many causes, and desegregation per se was not on the ballot. Nevertheless, despite ongoing opportunities for the workings of electoral politics to result in a repudiation of CMS' long-standing commitment to desegregation and to defeat some of the school board's most vocal proponents of this commitment, neither of those things happened during the turn-of-the century pupil assignment battles. Consequently, given the victory of the white plaintiffs in the reopened *Swann* case and the subsequent implementation of the race-neutral pupil assignment plan, one can plausibly argue that in those years the workings of the federal judiciary did more than the local electoral process to undermine Charlotte's pursuit of desegregation.

That argument leads to a further observation about how Charlotte's experience in those years contravenes the conventional wisdom about the federal courts and local control of educational policy. A declaration of unitary status is generally seen as increasing the authority of a local community. As the *Observer* put it in the subhead of its editorial after the Supreme Court refused to hear the appeal in the reopened *Swann* case, "Supreme Court decision puts the job in our hands."[22] Indeed, such statements are virtual truisms, if not tautologies. A finding of unitary status releases a school district from judicial supervision which, almost by definition, would seem to mean increased local control. However, up through and including the 2001 school board elections, the workings of local politics produced a school board majority that was more sympathetic to considering race in pupil assignment than the judicial finding of unitary status allowed it to do. In this respect, the courts' ruling that CMS was unitary can be viewed as undermining local control rather than strengthening it.

Spillover Benefits

Part of the ongoing support for desegregation in Charlotte can probably be attributed to its tranquil race relations. They are the most direct spillover effect of desegregation and have been repeatedly noted by civic leaders, scholars, and journalists. To remark on the benign aspects of Charlotte race relations since the 1970s is not to ignore the upheaval, student riots, and community turmoil earlier in that decade. Just the reverse; that tumult proved cathartic, helping Charlotteans become, in the words of the 1970s' school board chair, Bill Poe, "a whole lot better people than we were."[23]

The changes of the 1970s gave African Americans increased access to the corridors of corporate and political power, as suggested by the election of a black mayor, Harvey Gantt. Similarly, citizen participation, both black and white, in the implementation of the busing plan helped build the biracial coalition that won the 1977 referendum that changed Charlotte's city council from a body elected entirely at large to one in which a majority were elected from districts. "Because of the integration of the schools, we made contact through the PTAs—with the parents of our kids' friends in school—with the black community that we never had before," said Sam Smith, a white leader in the fight to change representation. "Had we still had separate school systems, it would have been much harder to form that coalition."[24] In the wake of that change, African American representation on the city council increased.

In those same years, spillovers from school desegregation affected Charlotte's public housing program in a way that benefited African Americans. In 1973, Julius Chambers filed suit in federal court, charging the Charlotte Housing Authority with furthering residential discrimination by concentrating public housing in predominantly black neighborhoods. Despite initial resistance to the suit by many local officials, a settlement was reached several years later, in part because of pressure from Judge McMillan and in part because of the lobbying by the same individuals and groups that had played a pivotal role in the development and implementation of the busing plan. Charlotte's initial scattered-site project opened in 1978, making it one of the first localities in the country to coordinate its school desegregation and public housing efforts.[25] By the time a combination of local and national developments brought the scattered-site program to an end a decade later, approximately 900 units had been built in twenty projects. Although not enough to make a significant dent in residential segregation, Charlotte's scattered-site program was generally considered one of the nation's most successful, and it made things somewhat easier for CMS. As Jay Robinson noted, such housing "cuts down on busing. It will not solve the problem, and it's only a small percentage, but it sure does help."[26]

Changed race relations also facilitated Charlotte's economic development. There is no way to compare quantitatively the importance of desegregation with other causes of Charlotte's boom, but virtually every civic leader, scholar, and journalist who has reflected on local growth has noted the link between it and school desegregation. Indeed, as suggested by both the statement from C. D. Spangler Jr. that provides the first epigraph for this chapter and the statement from Hugh McColl that provides an epigraph for the Introduction, Charlotte's most prominent business executives have viewed school desegregation as crucial to the area's prosperity. While Spangler's and McColl's comments might conceivably be discounted as those of business executives traditionally associated with racial liberalism, the same cannot be said of Bill Poe, who, as school board chair, spearheaded the appeal of McMillan's decision. As recently as 1995, Poe downplayed the educational significance of *Swann*, claiming that CMS was well on its way toward desegregating its schools even before judicial intervention. However, even he acknowledged that the way people came together to implement the Supreme Court decision "generated an era of racial good will in this community . . . Our compliance with court orders . . . and the general positive attitude of people here in race relations has contributed tremendously to the economics of the community."[27]

In addition, the workings of regime politics cannot be understood without reference to school desegregation. It was part of what might be called "the policy cement" that held together the coalition between black political leaders and the business elite that was necessary to elect pro-growth officials and pass the bond referenda that financed the infrastructure upon which development depended. To be sure, this coalition's origins antedate the business elite's support for the busing plan, but whether the coalition could have remained cohesive absent that support is extremely problematic. Urban regimes endure, as Stone emphasizes, because governance is not the "issue-by-issue process that pluralism suggests."[28] Thus, given very strong black support for school desegregation, the coalition might have frayed had the business elite not thrown its support behind the busing plan following the Supreme Court's 1971 decision. From this perspective, support for the busing plan may be considered as much the glue that held this coalition together, as were Fred Alexander's employment by C. D. Spangler Sr., a complex web of personal relationships, and a wide range of development projects.

Since regime theory emphasizes how informal arrangements and personal relationships allow governance to transcend the issue-by-issue process suggested by pluralism, it is useful to illustrate the way in which school desegregation strengthened long-standing relationships between the business elite and black political leaders in a way that facilitated governance and increased civic capacity. The illustration involves Leroy "Pop" Miller, one of CMS' most acclaimed teachers and principals. An African American, Miller had contact with Charlotte's business elite as early as the segregated 1940s. As a teacher at the all-black West Charlotte High School, he and students from the school's vocational education program catered dinner parties at the homes of some of Charlotte's wealthiest and most powerful white families, including that of developer James Harris. During one such party, the *Observer* reported, Harris's young son, Johnny Harris, earned a spanking from Miller for dirtying a dance floor that the latter had just waxed.[29] When twenty years later, CMS faced the politically delicate task of assigning the first-ever black principal to a historically white high school in affluent southeast Charlotte, it tapped Miller, by then the principal of a recently desegregated, historically white middle school in southeast Charlotte.

Miller's successful and almost legendary leadership at both the historically white middle school and high school gave him enhanced respect as well as direct contact with many of Charlotte's most powerful and influential white citizens. Among these white citizens was Eddie Knox, who as mayor subsequently appointed Miller a vice chair of a citizens committee created in 1983 to address—very successfully, as it turned out—the controversies swirling around proposals for construction of a new coliseum.[30] By then an adult and one of Charlotte's most prominent developers, Johnny Harris chaired that committee. Harris and Miller provided "a perfect combination," in the words of Knox's successor, Harvey Gantt: "Pop Miller, popular principal of a high school in Charlotte with a top academic reputation. Black, likeable, acceptable in the black community *and* the white community was exactly the kind of leader [that was needed] with a Johnny Harris developer/old Charlotte name."[31] Because of Miller's respected leadership of schools in southeast Charlotte, when he "would take a position," a white civic leader who also served on the coliseum committee would note that "people would listen to it in populations that wouldn't listen to other African Americans. So he had a very unique role. You always tried to get Pop Miller to embrace your side of an issue . . . It carried with it such respect."[32]

Finally, there is a more subtle but very important way that school desegregation facilitated economic development. This involves the contribution that desegregation made to the switch to district representation on the city council in 1977. Opponents of district representation feared that it would strengthen neighborhood political clout at the expense of growth, but that fear proved unjustified. The change in representation did lead to greater geographical equity in the dispersion of some resources, most notably emergency medical services, but there is no indication that it adversely affected Charlotte's growth. A 1984 comparative study of eleven cities, one of which was Charlotte, found "no evidence of major changes in the distribution of policy benefits, other than in the location of new facilities."[33] Three years later, a study focusing on Charlotte noted: "There is little evidence that district representatives on the Council have acted any different from at-large members. Nor is there any evidence that the five Councils from 1977 to 1987 have been 'anti-growth' or more parochial than earlier Councils. To the contrary, overall the decade from 1977 to 1987 witnessed one of the most significant economic and population expansions in Charlotte's history."[34]

Not only did the switch to districts not hurt Charlotte's growth, but there is considerable evidence that the switch helped development because district representation greatly facilitated the passage of the bonds necessary for the expansion of Charlotte's airport. When first placed on the ballot in 1975, the airport bonds failed, largely because a group of black leaders saw mobilization of a No vote as a way to indicate both dismay at the city's neglect of African American needs and anger at Charlotte's more established black political leadership that supported the bonds. Combined with the opposition of white neighborhoods, such as those on the westside, traditionally less likely than affluent southeast Charlotte to support bond referenda, the unusually strong black opposition helped defeat the bonds by a 54–46 percent margin. When the bonds subsequently appeared on the ballot in 1978, district representation had been implemented with the result that one of the main black leaders of the No campaign in 1975 was now on the council, and other opponents, both black and white, now felt that they had a place at the table. As Harvey Gantt would later remark, "There's a direct correlation between district representation in 1977 . . . and the passage of the [airport] bond referendum in 1978 . . . Some of the people who had got elected after district representation . . . brought along large constituencies that had voted against the airport bond before . . . People felt better about the city because they now had representation on the council."[35] While the bonds did better throughout Charlotte in 1978 than in 1975, the swing was especially large in the black precincts.[36]

Without the passage of the 1978 referendum and the subsequent expansion of the airport, Charlotte would not—indeed, could not—have grown the way it did in the 1980s and 1990s. For example, the mergers and acquisitions that led to the explosive growth of Charlotte's banks might very well have taken place had not the airport been expanded, but it is extremely unlikely that the merged banks' headquarters would have remained in Charlotte without such an expansion.

Insofar as school desegregation facilitated the area's dramatic economic growth, improved educational outcomes, and enhanced African American political mobility and access, it would seem a policy with many worthy spillovers benefiting a broad range of Charlotteans. There is some merit to that viewpoint, but it begs two related and troubling issues, the first of which is suggested by Bell's interest-convergence thesis and the second by Monti's claim that school desegregation distracts attention from more fundamental issues.

The Interest-Convergence Thesis and the Primacy of Developm

While the interest-convergence thesis indicates that whites as well as blacks can benefit from the latter's demand for racial equality, the thesis's cutting edge is that black interest in racial equality will receive short shrift unless it converges with white interests. In evaluating that thesis's relevance to Charlotte, two thorny issues must be addressed: Is there a distinct black interest—as opposed to diverse and perhaps conflicting black interests—in achieving racial justice? Is there a distinct white interest—again, as opposed to diverse and perhaps conflicting white interests—that must be accommodated to achieve this justice? For purposes of this discussion of school desegregation in Charlotte, my answer to the first question is yes, and to the second, no.

While important differences and conflicts certainly exist among African Americans, they are secondary in any discussion of school desegregation in Charlotte. From the 1970s, when Reverend Leake's support for busing trumped his dislike of the loss of identity of black schools, to 1999, when there was no organized opposition among African Americans to the school board's appealing Potter's decision, black Charlotteans have generally cohered around the position that a desegregated school system was a key aspect of the struggle for racial equality.[37] In this respect, Charlotte is an example of Peter Eisinger's claim that "there is justification for viewing black urban populations as constituting racial political communities, distinctive from white political communities and capable of independent and cohesive action" and able "to resolve internal tensions in order to present a united racial front."[38]

For whites, the situation is more complicated. Indeed, one of the key issues in U.S. history is which, if any, predominantly white groups, classes, or strata benefit from white supremacy and, if so, under what circumstances and for how long. Unable even to begin to address that complex issue here, I want to rephrase Bell's thesis by talking not about whites in general but about what, according to both intuition and regime theory, is the most politically influential social formation of whites in Charlotte, the business elite, which remained overwhelmingly white even at the start of the twenty-first century. Thus rephrased, the issue becomes, Do black interests in securing racial justice receive short shrift when they do not converge with the business elite's interest in economic growth and development?

Yes is the answer provided by much of Charlotte's desegregation experience. While racial justice and the education of black children have been important to some members of the business elite, concerns about civic tranquility and economic growth were generally more common and stronger motivations. Had the former concerns been primary, the business elite would not, in general, have stood on the sidelines during the tumultuous years between the initial desegregation order by federal district court judge James

McMillan and the Supreme Court's affirmation of it in 1971. But the Supreme Court's decision made clear that the most expeditious way to resolve the crisis roiling Charlotte's once placid educational waters was to satisfy the black plaintiffs and the federal court by politically intervening in support of a busing plan, as discussed in chapter 3. It is impossible to distinguish between a mere concern with civic tranquility per se and anticipation that the desegregation of the schools, like the successful desegregation of public accommodations, would be an important selling point in the struggle among localities for mobile capital. But even at that early date there is evidence that the quality (however defined) of Charlotte's school system affected its ability to lure new businesses to Charlotte. Bill Poe, school board chair during those tumultuous days, has recalled "sitting in any number of meetings where questions were asked about the school system" by representatives of businesses considering relocating to Charlotte.[39]

The business elite's support for desegregation was largely ancillary to its pursuit of development. To be sure, once the busing plan was implemented, civic boosters milked CMS' school desegregation accomplishments for all they were worth, deriving, as noted earlier, much mileage from Charlotte's being "The City That Made It Work" in contrast to being just another city, like Atlanta, merely too busy to hate. But in major conflicts between desegregation and development, the latter typically prevailed, as exemplified by the 1970s' controversy about the location of the outerbelt in the south of the county. W. T. Harris and other members of the business elite could wax quite lyrical about Charlotte's desegregation accomplishments, as evidenced by this chapter's second epigraph. However, as noted in chapter 4, they paid virtually no attention to how the outerbelt's construction would affect CMS. Harris preferred the southern route but did not really care where the road went as long as it was built, despite the especially grave implications of the southern route for CMS' ability to maintain a desegregated system. Similarly, warnings on the *Observer's* news and editorial pages about how southeastern Mecklenburg's growth was jeopardizing desegregation did nothing to abate growth in that area. Local government did make considerable effort in the 1970s and 1980s to promote growth in the northern part of the county, and, in those years, such growth posed fewer challenges to desegregation because the developing areas in the north of the county were closer to black neighborhoods than the developing areas in the south. However, while attempts to encourage growth in the north of the county were successful, those to limit it in the south generally failed. As a result, when the *Swann* litigation reopened in the late 1990s, there were a large number of recently constructed schools in the south of the county that were racially identifiable white by the definition adopted by Judge Potter in the trial.

Another example of the business elite's approach to education involves the scrapping of the busing plan. The growth facilitated by the plan helped undermine it by attracting newcomers to Charlotte who lacked attachment to CMS' desegregation accomplishments and were accustomed to smaller, more racially homogeneous school districts. Especially vocal in these criticisms were employees of Royal Insurance, at that point Charlotte's prize relocation plum. Fearing that future relocations and growth would be threatened, the established business elite threw its support behind dismantling the busing plan.

The resultant magnet plan was an attempt to have the cake and eat it too—to maintain a desegregated school system but to appease desegregation's critics and thus not jeopardize growth. Consequently, the magnet plan might be viewed as a policy that, like mandatory busing, fulfilled the interests of both the business elite and black Charlotteans. That view, however, encounters at least three difficulties. First, whatever racial inequities existed in the 1974 mandatory busing plan, it enjoyed considerable support from black political leaders as well as the business elite. But in the 1992 magnet plan, the overlap was much less, with the business elite pushing the plan very hard but with many blacks—including all major black political organizations and the law firm that had represented Swann a generation earlier—voicing doubts.

Second, many of these doubts turned out to be justified. As the C25, League of Women Voters, and Black Political Caucus noted, the years following the magnet plan saw increasing resegregation and increasing disparities between have and have-not schools. Yet in its enthusiasm for John Murphy and his reform program, the business elite paid little attention to these issues. Nor for all of its talk of accountability and the presumed concern with quantitative measures of academic achievement did the business elite make any attempt to marshal the considerable intellectual talent at its disposal to conduct an independent evaluation of the Murphy administration's claims of breathtaking gains in academic achievement.

Third, the dismantling of this nationally praised busing plan was allowed to occur without any evaluation of how it was affecting the education of either black or white children. Although ample time for such an evaluation existed between the explosion of dissatisfaction in the mid-1980s and the adoption of the magnet plan five years later, it was not attempted. For this omission, CMS obviously bears primary responsibility, but with accountability already a buzzword in business discourse about public education, it is striking that Charlotte's corporate elite made no attempt to assess the educational consequences of the mandatory busing plan. Rather, the main criteria were political ones that gave high priority to the dissatisfaction of whites, especially vocal transplants, seen as threatening Charlotte's ability to attract mobile capital. In this respect, the withdrawal of support for the mandatory busing plan was the mirror image of the early 1970's infusion of support for it. In the 1970s, African American political mobilization provided the greatest threat to local political tranquility and led—after the Supreme Court's decision in *Swann*—to business elite support for the busing plan. But by the late 1980s, African American demands were no longer the main threat to local political tranquility and economic growth. Rather, other wheels were squeaking much more loudly, and they were the ones that received the most attention from the business elite's political grease gun.

The aftermath of the 1999 trial again indicates how the business elite's focus on development trumped a concern with racial justice. Especially striking was the elite's desire in the months between the close of the trial and Potter's ruling to preempt a possible appeal by CMS of the likely ruling by arranging support for compensatory resources, construction, and renovation. Moreover, once CMS decided to appeal the ruling, the business elite's silence on the merits of the appeal was deafening. Rather, it pushed for adoption of a plan before the appellate courts ruled, believing that a speedy end to the controversy over pupil assignment would be good for CMS and Charlotte. But again, the criteria for deciding what was good or bad were primarily political, not educational.

A final example of how, in conflicts between the two, development took precedence over desegregation involves local housing policy. The same political forces, including a sympathetic federal judge, that played a critical role in the implementation of the busing plan also contributed to the development of Charlotte's scattered-site public housing program. Beyond that successful, but modest, effort, Charlotte was not able to sustain political initiatives aimed at alleviating the residential segregation that helps make pupil assignment so contentious. The most noteworthy effort to link school and residential segregation came in 1993–94 when, at the request of Arthur Griffin, the staff of the planning commission prepared a report, *Housing Strategies to Racially Integrate Schools*.[40] Some of the proposed measures such as monitoring and enforcing fair housing laws were unexceptional and provoked little controversy. However, other strategies were both more ambitious and controversial, with the suggested exploration of "the use of regulatory techniques and incentive programs such as inclusionary zoning, linkage ordinances, density bonuses, and low interest loans" provoking a storm of criticism.[41]

The school board supported the report and passed a resolution calling for the creation of an Affordable Housing Policy Task Force that would include members of the school board, city council, county commission, and representatives of the real estate, banking, and housing industries.[42] But other elected officials were less favorably inclined. In a lengthy memo, Charlotte Republican Mayor Richard Vinroot wrote that while many of the goals were appealing, the overall tone and approach smacked of "social engineering." Rather than create a special committee, he successfully urged that the matter be left in the hands of the planning commission.[43] The *Observer* endorsed that proposal as a way to nurture the city and "get past the hot rhetoric."[44] But leaving matters in the hands of the planning commission, rather than a task force focused on affordable housing, took wind out of the sails of efforts to pursue the report's more ambitious strategies. It is thus hardly surprising that a year later the *Observer* could report: "There has been talk of building affordable housing throughout the county as a way to naturally desegregate the schools, but there are no formal plans."[45] Indeed, as the 1990s wore on and the conflict between desegregation and neighborhood schools became increasingly salient, residential desegregation often was touted as a way of reconciling these frequently conflicting goals.[46] But the political will, ability, and muscle to undertake any meaningful steps in that direction were lacking.

These examples of how development trumped racial justice indicate that Charlotte provides considerable evidence for the interest-convergence thesis. The Charlotte experience also furnishes evidence that, as Monti suggests, busing distracted attention from other crucial issues. However, before discussing the nature and consequences of these distractions, it is important to consider CMS' response to the priority that the business elite gave development.

CMS' Latitude and Responsibility

The business elite's emphasis on development undoubtedly posed obstacles to CMS' efforts to pursue desegregation, as did the school system's lack of taxing authority. But CMS' leadership also frequently failed to make use of whatever latitude it did have. The most striking examples of these failures occurred in the early 1990s and involved teacher assignment, magnet schools, and planning issues. Although the court orders required CMS to maintain racially balanced faculties as well as student populations, the early 1990s saw a sharp increase in racial imbalance among CMS' faculties. The jump stemmed from the decreased oversight of faculty racial balance that accompanied the move to greater site-based management that was part of the Murphy administration's reform program. Whatever advantages site-based management might have, CMS had the latitude to implement it in a manner that would have allowed the central office to monitor faculty racial composition more closely than it did.

Similarly, the magnet plan stated that there would be no restrictions on the percentage of students who could go to magnets from the particular school to which they were otherwise assigned. That statement, a virtual invitation for whites to abandon certain schools, was part of a series of policies that gave preference to the magnets at the expense of other schools, a significant number of which became racially imbalanced and resource-poor as a result. Finally, during these years, the school board failed to adopt the 2002 Draft Master Plan. Prepared early in the Murphy administration, the plan was an unprecedented effort to overcome the fragmentation that historically

characterized school-related planning issues by bringing together staff from
CMS and the planning commission to develop a strategy for the siting of
new schools in a way that would accommodate growth and maintain a desegregated system. The plan emphasized the use of midpoint schools, with
one result being that none of the suggested locations was below Highway 51
in the southern, heavily white part of the county. However, the board never
adopted the 2002 Draft Master Plan, and within the next several years, CMS
began construction of at least three schools south of that road, two of which
would be approximately 95 percent white when they opened. Moreover, CMS'
decision to build all three of these schools fueled demands that it also ignore
desegregation guidelines when siting schools in the north of the county.

Both the Supreme Court and McMillan in *Swann* as well as the latter in
Martin had emphasized the importance of building new schools in locations
that would facilitate, not impede, desegregation. However, the board of education ignored its legal responsibilities, most strikingly in the locations of McKee
Road and Hawk Ridge, and the populating of Crestdale. The cumulative effect
of school siting decisions after McMillan's last (1980) pupil assignment order
in *Swann* was to impose much greater transportation responsibilities upon
black families if CMS were to maintain a desegregated system.

As the Fourth Circuit's three-judge panel noted, almost all of the twenty-
seven new schools in the previous twenty years were located in predominantly
white, generally outlying areas. During these same years, it should be emphasized, blacks accounted for approximately 55 percent of the increase in CMS'
enrollment. The siting of any one school or several schools might be explained by the complexities of the real estate market, severe fiscal constraints,
and other factors that constrained CMS' choices. But it is difficult to attribute
the cumulative discriminatory character of the location of these schools to
factors beyond the influence of CMS. The cumulative result of these siting
decisions, and the manner in which CMS drew attendance zones, was to
facilitate, beginning in the mid-1980s, growing racial imbalance in student
populations, despite the fact that, as witnesses for all three parties noted in
the 1999 trial, residential segregation in Mecklenburg was declining.

Pupil assignment was not CMS' only shortcoming in the early 1990s.
Despite the hype and national publicity accompanying Murphy's reform program, CMS' progress in improving outcomes was, with only one exception,
either the same or worse than that of comparable urban systems and the
entire state. As a result of such trends, CMS generally underperformed these
comparison school systems on state-mandated tests at the end of the Murphy
administration, just as it did at the start.

While part of CMS' problems may conceivably be attributable to
insufficient financial support, this is hardly the whole story. Rather, the reform program was characterized by woefully uneven implementation; a lack

of direction about how to achieve the reform vision; numerous examples of what Hess has called policy churn;[47] an esoteric accountability system that when communicated to the public (and many CMS personnel as well) concealed as much as it revealed; an eventually self-defeating emphasis on symbolic politics; and a superintendent whose ego, personal skills, and pre-occupation with his compensation undercut a vision of education that many in the community and CMS found inspiring. Indeed, given the initial enthu-siasm of both the business elite and a broad array of Charlotteans for Murphy's reform program, the most striking aspect of his administration may very well be the way it squandered this support and collapsed under the weight of its own contradictions.

Thus, budgetary constraints, Charlotte's explosive growth, a business elite for whom education was distinctly ancillary to economic growth, and the fragmentation of local political authority may not have provided the most supportive environment. But CMS' leadership can hardly be absolved of re-sponsibility for the school system's shortcomings in complying with court orders, pursuing racial equality in education more effectively, and improving opportunities and outcomes for all of its students.

Busing as a Distraction

Just as much of the Charlotte experience provides support for the interest-convergence thesis, so too does it furnish evidence for arguments, such as Daniel Monti's, that desegregation distracts attention from other crucial issues. To be sure, not all of Monti's analysis is applicable to Charlotte. In St. Louis, metropolitan fragmentation and a stagnating economy were key issues that were much less important in Charlotte where CMS was a consolidated school district in an economically booming area. Moreover, many of Monti's policy alternatives are commonplace, e.g., enhanced cooperation between school sys-tems and local corporations. Others are admittedly unrealistic, e.g., abolition by the courts of boards of education in segregated school systems.[48] Nonetheless, any analysis of the spillover benefits to blacks of school desegregation in Char-lotte must acknowledge the validity of the gist of Monti's argument: preoccu-pation with busing distracted attention from other crucial issues.

However, it is necessary to be precise in indicating which issues in Charlotte suffered from this lack of attention. Ever since *Swann*, critics have charged that CMS' preoccupation with desegregation distracted attention from more fundamental educational issues such as improving academic achieve-ment. However, this charge holds little water, even if its dubious assumption that pupil assignment and academic achievement are independent of each other is temporarily set aside. During the heyday of the mandatory busing plan, CMS undoubtedly devoted considerable energy to pupil assignment, but there is no question that the Robinson administration also paid considerable attention to academic achievement, especially as measured by scores on standardized tests. Similarly, a decade later, the magnet plan also required that CMS devote considerable energy to pupil assignment, but the Murphy administration also watched achievement very closely, as its complex accountability system indicates. Of course being concerned with academic achievement is no guarantee of success, and the gap between the Murphy administration's rhetoric and accomplishments was especially sharp. However, I know of no evidence that the reform program would have done more to boost achievement had CMS paid less attention to pupil assignment during the Murphy administration.

While the available data suggest that the Robinson administration did comparatively better than subsequent ones in boosting black academic achievement, it too fell far short of its academic goals. But again, critics of the mandatory busing plan have never demonstrated how more of these goals could have been achieved had the Robinson administration been less concerned about pupil assignment. Moreover, if the dubious assumption that pupil assignment and academic achievement are unrelated is no longer set aside, there is the evidence noted above that in CMS, segregated schooling adversely affects academic outcomes. Thus, there is little reason to claim that concern with desegregation has distracted attention from academic achievement in CMS. Other issues, however, do provide evidence of the distractive consequences of the busing plan.

Ironically, many of these other issues are not about the much ballyhooed and alleged conflict between equity and excellence; rather, they involve the tension between settling for a modicum of equity and pursing it more fully. As chapter 3 indicates, the late 1970s and early 1980s saw a political demobilization around education issues despite the many inequities among schools and numerous racially identifiable classrooms within them. That demobilization can largely be explained by political fatigue after the struggles to implement the busing plan, satisfaction with whatever success the busing plan had realized, the ability of savvy families to take advantage of these successes, and the assumption by many educational and desegregation activists of the responsibilities of governance. Similarly, the fear—both in CMS and among many community leaders—of jeopardizing the busing plan's accomplishments militated in the 1980s against pushing harder to realize desegregation's many unfulfilled promises. With political tranquility restored during the Robinson administration and Charlotte basking in the glow of its national reputation for progressive race relations, the politically influential business elite had scant motivation to pursue educational issues with any vigor.

Moreover, the fact that the busing plan allowed CMS to achieve high and nationally praised levels of racial balance ironically contributed to a failure to pursue other, more lasting desegregation strategies. That complacency was especially clear in the siting of McKee Road and Hawk Ridge elementary schools, two of the few land acquisitions for which there is a clear paper trail. The deputy superintendents who drafted the October 1987 memo urging acquisition of those sites in outlying, overwhelming white areas in the southernmost part of the county were strong proponents of desegregation, and the memo reflects their sensitivity to this issue. Yet as the memo made clear and subsequent history confirmed, long bus rides, especially for black children, would be necessary to achieve racial balance in the schools. Despite their length, such bus rides were less expensive and politically more expedient—especially because black children were being bused—than other desegregation strategies that CMS might have adopted, such as locating new schools at sites that were approximately midway between black and white neighborhoods. As messy as busing might have been, Charlotte found it less difficult than attempting to alleviate the residential segregation that gave rise to the need for busing, magnets, and other school desegregation strategies.

Finally, the busing plan allowed Charlotte to enjoy a reputation for exemplary race relations that is difficult to reconcile with the extent of the economic gap between black and white Charlotteans. As noted in chapter 2, in the years following the *Swann* decision, the economic condition of blacks in Charlotte improved significantly in relation to blacks in comparable areas. However, black/white disparities in Mecklenburg on income, poverty rates, and home ownership generally remained among the largest of the areas with which the county was compared. Moreover, as chapter 2 also indicated, Mecklenburg's progress in reducing the black/white economic gap on home ownership and especially per capita income lagged that of many other areas during the years in which Charlotte boomed and became the national economic player that it is today.[49]

The difference between the uneven progress in narrowing the black/white economic gap and the more ample and pervasive spillover benefits from busing that accrued to Charlotte and its business elite can be summed up in several ways. One is to note the distinction often made between policies designed to help a place and polices designed to help a group of people within a particular place. For example, the federal policies that transformed the Cotton Belt to the Sunbelt were, as historian David Schulman notes, "designed not so much to uplift poor people as to enrich poor places."[50] Desegregation, in contrast, was supposedly intended to uplift people, but in Charlotte its most distinctive economic spillover was to uplift a place, which, if not poor, was a far cry from the national economic player that it is today. A second way is in terms of the comparison with Atlanta that Charlotte's civic boosters have historically been so prone to make: from an economic standpoint, busing in Charlotte did more to help Charlotte's business elite catch up with the business elite of Atlanta than it did to help Charlotte's blacks catch up with Charlotte's whites.

In comparing the busing plan's economic benefits to the business elite with that to African Americans, I am making no claim about the extent to which African Americans who experienced a desegregated education subsequently earned more money than blacks who did not.[51] The comparison is not about individuals' life chances any more than this chapter's first epigraph—C. D. Spangler Jr.'s statement about racial harmony and Charlotte's economic progress—involves the claim that desegregation resulted in better educated and more productive workers. Rather, Spangler was talking about how the enhanced race relations that resulted from school desegregation facilitated Charlotte's economic progress by what I have called spillovers. However, while this racial harmony made a crucial contribution to Charlotte's boom, its effects on the black/white economic gap were uneven and more ambiguous. Undoubtedly, the kind of policies that would have facilitated greater black/white economic equality would be difficult for any locality to undertake. However, they are not impossible according to regime theory's claim that cities can develop political arrangements and the civic capacity to ameliorate the situation of economically disadvantaged residents despite the constraints of U.S. federalism and the imperatives of capitalist accumulation. The claim that such ameliorative political arrangements and civic capacity can be developed is what regime theory's rallying cry of "Politics Matters" is largely about.

REGIME POLITICS AND THE UPHILL FLOW OF CIVIC CAPACITY

The Asymmetric Transfer of Civic Capacity

The Charlotte experience furnishes support for the claim that politics matters in at least two ways. First, the Charlotte story provides several vivid examples of how mistakes and miscalculations in the most basic kind of nuts-and-bolts politics had important consequences. One such example involves the poor organization and overoptimism of the 1987 Harvey Gantt mayoral campaign that contributed to his upset defeat. Another example involves the May 1995 school bond referendum that saw CMS, the business elite, and bond proponents make a series of errors that facilitated the referendum's defeat, put CMS in an especially severe financial bind, and contributed to Superintendent John Murphy's abrupt departure from Charlotte.

Second, the Charlotte experience indicates quite clearly how politics mediates the structural imperatives of capitalist accumulation. Such mediation was the very essence of the coalition between the business elite and leadership of the black community that dominated much of local electoral politics from 1963 to 1987. Neither Charlotte's growth, the implementation of the busing plan, nor its dismantling can be adequately understood without considering the role that coalition played in helping elect pro-growth mayors and securing passage of the bond referenda necessary to support development. Additional evidence of this mediation involves another spillover from school desegregation: the switch from at-large to a combination of district and at-large representation on the city council that, it turned out, contributed heavily to the passage of the bond referendum to expand the airport. Insofar as the westside, the part of town that spearheaded the struggle for district representation, continued to suffer from a lack of development and government services in the 1980s and 1990s, there are striking parallels between school desegregation and the switch to mixed representation: both policies did more to help Charlotte boom than to improve the situation of the people who spearheaded the struggle to obtain them.

However, regime theorists' claim that politics matters involves much more than noting the costs of political miscalculation or the ways in which politics mediates the accumulation of capital. The claim that politics matters involves both the assertion and hope that cities can develop political arrangements and the resultant civic capacity to address the needs of disadvantaged citizens in a more effective manner than is anticipated by the varieties of Marxism and rational choice theory in opposition to which regime theory largely developed. From the standpoint of this much stronger and more important claim about politics mattering, the Charlotte story is very ambiguous. The ambiguity is especially evident in a discussion of civic capacity.

Drawing on the importance that regime theory attaches to the formation of durable coalitions in urban governance, civic capacity "brings to the forefront what multiple sectors can do when acting in concert" to fulfill key policy tasks.[52] While the concept of civic capacity was recently developed by Stone in connection with the study of urban education, the phenomena to which it refers have long existed. As several of Stone's collaborators point out, "This process of building civic capacity has taken place in many American cities, albeit to varying degrees and principally to accomplish development projects."[53] The creation of civic capacity in development projects is greatly facilitated by the opportunities they provide for selective material benefits, even in the face of opposition. Thus, in his study of Atlanta, Stone notes that redevelopment has been extremely divisive, but "selective incentives have enabled the biracial governing coalition to cohere while dividing the opposition."[54] In contrast, education provides fewer opportunities for selective incentives, since it is much more a public good.[55] Consequently, it is by no means certain that civic capacity developed in one policy area can be transferred to another. As Stone notes, the use of the term civic capacity "is not meant to imply that civic capacity in one area transfers easily into civic capacity in another area. Thus, a city could mobilize civic capacity for urban development or for specific projects, such as building a new sports arena, but not in children-and-youth policy."[56]

The example that Stone provides could easily have been taken from Charlotte. The civic capacity that, for example, aided the construction of new facilities for Charlotte's major league sports franchises in the late 1980s and early 1990s did not translate into a similarly effective multisector coalition focused on improving education. More importantly, the Charlotte experience indicates the need to elaborate on Stone's point that civic capacity may not readily transfer from one issue area to another. The ease with which civic capacity can be transferred between areas depends not only on the areas themselves but on the direction in which the transfer takes place. In issues such as district representation, the construction of sports facilities, and the passage of bond referenda, the biracial institutionalized relationships that developed in the struggle over school desegregation and that subsequently facilitated Charlotte's growth are the very stuff of civic capacity, its formation in one area, and its transfer to another. In all of these cases, the transfer of civic capacity from education to development was quite easy, although the transfer in the opposite direction is, as Stone and his collaborators note, very difficult.

Not only is it difficult to transfer civic capacity to education from development, but the civic capacity developed from the busing plan, an aspect of education, did not transfer very easily to other aspects of education. Historically, CMS' planning efforts have not been well coordinated with that of other governmental agencies, an indication of the lack of cross-sectoral cooperation essential to civic capacity. Moreover, even during the heyday of busing in the 1980s, Mecklenburg's support of public education was poor. Indeed, there is a striking contrast between the picture painted by this chapter's second and third epigraphs. However much people, such as W. T. Harris, may have bragged about CMS in national forums, back home there was insufficient civic capacity to fund public education at levels comparable to that of the state's two other large, consolidated urban districts. Like inadequate planning, these funding shortfalls are telling indicators of inadequate civic capacity because the county commission's influence over CMS' finances also places a premium on cross-sectoral cooperation.

Funding was even worse in the early 1990s, with those years also witnessing a huge discrepancy between inadequate local financial support for CMS and its dazzling national reputation (now for school reform, not desegregation). In fact, the asymmetry in the flow of civic capacity seems especially striking during the early 1990s. This was the time when many pieces of Charlotte's development puzzle came together brilliantly: Charlotte's banks and, consequently, Charlotte itself attained what for each of them was unprecedented financial eminence; Charlotte acquired its National Football League (NFL) franchise, and *Fortune* provided enthusiastic accounts of both

Charlotte's business climate and the accomplishments of its most prominent business executive, Hugh McColl.[57] While none of these developments depended on the Murphy administration's reform program, its high-profile national visibility—touted by the likes of Louis Gerstner and William Bennett—facilitated Charlotte's quest for mobile capital, as exemplified by Murphy's meeting with Transamerica Reinsurance executives prior to the firm's relocating its headquarters in Charlotte.[58]

Yet for all of Charlotte's development during these years and the contribution of CMS' high-profile reform program to this growth, there is little evidence of the successful transfer of civic capacity to education. The enthusiasm of the business elite for Murphy's program was insufficient to secure the passage of the crucial bond referendum of May 1995. As a result of both that loss and one on a smaller package in 1992, the Murphy administration suffered the only two school bond defeats that CMS experienced in over a generation. Moreover, the superintendent frequently found himself at loggerheads with influential African Americans and, most importantly, by the very criteria by which the Murphy administration most wanted to be judged, academic achievement, its progress in boosting outcomes was essentially the same or worse than school systems that were not receiving the kind of national publicity that CMS was.

So relatively easy has been the transfer of civic capacity from education to development over the past twenty-five years and so relatively hard has been the transfer to education that the difference resembles that between water flowing downhill and uphill. The political advantages possessed by development projects, especially the opportunity for selective incentives, allow civic capacity to flow almost naturally to it from education. For civic capacity to go from development to education is not impossible, but, to continue the hydraulic analogy, that transfer requires the political equivalent of a pump.

Of what might this pump consist? Stone and his collaborators on the Civic Capacity and Urban Education Project have called attention to the role of community-wide identity, problem definition, and leadership in building civic capacity necessary to improve urban education.[59] Without gainsaying the importance of these factors, I would argue that they are insufficient. To do so, I draw upon the distinction that Stone has made between development and opportunity expansion regimes discussed in the Introduction. While both require coordination among institutional elites, the coordination required by an opportunity expansion regime is more difficult to achieve because it cannot be obtained on a "purely voluntary basis" but requires regulation and coercion. Such regulation and coercion may be insufficient to effect major policy changes that will benefit African Americans, but the Charlotte experience strongly suggests that they are necessary. The single most important change of the past thirty years in Charlotte was school desegregation, and

however large a role Judge McMillan and the business elite may have played
in the ultimate implementation of the mandatory busing plan, the sine qua
non of desegregation was the mass insurgency of the civil rights movement.
That upsurge had many aspects and consequences, but the regulation and
coercion of institutional elites were clearly among the most important. Given
the importance that regulation and coercion have played in the past, it is
necessary to ask, To what extent is there empirical evidence that regulation
and coercion are no longer necessary to effect educational changes that will
benefit African Americans?

Are Regulation and Coercion Necessary?

A plausible case might be made that the improvement of education for
African Americans is less dependent on the regulation and coercion of institutional elites today than it was a generation ago. This case hinges on a claim
that the most important of these institutional elites, Charlotte's business elite,
has a much greater stake in improving education now than it did in the early
1970s. At that time, the fight over desegregation was largely seen as interfer-
ing with the political calm and stability considered a precondition of economic development. Similarly, the benefits accruing to the business elite were
largely the spillovers involving increased racial tranquility and the cementing
of the political alliance between the business elite and African American
political leaders. To be sure, there also were concerns about the relationship
between education per se and development, but they were relatively less than
today, when Charlotte's business elite views good schools as the sine qua non
of economic growth.

The actual relationship between education and economic performance is
an extremely complicated one. In the 1980s, *A Nation At Risk's* dismal appraisal of public education seemingly resonated with the United States' lagging economic performance, especially vis-à-vis Japan and Western Germany.
However, it is difficult—indeed, impossible—to attribute the dramatic reversal of the country's economic situation in the 1990s to any equally dramatic
improvement in public education. Nor did the fact that at the turn of the
century the United States was obviously once again the world's preeminent
economic powerhouse occasion any abatement in political concern about public
education. If anything, education was more of an issue in the 2000 presiden-
tial campaign than it was in prior ones.

Similarly, the weight that mobile capital actually attaches to the quality
of an area's educational system in making relocation and investment decisions
is extremely difficult to ascertain, especially because the subject has elicited
more than its share of self-serving rhetoric and school scapegoating from

business executives in Charlotte and around the country. The same executives so quick to lament the quality of the schools may be the very ones who oppose tax increases that help finance education, an irony not lost on local educators when the state's businesses opposed an increase in the corporate income tax.[60] Furthermore, as far as Charlotte's economic growth goes, it is doubtful that either the NFL or the National Basketball Association (NBA), two of the biggest economic prizes that Charlotte has landed, paid much attention to "the quality of the schools" in deciding to award franchises to the city.[61] As for the process that led other businesses to move, or not move, to Charlotte, there is virtually no hard evidence about the weight that the relevant corporate decision makers have attached to public education as opposed to tax rates, access to transportation, availability of real estate and/or office space, and so forth.

Such caveats notwithstanding, it is clear that Charlotte's business leaders believe that perceptions about "good schools" are an important part of the package that Charlotte offers in the cutthroat battle to attract mobile capital. Although such beliefs go at least as far back as the 1970s, they have become increasingly important since then. Indeed, by the late 1990s, the primacy of education in facilitating economic development had become a virtual staple of local economic discourse. A 1995 issue of the Charlotte Chamber of Commerce's quarterly magazine highlighted a statement from a relocation consultant that "the quality of K–12 public education as a location factor is probably growing in importance within the broad spectrum of business decision making faster than any other single factor."[62] Shortly thereafter, the *Observer's* editorial page prominently displayed a statement by Chamber Chair and NationsBank Chief Financial Officer James H. Hance Jr.: "Without question, the quality of our public school system is the best long-term economic development incentive we can offer."[63] Similarly, in a 1999 *Observer* article about his 15-year presidency of the Charlotte Chamber, Carrol Gray indicated that preK–12 public education was the Chamber's "No. 1 objective." The primacy of public education, the article continued, "is one of the key changes he's [Gray] noticed in business recruitment over the past fifteen years. When he moved . . . to Charlotte in 1984, the key concerns of relocating corporate decision makers were land and labor. Today, he said, 'Education is the top priority.' "[64]

In keeping with that view, the Chamber, together with prominent members of the business elite and various political leaders, launched a wide range of initiatives to improve public education and help CMS. These initiatives include the kind of cross-sector mobilization that, according to Stone, is the essence of civic capacity. Among the unprecedented attempts are the efforts of Charlotte's business elite to help deal with what is perceived as CMS' communication problem; increased attempts by CMS, the city, and the county to coordinate decisions about land use; numerous partnerships between local businesses and CMS; and the mayor's acknowledgment, in the aftermath of the 1999 trial, that CMS' financial needs were more pressing than the city's.

Despite this widespread cross-sector mobilization, there is simply no reason to assume that the business elite's educational interests will coincide with, or substantially overlap, those of African American families, especially low-income ones. There are several related reasons why such an assumption is a dubious one. First, the allocation of resources—physical, financial, and human—to meet the specific educational needs of the black poor can easily conflict with the allocation of resources to provide the strong college preparatory education highly valued by mid-level corporate employees whose hiring and retention businesses see as crucial.[65] Second, while the possibility for such conflict exists in many school systems, there are theoretical grounds for thinking that it will be more intense in CMS because of the district's consolidated character. In many urban areas, black children, especially from low-income families, find themselves isolated in school districts different from those enrolling more affluent, predominantly white children. That is not the case in Charlotte, where the school district covers all 530 square miles of Mecklenburg County, thus providing CMS with the potential to marshal more and broader resources to address the educational needs of black children. However, the fact that CMS is consolidated also provides a large number of white, middle-class claimants upon whatever resources CMS can marshal, and there is no assurance that in conflict over the allocation of these resources, the business elite will place the distinctive educational needs of black children, especially those from low-income families, at the top of its political agenda. In addition to there being no such theoretical guarantee, there is considerable empirical evidence from the discussion of the interest-convergence thesis that, at numerous key junctures in recent CMS history, the business elite has attached a higher priority to policies that it sees as facilitating economic growth than to policies that African American leaders and organizations have seen as facilitating the education of black children.[66]

Thus, while there may be little reason to question the business elite's increased interest in "good schools," there is considerable reason, both theoretical and historical, to question whether this increased interest will coincide with what African Americans perceive as their interest in "good schools." Consequently, there is also considerable reason to question whether the education that CMS provides to black children can be substantially improved without the regulation and coercion of institutional elites that are a defining characteristic of opportunity expansion regimes.

Regulation, as Stone notes, is "most sustainable when backed by a popular constituency."[67] However, the building of such a constituency requires broad political mobilization, most aspects of which Charlotte has not seen since the civil rights era. Indeed, even at the height of that insurgency, the coalition between African American political leaders and the business elite that would play so large a role in politics for the next thirty years was taking shape. The terms of that alliance were described by one of its principal architects, Fred Alexander, who, as indicated in chapter 2, stressed the stupidity of trying to scare the business elite and emphasized the primacy of the "conference approach" in dealing with political matters. The "conference approach" did not preclude all political mobilization but confined it largely to electoral politics. Alexander was an indefatigable advocate of increased black voter registration, and with few exceptions, the "conference approach" buttressed by electoral mobilization has been the main political way that black Charlotteans and their allies have sought to advance African American interests since the early 1970s.[68]

Electoral Mobilization and the Pursuit of African American Interests

Venerable as the "conference approach" might be, it experienced a major breakdown in the fall of 1999 as the school board voted to appeal Potter's ruling. As chapter 7 indicated, there is considerable dispute about whether a deal was made that CMS would not appeal, but there is little dispute that a series of meetings (i.e., "the conference approach") took place aimed at getting CMS to forsake an appeal. The attempt was a failure from the business elite's perspective. Within several months of those meetings, CMS did appeal—much to the general dismay of the business elite—and Arthur Griffin, who championed the appeal, was reelected to the board and maintained his position as chair. Moreover, in the aftermath of the election, Griffin continued to struggle against the resegregative aspects of the superintendent's choice plan and led the board in voting in December 2000 to postpone its implementation, again much to the dismay of the business elite.

Like the results of the school board election in 1995, the breakdown of the "conference approach" in 1999 indicated that in the late 1990s, the business elite faced greater difficulty in influencing the course of educational policy than it had in the 1970s or 1980s. The breakdown of the "conference approach" also indicated that, generally speaking, there was a greater divergence between the business elite and black school board members over desegregation-related issues than at any time since the implementation of the mandatory busing plan.[69]

The ability of black political leaders to resist the business elite is facilitated by voter mobilization in the same way that it improves African American clout at the conference table. Electoral mobilization played a large part in Griffin's and Rembert's 1999 electoral victories and helps explain the victory of white desegregation proponents such as Louise Woods in the elections of 1995 and 2001.

While black voter mobilization may be *necessary* to advance black interests, it is frequently *insufficient.* Here, as is often the case in talking about
Charlotte, the Atlanta experience is relevant. As Stone and Pierannunzi point
out, electoral mobilization in Atlanta was key to achieving "significant policy
responsiveness."[70] But even in that city with a black population much larger
than Charlotte's, electoral control has a "limited reach," and, they note, it
frequently provides fewer benefits for the poor and working class than for the
middle class.[71] In thinking about the limited reach of electoral mobilization,
it is worth recalling Adolph Reed Jr.'s observations about demobilization,
noted in chapter 3. The lack of effort required to vote and whatever successes
voting produces legitimize the ballot as the primary means of political participation. Political engagement is thus easily narrowed to its most passive
form. Reed's additional observations also are relevant:

> As popular participation narrows, the inertial logic of incumbency
> operates to constrict the field of political discourse. Incumbents re-
> spond to durable interests, and they seek predictability, continuity,
> and a shared common sense. This translates into a preference for a
> brokered "politics as usual" that limits the number and range of
> claims on the policy agenda. Such a politics preserve the thrust of
> inherited policy regimes and reinforce existing patterns of systemic
> advantage by limiting the boundaries of the politically reasonable.
> The same is true for the insider negotiation processes through which
> the nongovernmental organizations now define their roles, and those
> organizations often earn their insider status by providing a convinc-
> ing alternative to popular political mobilization.[72]

Charlotte's pupil assignment wars provide suggestive examples of the
insufficiency of electoral mobilization and the "conference approach" as a way
of achieving African American interests. Just as the fall of 1999 witnessed a
major breakdown of the "conference approach," it also saw the largest
glimmerings of a broad political mobilization around education by African
Americans and their allies since the implementation of the busing plan. As
chapter 7 indicates, these glimmerings were manifest in the rally urging CMS
to appeal, the mass turnouts at school board meetings, and the network of
organizations that came together to oppose adoption of the choice plan in the
months following Potter's decision. The breakdown of the "conference approach" and this broad, by Charlotte standards, mobilization reinforced each
other, with both being fueled by the threat of massive resegregation.

However, that broad mobilization could not be sustained. Consequently,
when all but one of the board's strongest proponents of desegregation finally
acquiesced in the adoption of the choice plan in July 2001, hardly a trace

remained of the political mobilization that had affected the political climate two years earlier. The 8–1 vote for adoption occurred, it should be remembered, at a time when the legal issues had not yet been settled. In fact, the most recent court ruling—that of the three-judge appellate panel—did not require a race-neutral plan such as the one the board adopted. Nor had the technical aspects of maintaining a race-conscious assignment plan become any more daunting than they were two years earlier, when the board's majority had resisted a very similar plan. But in the absence of a broader political mobilization, the "conference approach" and electoral politics were the only games in town, just as they had generally been since the 1960s.

Had the mobilization that occurred in 1999 been sustained, could it have altered the political climate in 2001? Could such mobilization have produced a situation in which the clamor to end uncertainty in pupil assignment was met with a louder roar that it was more important to alleviate racial and social injustice in education? Would such screeching wheels have attracted the business elite's ample supply of political grease, perhaps lowering pressure on the board to adopt a plan, any plan? Had the political climate been altered, could the board's majority have successfully insisted on a less resegregative plan— perhaps one that gave greater weight to FRL eligibility and concomitantly less weight to neighborhood schools and cohort continuity? Had the political environment been altered, would there have been greater support among the business elite and city and county officials for an aggressive, affordable housing program that, over the years, would have allowed the choice plan's emphasis on neighborhood schools to have fewer resegregative consequences?

I suspect—and would like to believe—that the answer to all of these questions is yes. But it is always easier to hypothesize—and to hope—about counterfactuals than to provide convincing evidence for them. Thus, rather than speculate about what might possibly have alleviated the resegregation that Charlotte has witnessed, it is easier, and probably more useful, to summarize Charlotte's desegregation past. The record is a mixed one. For all of its unfulfilled promises and inequities, from an educational standpoint, desegregation in CMS can be considered at least a partial success insofar as the best available data indicate that in Charlotte, as elsewhere, desegregation improved short- and long-term educational outcomes for African Americans. But when one turns to the broader picture and looks at spillovers, the conclusion is considerably less rosy, especially because both Charlotte and CMS exemplify many of the conditions generally viewed as favorable for African Americans. The area's economy boomed, and both the city of Charlotte's elastic boundaries and CMS' large size militate against the kind of geographically small governmental jurisdictions that exacerbate class and racial segregation in many metropolitan areas. Despite these favorable conditions, it is difficult to weigh Charlotte's boom and emergence as an economic powerhouse against a dismal record of local funding of public education, a lack of coordination in planning activities, a seventeen-year trend of increasing resegregation, the racially correlated disparities in educational opportunities and outcomes, and the uneven progress in reducing black/white economic disparities without reaching a somber conclusion: the rising tide of civic capacity that resulted from school desegregation—a struggle initiated by blacks seeking a greater measure of racial and social justice—has done much more to lift the yachts of Charlotte's business elite than the African American dinghies trailing behind.

Civic Capacity and The Charlotte-Mecklenburg Compromise

In some ways, these somber conclusions about the asymmetric flow of civic capacity and the disparities in spillover benefits would seem to provide empirical justification for what I have called the Charlotte-Mecklenburg Compromise. In seeking such empirical justification, one might say: The spillovers from school desegregation did so little to build the kind of civic capacity necessary to fund CMS adequately, facilitate educational planning, or improve the economic situation of black Charlotteans, how could the spillovers from the Charlotte-Mecklenburg Compromise do any worse? One could go even farther and argue that the Charlotte-Mecklenburg Compromise would enhance civic capacity. For supportive national evidence, such an argument could draw on the suggestion from the Civic Capacity and Urban Education Project, that those cities that have been under court order rank among the lowest in civic capacity.[73]

Looking for local evidence, this argument could draw on the C33, whose experience indicated that however much proponents of neighborhood schools may have disagreed with proponents of desegregation on pupil assignment, both recognized the importance of providing extra resources to schools with high percentages of at-risk students. By removing the contentious issue of desegregation from the policy agenda, the argument might continue, the Charlotte-Mecklenburg Compromise also could unite proponents of desegregation and neighborhood schools in support of increased funding for neighborhood schools with large percentages of children of color from low-income families.[74] Moreover, that kind of compromise would likely have the enthusiastic support of the business elite, as the 1999 Unity Rally made clear. Finally, this argument would conclude, opposition to the Charlotte-Mecklenburg Compromise may appear useless. Nationally, as the work of Orfield and his collaborators makes clear, there is a pervasive trend toward resegregation, even in the South, which, in the aftermath of the civil rights movement, had the highest levels of school integration.[75] Locally, whatever the differences among the educational agendas, political perspectives, and personal characteristics of Peter Relic, John Murphy, and Eric Smith, all three superintendents' administrations witnessed an increase in resegregation, as did the last years of Jay Robinson's.

There is merit to these arguments, but they are one-sided and/or ultimately wrong, for at least four reasons. The first has to do with the seeming inevitability of resegregation. Today's seeming inevitability is frequently the result of yesterday's choices, and that is largely the case with Charlotte's desegregation history. Consider, for example, something as mundane, but as crucial, as transportation times. Given Charlotte's growth and increased traffic congestion, were CMS to try to maintain the level of desegregation in 2002 that it had in 1982, transportation times for many children would undoubtedly be longer—in some cases unacceptably longer, by most standards—thus making a retreat from desegregation seem "inevitable." But those longer travel times stem in large part from choices made by CMS officials, government leaders, and the business elite on a range of key issues, e.g., the location of new schools, local funding for education, the outerbelt, and inadequate support for affordable housing. There was nothing inevitable about any of those choices.

Second, these arguments misread my somber conclusions about the asymmetric flow of civic capacity and the distribution of spillover benefits. These conclusions are primarily about the difficulties involved in the struggle for a full measure of racial justice as well as the ease with which power and privilege are reproduced in the absence of a broad political mobilization against them. But these conclusions are not arguments against school desegregation per se, which remains, in my view, an important goal in those parts of the country, such as Charlotte, where residential segregation, the balkanization of metropolitan areas into a plethora of school districts, and the long reach of *Milliken I* do not constitute virtually insurmountable barriers to desegregation.

School desegregation is an important goal—and this is the third reason the arguments for the Charlotte-Mecklenburg Compromise are wrong—because of its educational benefits. As indicated earlier in this chapter, there is considerable evidence that both black and white children have benefited from desegregation in Charlotte. Moreover, when the evidence on the benefits of desegregation in Charlotte is viewed in conjunction with the questionable effectiveness of *Milliken II* remedies nationally and the inauspicious experience of many other districts that have dismantled desegregation plans,[76] I find considerable reason to agree with Hochschild's view that "school desegregation is the worst option, except for the others."[77] To make that statement is not primarily to damn school desegregation with faint praise but to recognize the greater shortcomings of other options. Hochschild's thoughtful comments merit ample quotation:

When coupled with deep systemic reform of educational governance and content, it [school desegregation] is our only available option for ending the racial isolation and (possibly increasing) racial antagonism that separates cities and suburbs . . . Nor will racial integration develop on its own at a pace faster than all deliberate speed. We cannot afford to wait for the infinitesimally slow process of residential desegregation or racial intermarriage to dissolve black-white hostilities. Racial integration in the workplace *is* reasonably effective, but it requires that young adults be sufficiently well educated to be able to get a job in the first place.

And that leads to my final argument for school desegregation. We cannot afford to allow urban school systems to continue to deteriorate. There are 1,500 fourth graders in Hartford who attend schools where *fewer than 1%* of the children meet the state math and reading goals for their grade level. Putting them on a bus to Guilford will not by itself teach them how to read, but neither—demonstrably—will leaving them where they are. Ensuring that they attend a school where other children can read and add is, according to the scattered but consistent evidence, their best chance to become literate adults. Conversely, putting some of Guilford's children on a bus into Hartford—assuming they would go—would perhaps galvanize the Hartford school district and the state of Connecticut into taking the painful and expensive steps needed to blow up this nonfunctional system . . . In that context, even a little success in desegregating schools is worth pursuing.[78]

Finally, it is not at all clear that the Charlotte-Mecklenburg Compromise will increase civic capacity. In this context, it is worth recalling the results of its eponym. The Atlanta Compromise had questionable, if not disastrous, educational consequences.[79] Moreover, it did little to boost civic capacity. Indeed, just the reverse appears to be the case. Although Stone and his collaborators suggest that the cities under court order may rank low in civic capacity, they also find that Atlanta's civic capacity was among the lowest of the cities they studied.[80] "Despite the city's long history of biracial governance around urban redevelopment," they indicate that "Atlanta's education arena provides a striking example of weak civic capacity."[81] Moreover, they suggest, "Perhaps as an unintended legacy of the once-touted Atlanta Compromise, education has proved to be highly resistant to civic mobilization."[82] The Atlanta experience thus undermines any a priori claim that the Charlotte-Mecklenburg Compromise will enhance civic capacity or benefit the vast majority of black students.

To be sure, Charlotte has things going for it that Atlanta did not. Just as its consolidated character facilitated desegregation, CMS' large size provides access to the resources of middle-class whites in outlying areas that the smaller and landlocked Atlanta lacked. But as noted earlier, the whites who provide CMS with access to these resources also exert powerful political claims on them. It is all well and good that equity has become a local buzzword, and that many advocates of both choice and neighborhood schools recognize that the educational effectiveness and moral legitimacy of CMS' new race-neutral pupil assignment plan hinge on equity. But equity costs money, and there is no guarantee that it will be funded, especially in tough financial times, as CMS' recent budget battles indicate.

For all of these reasons, there is little reason to believe that the Charlotte-Mecklenburg Compromise in and of itself will be sufficient to enhance civic capacity. Rather, as in most matters pertaining to civic capacity, the relationship between its enhancement and the Charlotte-Mecklenburg Compromise will likely be a question of effective political intervention. In seeking models for such intervention, the 2000 bond referendum, discussed in chapter 7, merits additional attention because it exemplifies many scholarly comments about building civic capacity.

One such remark is Stone's observation that "civic capacity has strength to the extent that identity with, and therefore duty to, the larger community is strong enough to withstand competing claims."[83] In their well-financed campaign, bond proponents successfully sought to build precisely that identity. Some efforts involved banalities such as the bonds committee's brochure with headlines such as "Give all our children the chance to succeed," and "A quality education for all our children."[84] Others reflected the most obvious kinds of nuts-and-bolts political savvy. Thus, one of the volunteers speaking at community meetings on behalf of the bonds was a parent from North Mecklenburg High School, many of whose families were furious at the school board for removing the IB program from the school. "I don't care if you're mad at a board member or not," she was quoted as saying, "Not voting for the bonds is going to hurt children."[85] Yet other efforts of bond proponents were more profound and emotive. An example of these kinds of appeals was an *Observer* op-ed piece by H. Stephen Shoemaker, the senior minister at Myers Park Baptist Church. Entitled "School Bonds Will Reveal if Charlotte Has a Soul," the article reads like a textbook example of Stone's observation. "This issue asks us to feel the pain of every part of our city and calls us to exercise 'soul,' our capacity to be related to the whole," said Shoemaker. "I urge Charlotte's people and faith communities," he concluded, "to look beyond the welfare of their part alone to the welfare of the whole and support the 2000 School Bond Referendum."[86]

It also is useful to draw on Portz, Stein, and Jones's comparison of Pittsburgh, Boston, and St. Louis, in which they note that "all three cities have histories of racial divisions and discord that impact the development of civic capacity," but that the "role of race in explaining the development of civic capacity is best understood through the prism of institutions and leadership."[87] Much of this book's historical account—especially of the relationship between the business elite and black political leaders—testifies to the importance of that observation, and the history of the 2000 bond referendum is no exception. One of the co-chairs of the bond committee was the vice president of a construction company whose occupation helped refute claims by opponents that the bonds were unnecessary because CMS had money left over from previous packages. Thus, in an *Observer* op-ed piece that specified his occupation and was entitled, "There's No 'Unspent' School Bond Money," the construction executive pointed out that money from earlier packages not yet disbursed was committed to specific projects. Those who said that there was unspent money, he argued, did not understand the financing of school construction, or they were simply trying to confuse voters.[88]

Another co-chair of the bond committee was the pastor of one of Charlotte's leading black churches who a year earlier helped lead the fight for a less resegregative pupil assignment plan. That the black clergy should boost school bonds and oppose resegregation is hardly surprising. More problematic, but equally important, is the role of the white clergy. In the desegregation battles of the 1970s, the clergy at many of Charlotte's white churches played a key role in alleviating community tension, implementing the desegregation plan, and helping Charlotte emerge from the crisis "a whole lot better people than we were," as school board chair Poe said. Uniquely situated to make the kind of appeal that Reverend Shoemaker made for the bonds, Charlotte's white clergy have the potential to play a pivotal role developing cross-sectoral support for public education. The importance of the clergy in building this support also is apparent from the fact that the two community groups, HELP and the Swann Fellowship, most deeply involved in interracial community organizing in support of low-income children of color have consciously rooted themselves in Charlotte's faith community.

It remains to be seen whether future political intervention will be as effective as it was in the 2000 bond campaign. Also uncertain is the extent to which future attempts to build civic capacity will involve the regulation and coercion of institutional elites through broad political mobilization. In discussing the 2000 bond campaign, I have said little about such regulation and coercion. But having earlier called attention to their necessity, I want here to emphasize that they are not necessarily incompatible with developing the kind of identity with the larger community that, as Stone points out, contributes to civic capacity. Rather, as indicated by the effect of the civil rights movement on whites in Charlotte and nationally, the coercive and regulatory aspect of such mobilization can result in greater identity with the larger (interracial) community in a way that builds civic capacity.

Is There a Need to Limit Corporate Domination of Urban Regimes?

This chapter's observations about the uphill flow of civic capacity allow a modest comment on the exchange, discussed in the Introduction, between Clarence Stone and David Imbroscio about whether the situation of the urban poor can improve without "a fundamental change in the corporate-dominated character of most current urban regimes."[89] Much of the Charlotte story indicates the need for such a change.[90] Despite conditions seemingly favorable to improving the situation of African Americans, there have been profound asymmetries in the transfer of civic capacity and equally striking disparities in the spillover benefits from school desegregation. Moreover, the causes of these asymmetries and disparities ultimately stemmed from the systemic power accruing to the business elite by virtue of its control and/or ownership of land and mobile capital. Finally, Fred Alexander's reasons for relying on the "conference approach" indicate how one of the principal architects of the coalition with the business elite saw African American options circumscribed by corporate power. Alexander's comment and thirty-five years of subsequent local history are ample evidence that Stone's observation about Atlanta holds equally well for Charlotte: "The striking feature of the Atlanta experience is the inclination of those in positions of community responsibility to pull back from conflict with the business elite and seek accommodation. That is the recurring tendency particularly of the black middle class, but it is by no means unique to that group."[91]

Yet if one talks about incremental rather than sweeping changes in the situation of the urban poor, the Charlotte story requires a measure of agnosticism about the extent to which such improvements hinge on successfully challenging business domination of so many aspects of local politics. Such agnosticism hinges on recognizing that to assess fully the competing positions in the Stone-Imbroscio debate, it is necessary to study the consequences of a broad political mobilization, in particular, whether it improved the condition of the urban poor without any fundamental change occurring in the corporate domination of a particular regime. But in the years covered by this book, Charlotte has seen little of that kind of mobilization. The long shadow of corporate power goes a long way toward explaining why Charlotte has seen much more of "the conference approach" than a broad political mobilization, of which the "conference approach" is only a part. But to explain the hegemony of the "conference approach" solely by the corporate domination of Charlotte's regime is to fall into the kinds of reductionist explanations of urban politics that regime theory—with its shibboleth that politics matters—justifiably forswears. In other words, one cannot assume that a fundamental change in the corporate domination of Charlotte's regime is a precondition of broad political mobilization any more than such changes were a precondition of the mass insurgencies of the civil rights era.

Thus, whatever contribution that the Charlotte story presently makes to regime theory would be greater if the story included more multifaceted political mobilization, especially of the urban poor. More importantly, I strongly suspect, the urban poor also would benefit from such mobilization, an even more compelling reason for hoping that it will soon erupt onto Charlotte's seemingly progressive political landscape.

Appendix

Although there is considerable debate about the extent to which increased expenditures improve educational outcomes, I consider local funding a good measure of civic capacity for several reasons. First, because North Carolina law deprives CMS and almost all of the state's other school districts of taxing authority, they must rely on their county commissions to place bond referenda before voters as well as to supply a significant portion of their operating budget, in CMS' case, about 30 percent of annual expenditures. That reliance requires CMS to develop the kinds of arrangements with government officials, members of the business elite, other sectors of the community, and the public that are a defining characteristic of civic capacity. Second, there is growing evidence that properly targeted expenditures do improve outcomes.[1] And while all of the evidence about the relationship between funding and outcomes may not yet be in, perceptions are themselves relevant. As Stone and his collaborators note in explaining their use of financial support as a measure of civic capacity, "Local citizens and public officials strongly believe that money is very important. It seems most reasonable, therefore, to regard the commitment to raise and spend public funds as a necessary but not sufficient precursor to effective education. And high-mobilization cities [in their study] spend more of their own resources to educate their youth."[2]

To gauge local financial support for CMS, I draw comparisons with other large, consolidated North Carolina urban systems. Data comes from the Public School Forum of North Carolina. Since 1987, the forum has published yearly reports that compile data on local tax bases, school enrollments, and expenditures to rank each North Carolina county on its ability to fund public education, the amount it actually spends on K–12 public education, and the relationship between ability and expenditures. Over the years there has been some variation in the definition of key measures, but the reports have generally employed three main ones: Ability to Pay, Actual Effort, and Relative Effort (RE). Ability to Pay represents "a measure of a county's per student fiscal capacity to support local public schools," while Actual Effort "reflects the actual dollar effort of communities to fund local public schools without taking into account property wealth," and RE "is a measure comparing Actual Effort and Ability to Pay."[3] Because RE compares actual expenditures with a county's financial ability to support public education, it provides a useful gauge of civic capacity. Based on the values of Ability to Pay, Actual Effort, and RE, the Public School Forum also has computed what it calls a district's Overall Rank.

In the 1987 report, the computation of RE was based on the five-year average of expenditures for education for the school years 1981–82 through 1985–86. The second report (issued in 1989, there was none in 1988) differed from 1987's in that RE was computed based on expenditures for just the 1987–88 school year rather than a period of years. Beginning with the third report (issued in 1990), the forum began breaking down RE into Relative Current Effort (RCE) and Relative Total Effort (RTE). The former was based on county appropriations for just one school year, while the latter included both appropriations for one year and a several-year average of capital expenditures. These two measures of RE thus provide different, but complementary, ways of gauging civic capacity.

The use of these reports raises two sets of methodological concerns. The first involves the possibility that the manner in which the Public School Forum computes its measures biases comparisons among localities. For example, as the forum notes in its 1998 report, because of the way that RE is computed, "in general, low-wealth districts with comparatively high spending levels rank highest in this measure."[4] That helps explain why North Carolina's wealthiest counties never rank very high on this measure, and why it is thus important to compare Mecklenburg with other large, relatively wealthy urban counties rather than with every county in the state. As chapter 2 indicates, North Carolina historically has had five such counties: Durham, Forsyth, Guilford, Mecklenburg, and Wake. However, in two of these counties—Guilford and Durham—consolidation between the city and county school systems occurred too recently to allow meaningful historical comparisons with Mecklenburg. Thus, my analysis focuses on Mecklenburg, Wake (the county in which Raleigh is located), and Forsyth (in which Winston-Salem is located).

Of these three counties, Mecklenburg ranks highest on Ability to Pay on all but one of the reports. Until recently, it also ranked lowest on RE and RTE on most of the reports. Thus the question arises: Are Mecklenburg's generally lower rankings (compared to Wake and Forsyth) for RE and RTE an artifact of almost always ranking highest on its Ability to Pay? As best as can be determined, the answer to that question is no. Whatever may be the general tendency for North Carolina's 100 counties, among these three high-wealth counties, a higher rank on Ability to Pay does not necessarily translate into a lower rank on RE or RTE.

Given the small number of cases involved, the best way to see that there is no necessary relationship between Ability to Pay and RE or RTE is to look more closely at the rankings for Wake and Forsyth. For example, there is only one report (1989) where Mecklenburg does not rank highest on Ability to Pay. On that report, Wake ranks highest on both Ability to Pay and RE. Similarly, on the 1987 report, Forsyth ranks above Wake on both Ability to Pay and RE. Nor on the twelve reports (beginning with the one for 1990) for which RE is broken down into RTE and RCE does a higher rank on either of these two measures necessarily imply a lower rank on Ability to Pay. For example, Wake ranks ahead of Forsyth on both RTE and Ability to Pay on eight of the twelve reports. Given that for Wake and Forsyth there is no negative relationship between rankings for Ability to Pay and RE, it seems plausible to conclude that Mecklenburg's generally lower ranking for RE is not merely a by-product of generally ranking highest of the three counties on its Ability to Pay. Moreover, in the most recent reports, Mecklenburg's ranking on RTE has improved, even though it continues to rank highest on Ability to Pay.

The second set of methodological issues involves the linkages between the expenditure data in any particular report and the political decisions (and, hence, civic capacity) that affected those expenditures. The appropriations used to compute RCE come from a school year beginning two years prior to the date of the report. For example, the 1998 report draws on appropriations for the 1996–97 school year, budgeting decisions for which were finalized in the spring of 1996. There is thus a two-year lag between the time political events affecting RCE occurred and the date of a report. Moreover, given possible vagaries (in Mecklenburg and/or the comparison counties) in any particular budgeting cycle, it is important not to read too much into RCE in any one report but instead to look at several consecutive ones.

Since RTE includes a multiyear average of capital expenditures, there is an even greater lag between the time the relevant political decisions were made and the date of a report. Moreover, this lag is somewhat indeterminate because it is not apparent from the data when, during this six-year period, the actual funding decisions or referenda occurred. Moreover, the expenditures might even reflect decisions that took place prior to the six-year period, e.g., a bond referendum could have been passed eight years previously and the money spent over the next five years. Thus, the inclusion of the additional data that allows RTE to provide a more complete picture than RCE also makes it especially important not to rely on data for RTE from any one report.

Because of these lags and uncertainties, I will generally make inferences about local financial support of public education for a period of several years, e.g., the early 1990s rather than any one year. While such periods are admittedly imprecise, the data do not allow inferences that are any more precise. Moreover, it turns out that the data are amenable to the use of such periods.

Table 3.2 presents the Public School Forum's rankings for the three counties for all reports from 1987 to 2001. Inspection of the rankings for RCE, RTE, and RE indicates that, until very recently, Mecklenburg generally has ranked lower than the other two counties, especially on the last two measures. Given that these rankings indicate that for almost twenty years Mecklenburg did a generally poorer job than Wake or Forsyth in funding its public school system, another question arises, Was there any period during these many poor years that Mecklenburg did especially poorly?

That question cannot be answered solely on the basis of the Public School Forum's published rankings, which are primarily designed to compare school systems within any particular year rather than to track trends across years. However, based on these published rankings, it is possible to compute four indicators that do address this question: Difference in Relative Total Effort (DRTE), Difference in Relative Current Effort (DRCE), Difference in Overall Rank (DOR), and Ability/Effort Discrepancy (AED).

Table 4.1 provides values for these indicators. Given the way the first three of these indicators are calculated, a negative value generally means that Mecklenburg is doing worse than the comparison counties, and the larger the magnitude of the negative value, the worse is Mecklenburg's performance relative to Wake and Forsyth. The fourth indicator, AED, is a cruder indicator that has only two values, none or negative, with the latter indicating that Mecklenburg's support of public education is much poorer than that of Wake's and Forsyth's.

The DRTE is defined as:

(Wake's Rank on RTE-Mecklenburg's Rank on RTE)

+

(Forsyth's Rank on RTE-Mecklenburg's Rank on RTE)

The DRCE and DOR are defined analogously. As is evident, the calculations used to compute these three indicators treat the forum's rankings as interval variables, even though they are ordinal ones. Thus, these three indicators can only be considered approximations. Moreover, in some cases these three indicators can obscure important information, as the following example demonstrates: Consider two hypothetical rankings for DRTE: The first is Forsyth 1, Wake 2, and Mecklenburg 3; the second is Forsyth 1, Mecklenburg 9, and Wake 10. In the first case, the computed value of DRTE is −3, and in the second case, it is −7. The greater magnitude (7 as opposed to 3) presumably indicates that in this second case Mecklenburg is doing worse compared to the other counties than in the first case. However, in the first case, Mecklenburg is at the bottom of the pile, but in the second case, Mecklenburg is in the middle.

As this example suggests, these three indicators are most useful for looking at trends over a multiyear period when Mecklenburg's position relative to the other two counties is the same in each year. That is generally the situation with RTE and Overall Rank.

The fourth indicator, AED, avoids the problems inherent in treating ordinal variables as though they were interval ones but involves a different set of problems. It is computed in this way:

> If in any report, Mecklenburg ranks in the same place (whether it is highest, in the middle, or lowest) on both Ability to Pay and Actual Effort, there is no discrepancy.

> If on any report, Mecklenburg's rank on Ability to Pay (either highest or in the middle) is higher than its rank for Actual Effort (in the middle or lowest, respectively), there is a negative discrepancy.

> If on any report, Mecklenburg's rank on Ability to Pay (either lowest or in the middle) is lower than its rank for Actual Effort (in the middle or highest, respectively), there is a positive discrepancy.

This fourth indicator is a relatively crude one because it simply compares Mecklenburg's rank on Ability to Pay with its rank for Actual Effort without taking into account the Public School Forum's detailed calculations and rankings of Relative Effort and Overall Rank, both of which allow much more detailed comparisons. Consequently, AED shows a negative discrepancy when the other three indicators show an especially large difference between Mecklenburg and the controls, as is generally the case in the years covered by the 1990–94 reports. However, in cases (e.g., the reports from 1987 and 1989) where the other indicators show less of a difference, AED indicates that there is no discrepancy.

Because Mecklenburg ranks higher on Ability to Pay than the other two counties in eleven of the twelve reports, it is logically impossible for AED, given the way it is computed, to show a positive discrepancy on these eleven reports. In principle, that is an obviously severe limitation on this indicator. But with the possible exception of the reports at the turn of the century, that limitation is of minimal practical import, since the accumulated weight of all of the other more detailed indicators is that Mecklenburg's effort has generally been worse, not better, than that of the controls, given its generally higher ability.

A final note about Table 4.1: in computing RE, the 1987 report drew upon both capital expenditures and annual appropriations over a several-year period. Thus, in that report, RE was similar to what subsequent reports called RTE, and it is considered as such in the table. Analogously, the 1989 report's measure of RE is similar to what later reports called RCE, and in Table 4.1, RE for 1989 is treated as RCE.

Notes

CHAPTER 1

1. Editorial, "You Were Wrong, Mr. President," *Charlotte Observer*, October 9, 1984, p. 18A.

2. Hugh L. McColl Jr., "What Is, and What We Hope For," speech at the Governor's Emerging Issues Forum, Raleigh, North Carolina, February 24, 2000, available at <http://www.bankofamerica.newsroom/spe . . . speech.cfm?speech ID= speech.20000224.05ht>, accessed March 2000.

3. As quoted in Frye Gaillard, *The Dream Long Deferred*, (Chapel Hill: University of North Carolina Press, 1988), xv. Although my interpretation of Charlotte's desegregation experience is different and less rosy than Gaillard's, it is probably indicative of how much I owe his work that I begin with the same incident that his book does. My first extensive exposure to Charlotte's desegregation history came from *The Dream Long Deferred*, and it continues to embody many of the issues with which any account of this history must deal. The second edition of the book published shortly after the 1999 trial (Charlotte, N.C.: Briarpatch Press, 1999) provides insightful discussion of many of the people and events discussed below in chapter 6.

4. Ibid.

5. Rick Rothacker, "Wachovia Starts New Ad Campaign," *Charlotte Observer*, May 29, 2002, pp. 1D, 6D.

6. Dan Chapman, "Charlotte Crowned As 'Most Livable,'" *Charlotte Observer*, June 20, 1995, p. 1C.

7. Bob Meadows, "No. 1 Spot in Nation for Blacks: Charlotte," *Charlotte Observer*, May 20, 1998, p. 1C. See also a 2002 list compiled by Black Entertainment Television, in which Charlotte ranked fourth in the nation (Herbert L. White, "Life's Good in Charlotte," *Charlotte Post*, October 10, 2002, pp. 1A, 2A).
Following the usage of many contemporary scholars, I will use "black" and "African American" interchangeably. As Orr notes, "Good arguments have been made for the use of both, as each suggests different emphases in regard to racial and global identity, and the American experience" (Marion Orr, *Black Social Capital: The Politics of School Reform in Baltimore, 1986–1998* [Lawrence, KS: The University Press of Kansas, 1999], 198).

8. For a discussion of many aspects of the gap between black and white educational achievement, see Christopher Jencks and Meredith Phillips, *The Black-White Test Score Gap* (Washington, D.C.: Brookings, 1998). To call attention to ongoing shortcomings in black educational opportunities and outcomes is not to deny the considerable progress that was realized in the last half of the twentieth century. As Jeffrey Henig notes, "From the mid-1950s into the 1970s, it seems fair to say that improving racial equality was the dominant item on the nation's public-education agenda . . . [and] America's public schools accomplished much in this area" (Jeffrey Henig, *Rethinking School Choice* [Princeton: Princeton University Press, 1994], 36). Nor should these shortcomings be taken as evidence for a generic crisis in U.S. education, which, by both historical and cross-national standards, is doing much better than allegations of a crisis would lead one to expect, as numerous commentators have pointed out (e.g., Henig, op. cit., chapter 2 and David C. Berliner and Bruce Biddle, *The Manufactured Crisis* [Reading, Mass: Addison-Wesley, 1995]).

Finally, to discuss the shortcomings in educational opportunities for black students is not to deny the existence of shortcomings for many other students of color and for poor and working-class whites. But I generally confine the book's discussion to African Americans for several reasons. Until recently nonblack students of color comprised a minuscule percentage of CMS' enrollment, and organizations rooted in nonblack communities of color played an equally small role in Charlotte politics. Poor and working-class whites have, of course, always constituted a significant percentage of CMS' enrollment, but the inadequacies of their educational opportunities have not been anywhere near as pivotal an issue in Charlotte politics as desegregation and the education of black children have been. In this respect, Charlotte's experience over the past half century has not been all that different from the national one; in both cases, race has been a more salient political issue than class.

9. David L. Imbroscio, review of *Reconstructing Urban Regime Theory: Regulating Urban Politics in a Global Economy*, ed. Mickey Lauria, *Urban Affairs Review* 33, no. 1 (1997): 141.

10. Clarence N. Stone, *Regime Politics: Governing Atlanta, 1946–1988* (Lawrence: University Press of Kansas, 1989).

11. Stone, *Regime Politics*, 227.

12. Ibid.

13. Ibid, 230.

14. Talcott Parsons, "The Distribution of Power in American Society," *World Politics* 10 (1957): 123–43.

15. C. Wright Mills, *The Power Elite* (New York: Oxford University Press, 1959).

16. Stone's work on Atlanta has been heavily influenced by that of Floyd Hunter, whose work, like that of Mills, is generally considered to exemplify stratification theory. See Floyd Hunter, *Community Power Structure* (Chapel Hill: University of North Carolina Press, 1953).

17. Charles Lindblom, *Politics and Markets* (New York: Basic Books, 1977).

18. Stone, *Regime Politics*, 197.

19. Ibid., 222.

20. Clarence N. Stone, "Urban Regimes and the Capacity to Govern: A Political Economy Approach," *Journal of Urban Affairs*, 15, no. 1 (1993): 2.

21. The most influential exposition of this position is generally considered Paul Peterson's *City Limits* (Chicago: University of Chicago Press, 1981).

22. Despite its recognition of the importance of control of investment capital and its witheringly effective criticism of the classical urban pluralism formulated in works such as Robert Dahl's *Who Governs?* (New Haven: Yale University Press, 1961), regime theory can be categorized as an example of what John Manley calls Pluralism II (John F. Manley, "Neo-Pluralism: A Class Analysis of Pluralism I and Pluralism II," *American Political Science Review* 77 [1983]: 368–89). As Manley notes, the thinking of Dahl and Charles Lindblom, whose work exemplified the classical pluralism of the late 1950s, underwent considerable development in subsequent years. Among other things, these scholars' later work pays much more attention to the political consequences of economic inequality and what Lindblom calls the privileged position of business. This privilege is rooted in the structure of a capitalist economy because ownership/control—for the sake of brevity, I blur what in other contexts is a pivotal distinction—of capital, especially large, concentrated amounts of it, confers unique political advantages.

These empirical insights notwithstanding, Dahl's and Lindblom's later work is still best understood, Manley notes, as pluralism because it continues to bear the normative stamp of their earlier work. For example, as Manley points out, Dahl's and Lindblom's work still holds that the system's problems and failures "can be corrected without specifying how much structural change or redistribution of wealth and income are needed," and that whatever structural reforms are necessary do not "entail basic alterations in class structure or class power"(Manley, "Neo-Pluralism," 385).

Regime theory fulfills Manley's criteria of Pluralism II. Stone has drawn heavily upon Lindblom for his understanding of the political consequences of control of investment capital, and the exchange with David Imbroscio, quoted below, makes clear Stone's view that urban problems can be alleviated without fundamental changes in class structure and power. For these reasons, regime theory has more in common, at root, with the gist of classical pluralism than with the gist of even the non-deterministic Marxist analysis for which Manley calls. A similar line of argument has led Davies to recently emphasize the gap between regime theory and Marxism, as well as to argue that what he sees as the weaknesses of regime theory might be alleviated were its proponents "to reengage critically with variants of Marxism, which unlike Structuralism, recognize the possibility of agency" (Jonathan S. Davies, "Urban Regime Theory: A Normative-Empirical Critique," *Journal of Urban Affairs* 24, no. 1 [2002]: 1). I am sympathetic to Davies' concerns and, indeed, the Charlotte experience may provide empirical support for aspects of his argument. But at the risk of trying to bridge an unbridgeable theoretical gap between Marxism and regime theory, I would argue that, at the middle-range level of theory, regime theory as presently constituted is a powerful supplement to traditional Marxist lines of inquiry rather than an irreconcilably different approach. Whatever the more fundamental theoretical differences, regime theory addresses important issues to which Marxist scholarship often pays inadequate attention, e.g., the institutional arrangements that—in the absence of major political and economic changes—might ameliorate the condition of low-income urban residents.

23. Stone, "Urban Regimes and the Capacity to Govern," 8, 13.

24. Ibid., 9.

25. Stone's typology also includes maintenance and middle-class progressive regimes. In many ways, a middle-class progressive regime can be viewed as falling close to the middle of a continuum whose end points are development and lower-class opportunity regimes. Maintenance regimes are those in which little effort is made to effect significant change.

26. Stone, "Urban Regimes and the Capacity to Govern," 18–19.

27. Ibid., 20.

28. Stone, "Urban Regimes and the Capacity to Govern," 21. Although Stone talks only of regulation, I will typically talk of regulation and coercion. To be sure, my usage is largely redundant because regulation has inevitable coercive aspects. As Lowi and Ginsberg note, "As we have so often said, the key characteristic of regulatory policy is control of individual conduct by directly coercive techniques. Regulatory techniques are used to impose obligations, duties, or restrictions on conduct. The *politics* of regulation follows from this directly coercive character of regulatory *policy*" (Theodore Lowi and Benjamin Ginsberg, *American Government: Freedom and Power*, 3rd ed. [New York: W. W. Norton, 1994], 640). However, *coercion* has a harder edge than *regulation*, and I want to emphasize the difference between the governance processes associated with development and lower-class opportunity expansion regimes, in particular that the latter cannot rely solely on the voluntary coordination of elites.

29. Stone, "Urban Regimes and the Capacity to Govern," 25.

30. Ibid, 22.

31. Clarence N. Stone, "Introduction: Urban Education in Political Context," in *Changing Urban Education*, ed. Clarence N. Stone (Lawrence: University Press of Kansas, 1998), 15.

32. Ibid., 12.

33. Ibid., 15.

34. Ibid., 9.

35. Clarence N. Stone, "Civic Capacity and Urban School Reform," in Stone, ed., *Changing Urban Education*, 254.

36. Stone, "Introduction: Urban Education in Political Context," 15. As is frequently the case when terms from the natural sciences are applied to social phenomena, the analogy cannot be taken too literally. Absent mutations and copying errors, the information contained in one strand of the DNA double helix determines the information contained in the other. However, there is much more slippage between

the two strands of the school reform double helix, and a key political task is to make them more complementary by overcoming this slippage. Moreover, in a DNA double helix, neither strand is the inside or outside one. These important differences notwithstanding, the analogy is a useful one precisely because it invokes an image of two interwoven aspects of school reform, each of which shapes the other.

37. Stone, "Introduction: Urban Education in Political Context," 12.

38. I say "what is usually called social capital" because, as Jessica Kulynych and I have argued elsewhere, the empirical referents of the term *social capital* merit study, but the term itself befuddles key analytic distinctions and carries ponderous ideological baggage in a way that impedes rather than advances inquiry (see Stephen Samuel Smith and Jessica Kulynych, "It May Be Social, but Why Is It Capital? The Social Production of Social Capital and the Politics of Knowledge," *Politics and Society* 30, no. 1 [2002]: 149–86; Stephen Samuel Smith and Jessica Kulynych, "Liberty, Equality and . . . Social Capital?," in *Social Capital: Critical Perspectives on Community and "Bowling Alone,"* ed. Scott McLean, David Schultz, and Manfred Steger [New York: New York University Press, 2002], 127–46). The most comprehensive discussion of the putative importance of social capital in many areas of contemporary life is Robert D. Putnam's *Bowling Alone: The Collapse and Revival of American Community* (New York: Simon and Schuster, 2000).

39. Putnam, *Bowling Alone*, 19.

40. Stone, "Civic Capacity and Urban School Reform," 254.

41. Ibid., 270.

42. Putnam, *Bowling Alone*.

43. Clarence Stone, "The Politics of Urban School Reform: Civic Capacity, Social Capital, and the Intergroup Context" (paper presented at the 1996 annual meeting of the American Political Science Association, San Francisco), 16. The chapter in *Changing Urban Education* from which this paragraph's other quotations are taken draws upon this paper.

44. Stone, "Civic Capacity and Urban School Reform," 270.

45. An approach quite different from Stone's that also calls attention to the decisive role that durable political arrangements play in explaining educational policy and practice is the sweeping voucher plan advanced in John Chubb and Terry Moe's *Politics, Markets, and America's Schools* (Washington, D.C.: Brookings, 1989). Their cure for what allegedly ails U.S. education is predicated on the belief that this voucher plan, and it alone, will eliminate the prevailing institutional arrangements that, in their view, incapacitate the country's public schools. Whereas their proposal would eliminate public education "as we know it," Stone pays little attention to such panaceas and is more concerned with explicating the political arrangements that will allow a still-recognizable form of public education to address the academic needs of all students, especially economically disadvantaged ones. It is hardly coincidental that all three men are political scientists, a discipline long concerned with how political institutions and arrangements affect public policy.

46. For examples of these criticisms, see Bob Edwards and Michael Foley, "Social Capital and the Political Economy of Our Discontent," *American Behavioral Scientist* 40 (1997): 669–78; Bob Edwards and Michael Foley, "Civil Society and Social Capital beyond Putnam," *American Behavioral Scientist* 42 (1998): 124–40; Ellis Goldberg, "Thinking about How Democracy Works," *Politics and Society* 24, no. 1 (1996): 7–18; Margaret Levi, "Social and Unsocial Capital: A Review Essay of Robert Putnam's *Making Democracy Work*," *Politics and Society* 24, no. 1 (1996): 46–55; Alejandro Portes, "Social Capital: Its Origins and Applications in Modern Sociology," *Annual Review of Sociology* 24 (1998): 1–24; Smith and Kulynych, "It May Be Social, but Why Is It Capital?"; Smith and Kulynych, "Liberty, Equality, and . . . Social Capital?"

47. Smith and Kulynych, "It May Be Social, but Why Is It Capital?," p. 167.

48. Another reason to avoid viewing civic capacity as a category of social capital is that the *civic* in civic capacity calls to mind the lofty notion of public activity. However, the term *social capital* blurs the difference between public and private (see Smith and Kulynych, "It May Be Social, but Why Is It Capital?").

49. Stone, *Regime Politics*, 229.

50. Anthony Giddens, " 'Power' in the Recent Writings of Talcott Parsons," *Sociology* 2 (1968): 264.

51. Stone, "Civic Capacity and Urban School Reform," 254.

52. For a nuanced argument on the inadequacy of such models, especially those that view power from a zero-sum framework, see Joel F. Handler's *Down from Bureaucracy* (Princeton: Princeton University Press, 1996).

53. Ernesto Cortes, "Reweaving the Fabric: The Iron Rule and the IAF Strategy for Power and Politics, in *Interwoven Destinies: Cities and the Nation*, ed. Henry G. Cisneros (New York: W. W. Norton, 1993), 294–319. For a fuller discussion of the IAF's activities, see Dennis Shirley, *Community Organizing for Urban School Reform* (Austin: University of Texas Press, 1997).

54. These conflicts are amply illustrated by the case studies in Stone, ed., *Changing Urban Education*, the Baltimore experience discussed in Orr, *Black Social Capital*, and other studies based on the Civic Capacity and Urban Education Project: John Portz, Lana Stein, and Robin R. Jones, *City Schools and City Politics: Institutions and Leadership in Pittsburgh, Boston, and St. Louis* (Lawrence: University Press of Kansas, 1999); Clarence N. Stone, Jeffrey R. Henig, Bryan D. Jones, and Carol Pierannunzi, *Building Civic Capacity: The Politics of Reforming Urban Schools* (Lawrence: University Press of Kansas, 2001); and Jeffrey R. Henig, Richard C. Hula, Marion Orr, and Desiree S. Pedescleaux, *The Color of School Reform: Race, Politics, and the Challenge of Urban Education* (Princeton: Princeton University Press, 1999).

55. Mickey Lauria, "Introduction," in *Reconstructing Urban Regime Theory: Regulating Urban Politics in a Global Economy*, ed. Mickey Lauria (Thousand Oaks, Calif: Sage, 1997), p. 2.

56. Clarence N. Stone, "Regime Analysis and the Study of Urban Politics: A Rejoinder," *Journal of Urban Affairs*, 20, no. 3 (1998): 259.

57. David L. Imbroscio, "The Necessity of Urban Regime Change: A Reply to Clarence N. Stone," *Journal of Urban Affairs* 20, no. 3 (1998): 264. Davies' "Urban Regime Theory" develops a critique that in many ways parallels as well as expands Imbroscio's. Here I confine my attention to Imbroscio's because it was accompanied by a published rejoinder by Stone.

58. Jean Anyon, *Ghetto Schooling: A Political Economy of Urban Educational Reform* (New York: Teachers College Press, 1997), 168.

59. Stone, "Regime Analysis and the Study of Urban Politics," 254.

60. The Charlotte experience leaves crucial aspects of these questions unanswered in part because of the way this experience has unfolded. However, insofar as Charlotte is just one of this country's many cities, there are also compelling methodological reasons why even if this experience had unfolded differently, it could not provide a full and definitive answer. For more on the relationship between case studies and the construction of theory, see Harry Eckstein, "Case Study and Theory in Political Science," in *Handbook of Political Science*, vol. 7, ed. Fred Greenstein and Nelson W. Polsby (Reading, Mass.: Addison-Wesley, 1975), 79–137.

61. Jeffrey Mirel, *The Rise and Fall of an Urban School System: Detroit, 1907–81* (Ann Arbor: University of Michigan Press, 1993), xii.

62. Portz, Stein, and Jones, *City Schools and City Politics*; Stone et al., *Building Civic Capacity*; Henig et al., *The Color of School Reform*.

63. An early report of my work on Charlotte appeared in an edited volume, most of whose contributors were part of the Civic Capacity and Urban Education Project. See Stephen Samuel Smith, "Education and Regime Change in Charlotte," in Stone, ed., *Changing Urban Education*.

64. Most of the data for this book was gathered between 1994 and 2000. During this time, I conducted over 150 semi-structured interviews with a wide range of political and civic leaders, CMS personnel, and educational activists. Substantial portions of sixty-six of these interviews were tape-recorded. However, I was more interested in candor than having a taped record of the interview, and I willingly shut the machine off whenever a respondent so requested.

I also have benefited from the stock of knowledge that comes from more than fifteen years of residence in Charlotte and a long-standing involvement in many aspects of local educational affairs. Among other things, my children graduated from CMS schools, I was a member of the 1997 CMS citizen task force discussed in chapter 6, and I served as an expert witness for the black plaintiffs in the reopened *Swann* litigation, also discussed in that chapter.

65. I confine the comparisons to North Carolina because interstate variations in curriculum, standards, and funding make it much more difficult to compare districts in different states.

66. The effective use of class analysis in the United States requires a precise definition of the capitalist class and a careful demarcation of the boundaries between it and other classes, both of which are complicated efforts not necessary in this book.

For example, over the years, both Hugh McColl and Joe Martin have played key roles in local educational policy. The CEO of the Charlotte-based Bank of America during most of the years covered by this book, McColl was a member of the capitalist class by any plausible definition of the term. During the years that the forerunners of Bank of America were growing from a regional to a national powerhouse, Martin was, among other things, the bank's principal corporate affairs officer. He also was among McColl's closest advisors, frequently wrote his speeches, facilitated the bank's growth by drawing on the political connections that came with being the brother of North Carolina's governor, and, at McColl's request, ran (successfully) for the school board. Ascertaining Martin's position in the class structure is a complex empirical and theoretical endeavor largely irrelevant to this book's main inquiry, and one of the appeals of the term *business elite* is that it fudges issues such as this.

67. John R. Logan and Harvey Molotch, *Urban Fortunes: The Political Economy of Place* (Berkeley and Los Angeles: University of California Press, 1987).

68. Ibid., 70. They amplify this characterization by noting that the metropolitan newspaper often achieves "a statesmanlike position in the community" by serving as the "arbiter of internal growth machine bickering, restraining the short-term profiteers in the interest of more stable, long-term, and properly planned growth." The *Observer's* frequent magisterial assumption of such responsibilities is exemplified by an editorial discussing the competition between downtown and outlying sites for prestigious retail stores such as Nordstrom and Saks. Noting that it would be unwise to assume that such areas "are necessarily pitted against each other," the editorial concluded by saying that the conflict's best outcome "would be obtained by methods that could serve a growing community again and again. The worst would be an outcome in which some interests of the moment defeat other interests of the moment, and larger interests are left to fate and another day" (*Charlotte Observer*, "Separate Issues: Uptown, SouthPark not Either-or Question," February 24, 1999, p. 14A). For additional discussion of the *Observer's* role in Charlotte, see Timothy D. Mead, "The Daily Newspaper As Political Agenda Setter: The *Charlotte Observer* and Metropolitan Reform," *State and Local Government Review* 26, no. 1 (1994): 27–37.

Until stopping publication in 1985, the *Charlotte News* was the city's afternoon paper. Once the Carolina's largest afternoon paper, the *News* prided itself on extensive local coverage. But its circulation was hurt by the same economic and social trends that have killed afternoon papers throughout the country. (John Vaughan, "Stopping the Presses, the *News* Bids Farewell to Its City," *Charlotte Observer*, November 1, 1985, p. 1A). I will draw heavily on the *News's* news coverage of the desegregation battles of the 1970s. Also, in discussing the 1990s, I will occasionally draw on the coverage by two weekly newspapers—the *Charlotte Post*, which is targeted toward African Americans, and the *Leader*, which was targeted toward an upscale, primarily white readership and frequently provided in-depth coverage of educational issues, until it ceased publication in 2002.

69. The bank that bore the Wachovia name as of the spring of 2003 was a product of a merger in 2001 between the Winston-Salem-based Wachovia bank and the larger Charlotte-based First Union. The resultant bank bears the Wachovia name, but it is headquartered in Charlotte.

70. Logan and Molotch, *Urban Fortunes*, 207.

71. Pamela L. Moore, "Crutchfield, McColl Talk Banking, and Then Some," *Charlotte Observer*, April 1, 1999, p. 4C.

CHAPTER 2

1. Peter Applebome, *Dixie Rising: How the South Is Shaping American Values, Politics, and Culture* (New York: Times Books, 1996), 153.

2. Pat Watters, *Charlotte* (Atlanta: Southern Regional Council, 1964), 76.

3. Carol Leonnig, "Black Activists Disagree on Walton's Successor," *Charlotte Observer*, July 28, 1994, pp. A1, A8.

4. Scott Dodd and Ted Mellnik, "In Growth, Charlotte No. 2 in U.S," *Charlotte Observer*, March 31, 2001, pp. 1A, 16A.

5. Scott Dodd, "The Secret of Charlotte's High Growth? Annexation," *Charlotte Observer*, June 27, 2000, pp. 1A, 6A.

6. Data obtained on line on August 17, 2002, at <http://factfinder.census.gov/bf/_lang=en_vt_name=DEC_2000_SF1_U_DP1_geo_id=16000US3712000.html>.

7. Data obtained on line on August 17, 2002, at <http://factfinder.census.gov/bf/_lang=en_vt_name=DEC_2000_SF1_U_DP1_geo_id=05000US37119.html>.

8. Enrollment data are from Charlotte-Mecklenburg Schools Membership Reports, second month of 1990–91 and first month of 2002–03 school years.

9. Data obtained on line on August 17, 2002, at <http://factfinder.census.gov/bf/_lang=en_vt_name=DEC_2000_SF1_U_DP1_geo_id=05000US37119.html>.

10. *Swann v. Charlotte-Mecklenburg Board of Education*, 402 U.S. 1 (1971).

11. Figures on racial composition are from CMS' membership reports for the second month of the academic year.

12. In compiling and reporting data on Hispanic enrollment, CMS has generally considered Hispanic, white, and black mutually exclusive categories. Data for 1992–93 are from CMS' *Ethnic Report As of the End of the First School Month, 1992–93* (unpublished report, dated 9/21/92). Data for 2002–03 are from CMS' *Monthly Membership at End of Month 1* (unpublished report, dated 9/17/02).

13. Harold A. Stone, Don K. Price, and Kathryn H. Stone, *City Manager Government in Charlotte* (Chicago: Social Science Research Council, 1939).

14. Jack Claiborne, *Jack Claiborne's Charlotte* (Charlotte, N.C.: The Observer/Craftsman Printing Company, 1974), 63.

15. In 1995, when the new system of representation was instituted, all nine seats on the school board were on the ballot. However, in order to stagger terms, the at-large members served a full four-year term, but the district representatives had to stand for reelection again in 1997, with the winners of that year's election then serving the full four-year term.

16. Applebome, *Dixie Rising*, 154.

17. Ibid., 151.

18. *Charlotte Observer*, "Trashing Family," August 7, 1996, p. 16A.

19. Thomas Hanchett, *Sorting Out the New South City: Race, Class, and Urban Development in Charlotte* (Chapel Hill: University of North Carolina Press, 1998), 226.

20. Ted Reed, "Cargo, Coming and Going," *Charlotte Observer*, January 18, 1998, pp. 1D, 3D.

21. Hanchett, *Sorting Out the New South City*, 186–87.

22. As quoted in Hanchett, *Sorting Out the New South City*, 225.

23. William T. Moye, "Charlotte-Mecklenburg Consolidation: Metrolina in Motion," (Ph. D. diss., University of North Carolina at Chapel Hill, 1975), 16.

24. Mary Norton Kratt, *Charlotte: Spirit of the New South* (Winston-Salem, N.C.: John F. Blair, 1992), 59.

25. As quoted in Hanchett, *Sorting Out the New South City*, 187.

26. Howard E. Covington Jr., and Marion A. Ellis, *The Story of NationsBank: Changing the Face of American Banking* (Chapel Hill: University of North Carolina Press, 1993).

27. Covington and Ellis, *The Story of NationsBank*, 24.

28. Linda Grant, "Here Comes Hugh," *Fortune*, August 21, 1995, cover, 5.

29. John Huey, "The Best Cities for Business," *Fortune*, November 4, 1991, p. 70; Jon Talton, "Hearst Name to Go on N. Tryon Tower," *Charlotte Observer*, December 17, 1998, pp. 1D, 10D.

30. Doug Smith, "Banks Wage Fight for Height on Charlotte Skyline," *Charlotte Observer*, October 9, 1998, p. 1A.

31. Doug Smith, "Star Grad Moving Back Near UNCC," *Charlotte Observer*, April 27, 2000, pp. 1D, 2D.

32. Doug Smith, "Builder Bringing 3-Bedroom Townhomes to Ballantyne," *Charlotte Observer*, February 23, 1999, pp. 1D, 2D.

33. Clarence N. Stone, "Regime Analysis and the Study of Urban Politics, A Rejoinder," *Journal of Urban Affairs*, 20 no. 3 (1998), 258.

34. The extent of organized labor's influence in local politics in earlier periods remains a subject for future research, but it is worth noting that one of the leading members of the Central Labor Council, Claude Albea, held a seat on Charlotte's City Council for thirty-four years from the 1930s to the 1960s and was generally viewed as organized labor's representative on that body (John York, "Ex-Council Member Claude Albea Dies," *Charlotte Observer*, November 25, 1978, p. 3B). Moreover, from the 1930s until 1953, Charlotte was home to the *Charlotte Labor Journal* and *Dixie Farm News*, a weekly whose ability to fill Labor Day issues with advertisements and

congratulations from local businesses indicates that organized labor once had a presence in Charlotte that is now largely forgotten.

35. Clarence N. Stone, *Regime Politics: Governing Atlanta, 1946–1988* (Lawrence: University Press of Kansas, 1989), 198, emphasis in original.

36. The phrase is from Carl Abbott's *The New Urban America: Growth and Politics in the Sunbelt*, rev. ed. (Chapel Hill: University of North Carolina Press, 1987), 257. As the work of Abbott, Stone, and many other scholars makes clear, Charlotte has not been the only Southern city to be characterized by such a coalition, but as subsequent chapters will indicate, it was distinctive, and perhaps unique, in the extent to which school desegregation was so important a part of regime politics.

37. William B. A. Culp Jr. and Gerald Ingalls, "Charlotte Elections," in *Elections, Parties, and Politics in Mecklenburg County*, ed. Gerald L. Ingalls (Charlotte, N.C.: Charlotte-Mecklenburg Board of Elections, Department of Geography, and the Urban Institute of the University of North Carolina at Charlotte, 1988), p. 52.

38. As quoted in Hanchett, *Sorting Out the New South City*, 82.

39. Hanchett, *Sorting Out the New South City*, 83.

40. As quoted in Janette Thomas Greenwood, *Bittersweet Legacy: The Black and White "Better Classes" in Charlotte, 1860–1910* (Chapel Hill: University of North Carolina Press, 1994), 224.

41. A variety of suggestive examples of the activity of the members of the "black better class" can be found in the epilogue to Greenwood's *Bittersweet Legacy*.

42. "Brisk Voting Reported from All City Boxes," *Charlotte News*, May 7, 1935, p. 1.

43. Ibid.

44. "More Congratulations," *Charlotte News*, May 8, 1935, p. 4.

45. "New Mayor and Council Take Office," *Charlotte News*, May 8, 1935, pp. 1, 8.

46. Abbott, *The New Urban America*, 249.

47. Damaria Etta Brown Leach, "Progress under Pressure: Changes in Charlotte Race Relations, 1955–65" (master's thesis, University of North Carolina at Chapel Hill, 1976), 11.

48. As quoted in Leach, "Progress Under Pressure," 11.

49. Joe Doster, "Smith Winner in Hot Race," *Charlotte Observer*, May 3, 1961, p. 1A.

50. As quoted in Alex Coffin, *Brookshire and Belk: Businessmen in City Hall* (Charlotte: University of North Carolina at Charlotte, 1994), 8.

51. Editorial, "The Observer Recommends," *Charlotte Observer*, May 1, 1961, p. 2B.

52. Dick Young, "Redevelopment Body Filled Out," *Charlotte News*, December 5, 1957, pp. 1B, 13B.

53. Lu Stanton, "52,000 Bus Riders Had to Find New Way to Go," *Charlotte News*, November 8, 1976, p. 1B.

54. Harry Golden, "The Textile Workers and the South," *Carolina Israelite*, July–August 1959, 7.

55. Moye, "Charlotte-Mecklenburg Consolidation," 170.

56. I am grateful to Tom Hanchett for helping me identify the white working-class precincts.

57. Many key decisions about the early phases of urban renewal involving Brooklyn and Blue Heaven were made before the upsurge of the civil rights movements gave the business elite added incentive to develop its alliance with black political leaders. Moreover, knowing that there was considerable opposition to urban renewal among both blacks and whites (albeit for different reasons), Brookshire consciously chose to pay Charlotte's share through tax revenue rather than by putting bond referenda before the voters (Coffin, *Brookshire and Belk*, 72).

58. Drawing on accounts in the *Charlotte Observer*, Hanchett notes that the realty company run by the mayor's brother tried to evict tenants in one neighborhood with a view toward transforming it from one that was all white to one that was all black (*Sorting Out the New South City*, 334, n. 110).

59. Hanchett, *Sorting Out the New South City*, 251.

60. Leach, "Progress under Pressure," 168.

61. Ibid., 120.

62. See, for example, Frye Gaillard, *The Dream Long Deferred* (Chapel Hill, NC: University of North Carolina Press, 1988).

63. Stanford R. Brookshire, "Turning Point 25 Years Ago, Charlotte Began New Era in Race Relations, *Charlotte Observer*, May 29, 1988, p. 1D.

64. As quoted in Davison M. Douglas, *Reading, Writing, and Race: The Desegregation of the Charlotte Schools* (Chapel Hill: University of North Carolina Press, 1995), 102.

65. Ibid.

66. Watters, *Charlotte*, 8.

67. Ibid., 33.

68. Randy Penninger, "The Emergence of Black Political Power in Charlotte, North Carolina: The City Council Tenure of Frederick Douglas Alexander, 1965–74" (master's thesis, University of North Carolina at Charlotte, 1989), 82.

69. Victor K. McElheny, "City's Negro Leaders Split on Local Issues," *Charlotte Observer*, May 10, 1961, p. 1C.

70. James K. Batten, "Negroes Seeking More Subtle Progress," *Charlotte Observer*, June 7, 1965, pp. 1C, 3C.

71. Watters, *Charlotte*, 34.

72. Ibid., 37.

73. Penninger, "The Emergence of Black Political Power," 90.

74. James Pierce, interview with author, Charlotte, North Carolina, June 28, 1996.

75. Leach, "Progress under Pressure," 168.

76. Batten, "Negroes Seeking More Subtle Progress," p. 1C.

77. These difficulties are illustrated by the results of the 1968 Democratic gubernatorial primary that Hawkins entered with the support of the liberal wing of organized labor and some civil rights leaders. The campaign's foci resembled those of the roughly contemporaneous Poor People's Campaign: racial equality and economic justice for people of all races. In fact, on April 4, the day he was killed, Martin Luther King had been scheduled to campaign with Hawkins but canceled his trip to North Carolina to deal with the increasingly tense situation in Memphis that accompanied the sanitation workers' strike. Whether King's appearance might have significantly improved Hawkins's showing in black precincts is a what-if question to which a definite answer cannot be given. But the fact is, Hawkins fared poorly in the primary, especially in Mecklenburg County, where, even in the black precincts, he received fewer votes than Alexander had in his recent campaigns for city council (Leach, "Progress under Pressure," 165).

78. Penninger, "The Emergence of Black Political Power," 85.

79. Moye, "Charlotte-Mecklenburg Consolidation," 140.

80. Douglas, *Reading, Writing, and Race*, 142.

81. Frye Gaillard, who covered much of the desegregation controversy for the *Observer*, has called Belk "disgraceful in his silence during the busing controversy" and noted that when a reporter asked about the schools, Belk replied, " 'That comes under the county budget, not under the city budget' " (Gaillard, *The Dream Long Deferred*, 157).

82. Theodore S. Arrington, "Partisan Campaigns, Ballots, and Voting Patterns," *Urban Affairs Quarterly* 14 (1978): 253–61.

83. Covington and Ellis, *The Story of NationsBank*, 146.

84. I was a member of Charlotteans for a Free Southern Africa and participated in these activities.

85. Joe Martin, interview with author, Charlotte, North Carolina, September 15, 1994.

86. Harvey Gantt, interview with author, Charlotte, North Carolina, May 25, 1999.

87. Ibid.

88. Margaret Edds, *Free at Last* (Bethesda, Md.: Adler and Adler, 1987), 207.

89. Ibid.

90. Culp and Ingalls, "Charlotte Elections," in *Elections, Parties, and Politics*, 55.

91. Joe Martin, interview with author, Charlotte, North Carolina, September 15, 1994.

92. The one exception to Democratic control of Charlotte's mayoralty during this period was Republican Ken Harris's victory in the election of 1977, the first after Belk's retirement. A downtown executive, Harris was especially well connected to the business elite. His Democratic opponent, the much older Jim Whittington, was a longtime city council member and party activist who lacked the connections with the business elite that Brookshire, Belk, or even Harris had. Rather, Whittington ran a funeral home and suffered from the (well-deserved) reputation of being a "satchel man," a person who made sure the Election Day workers in working-class white and black precincts received financial compensation for their services. Whittington's nomination was a controversial one among Democratic leaders. Brookshire, in fact, endorsed Harris; Belk held off endorsing Whittington until late in the campaign; and Fred Alexander's support was lukewarm. For all of these reasons, Harris ran in many ways like a Democrat, winning approximately 30 percent of the vote of African Americans.

93. Hugh McColl, "A Vision for Charlotte's Future," *Charlotte Observer*, September 22, 1995, p. 13A.

94. Editorial, "Election Recap: A Summary of Our Endorsements," *Charlotte Observer*, May 5, 1998, p. 12A.

95. Mary Newsom, "Remember When Local Politics Was Genteel?" *Charlotte Observer*, December 5, 1997, p. 13A.

96. Timothy D. Mead, "The Regime Strikes Back: A Case Study" (paper presented at the annual meeting of the Urban Affairs Association, Fort Worth, Texas, April 1998, p. 26).

97. A Better Charlotte Political Committee, Disclosure Reports, on file with the Mecklenburg County Board of Elections.

98. The business elite also sought—and obtained relatively easily—African American support in the county commission race in one of the heavily black districts. Its representative, a black, had supported the cut in arts funding. Moreover, elected as a Democrat, he also had crossed party lines to join the commission's four Republicans in voting to replace the Democratic chair of the commission with a Republican. With the latter vote costing him dearly among black Democrats, he ended up trying to run as an Independent but did not even get on the ballot. The ABC Political Committee also intervened in the Republican district primaries, helping secure the defeat of one of the incumbents who had been a member of the so-called Gang of Five.

99. As a measure of central tendency, the use of means (such as per capita income), rather than medians has certain well-known difficulties, among which are that means can attach undue weight to extremely high and extremely low values. However, the 1970 Census reports county-level income data for blacks and for the county's entire population, but not for whites per se. It is thus difficult to calculate white median income without making various assumptions about income distribution. However, knowing per capita income for the entire population and for blacks, it is relatively easy to obtain good estimates of that for whites because in 1970, in none of the five counties of particular interest here did persons who were neither black nor

white comprise more than 1/2 percent of the county's total population. In particular, Table 2.2's data on white per capita income from the 1970 Census for the five counties represent the arithmetic mean resulting from two calculations of white per capita income. The first assumed that the per capita income of persons who were neither white nor black was the same as that of whites, and the second assumed that the per capita income of these same persons was the same as blacks. The results obtained from the two different calculations are virtually identical, and any differences between them have no substantive effect on the analysis. The data on per capita income come from the following Bureau of the Census sources:

For the 1970 Census: *General Social and Economic Characteristics, United States Summary*, p. 398; *General Social and Economic Characteristics, North Carolina*, pp. 220, 428, 429, 431, 434, 461, 462, 463, 466. For the 1980 Census: *General Social and Economic Characteristics, United States Summary*, p. 118; *General Social and Economic Characteristics, North Carolina*, pp. 84, 583, 584, 586, 591, 599. For the 1990 Census: Summary Tape File 3 (STF3A), Table P115A, accessed on line at http://homer.ssd.census.gov/cdrom/lookup/ on August 17, 2002. For the 2000 Census: American FactFinder Tables P157B and P157I, accessed on line at http://factfinder.census.gov on October 1, 2002.

100. Melvin L. Oliver and Thomas M. Shapiro, *Black Wealth/White Wealth: A New Perspective on Racial Inequality* (New York: Routledge, 1995), 108. The data on home ownership come from the following Bureau of the Census sources:

For the 1970 Census: *General Housing Characteristics, United States Summary*, p. 9; *General Housing Characteristics, North Carolina*, p. 8; *Detailed Housing Characteristics, North Carolina*, pp. 163, 164, 166, 170, 178. For the 1980 Census: *Detailed Housing Characteristics, United States Summary*, pp. 68, 69; *General Housing Characteristics, North Carolina*, pp. 37, 163, 164, 167. For the 1990 Census: Summary Tape File 3 (STF3A), Table H19 accessed on line at http://homer.ssd.census.gov/cdrom/lookup/ on August 17, 2002. For the 2000 Census: American FactFinder Tables H11 and H13, accessed on line at http://factfinder.census.gov on October 1, 2002.

101. As was the case with per capita income, the 1970 Census reported county-level poverty rates for all persons and for blacks. Table 2.4's data for white poverty rates for the five counties were obtained by an estimation procedure similar to that used to obtain Table 2.2's data on white per capita income, i.e., taking the mean of the results of two computations, the first assuming that the less than 1/2 percent of the population who was neither black nor white had a poverty rate identical to whites, and the second assuming that these same persons had a poverty rate identical to blacks. Again, any differences between the results of the two computations were minimal and of no substantive significance. Table 2.4 reports white poverty rates to only two significant digits because that is how many of these rates appeared in the published reports from the 1970 and 1980 censuses used to obtain the data. Thus, the black/white poverty rate ratios that appear in Table 2.5 are less precise than the ratios dealing with home ownership and per capita income. However, the magnitude of the differences between Mecklenburg and the other places is such that the poverty rate ratios are sufficiently precise to support the inferences that I draw from them. The data on poverty rates come from the following Bureau of the Census sources:

For the 1970 Census: *General Social and Economic Characteristics, United States Summary*, p. 400; *General Social and Economic Characteristics, North Carolina*, pp. 191, 428, 429, 431, 434, 461, 462, 463, 466. For the 1980 Census: *General Social and Economic Characteristics, United States Summary*, p. 113; *General Social and Economic Characteristics, North Carolina*, pp. 608, 609, 611, 616, 624. For the 1990 Census: Summary Tape File 3 (STF3A), Table P119 accessed on line at http://homer.ssd. census.gov/cdrom/lookup/ on August 17, 2002. For the 2000 Census: American FactFinder Tables P159B and P159I, accessed on line at http://factfinder.census.gov on October 1, 2002.

102. Thus, in 1999, blacks comprised approximately 39 percent, 26 percent, 29 percent, 28 percent, and 20 percent, respectively, of Durham's, Forsyth's, Guilford's, Mecklenburg's, and Wake's populations. Among these five counties, there is no readily discernible relationship between the size of their black populations and black economic status on the variables of interest here.

A fourth methodological question involves the technical considerations stemming from the way the 2000 Census dealt with race, especially the fact that it was the first to give respondents the opportunity to report more than one race. But that famous change does not appear to significantly affect the exploratory analysis presented here, especially because in the five counties upon which I focus, a relatively small percentage of the population (2 percent or less) reported more than one race. I thus confine my discussion to those who reported belonging to only one race. More important is the problem posed by the large jump in North Carolina's Hispanic population in the 1990s. Prior to the 2000 Census, Hispanics constituted a very small percentage of the counties' population, and much of the published census data upon which I draw did not disaggregate racial categories into Hispanic and non-Hispanic. Thus, neither do I in the data presented for 1970, 1980, and 1990. For 2000, the published census data that I use did distinguish between Hispanic and non-Hispanic whites. Given the large jump in Mecklenburg's Hispanic population during the 1990s and the fact that on the relevant variables there is a large difference between Hispanic and non-Hispanic whites, I draw only on the latter for my 2000 data on whites. However, my data for blacks make no attempt to distinguish between Hispanics and non-Hispanics for a combination of several reasons: (1) Hispanic blacks are a much smaller percentage of the five North Carolina counties' black populations than Hispanic whites are of the white populations; (2) data distinguishing between Hispanic and non-Hispanic blacks are more difficult to obtain than that for whites; and (3) the data that are readily available for Hispanic and non-Hispanic blacks show much less difference than that between Hispanic and non-Hispanic whites in the five counties of interest here.

103. The obvious downside of using the county as the level of analysis is that counties lack the economic and social integration that characterizes metropolitan statistical areas. However, in a study whose main concern is the political consequences of a busing plan in one county in a metropolitan statistical area that now crosses the state line, it is appropriate, initially at least, to use the county as the level of analysis.

104. Any particular census reports per capita income from the previous calendar year, but for convenience, both the tables and text refer to the data as coming from the year in which the census was taken. The same holds true for poverty rates.

CHAPTER 3

1. *Swann* v. *Charlotte-Mecklenburg* 300 F. Supp. 1358, 1360 (W.D.N.C. 1969).

2. *Martin* v. *Charlotte-Mecklenburg Board of Education* 475 F. Supp. 1318, 1347 (1979).

3. Editorial, "Playing with Fire: The Dangers of Resegregation," *Charlotte Observer*, March 19, 1986, p. 14A.

4. Davison M. Douglas, *Reading, Writing, and Race: The Desegregation of the Charlotte Schools* (Chapel Hill: University of North Carolina Press, 1995), 26. My account of much of the events leading up to the Supreme Court's decision in *Swann* draws heavily on this excellent book.

5. As quoted in Frye Gaillard, *The Dream Long Deferred* (Chapel Hill: University of North Carolina Press, 1988), 33.

6. The extent to which various kinds of desegregation plans produce white flight has been a subject of considerable research and scholarly debate. While such flight certainly takes place, it is worth emphasizing that the declining white enrollment of many urban districts has a variety of causes, including differential birth rates. White enrollment has declined in districts that have desegregated as well as those that have not, thus supporting the conclusion that "other factors had a much larger impact on [declining white enrollments] than did the implementation of school desegregation programs" (Steven G. Rivken, "Residential Segregation and School Integration," *Sociology of Education* 67 [1994]: 290).

7. Chris Folk, interview with author, Charlotte, North Carolina, May 28, 1998.

8. Douglas, *Reading, Writing, and Race*, 75.

9. Ibid., 92.

10. *Swann* v. *Charlotte-Mecklenburg* 300 F. Supp. 1358, 1360 (W.D.N.C. 1969).

11. Ibid.

12. Ibid., 1372.

13. Ibid., 1360.

14. Douglas, *Reading, Writing, and Race*, 202.

15. Ibid., 212.

16. *Martin* v. *Charlotte-Mecklenburg Board of Education* 475 F. Supp. 1318, 1321, 1346 (1979). The extent to which *Martin* constituted a unitary status hearing would be a key legal issue when *Swann* reopened twenty years later.

17. Most writers, including Judge McMillan himself, often refer to the *burden* of busing. In the Charlotte context, I find that word too pejorative and much prefer *responsibilities*. Busing was part of the educational landscape for many years prior to both *Brown* and *Swann*, both to maintain segregation and to transport students of all races to and from school. I doubt that any rigorous content analysis of educational discourse would find *burden* as frequently coupled to *busing* prior to 1954 as it has

been since. In fact, in a residentially segregated society, one might very well claim, as Judge McMillan did in a speech to local educators, that "sober reflection might lead us to believe that true education doesn't begin until we *leave* the neighborhood school" (Bradley Martin, "Old-Style Schools Miss Boat, *Charlotte Observer*, January 18, 1974, p. 1B, emphasis added). From that perspective, a polemicist might even venture to talk about the *opportunities* of busing rather than the burdens, but that would be bending the stick almost as far in one direction as *burdens* does in the other. Hence, *responsibilities* appears to hold the appropriate middle ground.

18. Editorial, "Playing with Fire: The Dangers of Resegregation."

19. As quoted in Douglas, *Reading, Writing, and Race*, 241.

20. William Poe, interview with Roslyn A. Mickelson, Charlotte, North Carolina, December 1998.

21. Nancy Brachey, "Haywood to Head 'Open' W. Charlotte," *Charlotte Observer*, July 10, 1974, p. 1B. See also Warren Barnard, "Haywood Heads W. Charlotte," *Charlotte News*, July 10, 1974, p. 1A.

22. Kay Reimler, "600 Pupils from Closed Schools to Attend Irwin Ave. Junior High," *Charlotte News*, August 28, 1969, pp. 1C, 14C.

23. Noting that Supreme Court justices are probably "not so isolated as some might think," Douglas calls attention to Justice William Brennan's use of newspaper surveys indicating decreased opposition to desegregation to lobby his colleagues against any language in the *Swann* decision that would encourage such resistance (*Reading, Writing, and Race*, 212).

More generally, it seems difficult to reconcile the Supreme Court's unanimous affirmation of comprehensive *intra*district remedies for school desegregation in *Swann* with its 5–4 vote in 1974 against similar *inter*district remedies in *Milliken v. Bradley* without taking some account of the country's generic retreat during those intervening three years from racial and social liberalism. By imposing high obstacles in *Milliken* to the use of interdistrict remedies, the Court made it difficult to achieve school desegregation in areas—such as Detroit, which gave rise to *Milliken*—in which predominantly black central cities are in a school district different from those of predominantly white outlying areas.

One of the ironies of the history of school desegregation involves the opinion of Justice Potter Stewart, who cast the decisive fifth vote in *Milliken*. Commenting on the demographic patterns precluding desegregation within Detroit itself, Stewart said "this essential fact of a predominantly Negro school population in Detroit" was caused by "unknown and perhaps unknowable factors" (*Milliken v. Bradley*, 418 U.S. 717, 756 [1974]). Pointing to the Supreme Court's reliance on the research of scholars such as Kenneth Clark in *Brown v. Board of Education*, critics often have claimed that this landmark case drew much too heavily on social science's understanding of the *consequences* of segregation. It thus seems appropriate to note that Stewart's decisive fifth vote in *Milliken* indicated an even greater unwillingness to draw upon social science's understanding of the *causes* of segregation in a Northern city such as Detroit.

24. Jennifer Hochschild, *The New American Dilemma* (New Haven: Yale University Press, 1984), 27.

25. Douglas, *Reading, Writing, and Race*, 113–29.

26. Jennifer Hochschild, "Is School Desegregation Still a Viable Policy Option?" *PS: Political Science and Politics* 30: 3 (1997): 459.

27. Douglas, *Reading, Writing, and Race*, 235.

28. Ronald P. Formisano, *Boston against Busing* (Chapel Hill: University of North Carolina Press, 1991), 214–15.

29. Douglas, *Reading, Writing, and Race*, 251.

30. Ibid., 148.

31. Ibid., 183.

32. William Poe, interview with author, Charlotte, North Carolina, April 3, 1995.

33. Douglas, *Reading, Writing, and Race*, 234.

34. Gaillard, *The Dream Long Deferred*, 145.

35. Staff writer, "Slate-Makers Tap Candidates for Funds," *Charlotte Observer*, May 4, 1972, p. 1A.

36. Gaillard, *The Dream Long Deferred*, 94, 108.

37. Covington and Ellis, *The Story of NationsBank*, 291; David Mildenberg, "Just Another Corporate Raider?," *Charlotte Observer*, March 5, 1995, pp. 1D, 7D.

38. Editorial, "School Board," *Charlotte News*, May 1, 1972, p. 18A; Editorial, "School Board Races," *Charlotte Observer*, May 4, 1972, p. 18A; Editorial, "We Recommend," *Charlotte Observer*, June 3, 1972, p. 12A.

39. Douglas, *Reading, Writing, and Race*, 234; Gaillard, *The Dream Long Deferred*, 145.

40. Polly Paddock and Nancy Brachey, "Huff Wins School Post, 4 in Runoff," *Charlotte Observer*, May 8, 1974, pp. 1A, 12A.

41. Gaillard, *The Dream Long Deferred*, 160.

42. Ibid.

43. Editorial, "Eloquent Words about Schools," *Charlotte Observer*, May 28, 1984, p. 18A.

44. Kay Reimler, " 'Best' Schooling? Negroes Disagree," *Charlotte News*, January 7, 1969, pp. 1A, 5A.

45. Rita Simpson, "Leake: Keep Metro School Regardless of Integration," *Charlotte News*, March 15, 1969, p. 2A.

46. Edward Cody, "Just Begun to Fight, Leake Says," *Charlotte Observer*, August 3, 1969, pp. 1B, 2B.

47. Kay Reimler, "Some Bus Confusion Evident," *Charlotte News*, September 2, 1969, p. 1A.

48. "Keep City Schools Open, Leake Says," *Charlotte Observer*, August 27, 1970, p. 1B.

49. Douglas, *Reading, Writing, and Race*, 182.

50. Theodore S. Arrington, "Personality and Issues," in *Elections, Parties, and Politics in Mecklenburg County*, ed. Gerald Ingalls (Charlotte: Charlotte-Mecklenburg Board of Elections, the Department of Geography and Earth Sciences and the Urban Institute at the University of North Carolina at Charlotte, 1988), 43.

51. Ibid.

52. Judy Gaultney, "3 Incumbents and Newcomer Win Seats on School Board," *Charlotte News*, June 30, 1982, p. 4A.

53. Ibid.

54. Editorial, "School Board: Choose Four Out of Seven," *Charlotte Observer*, June 24, 1982, p. 22A.

55. Judy Gaultney, "No Burning Issues for 7 School Panel Candidates," *Charlotte News*, June 23, 1982, p. 4A.

56. Editorial, "School Board: Choose Four Out of Seven."

57. Reflecting the history of desegregation and the fact that until recently almost all of CMS' nonblack students were non-Hispanic whites, the court orders in *Swann* dealt with only two categories of students, blacks and nonblacks, with the latter generally being referred to as whites. During the many years it was under court order, CMS typically did the same in reporting data on racial (im)balance. I will generally do so as well, since my analyses largely deal with the years in which almost all of CMS' students were either black or white, and few were Hispanic.

McMillan's last order in *Swann* was the one in 1980 that gave CMS additional latitude in meeting the court's criteria of racial balance. Whereas previous orders had prohibited all but one of CMS' schools from having a majority black enrollment, the 1980 order gave elementary schools more flexibility by specifying that none of them— with the exception of Hidden Valley—could have an enrollment of black students that exceeded the district-wide percentage of black students by fifteen percentage points. The exemption of Hidden Valley reflected McMillan's long-standing hope that it could be desegregated "naturally." In the mid-1970s, the area around Hidden Valley had recently become integrated, and the school was allowed to operate as a grades 1–6 neighborhood school, with McMillan viewing it "as a desirable experiment to encourage the neighborhood patrons to make a 'go' of a desegregated 'neighborhood school'" (*Swann v. Charlotte-Mecklenburg* 379 F. Supp. 1098, 1104 [1974]). As things turned out, that experiment failed, and black students soon comprised 80 percent, and then over 90 percent, of Hidden Valley's enrollment.

McMillan's 1980 order imposed no explicit limitation on the maximum percentage of white students that a school could have. But his previous orders were concerned with this issue, and in the reactivated *Swann* litigation, there was considerable dispute about what standards of racial balance McMillan's orders required CMS to follow. Reflecting on the standards in these earlier orders, Judge Potter, in his 1999 decision, called the situation "hazy" and "not a model of clarity." Rather than use a "mishmash of standards gleaned from several orders," the judge chose a +/–15 percent variance from the district-wide percentage of black enrollment for his definition of racial balance (*Capacchione* v. *Charlotte-Mecklenburg Schools* 57 F. Supp. 2d 228, 244, 246 [W.D.N.C. 1999]).

58. Data come from CMS' membership reports. Figure 3.1 starts with the first school year (1980–81) following McMillan's last order in *Swann*. Racial balance was at least as high in the late 1970s.

Racial balance can be measured in a variety of ways, each of which has its advantages and disadvantages. By tracking the percentage of CMS' black students in RIB schools, Figure 3.1 provides an intuitively satisfying measure of CMS' success in achieving one of school desegregation's major goals: minimizing the extent to which African Americans attend segregated black schools. Similarly, the figure also provides a straightforward measure of the extent to which white students attended racially balanced schools. However, this method suffers from the disadvantage that a slight change in the enrollment of a few large schools can lead to huge fluctuations in the amount of racial balance. For example, the precipitous drop in the percentage of white students in RIW schools between the 1987–88 and 1988–89 school years was caused by small changes in just three of CMS' 100-plus schools, but they were high schools with very large enrollments. In 1987–88, each of these three schools was less than three percentage points above the ceiling on white enrollment. In the following year, the three schools were exactly at that ceiling, with the result that all of those schools' white students (over 10 percent of the district's total white enrollment) were now counted as attending RB, as opposed to RIW, schools. That kind of simultaneous small change in the same direction in several large schools is relatively rare, but it emphasizes the importance of assessing changes in racial balance over a several-year period, not simply between any two years.

This problem can be avoided by counting the number of schools that are racially imbalanced, but that method has just the opposite problem: it gives equal weight to all schools in a district, no matter how many students they enroll. District-wide summary indices of racial balance and racial exposure also can be computed to measure desegregation, but their interpretation is more technical than these other methods.

59. Figures computed from Charlotte-Mecklenburg Schools, *1982–83 EEO5 Report Summary* (Charlotte, N.C.: Author, April 2, 1998).

60. Ricki Morell, "Split Board OKs Robinson Moves for Principals," *Charlotte Observer*, May 28, 1986, p. 1A.

61. Robert Hanes, interview with author, Charlotte, North Carolina, January 28, 1999.

62. See, e.g., Gaillard, *The Dream Long Deferred*, 179–81.

63. Southern Oral History Program, Southern Communities: Listening for a Change: Miscellaneous Projects, 1985–1999, Southern Historical Collection, Wilson Library, University of North Carolina, Chapel Hill, North Carolina.

64. For a more detailed treatment of the issues discussed in this paragraph, see Amy Stuart Wells and Robert L. Crain, "Perpetuation Theory and the Long-Term Effects of School Desegregation," *Review of Educational Research* 64 (1994): 531–55.

Importantly, David Armor, one of the academic world's leading skeptics about the benefits of desegregation, also notes that the case for the long-term benefits of desegregation is stronger than the case for the short-term benefits (David Armor, *Forced Justice* [New York: Oxford University Press, 1995], 113).

65. The data in Figures 3.2, 3.3, and 3.4 are from Charlotte-Mecklenburg Schools Assessment Services, "California Achievement Test—Results for Ethnic Groups, 1978–1992," unpublished report, November 1992.

66. For a typical report of such enthusiasm, see Charles E. Shepard, "Student Test Scores Rise Again," *Charlotte Observer*, July 2, 1981, p. 2D.

67. David Armor, transcript of testimony in *Capacchione* v. *Charlotte-Mecklenburg Schools*, April 29, 1999, p. 119. That Armor would dismiss the educational significance of CMS' rising CAT scores in the early 1980s is hardly surprising. Elsewhere (e.g., in *Forced Justice*), he has expressed considerable skepticism about the short-term educational benefits of desegregation, and he was testifying for white plaintiffs whose arguments against the utility of the district's desegregation practices would hardly be strengthened by evidence of increased black academic achievement during the years of peak racial balance in student and faculty assignment.

Unlike the white plaintiffs, the black plaintiffs and CMS, the case's other two parties, generally argued that desegregation was necessary to improve the education of African American students. Therefore, it may appear surprising that neither of these parties made a major effort to show that the years of peak racial balance saw improved academic outcomes for black students. The lack of effort in this regard was rooted, in part at least, in legal considerations that placed a premium on these two parties' showing that the situation of blacks in CMS in the late 1990s was a vestige of state-mandated segregation. Consequently, from the standpoint of courtroom strategy, it was to the advantage of both parties to downplay whatever desegregation accomplishments CMS may have achieved, lest such evidence undermine the claim that the situation of blacks in CMS in the late 1990s was rooted in years of *de jure* segregation.

Consequently and ironically, a two-month trial dealing with one of the nation's most successful desegregation experiences produced scant testimony about the extent to which the heyday of this experience, the early 1980s, improved outcomes for black students. Moreover, as part of its claim that CMS had still not achieved unitary status, CMS' legal team consistently emphasized the district's shortcomings rather than successes. While important to the courtroom strategy, the emphasis had unfortunate political consequences for the district, as chapter 6 will indicate.

68. The statewide data includes data from CMS. Insofar as CMS' enrollment comprised approximately 7 percent of the state's, any differences between CMS and the rest of the state are thus slightly larger than what the figures show.

69. One possible explanation of the difference between the early and late 1980s is that the 1986 changes in the CAT had an effect, in and of themselves, on CMS students that was different from the effect that they had statewide. However, there is no evidence for such an effect. Nor is it intuitively obvious what such an effect might be. A second possible explanation is that the characteristics of CMS and/or North Carolina students changed during the decade in a way that affected test scores. Of

such characteristics, one that is especially important is poverty, which is typically associated with lower academic achievement, all other things being equal. Since year-by-year racially disaggregated county poverty rates are not available, it is necessary to draw upon decennial census data. As Table 2.4 indicates, black and white poverty rates dropped in both Mecklenburg and North Carolina during the 1980s. For whites in North Carolina, the drop from a poverty rate of 10 percent to 8.6 percent translates into a relative decrease of 14 percent ([10–8.6]/10=14 percent), which is greater than the 11 percent relative decrease for whites in Mecklenburg. This greater relative decrease in statewide white poverty is consistent, all other things being equal, with the fact that North Carolina whites did better than CMS whites in the late 1980s than in the early 1980s, though this consistency is obviously insufficient to establish any causal relationship. However, for blacks, the relative decrease in poverty was greater in Mecklenburg than it was statewide (15 percent as opposed to 11 percent), thus leading one to expect, all other things being equal, that compared to black scores statewide, those in Mecklenburg would be higher at the end of the 1980s than at the beginning. But they were not higher; they were generally lower. The fact that black test scores did not change in the direction that would be anticipated by changes in black poverty rates adds weight to the suggestion that the relatively (compared to those statewide) higher black test scores in the early 1980s are attributable to changes in CMS rather than to changes in student characteristics during the decade.

70. Nay Howell, transcript of testimony in *Cappachione* v. *Charlotte-Mecklenburg Schools*, May 14, 1999, p. 101, and interview with author, Charlotte, North Carolina, August 19, 1999.

71. As noted in the Preface, my children attended First Ward during the last year of the Robinson administration and when, shortly thereafter, it received a National School of Excellence Award. My observations on the school and its PTA were confirmed by CMS personnel whose involvement with the school began much earlier in the Robinson administration, but who requested anonymity.

72. Although CMS occasionally tried to define quantitatively what constituted racial balance in the programs and classrooms within a particular school or system-wide, the efforts were sporadic and plagued by difficult methodological and substantive issues. Nor does Judge Potter's decision provide any guidance in formulating such a definition. Thus, I will not attempt one, but instead I will talk more generally about racially identifiable tracking. However, I will compute disparity ratios that show the magnitude of the over- and under-representation of African Americans in particular tracks. A disparity ratio of 1.2 or .80 is obviously much less troubling than one of 4.0 or .25, but the latter ratios are more representative, as Table 3.1 indicates, of the situation in the highest and lowest tracks.

I confine the discussion to racial disparities in track placement in CMS' high schools, because there is much less systematic data on analogous issues at the elementary school level (e.g., the racial composition of pull-out programs). However, both newspaper articles and CMS documents indicate that the racial composition of programs for "gifted" children was a major issue. See, for example, "Grouping and Achievement," *Charlotte News*, January 25, 1983, p. 8A; Judy Gaultney, "School Classes Reach Balance in Achievement, Racial Mix," *Charlotte News*, December 15, 1983, p. 10A;

Ricki Morell, "Relic Draws Praise for Candor," *Charlotte Observer*, September 10, 1987, pp. 1C, 8C; Ricki Morell, "Supt. Relic Stresses Reaching Black Children in Lower Grades," *Charlotte Observer*, October 15, 1987, p. 5C. The latter article pointed out that in a year when blacks comprised 39 percent of CMS' enrollment, only 10.4 percent of enrollment in academically gifted classes was African American.

73. Morell, "Relic Draws Praise for Candor," "Supt. Relic Stresses Reaching Black Children in Lower Grades." For information on the 1977 HEW grant, see Tom Bradbury, "HEW's Mandate: Racial Balance Over Education," *Charlotte News*, July 29, 1977, p. 12A.

74. Charlotte-Mecklenburg Schools, "Class Counts for High School English Classes," unpublished report, November 11, 1981, Defendant's Exhibit No. 61, *Cappachione v. Charlotte-Mecklenburg Schools.*

75. A basically identical version of this table first appeared in Roslyn Arlin Mickelson and Stephen Samuel Smith, "Race, Tracking, and Achievement among African Americans in a Desegregated School System: Evidence from the Charlotte-Mecklenburg Schools" (paper presented at the Stanford University Conference on Race, Stanford, Calif., November, 1999). My discussion of tracking draws heavily upon this paper.

The lowest track was what CMS called Skill Classes. The second lowest was called Regular, and the second from the top was called Advanced. The top track consisted of Advanced Placement and what CMS called Gifted and Talented. The survey lists the classes in this order; that is, in any given school, the Skill classes are listed first, followed by the Regular, then the Advanced, and so forth. The survey also lists the racial composition of specialized classes, for example, those labeled LD (learning disabled) and EMH (educable mentally handicapped). Such classes enrolled relatively few students and were not offered at all high schools. I have excluded them in preparing Table 3.1. It is worth noting, however, that the enrollment of most of these classes was predominantly African American.

76. For accounts of CMS' efforts to deal with the racial identifiability of classes in different tracks in both junior and senior high school in subsequent years of Robinson's administration, see Judy Gaultney, "Schools Alter Schedules in 55 Classes for Racial Balance," *Charlotte News*, January 24, 1983, p. 1A; Gaultney, "School Classes Reach Balance in Achievement, Racial Mix." The latter story's upbeat headline notwithstanding, the problem was not eliminated as Superintendent Relic's comments, previously noted, made clear.

Data from the 1990s show less racial disparity in twelfth-grade English tracks than there had been in 1981–82, but a considerable amount remained. For example, in the 1993–94 school year, the disparity ratio for the lowest track was 1.8, and for the highest track, it was .38 (Mickelson and Smith, "Race, Tracking, and Achievement"). A lack of available data for the late 1980s makes it impossible to pinpoint when the decrease in racially identifiable tracking occurred.

Even though the 1990s were characterized by a drop in the racial identifiability of the various tracks of twelfth-grade English, they also were years in which CMS witnessed growing resegregation at the building level. The fact that the years of minimal racial imbalance among schools were characterized by higher levels of racially identifiable track placement within schools, and that the years in which the latter decreased saw much greater racial imbalance among schools, is a telling indication of how far even a district widely praised for its desegregation efforts has been from ever fully realizing *Brown's* promise of equal educational opportunities for all children.

77. Charlotte-Mecklenburg Schools, "Class Counts for High School English Classes."

78. Charles E. Shepard, "Will Principal Shake Image with Move?," *Charlotte Observer*, December 28, 1980, pp. 1C, 8C.

79. Ibid.

80. Ricki Morell, Frye Gaillard, and Ed Martin, "Our Schools: Pass or Fail? Not Bad, but Not Equal," *Charlotte Observer*, April 23, 1988, p. 1A.

81. Ricki Morell, "Tale of Two Schools," *Charlotte Observer*, April 24, 1988, p. 1A.

82. Morell, Gaillard, and Martin, "Our Schools: Pass or Fail? Not Bad, but Not Equal."

83. Carrie Winter, interview with author, Charlotte, North Carolina, January 21, 2000.

84. Adolph Reed Jr., "Demobilization in the New Black Political Regime: Ideological Capitulation and Radical Failure in the Postsegregation Era," in *The Bubbling Cauldron: Race, Ethnicity, and the Urban Crisis*, ed. Michael Peter Smith and Joe R. Feagin (Minneapolis: University of Minnesota Press, 1995), 185.

85. Editorial, "Playing with Fire."

86. Rolfe Neill, "There Is Something Amiss in Schools Here: Let's Fix It," *Charlotte Observer*, March 13, 1988, p. 3C.

87. "Eloquent Words about Schools," *Charlotte Observer*, May 28, 1984, p. 18A.

88. Editorial, "Whose Priorities? County Shortchanges Schools," *Charlotte Observer*, May 31, 1984, p. 18A.

89. Carrie Winter, interview with author, Charlotte, North Carolina, January 21, 2000.

90. Public School Forum of North Carolina, *Local School Finance in North Carolina* (Raleigh, N.C.: Author, 1987). With the exception of 1988, a report has appeared every year since 1987.

91. Tom Bradbury, "Direct Growth for Schools' Sake," *Charlotte News*, October 25, 1979, p. 14A.

92. Ricki Morell and Mae Israel, "Critics Rap Schools' Planning," *Charlotte Observer*, August 27, 1987, p. 1A.

93. Ibid.

Chapter 4

1. Susan Jetton, "Hunt Hears Arguments on Beltway," *Charlotte Observer*, October 22, 1977, p. 1B.

2. Editorial, "Schools: Time for Change," *Charlotte Observer*, April 27, 1988, p. 14A.

3. For doubts about the existence of a crisis, see David C. Berliner and Bruce J. Biddle, *The Manufactured Crisis: Myths, Fraud, and the Attack on America's Schools* (Reading, Mass.: Addison-Wesley, 1995).

4. Mark Nadler, "Charlotte-Mecklenburg," in *Busing USA*, ed. Nicolaus Mills (New York: Teachers College Press, 1979), 315.

5. Ibid.

6. Charles E. Shepard, "Home Building Boom Overflows Schools," *Charlotte Observer*, September 27, 1979, pp. 1A, 24A.

7. Tom Bradbury, "Direct Growth, for Schools' Sake," *Charlotte News*, October 25, 1979, p.14A.

8. Thomas E. Norman, transcript of testimony in *Capacchione* v. *Charlotte-Mecklenburg Schools*, 57 F. Supp. 2d 228 (W.D.N.C. 1999), May 17, 1999, p. 6.

9. John Minter, "School Location Leaves Board in a Quandary," *Charlotte Post*, November 25, 1997, pp. 1A, 7A.

10. *Defendants' Post-Trial Brief* in *Capacchione* v. *Charlotte-Mecklenburg Schools*, filed July 20, 1999, p. 17. Because of ambiguity about what constitutes a new school and other definitional issues, some of the witnesses at the trial, such as myself, considered twenty-eight a more accurate count than twenty-seven. However, the latter was the figure used by the district court in its ruling (*Capacchione* v. *Charlotte-Mecklenburg Schools*, 57 F. Supp. 2d 228, 252 [W.D.N.C. 1999]), and it is the generally accepted one, which I will use in this book.

11. Ted DeAdwyler, "Gantt Urges Slower Pace in Southeast," *Charlotte Observer*, January 26, 1984, p. 1C; Jim Morrill, "For Developers, Elections Signal Tough Times Ahead," *Charlotte Observer*, November, 7, 1985, p. 1A; Harvey Gantt, interview with author, Charlotte, North Carolina, May 25, 1999.

12. Although called "the northern route," this route was in south Mecklenburg. But it was north of Highway 51, as opposed to the other proposed route, which was south of 51.

13. Susan Jetton, "Hunt Hears Arguments"; Henry Scott, "City Council Favors Belt North of 51," *Charlotte Observer*, March 21, 1978, p. 1A; Henry Scott, "N.C. Chooses Southern Belt Route," *Charlotte Observer*, April 22, 1978, p. 1A; Tom Bradbury, "The Belt Road: Protect the Path," *Charlotte News*, April 24, 1978, p. 4A; Earl Gullege, "City Leaders Followed Experts' Advice," *Charlotte Observer*, October 27, 1987, p. 18A.

14. Susan Green, "Busing Order Warned against Destabilizing Acts Like Outer Belt Decision," *Charlotte News*, February 7, 1979, p. 16A.

15. In 1999 interviews with the author, neither Harvey Gantt, who was deeply involved in the outerbelt debate, nor Tom Bradbury, who wrote about it extensively for the *News*, could recall any instance where school desegregation had figured in the debate. While twenty years may have dimmed their recollections, a search of the *Observer's* voluminous clipping file about the outerbelt turned up only one article in which school desegregation was discussed. That article was Green's letter, cited above.

16. Earl G. Gullege, "Northern Route Is Not the Best One," *Charlotte News*, March 20, 1978, p. 6A; Cathy Packer, "City-County Square Off in Outerbelt Road Dispute," *Charlotte News*, March 21, 1978, p. 6A; Bill Arthur, "County Favors Belt South of 51," *Charlotte Observer*, April 4, 1978, p. 1B; Robert J. Breedon and Karl M. Cates, "Belt Road, Facts Support Southern Route," *Charlotte Observer*, April 18, 1978, p. 15A.

17. This discussion of Morrison draws upon Heriot Clarkson, "A Biographical Sketch of Cameron Morrison," *Public Papers and Letters of Cameron Morrison*, ed. D. L. Corbitt (Raleigh: Edwards and Broughton Company, 1927) and Dan L. Morrill, *Survey and Research Report on Morrocroft*, unpublished report, October 3, 1979, Charlotte-Mecklenburg Public Library's North Carolina Room's file on Cameron Morrison. This file also contains a copy of a poster from Morrison's 1920 gubernatorial campaign, the subhead of which notes, "Cameron Morrison Fought a Glorious Fight for the Cause of White Supremacy in North Carolina in 1898–1900."

18. Ricki Morell, "Couple Symbolize City's Ambitions," *Charlotte Observer*, December 15, 1991, p. 1A. For an indication of Ballantyne's ambition, see the twenty-four page special advertising section "Ballantyne: A Better Way To Live, Play, Work, Stay," *Charlotte Observer*, April 11, 1999.

19. Ibid.

20. Lauro F. Cavazos, "Choice in Education," Remarks Made at Education Press Association Newsmaker Luncheon, National Press Club, Washington, D.C., May 19, 1989 (Washington, D.C.: U.S. Department of Education, 1989), 1. If the idiocy of Cavazos's comment and the trendy school bashing of the late 1980s were not apparent at the time, they surely were a decade later, when budget deficits had given way to surpluses, and the United States was once again the world's preeminent economic power, but few would credit public education for that turnaround.

21. Gordon Foster, *Expert Report*, in *Capacchione v. Charlotte-Mecklenburg Schools*, Table 4. National public school enrollment bottomed out the following school year, but neither national nor local enrollment changed materially in those two years. Between that trough and 1998–1999, the academic year in which the *Swann* trial occurred, enrollment in CMS increased 37 percent, while the national increase was 18 percent. (Computation for national increase based on data in U.S. Department of Education, *Digest of Education Statistics, 2000*, available on line at <http://nces.ed.gov/pubs2001/digest/dt003.html>, accessed June 2002.)

22. Bob Hanes and Bruce Irons, unpublished memo to Peter Relic concerning school sites, October 22, 1987, *Swann* Plaintiffs' Exhibit No. 134, *Capacchione v. Charlotte-Mecklenburg.*

23. Mecklenburg County Planning Commission, "Single-Family Preliminary Approvals, January 1, 1983–August 31, 1990," unpublished report.

24. Ricki Morell, "Vote to Build School Near Union County Assailed,"*Charlotte Observer*, March 10, 1988, p. 1D.

25. Editorial, "School Sites: A Better Option?" *Charlotte Observer*, March 15, 1988, p. 14A.

26. Ricki Morell, "Relic Hits New School," *Charlotte Observer*, September 9, 1987, p. 1A.

27. Ricki Morell, "Revision Stresses Athletics, Half to School's Changes for Sports," *Charlotte Observer*, September 24, 1987, p. 1D.

28. Bruce Henderson, "Watchdog Group Urges Votes to Reject School Bond Issue," *Charlotte Observer*, October 31, 1989, p. 1B.

29. On Relative Effort for Current Spending, Mecklenburg does better than on either Relative Total Effort or Overall Rank, but even on this measure, its aggregate record over the years is poorer than that of either of the other two counties.

30. Tucker Mitchell, "More Taxes . . . Again," *Leader*, July 2, 1993, p. 21.

31. Susan Burgess, interview with author, Charlotte, North Carolina, September 15, 1994.

32. As opposed to the more difficult challenge of opposition to the busing plan, the task force addressed the formal complaint about the lack of preparation of entry-level workers by emphasizing the need for increases in early childhood education and innovative programs aimed at at-risk children and their families. My summary of the task force's activity draws heavily upon Roslyn A. Mickelson, Carol A. Ray, and Stephen S. Smith, "The Growth Machine and the Politics of Urban Educational Reform: The Case of Charlotte, North Carolina," in *Education in Urban Areas: Cross-National Dimensions*, ed. Nelly P. Stromquist (Westport, Conn.: Praeger, 1994), 169–98 and Carol A. Ray and Roslyn A. Mickelson, "Corporate Leaders, Resistant Youth, and the Politics of School Reform in Sunbelt City," *Social Problems* 37 (1990): 101–13.

33. Joe Martin, interview with author, Charlotte, North Carolina, September 15, 1994.

34. Hugh McColl, "Our Schools Aren't Good Enough," *Charlotte Observer*, January 4, 1989, p. 19A.

35. Joe Martin, interview with author, Charlotte, North Carolina, September 15, 1994.

36. Ibid.

37. Ricki Morell, "Angry Parents Call for End of Busing," *Charlotte Observer*, January 22, 1988, p. 4C.

38. Editorial, "For the School Board," *Charlotte Observer*, April 30, 1986, p. 14A.

39. "Issues: Charlotte-Mecklenburg School Board Race," *Charlotte Observer*, May 4, 1986, p. 12A.

40. Editorial, "Schools: Time for Change."

41. Stephen Samuel Smith, "Hugh Governs? Regime and Education Policy in Charlotte, North Carolina," *Journal of Urban Affairs* 27, no. 3 (1997): 247–74.

42. Ricki Morell, "School Board Splinters," *Charlotte Observer*, October 14, 1988, p. 1A.

43. Joe Martin, "Needed: A New Consensus on Pupil Assignment," *Charlotte Observer*, February 17, 1990, p. 15A.

44. Editorial, "For the School Board," *Charlotte Observer*, May 4, 1990, p. 8A.

45. Joe Martin, interview with author, Charlotte, North Carolina, September 15, 1994; Frye Gaillard, "Relic's Care, Vision Couldn't Bridge Gaps," *Charlotte Observer*, July 29, 1990, pp. 1A, 12A.

46. John Minter, "Relic's Job on the Line at Annual Evaluation," *Charlotte Observer*, June 18, 1990, pp. 1A, 4A; Frye Gaillard, "Relic's Care, Vision Couldn't Bridge Gaps," *Charlotte Observer*, July 29, 1980, pp. 1A, 12A.

47. Joe Martin, interview with author, Charlotte, North Carolina, September 15, 1994.

48. Ibid.

CHAPTER 5

1. Charlotte-Mecklenburg School Board, *Minutes of Meeting of September 10, 1991.*

2. Kevin O'Brien, "School Experts Launch Search for Radical Change," *Charlotte Observer*, December 19, 1991, p. 1A.

3. Neil Mara, "Murphy Likes Job, but Not Ridicule," *Charlotte Observer*, December 10, 1995, p. 12A. Under the terms of Murphy's contract, CMS was obliged to pay all of his dental bills not covered by the school system's insurance plan, which allowed only $750 a year in benefits. Coming as it did after Murphy's frequent and controversial requests for pay increases (discussed later), his request for reimbursement of the $14, 000 attracted considerable attention, with several board members indicating that it had been a mistake to include such a provision in his contract (Neil Mara, "Murphy's Dental Bill Paid, but Contract Provision Questioned," *Charlotte Observer*, November 16, 1995, p. 1C).

4. Stephen Samuel Smith and Roslyn Arlin Mickelson, "All That Glitters Is Not Gold: School Reform in Charlotte-Mecklenburg, *Educational Evaluation and Policy Analysis* 22, no. 2 (2000): 101–28.

5. Gary Putka, "Forceful Educator Gets Teachers and Children To Be More Productive," *Wall Street Journal*, June 5, 1991, pp. 1A, 7A.

6. *Milliken II* programs get their name from the Supreme Court's decisions in *Milliken v. Bradley*. In 1974, the court in *Milliken I* rejected a metropolitan-area desegregation plan that would have involved busing between predominantly black Detroit and its predominantly white suburban school districts. Having blocked such a plan, the court in 1977 in *Milliken II* upheld a lower court's order establishing various programs (e.g., remedial reading, counseling, and career guidance) as compensation for segregation in Detroit's schools. See Gary Orfield, Susan E. Eaton, and the Harvard Project on School Desegregation, *Dismantling Desegregation: The Quiet Reversal of Brown v. Board of Education* (New York: The New Press, 1996).

7. The *Journal's* glowing account of improved test scores in Prince George's County notwithstanding, some scholars have questioned the extent to which outcomes actually improved during Murphy's tenure there (see Susan E. Eaton and Elizabeth Crutcher, "Magnets, Media, and Mirages: Prince George's County 'Miracle' Cure," in *Dismantling Desegregation*, pp. 265–89). Although Murphy denounced an earlier report about Prince George's County from the Harvard Project on School Desegregation as being ideologically motivated, his brief public responses did not address its specific claims (John Murphy, "The Numbers That Count," *Charlotte Observer*, May 3, 1994, p. 8A; "Busing Students Isn't the Answer, *Urban Advocate*, September 1994, p. 4).

8. See, e.g., Rolfe Neill, "Venture Capital for Schools," *Charlotte Observer*, February 20, 1994, p. 3D.

9. Ibid.

10. Kevin O'Brien, "Eye on Access: Districting for School Board on Ballot," *Charlotte Observer*, October 5, 1993, pp. 1A, 4A. Although few statistics are kept on the frequency with which the CEOs of major corporations—at the time, First Union was among the country's ten largest banks—cool their heels during the salary deliberations of local school boards, Crutchfield's attempted lobbying was presumably an unusual, if not a unique, event in U.S. educational history.

11. Liz Chandler, "School Bonds Loss Ignites Debate," *Charlotte Observer*, June 1, 1995, p. A6.

12. Neill, "Venture Capital for Schools."

13. Neil Mara, "Murphy's Possible Departure Rouses a Split Community," *Charlotte Observer*, April 21, 1994, p. 1A.

14. Roslyn Mickelson, Carol Ray, and Stephen Smith, "The Growth Machine and the Politics of Urban Educational Reform: The Case of Charlotte, North Carolina," in *Education in Urban Areas: Cross-National Dimensions*, ed. Nelly Stromquist (Westport, Conn.: Praeger, 1994), 169–98.

15. Louis Gerstner Jr., with Roger D. Semerand, Denis P. Doyle, and William B. Johnston, *Reinventing Education: Education in America's Public Schools* (New York: Dutton, 1994).

16. Denis P. Doyle and Susan Pimental, "A Study in Change: Transforming the Charlotte-Mecklenburg Schools, *Phi Delta Kappan* 74 (1993): 534–39.

17. Denis P. Doyle and Susan Pimental, *Raising the Standard* (Thousand Oaks, Calif.: Corwin, 1997).

18. John Murphy, "After Forty Years: The Other Half of the Puzzle," *Teachers College Record* 96 (1995): 743–50.

19. Alison Morantz, *Desegregation at Risk: Will Magnets Maintain Integration in Charlotte-Mecklenburg's Schools?* (Cambridge: Harvard Project on School Desegregation, 1995), 8.

20. The school board's vote took place on the same day, March 31, 1992, that the Supreme Court handed down the *Freeman* v. *Pitts* decision, making it easier for school districts to abandon the pursuit of desegregation. The coincidence was not lost upon those Charlotteans who worried that the school board's vote would facilitate CMS' resegregation.

21. John Murphy, comments at meeting of the Charlotte-Mecklenburg Board of Education, March 6, 1992.

22. Kevin O'Brien, "Charlotte's Black Community Divided over Magnet Schools," *Charlotte Observer*, March 1, 1992, pp. 1A, 7A.

23. Ibid.

24. James E. Ferguson II, *Statement to the Charlotte-Mecklenburg Board of Education*, February 25, 1992, *Swann* Plaintiffs Exhibit No. 128 in *Capacchione* v. *Charlotte-Mecklenburg Schools*, 57 F. Supp. 2d 228 (W.D.N.C. 1999).

25. Charlotte-Mecklenburg Board of Education, *Minutes of Meeting of March 31, 1992*; Kevin O'Brien and Rhonda Y. Williams, "School Plan Opponents Seek to Postpone Vote," *Charlotte Observer*, March 31, 1992, pp. 1A, 6A.

26. Mickelson, Ray, and Smith, "The Growth Machine and the Politics of Urban Educational Reform"; Roslyn Arlin Mickelson and Carol Axtell Ray, "Fear of Falling from Grace: The Middle Class, Downward Mobility, and School Desegregation," *Research in Sociology of Education and Socialization* 10 (1994): 207–38.

27. Charlotte-Mecklenburg Schools, *Charlotte-Mecklenburg Student Assignment Plan: A New Generation of Excellence, Swann* Plaintiffs' Exhibit No. 22, *Capacchione* v. *Charlotte-Mecklenburg Schools*.

28. Charlotte-Mecklenburg Board of Education, *Minutes of Meeting of March 31, 1992*, p. 6.

29. Ibid.

30. Ibid.

31. Kevin O'Brien, "School Board Debate Unearths No Discord Among Candidates," *Charlotte Observer*, April 23, 1992, p. 1C.

32. Editorial, "For the School Board," *Charlotte Observer*, April 27, 1992, p. 8A.

33. Charlotte-Mecklenburg Schools, *Charlotte-Mecklenburg Student Assignment Plan: A New Generation of Excellence*, pp. 14, 15.

34. Ibid., 38.

35. Charlotte-Mecklenburg Schools, *Magnet Schools . . . Coming Soon to Charlotte-Mecklenburg Schools* (Charlotte, N.C.: Author, 1992); Charlotte-Mecklenburg Schools, *1996–97 Magnet Programs* (Charlotte, N.C.: Author, 1996).

36. Charlotte-Mecklenburg Schools, *1994–95 Benchmark Goals Program: End of Year Summary* (Charlotte, N.C.: Author, 1995).

37. Kevin O'Brien, "Students' SAT Scores Rise," *Charlotte Observer*, August 26, 1992, p. 1A.

38. Editorial, "No Private Pay," *Charlotte Observer*, August 25, 1992, p. 6A.

39. Neil Mara, "Performance Goals Met at More Schools," *Charlotte Observer*, July 13, 1994, p. 1C.

40. John Murphy, "Introduction," *1994–95 Charlotte-Mecklenburg Schools Annual Report Card: Building a Legacy of Excellence*, special advertising section in the *Charlotte Observer*, October 26, 1995, p. 2.

41. Ed Williams, "Chasing Our Tails?," *Charlotte Observer*, April 2, 1994, p. 18A.

42. John Deem, "Superintendent of Sales," *Leader*, August 1, 1997, p. 14.

43. Kevin O'Brien, "School Chief's Pay Stirs Debate," *Charlotte Observer*, August 26, 1993, pp. 1A, 4A.

44. Editorial, "Just Stay Home," Charlotte Observer, August 23, 1993, p. 6A.

45. Rolfe Neill, "Dr. Murphy, Keep Your Word," *Charlotte Observer*, April 24, 1994, p. 3C.

46. Committee of 25, *Pupil Assignment Subcommittee Report* (Charlotte, N.C.: Charlotte-Mecklenburg Schools, 1994).

47. Ibid, 1–2.

48. Committee of 25, *Resource Subcommittee Report to the Board of Education* (Charlotte, N.C.: Charlotte-Mecklenburg Schools, 1994), 7.

49. Charlotte-Mecklenburg Schools Staff, *A Review of the Committee of 25's Report on Resources* and *A Review of the Committee of 25's Report on Student Assignment* (Charlotte, N.C.: Charlotte-Mecklenburg Schools, 1994).

50. The staff was correct, as Figure 3.1 indicates, that the years prior to the implementation of the magnet plan saw a much sharper increase in resegregation than did those afterward. Moreover, written after the first two years of the magnet plan's operation, the staff's rebuttal could plausibly point to certain favorable trends, but as Figure 3.1 shows, resegregation increased in the subsequent years of the magnet plan's operation. District-wide measures of racial imbalance and racial exposure computed by David Armor also indicate that resegregation increased following the implementation

of the magnet plan. From the school years 1991–92 to 1995–96, racial dissimilarity increased from approximately 24 to 27 for elementary schools, 22 to 23 for middle schools, and 20 to 26 for high schools. Similarly, racial exposure decreased from approximately 55 to 52 for elementary schools, 55 to 52 for middle schools, and 59 to 56 for high schools (David Armor, *Evaluation of Unitary Status in Charlotte-Mecklenburg*, Expert Report in *Capacchione* v. *Charlotte-Mecklenburg Schools*, Figures 4, 5, and 6).

Although these figures clearly indicate that there was a modest increase in resegregation following the implementation of the magnet plan, they do not explain why this resegregation occurred. That issue—as well as a similar one about the increase in resegregation since the early 1980s—figured prominently in the 1999 reactivated *Swann* litigation and is best postponed until the next chapter's discussion of that trial.

51. For a discussion of these debates with respect to desegregation, see Jennifer Hochschild, *The New American Dilemma: Liberal Democracy and School Desegregation* (New Haven: Yale University Press, 1984).

52. Figures computed by author from data from homogenous precincts and ecological regression analyses. See Stephen Samuel Smith, "Black Political Marginalization? Regime Change and School Reform in Charlotte, NC" (paper presented at the annual meeting of the American Political Science Association, Chicago, September 1995).

53. Comparisons with non-school county bonds are difficult and ambiguous because of, among other things, the small N's involved, but school bonds appear to have done worse than these other packages during the Murphy years. While 60 percent (three out of five) of the school bonds passed during this period, the corresponding figure for non-school bonds was 70 percent (seven out of ten).

54. Jeffrey Ball, "Law Puts Officials at Odds," *Charlotte Observer*, April 24, 1995, p. 4C.

55. Herbert L. White, "Committee to Recommend Bonds' Approval to Caucus," *Charlotte Post*, May 18, 1995, pp. 1A, 3A.

56. Neil Mara, "Bonds' Backers Say Needs Make Case," *Charlotte Observer*, April 16, 1995, p. 8B.

57. This figure is based on ecological regression estimates and actual returns from homogeneous precincts, the two techniques necessary to use in the absence of survey data. In the analysis of voting for Mecklenburg County bonds, these two techniques have generally yielded results that differ by no more than 5 percent. But on this referendum, the difference between the two results of the two techniques was 10 percent, and I have taken their arithmetic mean to arrive at the figure of 55 percent. For additional discussion of this issue, see Smith, "Black Political Marginalization?"

58. Calculations are my own, based on the data in "Black Political Marginalization?"

59. Liz Chandler, "County Pegs Tax Hike at 6 Percent, Gives School Board a Lecture," *Charlotte Observer*, June 15, 1993, p. 1A.

60. For additional discussion of these events, see Stephen Samuel Smith, "Hugh Governs? Regime and Policy Change in Charlotte, North Carolina" (paper presented at the annual meeting of the Southern Political Science Association, Atlanta, November 1994).

61. Kevin O'Brien, "Eye on Access: Districting for School Board on Ballot," *Charlotte Observer*, October 5, 1993, p. 1A.

62. Ibid.

63. Ibid.

64. Rolfe Neill, "Vote 'Yes' on Murphy," *Charlotte Observer*, November 5, 1995, p. 3C.

65. Charlotte-Mecklenburg Educational Foundation, *1995 Focus on School Board* (Charlotte, N.C.: Author, 1995), 2.

66. Ibid.

67. Charlotte Mecklenburg Alliance for Public Schools, pamphlet, 1995.

68. Tucker Mitchell, "Burgess Says New Group's Endorsements 'Smell' " *Leader*, September 22, 1995, pp. 1, 9.

69. Campaign finance data obtained from reports on file at the Charlotte-Mecklenburg Board of Elections. For a discussion of the methodological issues involved in using these reports, see Stephen Samuel Smith, "Education, Race, and Regime Change in Charlotte-Mecklenburg" (paper presented at the annual meeting of the Urban Affairs Association, New York City, March 1996).

70. In the at-large races, those $3,000 donations generally comprised between 10 and 15 percent of the total the Alliance-supported candidates raised during the campaign. In the district races, those $3,000 donations typically constituted at least 20 percent of all funds that a candidate raised.

71. Smith, "Black Political Marginalization?"

72. As noted earlier, the absence of polling data precludes a definitive explanation of black Charlotteans' voting on bond referenda. However, the events surrounding the 1993 and 1995 referenda strongly suggest that concerns about resegregation and resource allocation are an important part of the explanation of the drop in black support for these bonds.

73. Clarence N. Stone, *Regime Politics: Governing Atlanta, 1946–1988* (Lawrence, KS: University Press of Kansas, 1989), 197.

74. Susan Burgess, interview with author, Charlotte, North Carolina, September 15, 1994, emphasis added.

75. Ibid.

76. In addition to drawing on Smith and Mickelson, "All that Glitters," this section includes material that first appeared in two unpublished papers: Stephen Samuel Smith and Roslyn Arlin Mickelson, "Symbol and Substance in School Reform: The Case of Charlotte, North Carolina" (paper presented at the annual meeting of the

Southern Political Science Association, Norfolk, Va., November 1997); Stephen Samuel Smith and Roslyn Arlin Mickelson, "School Reform as Educational Alchemy: The Case of Charlotte-Mecklenburg, 1991–1995" (paper presented at the annual meeting of the American Educational Research Association, Seattle, Wash., April 2001).

77. Another equally important question is the extent to which many significant aspects of education can be appropriately measured by standardized tests. As a parent, citizen, teacher, and scholar, I have especially serious reservations about the extent to which quantitative accountability systems such as CMS' benchmark goals are science or scientism. But I put such issues aside here, and I do so for two related reasons. First, the question has been discussed many times and in many places, and there is no point in putting my plow to these well-worn fields. Second, I believe that the first step in appraising most policy innovations is to do so on their own terms, and the Murphy administration claimed success on both its system of benchmark goals as well as on other standardized tests such as the SAT.

78. Celeste Smith, "N.C. Schools Get Their Rankings," *Charlotte Observer*, August 8, 1997, pp. 1A, 13A; Foon Rhee, "Challenge of Aiding Urban Kids on Display," *Charlotte Observer*, August 8, 1997, p. 12A.

79. Charlotte-Mecklenburg Schools, *District Profile 1995–1996* (Charlotte, N.C.: Author, 1996); Curtis Sittenfeld, "2 Principals To Be Suspended, State Teams on Way to Schools," *Charlotte Observer*, August 8, 1997, p. 13A.

80. Smith and Mickelson, "All That Glitters."

81. Among the evidence for these statewide gains is the National Assessment of Educational Progress. Between 1992 and 1994, North Carolina's fourth-grade scores increased more than any other state's except Maine's (Drew Lindsay, "North Carolina: Random Acts of Reform, *Education Week*, January 22, 1997, pp. 177–80). For additional evidence of statewide gains in the early 1990s, see Suzanne Triplett, "Gains in N.C. Schools," *Charlotte Observer*, August 17, 1997, p. 2C.

82. Tim Simmons, "Gap Widens between National, State SAT Scores," *Raleigh News and Observer*, August 25, 1995, pp. 1A, 10A.

83. O'Brien, "Students' SAT Scores Rise."

84. A fuller analysis of SAT scores would have to examine racially disaggregated longitudinal participation rates, data that are difficult to obtain. However, in 1994–95, Murphy's last full year in office—a year for which data are available—the percentage of black students taking the SAT was lower in CMS (40 percent) than it was in Wake (47 percent) and Forsyth (45 percent), and the same as it was in the entire state (North Carolina Department of Public Instruction, *North Carolina 1995 Scholastic Assessment Test Report* [Raleigh, N.C.: Author, 1995]). The low (compared to the other urban districts) rate of participation of black students in CMS also calls into question any claims, such as those in Murphy's article in *Teachers College Record*, that black SAT scores are evidence for the success of CMS' reform program.

85. Smith and Mickelson, "All That Glitters," 120.

86. Patricia Holleman, interview with author, Charlotte, North Carolina, October 16, 1996.

87. The name and character of these alternative schools changed during the Murphy administration, making it hard to provide precise data on the increase in enrollment in alternative schools. But if schools for students who were pregnant and whose handicaps were other than behavioral and emotional are excluded, then the membership in the alternative schools increased approximately 141 percent from October of Murphy's first year to October of his last, while CMS' membership during this time increased only 15 percent (figures based on my calculations of data contained in October membership reports).

88. In other words, students at risk for dropping out were unlikely to enroll in higher-level courses. Their staying in school would increase the base upon which percentage enrollment in higher-level courses was calculated, thus decreasing that percentage.

89. Michael Arim, interview with author, Charlotte, North Carolina, November 4, 1996.

90. Roslyn Arlin Mickelson, "International Business Machinations: A Case Study of Corporate Involvement in Local Educational Reform," *Teachers College Record* 100, no. 3 (1999): 476–512.

91. Ibid., 484.

92. Rolfe Neill, interview with author, Charlotte, North Carolina, October 24, 1997.

93. More precisely, the figure tracks the value of the Pearson product moment coefficient of correlation, r, between the percentage of a school's students and teachers who were black. To help put that correlation in perspective, the figure also indicates the percentage of CMS' students and teachers who were black. If the system-wide totals are broken down into data for elementary, middle, and high schools, the same general trend in r is observed. Student data are from membership reports and teacher data are from EEO5 Report summaries that CMS provided to parties in the reactivated *Swann* litigation. While student data are available for all years, teacher data are available only for the years indicated in the chart.

94. Gwendolyn C. Bradford, testimony in *Capacchione v. Charlotte-Mecklenburg Schools*, May 28, 1999, pp. 26, 29. In trying to minimize the impact of Bradford's testimony about how the move toward site-based management explained the jump in faculty racial imbalance, attorneys for the white plaintiffs called attention, during cross-examination, to the constraints imposed upon CMS by the growing teacher shortage. While that shortage may have allowed teachers to be pickier about their assignments, the Murphy administration made no significant effort to counteract the manner in which site-based management was facilitating faculty racial imbalance.

95. Frederick M. Hess, *Spinning Wheels: The Politics of Urban School Reform* (Washington, D.C.: Brookings, 1999), 9.

96. Charlotte-Mecklenburg Schools, *Building a Legacy of Excellence, Charlotte Observer*, October 26, 1995, special advertising section.

97. Jeff Schiller and Susan Henry, "Memorandum," January 12, 1995, Defendant's Exhibit No. 238, *Capacchione v. Charlotte-Mecklenburg Schools*. Of these shortcomings,

the last two are especially important because they call attention to rates of change in outcomes, not their levels.

CHAPTER 6

1. Celeste Smith, "Dueling Crusades," *Charlotte Observer*, October 26, 1997, p. 4D.

2. A. Lee Parks, transcript of closing argument in *Capacchione* v. *Charlotte-Mecklenburg Schools*, June 22, 1999, p. 21.

3. *Capacchione* v. *Charlotte-Mecklenburg Schools*, 57 F. Supp. 2d 228, 294 (W.D.N.C. 1999).

4. John Deem, "School Board Pays a High Price for a Piece of Free Land," *Leader*, May 31, 1996, p. 11.

5. Charlotte-Mecklenburg School Board, *Minutes of Meeting of May 28, 1996*, p. 4.

6. Celeste Smith, "Free Land at a Price," *Charlotte Observer*, December 22, 1997, pp. 1A, 10A; Steve Moshier, "Highland Creek Has Reasons To Be Upset," *Charlotte Observer*, May 10, 1998, p. 17M.

7. John Deem, "Superintendent of Sales," *Leader*, August 1, 1997, p. 14.

8. Debbie Cenziper, "Backers Say Building Needs Are Clear," *Charlotte Observer*, November 2, 1997, p. 14A.

9. Deem, "Superintendent of Sales."

10. Editorial, "Organizing for Success," *Charlotte Observer*, August 12, 1996, p. 10A.

11. Debbie Cenziper, "Rising Sophomore," *Charlotte Observer*, August 3, 1997, p. 4C.

12. Editorial, "Organizing for Success."

13. Eric Smith, "Achieving Equity: Why Diversity, High Expectations Matter," *Charlotte Observer*, March 9, 1999, p. 13A.

14. However, shortly after Murphy left Charlotte, controversy erupted over his agreement with IBM, which was collaborating with CMS on the Education Village, that one-third of the seats in the complex would be reserved for students whose parents worked in the nearby University Research Park in which IBM had a major facility (Roslyn Arlin Mickelson, "International Business Machinations: A Case Study of Corporate Involvement in Local Educational Reform," *Teachers College Record* 100, no. 3 [1996]).

15. Dianne Whitacre, "Planning Board Studies Proposed High School in Matthews," *Charlotte Observer*, March 5, 1995, p. 11M.

16. See the comments of Assistant Superintendent Jeffry Schiller at the April 26, 1994, meeting of the school board (Charlotte-Mecklenburg Schools, *Minutes of Meeting of the Board of Education*, April 26, 1994, p. 5).

17. For a discussion of the cost of the Crestdale land, see Taylor Batten, "Matthews School Site Purchase Price Scrutinized," *Charlotte Observer*, May 17, 1997, p. 4C. For the 35 percent figure, see the comments of board member George Dunlap at the school board meeting of February 3, 1998 (Charlotte-Mecklenburg Schools, *Minutes of School Board Meeting of February 3, 1998*, p. 15).

18. Charlotte-Mecklenburg Schools, *Minutes of Meeting of February 10, 1998*, p. 12.

19. Charlotte-Mecklenburg Schools, *Minutes of Meeting of February 3, 1998*, p. 15.

20. I was a member of the C33. For a perceptive account of the views of several members of the C33, see Frye Gaillard, *The Dream Long Deferred*, 2d ed., (Charlotte, N.C.: Briarpatch Press, 1999), 215–20.

21. Future School Planning Task Force, *A Vision to Overcome Barriers to Educational Excellence Related to Future School Planning and Student Assignment* (Charlotte, N.C.: Charlotte-Mecklenburg Schools, 1997).

22. For a discussion of the reasons for being skeptical about any putative generic benefits of citizen participation in advisory councils and planning efforts, see Jennifer Hochschild, *The New American Dilemma: Liberal Democracy and School Desegregation* (New Haven: Yale University Press, 1984), chap. 5.

23. Celeste Smith, "Opponents Ticked at School Board," *Charlotte Observer*, November 2, 1997, pp. 1A, 14A.

24. Thomas R. Dye, *Understanding Public Policy*, 7th ed. (Englewood Cliffs: Prentice Hall, 1992), 335.

25. "District 5 Forum," *Charlotte Observer*, October 27, 1997, p. 10A.

26. Celeste Smith, "Voters Have Clear Goals for Schools," *Charlotte Observer*, October 5, 1997, pp. 1A, 12A.

27. Charlotte-Mecklenburg Educational Foundation, *1999 Community Assessment* (Charlotte, N.C.: Author, 1999), 9. In 1999, "improving equity of facilities" and "renovating/updating schools" received strong support from 77 percent of respondents, slightly less than the 79 percent who supported "increasing teacher salaries." In 1998, support for these two items ranked slightly ahead of increasing salaries. In both years, the two items ranked considerably ahead of "more computers/high-tech resources and providing a diverse environment (both at approximately 70 percent) and "building new schools" (approximately 60 percent). Much lower on the list in both years were tax increases, neighborhood schools, vouchers, and busing for racial balance.

28. Smith, "Dueling Crusades."

29. Ibid.

30. Campaign for a Color-Blind America <http://www.equalright.com/mission.html>, accessed December 21, 1999.

31. *Martin* v. *Charlotte-Mecklenburg Bd. of Ed.* 475 F. Supp. 1318, 1321 (1979).

32. *Capacchione* v. *Charlotte-Mecklenburg Schools* 57 F. Supp. 2d 228, 242 (W.D.N.C. 1999).

33. *Green* v. *County School Board of New Kent County*, 391 U.S. 430 (1968).

34. In addition to its general counsel and McMillan's firm, CMS also was represented by Hogan & Hartson, a law firm with extensive desegregation experience based in Washington, D.C.

35. For discussions of these cases from two different perspectives, see Gary Orfield, Susan E. Eaton, and the Harvard Project on School Desegregation, *Dismantling Desegregation: The Quiet Reversal of Brown v. Board of Education* (New York: The New Press, 1996) and David Armor, *Forced Justice: School Desegregation and the Law* (New York: Oxford University Press, 1995).

36. Jim Maxwell, "Potter in Line for Judgeship," *Charlotte News*, April 9, 1981, p. 1C.

37. Jim Morrill, "Trial Brings School Case Full Circle," *Charlotte Observer*, April 18, 1999, p. 16A. For additional observations on Potter and the trial see Gaillard, *The Dream Long Deferred*, 2d ed., chapter 14.

38. Celeste Smith and Debbie Cenziper, "John Murphy Strikes Back," *Charlotte Observer*, April 27, 1999, p. 11A. In his testimony during the trial, Michael Stolee, the consultant who had drafted the 1992 magnet plan, recounted a recent telephone conversation with Murphy in which the former superintendent had said "that goddamn Eric Smith has been running around town telling people that I misadministered the school district, and I am going to come in and testify and fix that son of a bitch" (Michael Stolee, transcript of testimony in *Capacchione* v. *Charlotte-Mecklenburg Schools*, May 25, 1999, p. 94). In his testimony, Murphy denied making such statements.

Whether Murphy made that statement or not, there was more than a little historical irony in the former superintendent's eagerness to testify for the white plaintiffs. As noted earlier, it was the magnet plan, a centerpiece of his reform program, which triggered the reactivation of *Swann*. Moreover, one of the key claims of the white plaintiffs was not only that the magnet plan unconstitutionally took race into account, but that Murphy had failed to seek unitary status, even though he thought CMS had achieved such status (*Plaintiff-Intervenors' Index of Relevant Testimony and Documentary Evidence* [July 20, 1999], pp. 46–47). In his opinion, Potter noted that Stolee's plan had emphasized the importance of CMS' seeking approval from the court to change its desegregation strategies, but that CMS had failed to do so. It was, of course, on Murphy's watch that this failure had occurred. Murphy was thus in the unseemly position of testifying on behalf of plaintiffs whose case was buttressed not only by what he said on the stand but also by his failure to fulfill what the court considered his legal obligations as superintendent.

39. I was the black plaintiffs' third expert witness; it was my first time serving in such a capacity. My testimony focused on school siting decisions, faculty racial balance, and disparities in teacher qualifications.

40. David Armor, *Evaluation of Unitary Status in Charlotte-Mecklenburg*, Expert Report in *Capacchione* v. *Charlotte-Mecklenburg Schools*, pp. 16–17.

41. David Armor, transcript of testimony in *Capacchione* v. *Charlotte-Mecklenburg Schools*, April 29, 1999, pp. 159–60.

42. The six *Green* factors involved student assignment, faculty hiring and assignment, staff hiring and assignment, facilities, transportation, and extracurricular activities.

43. Armor relied on a self-selected sample of CMS students whose parents had returned questionnaires in his key analysis of student-level data on achievement. After data were entered for each of the variables that he analyzed, his N had shrunk to less than 20 percent of CMS' eighth graders (David Armor, transcript of testimony, April 29, 1999, pp. 235, 237). That group cannot be considered statistically representative of the entire population, especially given the self-selection of his respondents. Moreover, Armor's definition of several key variables also was highly problematic. Among other measures of socioeconomic status (SES), he used a student's second-grade test score as a proxy for family background and for ability prior to the influence of schooling because it was the earliest indicator that he could obtain. But second-grade test scores reflect achievement after three years of schooling and thus are not a proxy for family background and/or student ability, independent of schooling. In contrast, Trent and Mickelson used conventional measures of family background, such as parents' education and occupation.

Finally, the linear regression technique employed by Armor is of dubious validity in dealing with the relationships among SES, race, and academic achievement. It is one that, he testified, has never appeared in any of his peer-reviewed academic publications dealing with these issues (transcript of testimony, April 29, 1999, pp. 240–41). Employing a so-called gap analysis, the technique involves a series of stepwise multiple regressions that begins by regressing achievement on race and then introducing various SES variables in subsequent steps. The result of the introduction of these SES variables is to reduce the relationship between race and achievement, thus purportedly providing evidence that the black/white achievement gap can be explained by differences in SES. However, because race is correlated with these various SES variables, the reduction of the relationship between race and achievement is mathematically inevitable in much the same way that the introduction of race would reduce the effect of SES if the stepwise regression had begun with the latter. Had the stepwise regression technique thus begun with SES, one could then interpret its results as showing that the SES gap could be explained by race. A more valid linear regression technique in dealing with the relations among achievement, race, and SES involves the simultaneous entry of all variables in the first step, as Mickelson did in her analyses. For an additional discussion of the flaws in Armor's regression techniques, see Jan de Leeuw: "Regression Analysis in the Wilmington Case," UCLA Statistical Series #175 (Department of Statistics, University of California at Los Angeles, 1995) and "Dr. Armor's Regressions," UCLA Statistical Series #249 (Department of Statistics, University of California at Los Angeles, 1999), accessed on line at <http://preprints.stat.ucla.edu/175> and <http://preprints.stat.ucla.edu/249> on July 3, 2002.

While the flaws in Armor's discussion of achievement were especially marked, the analyses of CMS' expert witnesses also had crucial problems. For example, Trent's regression analysis had methodological weaknesses, and a key variable in Mickelson's analysis was coded incorrectly in a small number of cases. Revealed during cross-examination, the mistake turned out to have relatively little effect upon her findings, but the court would not admit a corrected analysis into evidence, and the coding error drastically undermined the weight of her testimony. The findings reported in her testimony subsequently appeared in Roslyn Arlin Mickelson, "Subverting *Swann:* First- and Second-Generation Segregation in the Charlotte-Mecklenburg Schools," *American Educational Research Journal* 38 (2001): 215–52.

44. *Capacchione* v. *Charlotte-Mecklenburg Schools*, 57 F. Supp. 2d 228, 244 (W.D.N.C. 1999).

45. Given their claim that CMS was not yet unitary, it was to the obvious advantage of CMS and the black plaintiffs to call attention to this decrease in racial balance, but even Armor's report to the court showed significant changes with, for example, racial imbalance in elementary schools approximately doubling between the late 1970s and late 1990s (Armor, *Evaluation of Unitary Status*, Figure 4).

46. Armor's report, for example, showed a decrease in racial exposure and an increase in racial imbalance at the elementary, middle, and high school levels (Armor, *Evaluation of Unitary Status*, Figures 4, 5, and 6).

47. Armor, *Evaluation of Unitary Status*, p. 10.

48. Ibid., p. 8.

49. Fred M. Shelley, *Can Racial Imbalance in the Mecklenburg County Schools Be Attributed to Natural Demographic Change?* Expert report in *Capacchione* v. *Charlotte-Mecklenburg Schools*, p. 14.

50. Ibid., p. 15.

51. See chapter 4 for the developer's remarks about McAlpine School and for data on building permits near McKee Road School.

52. *Plaintiff-Intervenors' Index of Relevant Testimony and Documentary Evidence* in *Capacchione* v. *Charlotte-Mecklenburg Schools*, p. 127.

53. *Martin* v. *Charlotte-Mecklenburg Bd. of Ed.*, 475 F. Supp. 1318, 1329, 1338, 1340 (1979).

54. For example, of the sixty-nine satellite areas in 1998–99, sixty-two were in predominantly black neighborhoods, and blacks constituted approximately 78 percent of all students who were satellited (Gordon Foster, *Expert Report* in *Capacchione* v. *Charlotte-Mecklenburg Schools*, Table 7).

55. This controlled choice plan is considered in the next chapter as part of the discussion of the pre- and post-trial political battles over pupil assignment. The black plaintiffs had reservations about the plan; their trial brief deferred detailed comment on the plan and expressed concern "that the Board's plan to move to a 'controlled choice' scheme is unwarrantedly optimistic about the time it will take to rebuild and renovate the sixteen predominantly black schools identified in the plan" *(Swann Plaintiffs Trial Brief, Capacchione* v. *Charlotte-Mecklenburg Schools).*

56. *Capacchione* v. *Charlotte-Mecklenburg Schools*, 57 F. Supp. 2d 228, 280 (W.D.N.C. 1999).

57. Ibid., 260, 261.

58. Ibid., 272.

59. Ibid., 267.

60. Ibid., 244, 246.

61. Ibid., 247, 248.

62. Ibid., 250.

63. Ibid., 293.

64. Ibid., 294.

65. Ibid.

66. Jennifer Wing Rothacker, "Justice Prevails in Eyes of Plaintiffs," *Charlotte Observer*, September 11, 1999, p. 19A.

67. Karen Long, "I'm CMS teacher, and I Do 'Teach Black Children,'" *Charlotte Observer*, June 18, 1999, p. 12A.

CHAPTER 7

1. Wilhelmenia Rembert, comments at meeting of the Charlotte-Mecklenburg School Board, October 6, 1999.

2. Ed Williams, "How Will We Educate Disadvantaged Children?," *Charlotte Observer*, December 12, 1999, p. 3C.

3. Jennifer Wing Rothacker, "Businesses Feel Stress of Limbo in Schools," *Charlotte Observer*, December 24, 2000, p. 1B.

4. In the years immediately before and after *Brown*, many Southern states pumped resources into black schools in a last-minute effort to try to fend off desegregation by making the separate school systems equal ones, at least in terms of funding (Davison M. Douglas, *Reading, Writing, and Race: The Desegregation of the Charlotte Schools* [Chapel Hill: University of North Carolina Press, 1995], 21–22; Richard Kluger, *Simple Justice* [New York: Vintage, 1977], 334–35). In a different context, the Supreme Court's 1977 decision in *Milliken II* gave the high court's approval to the concept of additional and compensatory educational programs for students in segregated schools.

5. Gary Orfield and Carole Ashkinaze, *The Closing Door* (Chicago: University of Chicago Press, 1991). Given the Supreme Court's decision in *Milliken*, such deals have frequently been the best that African Americans could hope for, but the Atlanta Compromise was made before that court decision.

6. Editorial, "Our Schools' Future," *Charlotte Observer*, September 11, 1999, p. 20A.

7. Charlotte-Mecklenburg Schools, "Judge Declares CMS Unitary, Dissolves Court Order," press release, September 10, 1999.

8. Jennifer Wing Rothacker and Celeste Smith. "Leaders Unite Behind Schools," *Charlotte Observer*, August 24, 1999, p. 8A.

9. Arthur Griffin, "Things That Must Be Done," *Charlotte Observer*, August 24, 1999, p. 11A.

10. Rothacker and Smith, "Leaders Unite Behind Schools," p. 1A.

11. Rothacker, "Businesses Feel Stress of Limbo in Schools." Allegations of a deal were not made public until after CMS voted to appeal. During the height of the school board election campaign, the *Leader* ran several lengthy stories about this alleged deal and the sentiment among some Charlotte business and political leaders that Griffin had reneged on it. He insisted that such a deal had never taken place, and there was considerable variation in others' accounts of the meetings during which it was allegedly made. Much of the variation occurred, not surprisingly, along party lines with Republican Mayor McCrory claiming that there had been a deal, and Democratic County Commission Chair Helms denying that there had been one. Moreover, media coverage also reflected political positions. Critical of CMS policy, its legal stance during the trial, and Griffin's campaign, the *Leader* devoted considerable space in two issues to the alleged deal. More sympathetic to CMS and Griffin's candidacy, the *Observer* viewed the alleged deal as a nonevent and did not mention it either in its editorial or news pages during the 1999 campaign (the article quoting Campbell cited in the text appeared in December 2000 as part of a story about the business elite's frustration with that month's developments). For the *Leader's* account of the alleged deal, see Tucker Mitchell, "What's the Deal with Arthur Griffin," *Leader*, October 29, 1999, pp. 1, 3.

12. Rothacker, "Businesses Feel Stress;" Arthur Griffin, "Reporting on Failure and Divisiveness Is Sensational and Easy," *Leader*, October 29, 1999, p. 16.

13. As chapter 2 indicates, these two organizations were initiated by the business elite in 1997 as part of its battle against the Gang of Five on the county commission. They remained active in local civic and political affairs.

14. The main reason the reports provide little evidence for Campbell's claim is that, compared to John Lassiter, Griffin got relatively few donations from the business elite, either before or after the appeal. As discussed later, Lassiter's campaign received wide and extensive financial support from the business elite. Griffin received much less. Of the ten people who gave more than $100—smaller contributions need not be itemized—to both Griffin and Lassiter, seven were, by most plausible definitions, members of the business elite and/or prominent developers. Of these seven, as best as can be determined from dates on the campaign finance reports, two gave to Griffin after the board voted to appeal and to Lassiter within a week of the donation to Griffin. Another three gave to Griffin at least two weeks before the appeal, and to Lassiter within two weeks, either before or after, of giving to Griffin. There is thus considerable evidence that those who gave to both candidates generally made their donations around the same time. Had the business elite supported Griffin believing he would oppose an appeal, his reports would presumably show large numbers of donations from corporate executives prior to the appeal, just as Lassiter's do. But they do not.

15. Ann Doss Helms and Pam Kelley, "Ruling Met with Joy, Dread," *Charlotte Observer*, September 11, 1999, p. 17A.

16. The black clergy's activity in building support for the appeal after the trial was prefigured by mobilizations prior to the trial, especially around the March 1999 pupil assignment plan, discussed later.

17. Jen Pilla, "1,500 People Attend Rally for Schools," *Charlotte Observer*, October 4, 1999, p. 1C.

18.Wilhelmenia Rembert, remarks at school board meeting, October 8, 1999.

19. The only other school board election since the 1970s in which so much of the campaign involved desegregation-related issues was that of 1988. However, in that election, the issue was more one of support or opposition to the busing plan rather than to desegregation itself. Of the four challengers who won seats in that election, only one, Jan Richards, was an outspoken advocate of neighborhood schools. None of the other leading candidates in 1988 posed anywhere near as sweeping a challenge to desegregation as did Gauvreau, Lassiter, and Haisley in 1999.

20. Counterfactual discussions of how variations in the size of the black electorate might have affected electoral outcomes are complicated because they require assumptions about black voting behavior and both the size and behavior of the white electorate. In this brief note, such complications can be ignored and a few suggestive figures proffered.

In 1970 African Americans constituted 24 percent of Mecklenburg's population and approximately 14 percent of the registered voters. By 1999 the black share of the population had increased to 27 percent, but the black share of the electorate had jumped much more sharply to approximately 24 percent. Had blacks constituted 24 percent of the electorate in 1970, I estimate—based on 1970 newspaper reports of turnout and my own analysis of racially homogeneous precincts—that at least 3,300 more blacks would have voted. If only 75 percent of them had voted for Kerry, he would have received enough votes to have been elected in the first round and avoided the run-off (which he lost). Similarly, had blacks constituted only 14 percent of the electorate in 1999, I estimate that approximately 10,000 fewer African Americans would have voted. Since Rembert beat Gauvreau by 2,125 votes, the outcome of that election would also likely have been different.

21. Jennifer Wing Rothacker, "Citing Cost, School Board Candidate to Drop Out of Race," *Charlotte Observer*, September 24, 1999, p. 6C.

22. John Minter, "Black Voters May Decide '99 Election," *Charlotte Post*, October 19, 1999, pp. 1A, 3A.

23. Bill James, "*Observer* Endorsements Expose Double Standard," *Charlotte Observer*, October 27, 1999, p. 20A.

24. Eric Douglas, " 'Gang of Five' " Influence Would Damage Board," *Charlotte Observer*, October 29, 1999, p. 12A.

25. In a telling indication of how local politics differed from that prior to 1987, the mayor's race provided much less motivation to mobilize black voters, even though an African American, former city council woman Ella Scarborough, was challenging two-term Republican incumbent Pat McCrory, a white. A one-time stalwart of Charlotte's black political leadership, Scarborough had alienated some former friends and allies. Moreover, few observers gave her a chance of winning, and McCrory often was credited with paying more attention to black Charlotteans than had his Republican predecessors. Thus, enthusiasm for Scarborough among Charlotte's black politi-

cal leadership was uneven. Her endorsement, for example, by the Black Political Caucus was the only one on which the vote was not unanimous ("Black Caucus Divides over Scarborough," *Charlotte Observer*, October 19, 1999, p. 3C). Although she ran well in black precincts, she received only 39 percent of the city-wide vote.

26. Editorial, "For School Board," *Charlotte Observer*, October 26, 1999, p. 12A.

27. Lassiter's campaign finance reports indicate that he received donations from many prominent developers and leading executives of a range of companies that included Charlotte's natural gas utility, telephone company, largest supermarket chain, and largest department store. With PACs associated with Bank of America, Coca-Cola, Piedmont Natural Gas, the tourist industry, and a local architectural firm donating to his campaign, Lassiter received considerably more money from corporate PACs than any other candidate.

28. Moreover, as best as can be determined from the sometimes ambiguous data in the campaign finance reports, the overlap among the donors to the three Republicans, taken as a group, was less than among the donors to the three incumbents, taken as a group, though the latter also was small. In particular, nine individuals gave donations of $100 or more to the three incumbents, but only four (different) individuals gave donations of $100 or more to the three Republicans.

29. I donated to both Griffin and Rembert.

30. Lauren Markoe, "GOP Boss Faults Low Turnout Tuesday," *Charlotte Observer*, May 4, 1999, p. 10A.

31. Charlotte-Mecklenburg Schools, *Achieving the CMS Vision: Equity and Student Success* (Charlotte, N.C.: Author, 1999), 29.

32. Ibid., 28, 29.

33. Jim Puckett, "Controlled Choice Is Wrong Choice for Charlotte Schools," *Charlotte Observer*, March 12, 1999, p. 11A.

34. Lucy Bush and B. B. DeLaine, " 'Controlled Choice' Plan Raises Serious Questions," *Charlotte Observer*, March 16, 1999, p. 15A.

35. Roslyn Mickelson, Carol Ray, and Stephen Smith, "The Growth Machine and the Politics of Urban Educational Reform: The Case of Charlotte, North Carolina," in *Education in Urban Areas: Cross-National Dimensions*, ed. Nelly Stromquist (Westport, Conn.: Praeger, 1994), 187.

36. Celeste Smith and Jennifer Wing Rothacker, "Legal Challenge to Order Will Focus on 4 Points," *Charlotte Observer*, October 7, 1999, p. 1A.

37. Jennifer Wing Rothacker and Ted Mellnik, "Study Details the Transformation Plan Would Make in Student Bodies," *Charlotte Observer*, November 14, 1999, pp. 1A, 12A.

38. Ibid.

39. That threat met with two responses. The first was that CMS had repeatedly risked being hauled back to court thirty years ago in fighting a desegregation order, so why not do the same now in fighting a resegregation one? Moreover, it was noted,

given segregated housing patterns, residence could just as easily be viewed as a proxy for race, but that did not stop the proposed plan from giving it (residence) top priority.

40. Ed Williams, "Smith Thinks Parents Must Help Shape Schools," *Charlotte Observer*, November 28, 1999, p. 3C.

41. Ed Williams, "How Will We Educate Disadvantaged Children?," *Charlotte Observer*, December 12, 1999, p. 3C.

42. Editorial, "Don't Rush the Job," *Charlotte Observer*, December 10, 1999, p. 20A.

43. Jennifer Wing Rothacker and Celeste Smith, "Board Compromises, Votes 7–1 to OK Plan," *Charlotte Observer*, December 17, 1999, p. 14A.

44. Charlotte-Mecklenburg Schools, *Minutes of the Meeting of the Charlotte-Mecklenburg Board of Education*, December 16, 1999, p. 13.

45. Arthur Griffin, "The Court's Gift of Time Must Be Used Wisely," *Charlotte Observer*, January 4, 2000, p. 9A.

46. Celeste Smith and Jennifer Wing Rothacker, "Value of Magnet at School Debated," *Charlotte Observer*, May 14, 2000, pp. 1A, 8A. In each of the previous six years, as this article notes, a senior at West Charlotte was a finalist for a prestigious Morehead scholarship, and four of these seniors won it.

47. Jennifer Wing Rothacker, "High School IB Options Upset Some Parents," *Charlotte Observer*, May 6, 2000, p. 5B.

48. Ibid.

49. Jennifer Wing Rothacker, "Board Again Rejects Smith's Proposal," *Charlotte Observer*, May 10, 2000, p. 13A.

50. Araminta Stone Johnston, "Don't Blame Griffin for Plan's Defeat," *Charlotte Observer*, May 17, 2000, p. 15A.

51. Ed Williams, "School Board Should See Itself As Public Sees It," *Charlotte Observer*, May 14, 2000, p. 3C.

52. Fannie Flono, "School Board Must Tackle Eroding Public Trust," *Charlotte Observer*, May 12, 2000, p. 17A.

53. Ibid.

54. Jennifer Wing Rothacker, "McCrory Urges Schools Summit," *Charlotte Observer*, May 13, 2000, p. 1B.

55. Jennifer Wing Rothacker and Jon Goldberg, "School Secession Urged," *Charlotte Observer*, May 12, 2000, pp. 1A, 9A.

56. Jennifer Wing Rothacker and Jen Pilla, "Assignment Limbo Stirs Frustration," *Charlotte Observer*, May 11, 2000, p. 1A.

57. Jennifer Wing Rothacker, "School Board OKs Assignment Plan," *Charlotte Observer*, June 2, 2000, p. 1A.

58. Ibid., p. 12A.

59. *Belk* v. *Charlotte-Mecklenburg Board of Education* 233 F. 3d 232, 256 (4th Cir. 2000) (vacated).

60. Ibid. In addition to indicating the importance that McMillan attached to school siting, the opinion also noted that the Supreme Court had considered this a crucial issue in affirming his ruling.

61. Rothacker, "Businesses Feel Stress," p. 1B.

62. Ibid.

63. Celeste Smith and Michelle Crouch, "Reassignment Back on Agenda," *Charlotte Observer*, June 22, 2001, p. 1C.

64. Celeste Smith, "Parents Resentful, Cynical about Plan," *Charlotte Observer*, July 1, 2001, p. 1B. Nor was fatigue over pupil assignment wars confined to white parents who had often been the harshest critics of the board's majority. A longtime desegregation activist and officer of the League of Women Voters also was quoted as saying, "I, for one, am about tired."

65. Jennifer Wing Rothacker and Celeste Smith, "Board OKs Assignment Plan for '02–03," *Charlotte Observer*, August 1, 2001, p. 1A.

66. Celeste Smith, "Behind the Scenes Look at Board Vote," *Charlotte Observer*, October 21, 2001, p. 10B.

67. *Belk* v. *Charlotte-Mecklenburg Board of Education*, 269 F. 3d 305, 322 (4th Cir. 2001).

68. Ibid., 324.

69. Editorial, "Let It Be," *Charlotte Observer*, September 23, 2001, p. 6D.

70. Gary Orfield, "Turning Back to Segregation," in Gary Orfield, Susan E. Eaton, and the Harvard Project on School Desegregation, *Dismantling Desegregation: The Quiet Reversal of Brown v. Board of Education* (New York: The New Press, 1996), 2.

71. Celeste Smith and Ann Doss Helms, "High Court Won't Hear School Case," *Charlotte Observer*, April 16, 2002, p. 1A.

72. *Swann* attorneys and plaintiffs, "Equal Opportunity for All?" *Charlotte Observer*, April 17, 2002, p. 16A.

73. Editorial, "Educating Our Kids," *Charlotte Observer*, April 16, 2001, p. 12A.

74. Insofar as the *Observer* endorsed both Woods and her opponent, one can argue that business elite opposition to her candidacy was not unanimous. But as the campaign finance reports discussed later make clear, whatever support she did receive from the business elite was dwarfed by that given to her opponent.

In Districts 2, 3, and 5, incumbents Vilma Leake, George Dunlap, and Molly Griffin ran unopposed. In District 6, the decision of Lindalyn Kakadelis not to seek reelection created an open seat, but in this heavily white, Republican district, neither candidate focused on desegregation or equity, and the election's outcome was not expected to affect significantly the board's votes on these issues. District 1 also had an open seat; in 2000, the schoolboard had appointed a replacement for Jim Puckett, who had been elected to the county commission, but the replacement decided against running. The resulting race pitted Pam Mange, former school board member and witness for the black plaintiffs, against Larry Gauvreau, an unsuccessful at-large candidate in 1999. With Gauvreau drawing upon the same support that had allowed Puckett to oust Mange from the board in 1997, the battles lines in 2001 largely resembled those four years earlier, as did the outcome.

75. Bill Hewitt, "District 4 Race Key to School Board Balance," *The Leader*, September 7, 2001, p. 8. As noted earlier, *The Leader* was targeted at affluent whites.

76. For example, educational activist Annelle Houk, who had testified on behalf of the black plaintiffs, publicly indicated that she could support either candidate if they were not running against each other (Annelle Houk, "Close Call, but My Vote Goes to Louise Woods," *Charlotte Observer*, October 31, 2001, p. 14A).

77. Julian Wright, "Vote for Effective Leadership," *Charlotte Observer*, October 25, 2001, p. 12A.

78. Campaign finance data obtained from reports on file at the Mecklenburg County Board of Elections. Some of these reports also are available at <www.meckboe.org>.

79. Of course, she also received contributions from people outside of District 4. I was one such donor.

80. The correlation (Pearson) between the percentage of a precinct's vote that went to Woods and the percentage of registered Democrats among those who voted is .60. The correlation (Pearson) between the percent of a precinct's vote that went to Woods and the percent of the voters who were black is .73.

These analyses are of necessity imprecise because figures on turnout include anyone who voted in the election, not those who voted for the school board (district-wide, only 73 percent of those who voted cast a ballot in the race for the school board). Precinct-level data on support for Woods and Wright are available at <www.meckboe.org>. Data on racial and partisan turnout were obtained from a Mecklenburg County Board of Elections report, dated January 24, 2002: "2001 General Election Voting Analysis by Sex/Race/Pty./Prec."

81. Unpublished letter, "From the Desk of John W. Lassiter, Vice Chairman, Charlotte-Mecklenburg Board of Education" to "Dear Fellow Republican," dated October 31, 2001, in author's possession.

82. Given Potter's finding that CMS was unitary, the categories RIB (racially identifiable black), RB (racially balanced), and RIW (racially identifiable white) lacked the legal significance in the years following his decision that they had prior to it, but they remain a good empirical measure of racial segregation, independent of their legal relevance.

As in previous chapters, I am here defining an RIB school as one in which the percentage of black enrollment was more than 15 percent above the system-wide black enrollment (43 percent in 2002–03). These earlier chapters, it will be recalled, generally used white as a synonym for nonblack in accordance with the court orders in

Swann, CMS' usage, and the fact that for most of the years covered by this book, almost all of CMS' nonblack students were non-Hispanic whites. However, by 2002–03, the sharp increase in Hispanic enrollment coupled with CMS' practice of considering Hispanic, white, and black as mutually exclusive categories had made it increasingly problematic to use nonblack as a synonym for white. However, it is useful to temporarily ignore these problems to allow direct comparability with Figure 3.1, in which an RIW school was defined as one in which the percentage of white (defined as nonblack) students exceeded the system-wide percentage of white (again, defined as nonblack) students by more than 15 percent. Using that definition of white, the percentage of white students in RIW schools increased slightly from 29 percent in 2000–01 (the last year in Figure 3.1) to 31 percent in 2001–02. But in 2002–03, the first year of the choice plan, that figure skyrocketed to 48 percent. If white is defined as non-Hispanic white (as CMS' membership report did in 2002–03), and white in the definition of an RIW school correspondingly changed, then 58 percent of CMS' white students were in RIW schools in 2002–03.

After only one year of the choice plan, it is difficult to anticipate whether subsequent years will see additional jumps in resegregation as sharp as the first year's. As noted in chapter 6, the previous thirty years have seen a decline in residential segregation in Mecklenburg, especially as blacks have moved into previously white neighborhoods located roughly midway between downtown and the county's periphery. That decline in residential segregation combined with the school system's countywide scope and Mecklenburg's demographics and relatively large size may allow the choice plan to result in a number of racially and socioeconomically diverse schools whose existence would keep CMS from becoming as intensely segregated as many other urban school districts.

For additional discussion of resegregation in the first years of the post-*Swann* era, see Roslyn Arlin Mickelson, "The Academic Consequences of Desegregation and Segregation: Evidence from the Charlotte-Mecklenburg Schools," *North Carolina Law Review* 81 (2003): 1513–62; and Roslyn Arlin Mickelson and Stephen Samuel Smith, "Consequences of Judicial Withdrawal from the Charlotte-Mecklenburg Schools," (paper presented at the Fall Research Conference of the Association for Public Policy Analysis and Management, Dallas, Texas, November 2002).

83. Louise Woods, "Schools Leading Again: New Policies Will Lead to the Removal of Inequities," *Charlotte Observer*, September 26, 2001, p. 18A.

84. To allow comparisons between the years following Potter's decision and earlier ones in which CMS was under court order, defined white as nonblack, and reported data this way, Table 7.1 also defines white as nonblack, thus overlooking, among other things, the significance of the increased enrollment of Hispanics and Asians. Despite these problems, Table 7.1 provides a very good indication of the extent to which schools with disproportionately large percentages of African American students had, on average, the same percentage of experienced teachers as other schools.

Because the table aggregates data within each of the three groups (RIB, RB, RIW) of schools, it does not provide information on variation among the schools within each group. Although this within-group variation is considerable, the differences among groups are both obvious and marked. For example, in 2001–02, 13 percent of all CMS' teachers were new. That system-wide percentage was exceeded in

54 percent of the schools that were RIB, 41 percent of the schools that were RB, but only 16 percent of the schools that were RIW. Conversely, only 38 percent of the RIB schools had faculties in which fewer than 13 percent of the teachers were new. For RB schools, the corresponding figure was 54 percent, and for RIW schools, 84 percent. Similar patterns are observed in other years as well. Also, if the data are broken down by elementary, middle, and high schools, the disparities are basically similar to those shown in Table 7.1.

Student data are from CMS' monthly membership reports; teacher data for 1996–97, 1997–98, and 1998–99 are from machine-readable files supplied by CMS to parties involved in the reactivated *Swann* litigation prior to trial; and teacher data for 2000–01 and 2001–02 are from hard copies of *CMS' Instructional Staff Counts by School as of 9/11/00* and *2001–2002 Teacher Summary As Of 5/22/02*, respectively. CMS' special schools (e.g., for pregnant students, exceptional students) are excluded from this analysis. Teacher data for 1999–2000 were not available.

85. Because the disparity ratios indicate aggregated differences between groups of schools, and teacher quality has many aspects, not just experience, the educational significance of any particular disparity ratio is ambiguous as, presumably, are small differences between them (e.g., the difference between a ratio of 1.5 and 1.4). However, many of the differences, especially between RIB and RIW schools, are much greater, and they are persistent. In no year, for example, did RIB schools have, on average, fewer than 50 percent more new teachers than did RIW schools, and the difference was typically closer to 100 percent.

Like Table 7.1, Table 3.1 also presents what I call disparity ratios. Because the former deals with teacher qualifications and the latter deals with track placement, the disparity ratios in the two tables are not computed in the same way. However, in both cases, these ratios indicate racial differences (in track placement or teacher assignment, as the case may be), with a disparity ratio = 1 indicating the absence of such differences.

86. To allow comparability with Figure 5.3, teachers and students were considered either black or nonblack in computing the correlation coefficient for 2001–02. Data are from *2001–2002 Teacher Summary As Of 5/22/02*.

87. See, for example, Woods, "Schools Leading Again," and, more generally, Orfield et al., *Dismantling Desegregation*.

88. As the Appendix indicates, the data in any given year's report typically reflect spending decisions that were made at least two years before the date of the report.

89. Jen Pilla, "County Holds Line on Property Taxes," *Charlotte Observer*, June 21, 2000, pp. 1B, 5B.

90. As is frequently the case in local politics, these electoral considerations had racial aspects. The most vulnerable of the three Democratic incumbent at-large county commissioners was generally considered to be African American Jim Richardson. The four Democrats who argued against a tax increase included the three black county commissioners and the white chair, Helms, upon whom fell especial responsibility for tending to the party's electoral fortunes and seeking racial unity within the party.

91. Editorial, "No Tax Increase," *Charlotte Observer*, June 17, 2000, p. 20A.

92. Celeste Smith, "54 Struggling Schools Will Get Extra Help in 2002–03," *Charlotte Observer*, March 22, 2002, p. 5B.

93. Debbie Cenziper, "Smith Wants $355 Million Bond Issue," *Charlotte Observer*, February 24, 1999, pp. 1C, 4C; Jennifer Rothacker, "$1.3 Billion Bond Issue Requested," *Charlotte Observer*, March 10, 1999, p. 1A.

94. Mary Elizabeth DeAngelis, "County May Skip Vote on School Bonds," *Charlotte Observer*, June 24, 1999, p. 1A.

95. Celeste Smith, "Kickoff for Bonds Cramped, Purposely," *Charlotte Observer*, September 15, 2000, pp. 1C, 6C.

96. Celeste Smith, "School Bonds Approach Finals," *Charlotte Observer*, November 4, 2000, p. 3B.

97. Celeste Smith, "Firms Support Bonds," *Charlotte Observer*, October 30, 2000, pp. 1B, 7B.

98. Precinct-level voting data obtained from the Mecklenburg County Board of Elections, available on line at <http://meckboe.org/e_info/general00/>, accessed November 22, 2000.

CHAPTER 8

1. Debbie Cenziper and Celeste Smith, "School Plan Is Greeted Cautiously," *Charlotte Observer*, February 14, 1999, p. 21A.

2. Editorial, "Eloquent Words about Schools," *Charlotte Observer*, May 28, 1984, p. 18A.

3. Editorial, "Whose Priorities? County Shortchanges Schools," *Charlotte Observer*, May 31, 1984, p. 18A.

4. Gary Orfield and John Yun, *Resegregation in American Schools* (Cambridge: Harvard University Civil Rights Project, 1999); Gary Orfield, Susan Eaton, and the Harvard Project on School Desegregation, *Dismantling Desegregation: The Quiet Reversal of Brown v. Board of Education* (New York: The New Press, 1996). For the way an influential newsweekly saw things, see the April 19, 1996, *Time*, whose cover read "Back to Segregation: After Four Decades of Struggle, American Has Given Up on School Integration. Why?"

5. Of course, one could hardly expect opponents of desegregation to champion policies supporting it. But views that desegregation has not and/or cannot work acquire a distinctly self-fulfilling aspect when, as in the Reagan administration, they lead to policies (e.g., cutting funding for research on ways of making desegregation work better, cuts in federally funded Desegregation Assistance Centers) that adversely affect school districts' desegregation efforts.

6. *School Desegregation: A Social Science Statement*, a statement signed by fifty-two social scientists in the brief of the NAACP et al., as amicus curiae in *Freeman* v.

Pitts (1991), 12a. Although widely reported and quoted, the statement has never, to my knowledge, been published. For background on the statement, see Ellen K. Coughlin, "Amid Challenges to Classic Remedies for Race Discrimination, Researchers Argue Merits of Mandatory School Desegregation," *Chronicle of Higher Education*, October 9, 1991, pp. A9, A11.

  7. *School Desegregation: A Social Science Statement*, 7A.

  8. David Armor, *Forced Justice: School Desegregation and the Law* (New York: Oxford University Press, 1995), 71–76.

  9. Michael Goldfield, *The Color of Politics: Race and the Mainsprings of American Politics* (New York: The New Press, 1997).

  10. A suggestive account of how the complex dynamic of race and class played out in one Charlotte labor organization comes from the recollections of Bill Brawley, a leader of the local firefighters' union. Involved during the 1960s in a protracted political and legal fight over issues that threatened its existence, the union, Brawley recounts, sought an attorney to whom "the city didn't have no strings tied to," and "threw the city a curve . . . a mean, nasty slider down in the dirt . . . We went to Julius [Chambers], and a lily-white fire department hired a black civil rights lawyer." Brawley recalls being subsequently called into an office with several city officials and fire chiefs, and "our assistant chief told me . . . 'get rid of the nigger lawyer, or we are going to hire them here' " (Bill Brawley, interviews with author, Charlotte, North Carolina, July 12 and August 1, 1996).

  The union leadership refused, and shortly thereafter, Charlotte hired its first black firefighter. Whatever tension may have been created within the union by the hiring of a black firefighter was exacerbated by McMillan's desegregation order. Many white firefighters joined anti-busing organizations and demanded that the union fire Chambers. The union leadership again refused, prompting a decline in membership. What kept the decline from being "devastating," in Brawley's words, was Chambers's victories in grievance hearings and lawsuits, as well as the union's ability to secure large pay raises during this period.

  The dynamic of class and race also was evident in the events recounted in chapter 3 that led to the assignment of affluent white families in the Eastover neighborhood to the historically black West Charlotte High School. But in this case, the primary locus of struggle was not within any particular working-class organization. Rather, events unfolded in a manner that led whites from a range of strata and income levels to see their interests as being very different from those of the affluent and powerful whites of Eastover.

  The school board's early attempt to comply with the Supreme Court's decision involved a plan that largely exempted wealthy whites in southeast Charlotte from busing. The plan prompted white parents in other areas to petition McMillan to address "class discrimination" (Davison M. Douglas, *Reading, Writing, and Race: The Desegregation of the Charlotte Schools* [Chapel Hill: University of North Carolina Press, 1995], 221). Acknowledging the existence of such discrimination, McMillan viewed it as a political, not legal issue, and he refused to give the petitioners any relief. That denial notwithstanding, McMillan increasingly came to see the need to include southeast Charlotte in the busing plan, a view that resonated with both the Citizens

Advisory Group and many whites. Ironically, many of these whites had once opposed desegregation and detested McMillan, but as it became clear that a mandatory busing plan was inevitable, they looked to him to ensure that it was fair and included all whites (Douglas, *Reading, Writing, and Race*, 230). There is thus no question that the inclusion of this very affluent white neighborhood in the mandatory busing plan facilitated its success, though as chapter 3 indicates, many steps were taken to make the West Charlotte assignment an acceptable one to Eastover families.

11. Daniel Monti, *A Semblance of Justice: St. Louis School Desegregation and Order in Urban America* (Columbia: University of Missouri Press, 1985), 182.

12. Ibid.

13. Derrick Bell, "*Brown* and the Interest-Convergence Dilemma," in *Shades of Brown: New Perspectives on School Desegregation*, ed. Derrick Bell (New York: Teachers College Press, 1980), 95.

14. Roslyn Arlin Mickelson, "Subverting *Swann:* First- and Second-Generation Segregation in the Charlotte-Mecklenburg Schools," *American Educational Research Journal* 38 (2001): 215–52.

15. As chapter 6 indicates, in 1998–99, 78 percent of the students who were satellited were African American, even though blacks comprised only 42 percent of CMS' enrollment.

16. On a Charlotte-Mecklenburg Education Foundation (CMEF) survey of registered voters conducted in March 2001, respondents were asked to indicate their support for "busing students to achieve racial balance" on a scale of 1–10, with 10 being "strongly support" and 1 being "not at all support." For blacks, the distribution of responses was:

1–3:	11 percent
4–7:	23 percent
8–10:	63 percent
Don't know/refused to answer:	3 percent

That figure of 63 percent in the top bracket was the highest in the seven years that the CMEF had asked the question, but in all but one of the previous years, the figure was over 50 percent (Charlotte-Mecklenburg Education Foundation, *2001 Community Assessment* [Charlotte, N.C.: Author, 2001], 22–24).

17. Nine months after Potter's decision in Charlotte, a federal district court judge in Louisville, Kentucky, lifted that school district's desegregation order in response to a lawsuit by black parents seeking admission for their children into what had once been the district's sole black high school and was now a magnet. Because a limited number of whites had opted to attend that magnet, black enrollment also was limited, prompting the lawsuit (Mike Chambers, "Judge in KY Lifts Order to Desegregate Schools," *Charlotte Observer*, June 21, 2000, p. 4A).

As CMS struggled to develop a new assignment plan in the two years following the trial, there was more public disagreement among black Charlotteans about the relative merits of neighborhood, albeit highly segregated, schools than there had been at the time the board voted to appeal Potter's decision. Much of this disagreement centered on the attendance zone of an elementary school scheduled to open in Greenville Park, a predominantly black, inner-city neighborhood. Despite NAACP and CMS worries about the school becoming a de facto segregated one, Thomas "Pop" Sadler, head of a neighborhood association, led a group of black Greenville parents who downplayed such worries, touted the virtues of neighborhood schools, and lobbied the board to assign Greenville students to the school. Sadler went on to endorse Larry Gauvreau in the 2001 school board election, saying the two had developed a "partnership" when the issue of assignment to the Greenville Park school had arisen (Jennifer Wing Rothacker, "Black Families Shake Up Notions On School Busing," *Charlotte Observer*, January 14, 2001, pp. 1B, 2B; Celeste Smith, "Sadler's Beliefs Are Colorblind," *Charlotte Observer*, November 4, 2001, p. 2B).

18. Jennifer Hochschild, "Is School Desegregation Still a Viable Policy Option?," *PS* 30, no. 3 (1997): 464. In noting the lack of black opposition to CMS' appeal of Potter's decision, as well as the extent to which school desegregation has enjoyed widespread support among black Charlotteans, I have no desire to downplay the importance of divisions, class and otherwise, among African Americans. Indeed, as Adolph Reed Jr. has forcefully argued, it is crucial from both a theoretical and practical standpoint to recognize "that all black people are not affected in the same ways by public policy and government practice" (Adolph Reed Jr., "Demobilization in the New Black Political Regime: Ideological Capitulation and Radical Failure in the Postsegregation Era," in *The Bubbling Cauldron: Race, Ethnicity, and the Urban Crisis*, ed. Michael Peter Smith and Joe R. Feagin [Minneapolis: University of Minnesota Press, 1995], 203).

Over thirty years of national history since the civil rights era bespeaks the importance of Reed's point, as does the Charlotte experience. For example, even during the busing plan's heyday, there were numerous disparities among the district's schools, with those in the poorest part of town frequently getting the shortest end of the policy stick. However, even if many socioeconomic- and class-related disparities are taken into account, race per se matters tremendously in shaping educational opportunities and outcomes. For example, in Charlotte, as the reactivated *Swann* litigation made clear, there are profound racial differences even when poverty status is taken into account, with black students who are not eligible for free or reduced lunch (FRL) frequently achieving at approximately the same level as whites who are FRL-eligible. This local picture generally parallels the national one in which, as Jencks and Phillips note, the black/white test score gap remains, even when black and white families have similar amounts of education, income, and wealth (Christopher Jencks and Meredith Phillips, *The Black-White Test Score Gap* [Washington, D.C.: Brookings, 1998], 2).

Moreover, whatever the distribution of attitudes on educational issues among African Americans nationally, in Charlotte there appears to be considerable similarity of outlook, as suggested by the data in note 16. Additional evidence for this position comes from the best available study of local public opinion about education issues. Drawing on a January 1995 survey of views about school reform and the magnet program, the study found that "while whites speak according to class, blacks speak with one voice," and that there was generally no difference among blacks in high-poverty neighborhoods and blacks in other neighborhoods on education-related issues

(Mary Elizabeth Van Deren Belew, "Attitudes toward Education Reform: Issues of Race and Class," [master's thesis, University of North Carolina at Charlotte, 1998], 42, 43).

19. Charlotte-Mecklenburg Education Foundation, *2001 Community Assessment*, pp. 22–24. From 1995 to 1997, the survey asked respondents if they supported "assigning children to neighborhood schools." Between 75 percent and 80 percent of white responses were in the three highest categories on a ten-point scale. Beginning in 1998, the question was changed to "assigning children to neighborhood schools, even if it means that a number of schools will become racially segregated." With that change, the percentage of white responses in those top three categories fell to between 40 percent and 55 percent.

20. Jennifer Hochschild, *The New American Dilemma: Liberal Democracy and School Desegregation* (New Haven: Yale University Press, 1984).

21. Hochschild, "Is School Desegregation Still a Viable Policy Option?," 459.

22. Editorial, "Educating Our Kids," *Charlotte Observer*, April 16, 2001, p. 12A.

23. William Poe, interview with author, Charlotte, North Carolina, April 3, 1995.

24. Sam Smith, interview with author, Charlotte, North Carolina, February 2, 2000.

25. Douglas, *Reading, Writing, and Race*, 248.

26. Ted Mellnik, "Scattered-Site Public Housing Remains Policy, Charlotte Says," *Charlotte Observer*, October 19, 1987, p. 4D.

27. William Poe, interview with author, Charlotte, North Carolina, April 3, 1995.

28. Clarence N. Stone, "Urban Regimes and the Capacity to Govern: A Political Economy Approach," *Journal of Urban Affairs* 15, no. 1 (1993): 8.

29. Ricki Morell, "Couple Symbolize City's Ambitions," *Charlotte Observer*, December 15, 1991, p. 1A.

30. Leroy Miller, interview with author, Charlotte, North Carolina, January 21, 2000.

31. Harvey Gantt, interview with author, Charlotte, North Carolina, May 25, 1999, emphasis in original.

32. Sam Smith, interview with author, Charlotte, North Carolina, February 2, 2000.

33. Peggy Heilig and Robert J. Mundt, *Your Voice at City Hall* (Albany: State University of New York Press, 1984), 151.

34. William B. A. Culp Jr. and Gerald L. Ingalls, "Charlotte Elections," in *Elections, Parties, and Politics in Mecklenburg County*, ed. Gerald L. Ingalls (Charlotte, N.C.: Charlotte/Mecklenburg Board of Elections, the Department of Geography and Earth Sciences, and the Urban Institute at the University of North Carolina at Charlotte, 1988), 53.

35. Harvey Gantt, interview with author, Charlotte, North Carolina, May 25, 1999.

36. In 1975, 40 percent of the voters in predominantly (> 95%) black precincts voted for the airport bonds, while 48 percent of the voters in predominantly (>95%) white precincts voted for them. In 1978, the Yes vote in predominantly black precincts was 81 percent, and in predominantly white precincts it was 71 percent. (Calculations are based on data obtained from the Charlotte-Mecklenburg Board of Elections.)

37. Although the dismantling of the busing plan and its replacement by other desegregation strategies, most notably magnets, occasioned considerable differences among African Americans, these differences were much more about the best way of pursuing desegregation rather than its importance as a policy goal. Moreover, as indicated in note 18, a study of public opinion found that by the magnet plan's third year, blacks generally spoke with one voice on educational issues, as opposed to whites, among whom class played a much larger role. As also indicated in that note, race per se matters tremendously in shaping educational opportunities and outcomes in Charlotte.

In emphasizing what black Charlotteans have generally said and done about desegregation, I am assuming that preferences and actions reflect interests in the sense that Bell uses the term. That assumption avoids all of the complex epistemological and methodological issues inherent in the concept *interests*. But dealing with those issues would take my discussion much too far afield.

38. Peter K. Eisinger, *Patterns of Interracial Politics: Conflict or Cooperation in the City* (New York: Academic Press, 1976), 6.

39. William Poe, interview with author, Charlotte, North Carolina, April 3, 1995.

40. Charlotte-Mecklenburg Planning Staff, *Housing Strategies to Racially Integrate Schools: Report to the Charlotte City Council, Board of County Commissioners, and Board of Education* (Charlotte, N.C.: Author, 1994).

41. Ibid, ii.

42. Charlotte-Mecklenburg Schools, *Minutes of School Board Meeting of April 12, 1994.*

43. Richard Vinroot, "Integration Task Force Not Necessary," *Charlotte Observer*, September 19, 1994, p. 13A.

44. Editorial, "Nurturing the City," *Charlotte Observer*, September 19, 1994, p. 12A.

45. *Charlotte Observer*, "School Desegregation Options," October 8, 1995, p. 6A.

46. See, for example, Future School Planning Task Force, *A Vision to Overcome Barriers* (Charlotte, N.C.: Charlotte-Mecklenburg Schools, 1997); Fannie Flono, "Home and School—Tackling the Tie That Binds," *Charlotte Observer*, February 4, 1998, p. 13A.

47. Frederick M. Hess, *Spinning Wheels: The Politics of Urban School Reform* (Washington, D.C.: Brookings, 1999), 8.

48. Monti, *A Semblance of Justice*, 185–90.

49. Although noting variations among these seven places in the rate at which racial economic inequality has been reduced, I make no attempt to investigate the causes of such differences. Any such effort would have to employ complex, multivariate statistical models that consider a wide range of variables, many of them demographic. Such an attempt is well beyond this book's scope, especially because there is relatively little scholarly literature investigating racial differences at the county level in per capita income, poverty rates, and home ownership. Here it suffices to note the existence of these geographical variations and to emphasize, as I do shortly, regime theory's core perspective, that political intervention can improve the situation of economically disadvantaged urban residents.

50. David Schulman, *From Cotton Belt to Sun Belt: Federal Policy, Economic Development, and the Transformation of the South* (New York: Oxford University Press, 1991), viii.

51. A variety of factors (e.g., population movement to/from a county) make it difficult to use county-level data, the basis for this discussion of black economic progress in Charlotte, to ascertain the extent to which a person's earnings are affected by the extent to which his or her education was a desegregated one.

52. Clarence N. Stone, "Civic Capacity and Urban School Reform," in *Changing Urban Education*, ed. Clarence N. Stone (Lawrence: University Press of Kansas, 1998), 254.

53. John Portz, Lana Stein, and Robin R. Jones, *City Schools and City Politics: Institutions and Leadership in Pittsburgh, Boston, and St. Louis* (Lawrence: University Press of Kansas, 1999), 19.

54. Clarence N. Stone, *Regime Politics: Governing Atlanta, 1946–1988* (Lawrence: University Press of Kansas, 1989), 187.

55. Marion Orr, "Urban Regimes and Human Capital Policies: A Study of Baltimore," *Journal of Urban Affairs* 14, no. 2 (1992): 173–87.

56. Stone, "Civic Capacity and Urban School Reform," 254.

57. John Huey, "The Best Cities for Business," *Fortune*, November 4, 1991, pp. 52–84; Linda Grant, "Here Comes Hugh," *Fortune*, August 21, 1995, pp. 42–52.

58. Doug Smith, "Charlotte Chamber Focuses on the 3R's As Well As Dollars, Cents," *Charlotte Observer*, November 30, 1992, p. 2D.

59. Stone, "Civic Capacity and Urban School Reform."

60. Ricki Morell, "Corporate Heat Is on the Schools," *Charlotte Observer*, July 13, 1991, pp. 1A, 4A.

61. And, of course, the 2002 decision of the Charlotte Hornets, the local National Basketball Association team, to move to New Orleans had nothing to do with public education.

62. Barbara Russell, "Striking a Balance in Education," *Quarterly* (Fourth Quarter 1995): 22.

63. James Hance Jr., "Quotable," *Charlotte Observer*, February 22, 1996, p. A6.

64. Doug Smith, "Gray Knows Now; He's in the Right Job," *Charlotte Observer*, November 2, 1999, p. 1D.

65. This is not to imply that low-income black families lack interest in a strong college-preparatory education for their children. But providing that kind of education to the black poor typically requires allocating resources (e.g., pre-kindergarten programs and differentiated staffing) that children from more privileged backgrounds are less likely to need.

Nor do these comments imply that the business *qua* business stake in improving public education involves nothing more than CMS providing a strong college preparatory education that will make Charlotte an attractive place for mid-level corporate employees. Business has other interests, including, obviously, the preparation of its entry-level workforce. Again, however, there is no guarantee that what the business elite considers adequate preparation for its entry-level workers will coincide with the interests of black children. In the early 1990s, the business elite paid scant attention to the complaints of African Americans about CMS' reform program, with some of its most prominent members publicly championing the program until Murphy's abrupt resignation. But there was much less to champion about trends in either racial balance or the academic achievement of black students (as well as of white students) than the business elite generally recognized. Among other things, CMS was making less progress than comparable districts or the entire state in boosting grades 3–8 reading and math proficiency, presumably important aspects of the preparation of entry-level workers.

66. Of course, at none of these junctures can one simply assume that Charlotte's black clergy, civic organizations, and political leaders had the best understanding of what educational programs and policies would best serve the needs of African American children, especially those from low-income families. However, it is even more problematic to assume that the economically privileged and overwhelmingly white business elite might have had a better understanding, as the previous note's discussion of the early 1990s indicates.

67. Stone, "Urban Regimes and the Capacity to Govern," 21.

68. Perhaps the most notable example of the failure to resolve issues through the "conference approach" in areas outside of education was the battle over district representation on Charlotte's city council, which had to be settled through a hard-fought referendum campaign. However, the incorporation of many of the leaders of that struggle into Charlotte's governance structures contributed to the hegemony of the "conference approach."

69. The heyday of that plan—generally speaking, the years in which Jay Robinson was superintendent—was characterized by an extensive overlap between the two group's positions, whatever differences there may have been in their motives. That amount of overlap decreased with the implementation of the magnet plan during the Murphy administration, but portions still remained if only because African American opinion, exemplified by the positions of the board's two black members, was divided on the merits of the magnet plan. By 1999, the overlap had decreased significantly as the business elite and superintendent pushed hard for the

Charlotte-Mecklenburg Compromise, but black school board members placed a much higher priority on desegregation.

70. Clarence Stone and Carol Pierannunzi, "Atlanta and the Limited Reach of Electoral Control," in *Racial Politics in American Cities*, 2d ed., ed. Rufus P. Browning, Dale Rogers Marshall, and David H. Tabb (White Plains, N.Y.: Longman, 1997), 165.

71. Ibid.

72. Reed, "Demobilization in the New Black Political Regime," 185.

73. Clarence N. Stone, Jeffrey R. Henig, Bryan D. Jones, and Carol Pierannunzi, *Building Civic Capacity: The Politics of Reforming Urban Schools* (Lawrence: University Press of Kansas, 2001), 84, 96. Their suggestion arises from the following observation: "Significantly, three of the four cities weakest in civic mobilization (Denver, San Francisco, and St. Louis) have been under broad desegregation orders, and some observers believed that court action has preempted local leadership." However, the fourth city weakest in civic mobilization is Atlanta. Given that Atlanta's experience was characterized by the explicit abandonment of desegregation, and that it is one of the four cities weakest in civic mobilization, I have difficulty viewing Stone and his colleagues' data as providing anything other than the most tentative association between the pursuit of desegregation and levels of civic capacity. Rather, it seems to me that their study is equally consistent with a view that the relationship between civic capacity and the pursuit/abandonment of court-supervised desegregation is historically contingent and dependent upon the nature of the court supervision and the local political response to it. In this regard, it is useful to compare what happened in Charlotte with Boston's desegregation experience in the mid-1970s. My argument about the minimal spillover benefits from the busing plan notwithstanding, it is clear that in the early 1970s, both Judge McMillan's political acumen and local conditions in Charlotte facilitated favorable civic mobilization around education in a way that did not occur in Boston, where very different (from Charlotte) local conditions and judicial intervention eroded civic capacity, at least in those years.

74. Evidence linking the Charlotte-Mecklenburg Compromise to increased civic capacity might be sought from Table 4.1, which appears to show a dramatic increase in local financial support for CMS during the very years that the system was moving toward the compromise. However, these appearances are deceiving, because, as the Appendix points out, there is a two-year difference between the date of a report and the period from which its data comes. Thus, the dramatic improvement shown in the 1999, 2000, and 2001 reports largely reflects events that took place when the future of pupil assignment was very much up in the air (e.g., the 1997 bond package and full funding of CMS' budget during Smith's first two years). If future reports present a picture similar to those of 1999, 2000, and 2001, they could strengthen the case for the Charlotte-Mecklenburg Compromise, though it would be important to investigate which schools were receiving the additional funding.

75. Orfield and Yun, *Resegregation in American Schools*.

76. Orfield et al., *Dismantling Desegregation*.

77. Hochschild, "Is School Desegregation Still a Viable Policy Option?," 464.

78. Ibid. Although my position draws heavily on Hochschild's, I would add the following important qualification: Emphasizing the importance of blacks having access to a desegregated education is not equivalent to claiming, especially if the claimant is white, that use should be made of that access. For any number of reasons, African Americans may not want a desegregated education, and I think that whites, such as myself, are obliged to respectfully take that view into account, especially because of the long and unfortunate history of whites presuming to know what is best for blacks. However, to acknowledge this obligation is not to diminish whites' responsibility to support blacks' having the opportunity to receive a desegregated education, an opportunity that is increasingly foreclosed by trends both nationally and in Charlotte.

79. For a very critical account of the Atlanta Compromise's effect on education, housing, and black opportunity, see Gary Orfield and Carol Ashkinaze, *The Closing Door* (Chicago: University of Chicago Press, 1991). Jeffrey Henig, Richard Hula, Marion Orr, and Desiree S. Pedescleaux's account (*The Color of School Reform* [Princeton: Princeton University Press, 1999]) focuses on education and calls attention to both the community mobilization and rising test scores that followed the compromise, but it also quotes newspaper accounts of how pressure to raise test scores not only led teachers to teach to the test but also allowed groups of students to work together during the test. It also indicates how reform unraveled and how the board of education fell into disarray in the 1980s.

80. Stone et al., *Building Civic Capacity*, 77. More precisely, Stone and his colleagues view the cities as falling into three groups: three at the upper end of civic mobilization, four that are intermediate, and four (including Atlanta) that are "quite low."

81. Ibid., 15.

82. Ibid.

83. Stone, "Civic Capacity and Urban School Reform," 270.

84. *Put Our Children First*, brochure of the Vote YES! All Bonds 2000 Committee, Charlotte, North Carolina.

85. Celeste Smith, "Parents, Business Leaders Pound Pavement for Schools," *Charlotte Observer*, October 15, 2000, p. 2M.

86. H. Stephen Shoemaker, "School Bonds Will Reveal if Charlotte Has a Soul," *Charlotte Observer*, October 16, 2000, p. 11A.

87. Portz, Stein, and Jones, *City Schools and City Politics*, 137.

88. David Dooley, "There's No 'Unspent' School Bond Money," *Charlotte Observer*, September, 24, 2000, p. 2C.

89. David L. Imbroscio, "The Necessity of Urban Regime Change: A Reply to Clarence N. Stone," *Journal of Urban Affairs* 20, no. 3 (1998): 264.

90. To be sure, this book focuses on black Charlotteans, not Charlotte's urban poor. The two groups are not identical, and the terms are hardly synonymous. But a disproportionate percentage of the urban poor are black, and the obstacles facing both

groups, as groups, are not all that different. Thus, at the risk of further downplaying the role of class, it is useful to explore briefly how the experience of black Charlotteans bears on scholarly debates on the political situation of the urban poor.

91. Stone, *Regime Politics*, 222.

APPENDIX

1. See, for example, Ronald F. Ferguson and Helen F. Ladd, "How and Why Money Matters: An Analysis of Alabama Schools," in *Holding Schools Accountable: Performance-Based Reform in Education*, ed. Helen Ladd (Washington, D.C.: Brookings, 1996), 265–98.

2. Clarence N. Stone, Jeffrey R. Henig, Bryan D. Jones, and Carol Pierannunzi, *Building Civic Capacity: The Politics of Reforming Urban Schools* (Lawrence: University Press of Kansas, 2001), 129.

3. Public School Forum of North Carolina, *1998 Local School Finance Study* (Raleigh, N.C.: Author, 1998), 11.

4. Ibid.

Index